Fernando Pessoa's Shakespeare:
The Invention of the Heteronyms

Mariana Gray de Castro

D1477466

Critical, Cultural and Communications Press
London
2016

Fernando Pessoa's Shakespeare: The Invention of the Heteronyms
by Mariana Gray de Castro

First published in Great Britain by Critical, Cultural and Communications Press, 2016.

Cover design by Hannibal, incorporating an image by Mark Cousins.

ISBN 978-1-905510-46-7

CONTENTS

To Helder and Suzette Macedo

FOREWORD

In this welcome book, Mariana Gray de Castro convincingly demonstrates the significance of Shakespeare for Fernando Pessoa's intellectual and creative development. Another fundamental reference for Pessoa was Luís de Camões, but with an important difference: Camões was the father Pessoa needed to kill. He had become a stultifying presence in Portuguese literature and Pessoa sought to liberate himself by proclaiming the need for the emergence of a "super-Camões" whom, implicitly, he himself could become. Paradoxically, however, by doing so, he would be paying a grudging homage to the bard who had become emblematic of Portuguese identity.

Portuguese literary criticism has overemphasized the rivalry Pessoa felt in relation to Camões, which is, I think, a perverse way of keeping the former under the shadow of the latter. I consider it more fruitful to relate these two major poets in terms of complementarity. The fragmentation experienced by Camões in "a life lived in fragments scattered through the world" ("*a vida pelo mundo em pedaços repartida*") finds a correspondence in Pessoa's imagined fragmentation of the self in different personalities or "heteronyms".

A great deal has been written on Fernando Pessoa's creation of his heteronyms, the alternative selves in whose names he wrote much of his work. The idea of multiple personalities was very much in the air at the time, as can be seen from Sigmund Freud's exploration of the unconscious and the studies of William James as well as in Oscar Wilde's insights into semblance and truth. Portugal's most influential literary essayist, Eduardo Lourenço, has made a perceptive comment on the nature of Pessoa's heteronyms, stating the simple but fundamental fact that the imagined alternative selves exist only in the writings which Pessoa attributed to them. They are dramatic constructs, *dramatis personae* in a theatre of the imagination. In other words, the bucolic Alberto Caeiro, the futurist Álvaro de Campos and the classicist Ricardo Reis – the only fully developed heteronyms among the many others Pessoa experimented with – are only the words he wrote under their names.

From this perspective, Shakespeare's importance for Pessoa as a dramatic poet becomes more evident. Mariana Gray de Castro conclusively argues that Pessoa's Shakespeare was not only a constant presence in his intellectual development but also a model for his multifaceted poetic identity. She highlights Pessoa's interest in the controversy about whether the actor from Stratford-on-Avon known as William Shakespeare could have been the author of the plays written in his name. In my view, this interest is particularly relevant not so much in relation to Shakespeare but in relation to Pessoa himself, as if Fernando Pessoa identified himself not with a factual Shakespeare but with the assumption that the identity of the author is only in the writing, thus understanding the literary work as the real body of a hidden identity, as Pessoa himself was in his heteronyms.

As we know, Fernando Pessoa's basic schooling was in the English language and English literature became extremely important for him. He even sought to be an English language poet, publishing poems with an evident but not always beneficial Shakespearean diction. But it was in the language of Camões that he found his own incomparable voice as a modern poet. Nevertheless, his concept of what poetry should be may owe more to Shakespeare's theatre than to the poetry of Camões.

Helder Macedo

ACKNOWLEDGEMENTS

It gives me great pleasure to acknowledge the many people who have helped me over the course of my research.

I have benefitted enormously from the help of fellow Pessoa scholars and experts in Portuguese and English literature. Juliet Perkins and Max Saunders supervised the doctoral dissertation that led to this book, and Francisco Bettencourt deposited much confidence in me during my time at King's College London.

This book would not have been possible without the doctoral Studentship of the *Espírito Santo Financial Group* in London, during my time at King's College.

Helder and Suzette Macedo generously gave me their time, support and feedback over several years. Richard Zenith shared with me all aspects of his research and ideas, and helped me to decipher Pessoa's unpublished texts on Shakespeare. Jerónimo Pizarro introduced me to the world of textual criticism, teaching me the methodology of critical editions, and discussed with me Pessoa's genius, madness and invisible authorship. José Blanco shared his encyclopaedic knowledge of all things Pessoan. Ann Thompson set me on the right Shakespearean track. Bernard McGuirk encouraged me in my work.

My remarkably gifted supervisors, colleagues and students at the University of Oxford and the University of Lisbon have been an unfailing source of intellectual stimulation, exchange and challenge. I am grateful to Claudia Pazos-Alonso, Bernard O'Donoghue, Thomas Earle, and the rest of the team at Oxford for nurturing my early interest in comparative literature, and for their continued encouragement and support, and to António Feijó and Miguel Tâmen for our fruitful discussions in Lisbon.

I am grateful to the *Casa Fernando Pessoa* for granting me access to Pessoa's personal library, and to the *Portuguese National Library* (Biblioteca Nacional de Portugal) for allowing me to access Pessoa's archive in digital form. The images reproduced in this book (all in the public domain) are from these two sources.

Thank you to Mark Cousins for the cover image and for proof-reading my book, and to Keir and the rest of the team at CCC Press for their excellent work.

ABBREVIATED TITLES

Fernando Pessoa

AC
Alberto Caeiro: Poesia [Alberto Caeiro: Poetry], ed. Fernando Cabral Martins and Richard Zenith (2nd ed., Lisbon: Assírio e Alvim, 2004).

AdC
Álvaro de Campos: Poesia [Álvaro de Campos: Poetry], ed. Teresa Rita Lopes (Lisbon: Assírio e Alvim, 2002).

LD
Livro do Desassossego [The Book of Disquiet], ed. Richard Zenith (3rd ed., Lisbon: Assírio e Alvim, 2001).

Corr I
Correspondência 1905-1922 [Correspondence 1905-1922] ed. Manuela Parreira da Silva (Lisbon: Assírio e Alvim, 1998).

Corr II
Correspondência 1923-1935 [Correspondence 1923-1935] ed. Manuela Parreira da Silva (Lisbon: Assírio e Alvim, 1999).

GL
Fernando Pessoa: Escritos sobre génio e loucura [Writings on Genius and Madness], 2 vols., ed. Jerónimo Pizarro (Lisbon: IN-CM, 2006).

H
Heróstrato e a busca da imortalidade [Erostratus and the Search for Immortality], ed. Richard Zenith (Lisbon: Assírio e Alvim, 2000).

PC I
Pessoa por conhecer I: Roteiro para uma expedicão [The Unknown Pessoa I], ed. Teresa Rita Lopes (Lisbon: Estampa, 1990).

PC II
Pessoa por conhecer II: Textos para um novo mapa [The Unknown Pessoa II], ed. Teresa Rita Lopes (Lisbon: Estampa, 1991).

PETCL
Páginas de estética e de teoria e crítica literárias [Pages on Aesthetics and Literary Theory and Criticism], ed. Georg Rudolf Lind and Jacinto do Prado Coelho (Lisbon: Ática, n.d. [1966]).

PI
Pessoa inédito [The Unpublished Pessoa], ed. Teresa Rita Lopes (Lisbon: Horizonte, 1993).

PIAI
Páginas íntimas e de auto-interpretação [Personal pages and

Self-Analyses], ed. Georg Rudolf Lind and Jacinto do Prado Coelho (Lisbon: Ática, n.d. [1966]).

PPP   *Páginas de pensamento político* [*Pages of Political Thought*], 2 vols., ed. António Quadros (Mem Martins: Europa-América, 1986).

RR   *Ricardo Reis: Prosa* [*Ricardo Reis: Prose*], ed. Manuela Parreira da Silva (Lisbon: Assírio e Alvim, 2003).

William Shakespeare

CW   *The Complete Works of William Shakespeare*, ed. W. J. Craig (Oxford: Clarendon, n.d. [1892]). Pessoa's personal copy.

Introduction

This study sets out to explore the impact of the Portuguese writer Fernando Pessoa's readings of William Shakespeare on his own work, in particular the invention of the heteronyms.

It makes a distinction, from the outset, between Pessoa's heteronyms, as he conceives and explains them, and his other dramatic voices: masks, pseudonyms, pseudo– or proto-heteronyms, or whatever else we choose to label them. Over seventy putative authors have emerged from Pessoa's archive (Portuguese National Library), although it is debatable how many represent alternative, autonomous personalities rather than slighter literary experiments. The current vogue, in a direct line from Teresa Rita Lopes's decision to list over seventy *dramatic personae*, many previously unknown, in the two volumes of *Pessoa por conhecer* [*The Unknown Pessoa*] (1990-1991) (*PC I* and *PC II*), is to classify every dramatic character Pessoa ever created as a heteronym. This tendency led Michael Stoker to propose a list of 83 heteronymic entries in 2009, including such names as 'Ibis' (a character Pessoa impersonated to amuse young children and his girlfriend Ophélia, whom he sometimes also addressed as 'Ibis' in his letters to her), 'Voodooist' (one of the spirits he communed with during his sessions of automatic writing), 'Maria José' (the fictional author of a single letter) and 'Abílio Quaresma' (the protagonist of his detective stories).[1] It culminated in Jerónimo Pizarro and Patrício Ferrari's *Eu sou uma antologia* [*I Am An Anthology*] (2013), presenting writings by '136 autores fictícios' [136 fictional authors].[2]

In *Fernando Pessoa's Shakespeare: The Invention of the Heteronyms*, Pessoa's 'heteronyms' refers to the four that he himself described as such: Alberto Caeiro, Álvaro de Campos, Ricardo Reis and Bernardo Soares (the last as a 'semi' heteronym, because Pessoa argues that his personality is a limited version of his own rather than a dramatic departure like the other three). No previous writer had ever granted his fictional voices such autonomy, for the heteronyms interact with each other, hold literary and philosophical discussions, write letters, and respond to each other's work. Each has a distinctive poetic idiom, thematic core, and context of literary influence. Pessoa went as far as to describe their physical appearances and to provide them with fictional biographies and astrological charts. The 'heteronymic project', however, or words to that effect, refers to the wider universe of Pessoa's dramatic personalities, with the heteronyms firmly at its centre, including their complex network of interrelationships, and their relation to himself as author.

As Eduardo Lourenço argues, an understanding of Pessoa's work and an understanding of his 'jogo heteronímico vão de par' [heteronymic game go hand

---

[1] Michael Stoker, *Fernando Pessoa: De Fictie Vergezelt Mij Als Mijn Schaduw* (Utrecht: Uitgeverij IJzer, 2009), pp. 219-248.
[2] *Fernando Pessoa, Eu sou uma antologia: 136 autores fictícios*, ed. Jerónimo Pizarro and Patricio Ferrari (Lisbon: Tinta da China, 2013).

in hand].[3] As he puts it more forcefully elsewhere, 'A compreensão do mecanismo heterónimo é essencial para *a compreensão* da poesia de Pessoa na sua totalidade' [An understanding of the heteronymic mechanism is essential to the *understanding* of Pessoa's poetry as a whole].[4] The heteronymic phenomenon is easily the aspect of Pessoa's work that has generated the most critical attention, and it continues to fascinate; José Blanco's bibliography lists almost a thousand different studies of it up to 2004.[5]

Pessoa's most elaborate explanation is in his letter of 13 January 1935 to Adolfo Casais Monteiro (*Corr II*, pp. 337-348), which features in almost every study of the heteronyms, and will be cited in the chapters that follow.

Arnaldo Saraiva, in an essay of 1987, charts the critical heritage of the heteronymic project until that date, listing the most significant interpretative theses it has generated:

> – a tese psicológica ou psicanalítica de João Gaspar Simões ('perda' da mãe);
> – a tese sociológica de Mário Sacramento (comportamento histórico típico de uma classe sem futuro);[6]
> – a tese estruturalista de Roman Jakobson (estruturação das forças psíquicas);[7]
> – a tese religiosa (ou arreligiosa) de Angel Crespo (paganismo de raiz panteísta: cada sentimento da natureza, onde não há unidade, pede um heterónimo);[8]
> – a tese esotérica de António Quadros (a necessidade de conhecer ou compreender as forças ocultas ou simbólicas que regem o mundo ou o destino do homem);[9]

---

[3] Eduardo Lourenço, *Pessoa revisitado: leitura estruturante do drama em gente* [*Pessoa Revisited*] (1973; Lisbon: Gradiva, 2003), p. 25.

[4] 'Poesia e heteronímia: Resposta (sem metáfora) ao Snr. Prof. Jacinto do Prado Coelho' [Poetry and Heteronymity: A Reply (Without Metaphor) to Prof. Jacinto do Prado Coelho], *Colóquio-Letras* 171 (*Eduardo Lourenço, Uma ideia do mundo* [*An Ideia of the World*], May-August 2009), 376-387, p. 381.) Original emphasis. All translations are my own unless otherwise noted.

[5] José Blanco, *Pessoana: Bibliografia passiva, selectiva e temática*, 2 vols. [*Pessoana: A Secondary, Selective, Thematic Bibliography*] (Lisbon: Assírio e Alvim, 2008), II (*Índíces*), pp. 50-57.

[6] See Mário Sacramento, *Fernando Pessoa, Poeta da hora absurda* [*Poet of the Absurd Hour*] (1958; Porto: Inova, 1970).

[7] See Roman Jakobson, 'Os oximoros dialécticos de Fernando Pessoa' [Fernando Pessoa's Dialectical Oximorons], in *Roman Jakobson: Linguística, poética, cinema* [*Linguistics, Poetry Cinema*] (São Paulo: Editora Perspectiva, 1970), pp. 93-119.

[8] See Ángel Crespo, 'El paganismo de Fernando Pessoa (Para una interpretación de los heterónimos)' [Fernando Pessoa's Paganism (Towards an Interpretation of the Heteronyms)], *Hora de Poesia* [*Poetry Time*] 4-5 (n.d.), 140-157.

[9] Quadros outlines this thesis most succinctly in the essay 'Dos mitos dos heterónimos aos heterónimos dos mitos' [From the Myth of the Heteronyms to the Heteronyms of Myths], in *Encontro internacional do centenário de Fernando Pessoa: Um século de Pessoa*

– a tese da intransitividade, defendida por Gilberto de Mello Kujawsky (Pessoa, pouco interessado na acção, era vocacionado para a contemplação ou para a reflexão sobre a acção);[10]

– a tese da exuberância genial, defendida por Eduardo Lourenço e outros (Pessoa como personalidade rica e excessiva, justificadora de metáforas cósmicas como a de uma constelação ou de uma galáxia – não de uma simples estrela, star);[11]

– a tese da carência, de Leyla Perrone Moisés, para quem o desdobramento heteronímico 'não é fruto da riqueza de uma personalidade, mas a indicação lúdica da falta profunda em que se fundamenta o ser humano. [12]

[– João Gaspar Simões's psychological or psychoanalytical thesis ('loss of the mother')

– Mário Sacramento's sociological thesis (a historic behaviour typical of a class with no future)

– Roman Jakobson's structuralist thesis (the structure of psychic forces)

– Angel Crespo's religious (or irreligious) thesis (a pantheist paganism: each feeling about nature, where there is no unity, calls for a heteronym)

– António Quadros's esoteric thesis (the need to know or understand the occult or symbolic forces that rule the world or man's destiny)

– the thesis of intransitivity, defended by Gilberto de Mello Kujawsky (Pessoa, not interested in action, had a tendency for contemplation, or reflecting upon action)

– the thesis of brilliant exuberance, defended by Eduardo Lourenço and others (Pessoa as a rich, excessive personality, which calls for cosmic metaphors like a constellation or a galaxy – not just a simple star)

– the thesis of lack, by Leyla Perrone Moisés, for whom the heteronymic unfolding 'is not the product of a richness of personality, but a playful signal of the profound lack that characterises human beings']

Saraiva adds his own theory at the end of this overview:

Por mim, sem desprezar as teses que correm, sobretudo as que se valem de referências psicanalíticas pós-freudianas, tenho defendido a tese (também de cariz psicanalítico) da orfandade Pessoana, que incluive [sic] me permite

---

[International Conference on Pessoa's Centenary: A Century of Pessoa], ed. Isabel Tamen (Lisbon: Secretaria de Estado da Cultura, 1990), pp. 247-251.

[10] A representative exposition of his view appears in 'Bernardo Soares e o Velho do Restelo' [Bernardo Soares and the Old Man of Restelo], in Encontro internacional, pp. 281-282.

[11] First proposed by Lourenço in Pessoa revisitado, and developed in subsequent studies.

[12] See Leyla Perrone-Moisés, 'O Vácuo-Pessoa' [The Pessoa-Vaccum], in Fernando Pessoa: Aquém do eu, além do outro [Before the Self, Beyond the Other] (São Paulo: Martins Fontes Editora, 1982), pp. 71-113.

relacionar a epifania heteronímica com o *Orpheu*, e com o *Marinheiro*.[13]

[As for me, without discounting the current theses, particularly those that make use of post-Freudian psychoanalysis, I have defended the thesis (also psychoanalytical in nature) of Pessoa's orphanhood, which has also allowed me to make the connection between the heteronymic epiphany and *Orpheu*, as well as the play *The Mariner*.]

To these interpretative approaches must be added Jacinto do Prado Coelho's influential thesis of mediumistic creativity:

Cerebral e retraído, Fernando Pessoa concebeu o projecto de se ocultar na criação voluntária, *fingindo* indivíduos independentes dele – os heterónimos – e inculcando-os como produtos de um imperativo alheio à sua vontade: eles o teriam forçado a escrever, na atitude submissa do *medium*, a poesia heterónima.[14]

[Being cerebral and withdrawn, Fernando Pessoa conceived the project of hiding himself in deliberate creation, *feigning* individuals independent from himself – the heteronyms – and viewing them as products of an order outside his will: they forced him to write the heteronymic poetry, in the submissive attitude of a medium.]

Lourenço, in *Pessoa revisitado* (1973), criticises what he considers to be the three major approaches to the heteronyms into which most can be classified: the psychological, the literary, and the sociological, represented by João Gaspar Simões, Jacinto do Prado Coelho and Mário Sacramento respectively. Lourenço gives a valuable summary of the three:

a primeira constituiu em encontrar na *vida* do Poeta, na sua psicologia real ou suposta, as motivações dessa diversificação em poetas, característica da sua criação literária; a segunda, em mostrar, através da análise de cada um dos poetas que Pessoa pretendeu ser, que a apregoada autonomia não resiste a um exame, nem dos temas, nem das particularidades estilísticas; a terceira, finalmente, reenvia essa estranheza, diagnosticada como simples difracção de um comportamento histórico absurdo característico de uma classe sem futuro inteligível para essa mesma história de que é reflexo.][15]

---

[13] Arnaldo Saraiva, *Fernando Pessoa e o Supra-Camões e outros ensaios pessoanos* [*Fernando Pessoa and the Supra-Camões and Other Pessoa Essays*] (Lisbon: Academia das Ciências de Lisboa, 1987), p. 119.

[14] Jacinto do Prado Coelho, *Diversidade e unidade em Fernando Pessoa* [*Diversity and Unity in Fernando Pessoa*] (Lisbon: Revista do Ocidente, 1949), p. 9.

[15] *Pessoa revisitado*, pp. 25-26.

[The first constituted the discovery in the poet's *life*, in his real or supposed psychology, of the motivation behind that multiplication into poets which characterises his literary creation; the second, in showing, via an analysis of each poet Pessoa pretended to be, that their autonomy does not stand up to scrutiny, neither thematically, nor stylistically; the third, finally, diagnoses this strangeness as the simple representation of an absurd historical behaviour characteristic of a class with no intelligible future, to the history it is a reflection of.]

The problem with psychological interpretations, in particular, is that for Lourenço the heteronyms are not the putative authors of specific poems but are instead created by the poems ascribed to them, it therefore being meaningless to speak of their non-literary existence. 'Caeiro não é *ninguém*', he argues in one essay. 'Caeiro não é o autor de "O Guardador de Rebanhos." Caeiro *é* o *Guardador de Rebanhos*, o poema claro está. [...] O *retrato* de Caeiro não cria um "sujeito de poemas". Pertence ao mesmo processo que criou *os poemas* que "são" Caeiro' [Caeiro is *nobody*. Caeiro is not the author of *The Keeper of Sheep*. Caeiro *is* the *Keeper of Sheep*, as the poem makes clear. Caeiro's *portrait* does not create a 'poetic subject'. It belongs to the same process which created the *poems* which 'are' Caeiro].[16]

Following in the footsteps of the above critics, I propose in this book a new interpretative approach to the heteronyms and the heteronymic project: Pessoa's Shakespeare. Not an 'objective' Shakespeare, but rather Shakespeare as Pessoa read, understood, fashioned, cited, assimilated and appropriated him. I hope to establish that Pessoa's engagement with Shakespeare was instrumental to the invention of the heteronyms and their universe, and that an insight into Pessoa's vision of Shakespeare is therefore essential to our understanding of them.

That an insight into Pessoa's image of Shakespeare might illuminate our understanding of the heteronymic project was first posited by Pessoa himself, the heteronyms' first theorist, who continually cited the Bard's example as a model in critical writings and personal letters. The notion has been parroted so often since that it has become a critical commonplace, one that scholars regularly alight upon but rarely dwell on.

Studies of Pessoa's intellectual and poetic development tend to mention Shakespeare in passing, a representative example being Maria da Encarnação Monteiro's *Incidências inglesas na poesia de Fernando Pessoa* [*English Influences in Pessoa's Poetry*] (1956), in which the dramatist is evoked in the context of Pessoa's *35 Sonnets* (1918).[17] Since Pessoa openly offers Shakespeare's *Sonnets* (1609) as the model for his own sonnets in English, the Bard invariably features in introductions to, and studies of, the compositions, such as Yara Frateschi Vieira and Brian F. Head's '"35 Sonnets": Uma leitura de Shakespeare' [35 Sonnets: A

---

[16] 'Poesia e heteronímia', *Colóquio-Letras* 171, p. 831.
[17] Maria da Encarnação Monteiro, *Incidências inglesas na poesia de Fernando Pessoa* (Coimbra: Coimbra Editora, 1956), p. 27.

Reading of Shakespeare] (1990).[18] Maria do Céu Saraiva Jorge, the author of a number of articles on Shakespeare's reception in Portugal, as well as an unpublished doctoral dissertation of 1949, declares that 'A obra de Fernando Pessoa, só por si, daria assunto para uma longa monografia, neste campo. Basta lembrar que o próprio 'Times' considerou os seus sonetos ingleses imbuídos de "ultra-shakespearean shakespeareanisms"' [Fernando Pessoa's work, alone, provides enough material for a long monograph in this field. We need only remember that the *Times* considered his English sonnets full of 'ultra-Shakespearean Shakespeareanisms']; however, she does not embark on such a project herself.[19] Despite Pessoa's direct reference to Shakespeare in the context of *35 Sonnets*, some commentators bypass the influence of Shakespeare on Pessoa entirely: Carlos Estorninho, in an article charting 'Shakespeare na Literatura Portuguesa' [Shakespeare in Portuguese Literature] up to 1960, makes no mention of Pessoa.[20]

Blanco's bibliography lists thirteen studies about Pessoa's encounter with Shakespeare. Some contain only fleeting references to the Bard, as is the case of John Pilling's entry on Pessoa in *An Introduction to Fifty Modern European Poets* (1982).[21] Others point to perceived affinities between the two writers, suggest parallels, and chart possible influences: João Medina, in an essay of 1976, proposes that Álvaro de Campos's emblematic poem 'Tabacaria' [Tobacco Shop](1928) should be viewed as a static drama, written by a lusophone Hamlet living in exile and disgrace; and Christine Buci-Glucksmann, in 1990, compares Pessoa, not Campos, to Hamlet.[22]

Alex McNeil, in 'What's in a "Nym?" Pseudonyms, heteronyms and the remarkable case of Fernando Pessoa' (2003), argues that Pessoa had remarkably similar creative impulses and talents to Shakespeare, and a keen insight into his mind.[23] The object of McNeil's essay is to further the Oxfordian cause, the position that 'Shakespeare' was a pseudonym adopted by the concealed author of the Shakespearean canon, in this case Edward de Vere, 17th Earl of Oxford. The so-

[18] Yara Frateschi Vieira and Brian F. Head, '"35 Sonnets": Uma leitura de Shakespeare', *U.S.D.P.* (1990), 276-281.
[19] Maria do Céu Saraiva Jorge, 'Shakespeare e a literatura oitocentista posterior a Garrett e Herculano', [Shakespeare and Ninteenth-century Literature after Garrett and Herculano] *Palestra* 23 (1965) 56-82, p. 82.
[20] Carlos Estorninho, 'Shakespeare na Literatura Portuguesa' [Shakespeare in Portuguese Literature], *Ocidente* LXVII (1964), 114-125.
[21] John Pilling, 'Fernando Pessoa (1888-1935)', in *An Introduction to Fifty Modern European Poets* (London/Sidney: Pan Books, 1982), pp. 173-180.
[22] João Medina, 'Hamlet morou defronte da Tabacaria' [Hamlet Lived Facing the Tobacco Shop], *Diário de Notícias* (1 August 1974); repr. in *Portugal: Informação* 2:1 (1976) 3-6; Christine Buci-Glucksmann, 'La place d'Hamlet' [Hamlet's Place], in *Tragique de l'ombre: Shakespeare et le maniérisme* [*Shadow Tragedy: Shakespeare and Mannerism*] (Paris: Galilée, 1990), pp. 147-157.
[23] Alex McNeil, 'What's in a "Nym?": Pseudonyms, heteronyms and the remarkable case of Fernando Pessoa', *Shakespeare Matters* 6 (Winter 2003), 16-20.

called Shakespearean authorship controversy has generated much of the international interest in the Pessoa-Shakespeare relationship, with authors like McNeil citing Pessoa as an extreme example of a writer who used pseudonyms; if he could do it, why not someone like de Vere? McNeil is unaware that Pessoa was fascinated by the Shakespearean authorship controversy himself, a fascination which has attracted some attention in Portugal, most notably by João Almeida Flor in an essay of 1984.[24]

A handful of critics have wrestled with Shakespeare's influence on Pessoa's heteronyms, the topic of this book, such as Vitorino Nemésio in 'O Sincero Fingido' [The Sincere Feigner] (1945), Jacinto do Prado Coelho in 'Fernando Pessoa ou a estratégia da razão' [Fernando Pessoa or the Strategy of Reason] (1981), and Alexandrino E. Severino in 'Fernando Pessoa e William Shakespeare: Um estudo comparativo de heteronímia' [Fernando Pessoa and William Shakespeare: A Comparative Study of the Heteronyms] (1990).[25] In the same year, Flor penned an article arguing that Pessoa fashions Shakespeare as a supreme faker, whom he can thus praise as his fellow-poet.[26]

In recent years there has been a wave of renewed interest in Pessoa's engagement with Shakespeare. Jerónimo Pizarro published in 2006 Pessoa's writings on genius and madness, together with the accompanying study *Fernando Pessoa: entre génio e loucura* [*Fernando Pessoa: Between Genius and Madness*] (2007); there are numerous references to Shakespeare in both.[27] In 2008, Onésimo de Almeida wrote of Pessoa's admiration for the Bard in an essay ostensibly on Pessoa and Antero de Quental.[28] In the same year, Richard Zenith penned the entry on Shakespeare for the *Dicionário de Fernando Pessoa e do Modernismo Português* [*Dictionary of Fernando Pessoa and Portuguese Modernism*] (2008), in which he mentions *35 Sonnets*, Pessoa's interest in the Shakespearean authorship controversy, and the way in which Pessoa's writings on Shakespeare tend to be autobiographical.[29] Still in 2008, Rita Patrício defended the doctoral

[24] João Almeida Flor, 'Fernando Pessoa e a questão shakespeariana' [Fernando Pessoa and the Shakespeare Question], in *Afecto às Letras: Homenagem da literatura portuguesa contemporânea a Jacinto do Prado Coelho* [*Loving Literature: A Tribute by Contemporary Portuguese Literature to Jacinto do Prado Coelho*] (Lisbon: IN-CM, 1984), pp. 276-283.
[25] Vitorino Nemésio, 'O Sincero Fingido', *Diário Popular* (26 December 1945), 4-7; Jacinto do Prado Coelho, 'Fernando Pessoa ou A estratégia da razão', *Jornal de Letras* (17 March 1981), 12-13; repr. in *Camões e Pessoa, Poetas da utopia* [*Camões e Pessoa, Utopic Poets*] (Lisbon: Europa-América, 1983), pp. 114-118; Alexandrino E. Severino, 'Fernando Pessoa e William Shakespeare: Um estudo comparativo de heteronímia', *Actas IV – Secção Brasileira* (São Paulo: Perspectiva, 1990), pp. 13-22.
[26] Flor, 'Shakespeare em Pessoa' [Shakespeare in Pessoa], in *Shakespeare* (Lisbon: Gulbenkian – Acarte, 1990), pp. 51-63.
[27] *Fernando Pessoa: Escritos sobre génio e loucura*, 2 vols., ed. Jerónimo Pizarro (Lisbon: IN-CM, 2006); Pizarro, *Fernando Pessoa: entre génio e loucura* (Lisbon: IN-CM, 2007).
[28] Onésimo T. Almeida, 'Fernando Pessoa and Antero de Quental (with Shakespeare in between)', *Portuguese Studies* 24:2 (*The Future of the* Arcas, 2008), 51-68.
[29] Richard Zenith, 'Shakespeare', in *Dicionário de Fernando Pessoa e do Modernismo*

dissertation *Episódios da teorização estética em Fernando Pessoa* [*Instances of Fernando Pessoa's Aesthetic Theory*], which contains a section devoted to Shakespeare, and a year later published an article on the impact of Shakespeare on Pessoa. [30] George Monteiro has also turned his critical gaze to Pessoa-Shakespeare; his first article on the subject was published in 2008, and more are in progress.[31]

The existing studies on Pessoa and Shakespeare are discussed in the chapters that follow. Although insightful and full of tantalising leads, they lack the scope to explore in depth the ways in which Pessoa's vision of Shakespeare informs the heteronymic project, so the time seems propitious for a full-length book devoted to the subject.

How and why Pessoa's Shakespeare underpins the heteronymic project can only be understood following a detailed exploration of Pessoa's various readings of, responses to, identifications with, and appropriations of the Bard: in other words, a comprehensive overview of Pessoa's vision of the dramatist. In analysing the intricacies of how Pessoa's readings of Shakespeare inform his own heteronymic art, this book also presents the most thorough picture of Pessoa's relationship with Shakespeare to date.

Pessoa cites Shakespeare surprisingly few times in his poetry and creative prose, but alludes to him continually in his correspondence, as well as in theoretical writings on such topics as celebrity, authorship, genius, madness, and sexuality. Shakespeare also assumes pride of place in Pessoa's reflections on his own work.

Until the closing decades of the twentieth century, it was common practice to take Pessoa's self-explanations and theoretical writings at face value. Lourenço begins his title essay in *Fernando, rei da nossa baviera* [*Fernando, King of Our Bavaria*] (1984) with the assertion: 'Custa-me imaginar que alguém possa um dia falar melhor de Fernando Pessoa que ele mesmo' [I find it difficult to imagine that anyone might one day speak about Fernando Pessoa better than Pessoa himself].[32] Ivo Castro was surprised to discover, in 1986, that Pessoa's account of Alberto Caeiro's appearance was a statement of intent rather than a matter of fact.[33] The current, Postmodernist trend is to start instead from a position of complete mistrust, taking literally Pessoa's poetic admission that he is a faker. The stance is

Português [*Dictionary of Fernando Pessoa and Portuguese Modernism*], ed. Fernando Cabral Martins (Lisbon: Caminho, 2008), pp. 798-800.

[30] Rita Patrício, 'Shakespeare, "a fatal influence"', in *Episódios da teorização estética em Fernando Pessoa* [*Instances of Aesthetic Theory in Fernando Pessoa*] (unpublished doctoral dissertation, University of Minho, July 2008), pp. 172-187; 'Shakespeare e Pessoa', in *Fernando Pessoa: O guardador de papéis* [*The Keeper of Papers*], ed. Pizarro (Lisbon: Texto Editores, 2009), pp. 83-99.

[31] Monteiro, 'Shakespeare, the "Missing All"', *Portuguese Studies* 24:2 (2008), 33-49.

[32] Lourenço, title essay, *Fernando, Rei da nossa baviera*, (Lisbon: IN-CM, n.d. [1984]), p. 9.

[33] *Fernando Pessoa: O manuscrito de* O Guardador de Rebanhos *de Alberto Caeiro: edição facsimilada* [*The Manuscript of* A Keeper of Sheep: *Facsimile Edition*], ed. Ivo Castro (Lisbon: Dom Quixote, 1986).

equally unproductive, for as Onésimo de Almeida vehemently argues, Pessoa's hundreds of theoretical writings about his art cannot be discounted *a priori* as irrelevant fictions.[34] In this book, Pessoa's writings on Shakespeare, and on his own work, are admitted as evidence; they are treated with suspicion when there is good reason to do so. As an example, there is no reason to doubt that Pessoa's main conclusions about the nature of the Bard's genius, invisibility, madness and sexuality were anything other than firmly held beliefs, but it is of course worth probing the reasons behind these beliefs, and their implications in the context of his own work and self-fashionings.

In addition to Pessoa's published writings on Shakespeare, there is a wealth of untapped material available, for his archive (in the Portuguese National Library, in Lisbon) contains close to three hundred unpublished manuscripts either exclusively or principally devoted to the dramatist. If we discount Pessoa's letters, and passing allusions in texts on other topics, I estimate that close to eighty per cent of Pessoa's major writings on Shakespeare remain unpublished. Most of these are handwritten, fragmentary, and in English. To locate Pessoa's disparate writings on the Bard and, in the case of unpublished texts, to decipher and transcribe them, was my first step towards an understanding of his vision of Shakespeare.

Further to his writings on Shakespeare, published and unpublished, Pessoa left behind valuable evidence of his reading on him. Books surrounded Pessoa his entire adult life, although how far they shaped his own creativity or simply bolstered ideas that had already germinated is open to question. Almost thirty books either by Shakespeare, or with him as their chief subject-matter, survive in Pessoa's library. There is a heated debate over what exactly constitutes Pessoa's library, with some scholars including the books that once belonged to Pessoa in private collections, at the National Library in Lisbon, and / or with Pessoa's heirs. In this book, 'Pessoa's library' refers exclusively, unless otherwise stated, to the almost 1,200 books now housed at the *Casa Fernando Pessoa* [*Fernando Pessoa House*], by far the largest of the collections.

The most important of Pessoa's Shakespearean books is a handsome, leather-clad, single-volume, 1892 edition of Shakespeare's *Complete Works*, awarded to Pessoa as a school prize in Durban in 1905.[35] Its frontispiece is reproduced on the following page.

The marginalia inside this and Pessoa's other Shakespearean books comprises the second major source of primary material essential to our understanding of his encounter with Shakespeare.

---

[34] See Onésimo de Almeida, 'Fernando Pessoa and Antero de Quental (with Shakespeare in between)', *Portuguese Studies* 24:4.

[35] William Shakespeare, *The Complete Works of William Shakespeare*, ed. W. J. Craig (Oxford: Clarendon, n.d. [1892]); henceforth *CW*.

The Oxford Shakespeare

THE

COMPLETE WORKS

OF

WILLIAM SHAKESPEARE

EDITED, WITH A GLOSSARY

BY

W. J. CRAIG, M.A.

Trinity College, Dublin

Oxford

AT THE CLARENDON PRESS

LONDON: HENRY FROWDE

OXFORD UNIVERSITY PRESS WAREHOUSE, AMEN CORNER, E.C.

NEW YORK: 91 & 93, FIFTH AVENUE

Pessoa's library offers us a treasure trove that has only recently begun to be acknowledged as such: in 2008 it was digitalised and made available online (http://casafernandopessoa.cm-lisboa.pt), and a year later Maria do Céu Lucas Estibeira defended the first doctoral thesis devoted to the study of Pessoa's marginalia, which includes a section on that in his Shakespearean books.[36] Numerous studies of Pessoa's work have demonstrated the insights to be gained from examining the ways in which his reading informs his creativity, and pointed to sources for his ideas and expressions, such as Patrício Ferrari's 'A biblioteca de Fernando Pessoa na génese dos heterónimos' [Fernando Pessoa's Library and the Genesis of the Heteronyms] (2009).[37]

As Ralph Waldo Emerson declares in an unpublished text, 'While you are reading, you are the book's book.'[38] In his essay 'History', a copy of which Pessoa owned and read, underlining certain passages, Emerson argues that 'the student should read actively and not passively; to esteem his own life the text, and books the commentary.'[39] The vast majority of Pessoa's Shakespearean sources are English ones, and his immensely wide reading on the Bard is both active and creative in the manner Emerson calls for: he picks up from his books, like a magpie, the more glittering ideas and observations to appropriate, or misappropriate, for his own work.

'Mature poets', T. S. Eliot famously declared, 'steal' – the best ones transform their sources into 'something better, or at least something different' – and the same is true of good magpies.[40] A vision of the poet as magpie is particularly pertinent to Pessoa's engagement with Shakespeare, so this book compares his reading on the playwright to his writings on him throughout. We will see numerous examples of Pessoa occulting, misquoting, or downright misappropriating his Shakespearean sources. Interestingly, Pessoa rarely names his sources, perhaps in a bid to create an impression of greater originality than in reality exists. As a capital example, when he has Álvaro de Campos make insinuations about Ricardo Reis's sexuality (more on this in Chapter 4), Campos

---

[36] Maria do Céu Lucas Estibeira, *A Marginalia de Fernando Pessoa* [*Fernando Pessoa's Marginalia*] (doctoral dissertation, University of Lisbon: Faculdade de Letras, 2009), pp. 240-254. The date on its cover and title page appears erroneously as 2008. See also her article 'Uma perspectiva da *Marginalia* de Fernando Pessoa', [A Vision of Fernando Pessoa's *Marginalia*] *Romântica* 18 (2009), 91-108.
[37] Patrício Ferrari, 'A biblioteca de Fernando Pessoa na génese dos heterónimos', in *Fernando Pessoa: O Guardador de papéis*, pp. 155-218.
[38] Robert D. Richardson, *First We Read, Then We Write: Emerson on the Creative Process* (Iowa City: University of Iowa Press, 2009); cited in John Banville, 'Emerson, "A Few Inches From Calamity"', *The New York Review of Books* (21 November 2009), 2-4, p. 2.
[39] Ralph Waldo Emerson, in *Works of Ralph Waldo Emerson: Essays, First and Second Series, Representative Men, Society and Solitude, English Traits, The Conduct of Life, Letters and Social Aims, Poems, Miscellanies Embracing Nature, Addresses, and Lectures* (London: George Routledge & Sons, 1902), p. 8.
[40] T. S. Eliot, *Selected Prose of T.S. Eliot*, ed. Frank Kermode (London: Faber and Faber, 1975), p. 153.

accuses Reis of using a 'delgado sendal, ou o que quer que seja, que cobre as partes do discurso' [light veil, or whatever it is, to cover the discourse's parts] as a deflecting tactic (*PC II*, p. 474). António M. Feijó first noticed that this phrase derives directly from Camões's poem II:37 in *Os Lusíadas* [*The Lusiads*] (1573), a derivation Pessoa does not point out himself.[41]

Pessoa's debt to specific sources informs my decision to present direct quotations rather than paraphrases in the case of his unpublished writings on Shakespeare: set out in this manner, it is easier for the reader to follow how Pessoa's words are often reminiscent of earlier commentators'. Full transcriptions of all cited unpublished manuscripts are in the Appendix.

Emerson further declares, in his essay 'Shakespeare; or the Poet', which Pessoa also read: 'The greatest genius is the most indebted man. A poet is no rattlebrain, saying what comes uppermost, and, because he says everything, saying, at last, something good; but a heart in unison with his time and country.' He concludes that 'all originality is relative. Every thinker is retrospective.'[42] This book fully subscribes to this view. Pessoa is, like Shakespeare, of an age as well as for all time, and there are precedents for his appraisals of the dramatist which it is possible to confidently trace. Therefore, an examination of Pessoa's alignment with, or departure from, the spirit of his day, as well as the impact of specific books he read, is favoured over the application of any particular theoretical models to his readings of Shakespeare. As examples, Pessoa's reaction to psychoanalysis is deemed more significant, for the purposes of this study, than an attempt to place him on the psychoanalytic couch, and his appropriation of topical notions of genius and madness are explored rather than a diagnosis of his mental condition advanced. Insofar as this constitutes a critical approach, it tends towards historicism. Interestingly, historicism is the pervasive critical approach to Shakespeare (excepting Harold Bloom's, as we shall see in Chapter 1): Stephen Greenblatt's *Will in the World: How Shakespeare Became Shakespeare* (2004), Stanley Wells's *Shakespeare and Co.: Christopher Marlowe, Thomas Dekker, Ben Jonson, Thomas Middleton, John Fletcher and the Other Players in his Story* (2006), and Jonathan Bate's *Soul of the Age: The Life, Mind and World of William Shakespeare* (2008) are representative titles in this vein.

My approach is thematic, rather than chronological, because Pessoa's appraisal of Shakespeare is both coherent and consistent over time, despite characteristic surface contradictions; broad chronological brushstrokes are proposed whenever relevant, for example when attempting to narrow the period of Pessoa's most profound engagement with the Shakespearean authorship controversy in Chapter 2. A thematic approach has the advantage of permitting us to concentrate on those

---

[41] António M. Feijó, 'Ricardo Reis, [A flor que és, não a que dás, eu quero]' [I want the flower you are, not the one you give], in *Século de Ouro: Antologia crítica da poesia portuguesa do século XX* [*Golden Century: A Critical Anthology of Twentieth-century Portuguese Poetry*] , ed. Osvaldo Manuel Silvestre and Pedro Serra (Braga, Coimbra, Lisbon: Angelus Novus & Cotovia, 2002), p. 470.

[42] Emerson, *Works*, pp. 187, 189.

aspects of Shakespeare's work that Pessoa himself focussed on. I have chosen a circular structure for the first four chapters: each one begins with one of Pessoa's thematic readings of the Bard – of his genius, his perceived invisibility, his possible madness, and his sexuality, respectively – goes on to contextualise it and examine its sources, then explores the issues and problematics that arise from it in the context of Pessoa's own creativity, finally relating it back to the heteronymic project. This circularity is also intended to mirror Pessoa's thought-process, and it highlights the way in which he is ultimately, and almost exclusively, interested in making use of his vision of Shakespeare for the invention of the heteronyms.

In Chapter 1, 'Shakespeare's Genius', I begin by surveying Shakespeare's place in Portuguese culture in Pessoa's day, and describe how Pessoa encountered his work. I go on to examine Pessoa's ambition to establish the Bard more prominently on the Portuguese literary landscape, largely via ambitious projects to translate his writings. I then turn to Pessoa's poetic appropriations of Shakespeare, both for *35 Sonnets* (1918) and for the poem ascribed to Álvaro de Campos which begins 'Se te queres matar, porque não te queres matar?' [If You Want to Kill Yourself, Why Don't You Want to Kill Yourself?] (1926), which I propose is a poetic response to the most famous speech in all of Shakespeare, Hamlet's 'To be, or not to be' soliloquy. Turning from Pessoa's literary appropriations of Shakespeare to his critical appraisals of him, I investigate the latter's place in Pessoa's canon, showing that Shakespeare is the writer Pessoa most admires, which fact alone justifies the existence of this book. Pessoa's vision of Shakespeare's genius is indebted to Romantic character criticism, as well as to the Modernist ideal of impersonality, so both spheres of influence are charted. It is also, as I attempt to show, largely autobiographical, based on self-projection. Finally, I explore how Pessoa appropriates, in his conception of and explanation for the heteronymic project, what he considers to be the essence of Shakespeare's genius.

The three chapters that follow examine Pessoa's most important corollary readings of Shakespeare, and explore how these, too, inform his thinking on the heteronyms and their universe.

Chapter 2, 'Shakespeare's Invisibility', is devoted to Pessoa's engagement with the Shakespearean authorship controversy, in greater depth than has hitherto been attempted. Doubts as to whether Shakespeare in fact penned the works that go under his name were fuelled by the perceived nature of his genius, and Pessoa engaged with the conspiracy theory at length, reading dozens of books on the topic, which he responded to in almost two hundred manuscripts, the majority of which are unpublished. I examine Pessoa's most developed piece of writing on the subject to provide a context for his ideas on it, in which his appropriations and misappropriations of authorship sources provide us with a wonderful illustration of the poet as magpie. I then question the established wisdom that Pessoa doubted the traditional attribution of Shakespeare's writings, and go on to explore the reasons behind his fascination with the controversy. Finally, I examine how and why Pessoa's thinking on Shakespeare's perceived invisibility informed his own creativity, its key sites of contention providing him with a valuable mirror for the chief problematics of the heteronymic project.

Chapter 3, 'Shakespeare's Madness', begins with Pessoa's most original contribution to the Shakespearean authorship debate, his proposed solution to the Bard's apparent unconcern with the publication of his brilliant works. This solution is grounded in Pessoa's diagnosis of Shakespeare as a fellow madman as well as fellow genius, for he discovers in the dramatist the very same mental condition he ascribes to himself, namely hystero-neurasthenia. I examine Pessoa's derivation and understanding of the neurosis, and the ways in which he employs the 'madness' he discovers in Shakespeare and his dramatic characters, Hamlet in particular, in his own art, especially the poetry of Álvaro de Campos. I then explore why Pessoa should offer the 'madness' he ascribes to Shakespeare and himself as the psychological explanation for both men's genius, the creation of dramatic others.

In Chapter 4, 'Shakespeare's Sexuality', I describe how Pessoa deduces, from his reading of Shakespeare's *Sonnets*, their author's real-life sexuality. Pessoa's biographical reading of the *Sonnets* is again evidence of his immersion in nineteenth-century Shakespearean criticism, so I trace the impact of Romantic readings of the problematic compositions, particularly Oscar Wilde's, on Pessoa's conviction that Shakespeare was homosexual. I then analyse the implications of Pessoa's biographical approach to Shakespeare's poetry, the main one being that it contradicts his insistence on impersonality, particularly evident in his explanations for his own homoerotic writings. But Pessoa's homoeroticism, I posit, is directly informed by the chief characteristics he discovers in Shakespeare's *Sonnets*. His contradictory stance towards both men's literary sexuality has the scope to illuminate our understanding of his encounter with Freudian psychoanalysis, the most intrusive biographical approach of the day. Finally, it also reveals his differing approach to lyric poetry (the *Sonnets*) and dramatic poetry (Shakespeare's plays; his own heteronymic output).

Chapter 5, 'Shakespeare and the Invention of the Heteronyms', explores in greater depth the overriding analogy that Pessoa's readings of Shakespeare's genius, invisibility, madness and sexuality all set up: that of Shakespeare's characters as akin to his own heteronyms. I begin by questioning the validity of the approximation, and propose the existence of what I call a 'kinship fallacy' in Pessoa's retrospective projection of affinity, one that has been echoed by numerous scholars. I then examine whether Shakespeare is, as Pessoa claims, the best possible model for the heteronymic project, when there are alternative precedents in the Modernist masks and dramatic monologues of his own period, before going on to ponder the main reasons behind Pessoa's continual evocation of the Bard in this regard. I explore how Pessoa, in his heteronymic project, appropriates the defining features he discovers in Shakespearean drama: his characters' unprecedented self-consciousness, their dramatic play-acting, their tendency to transgress their set roles, and their representation of the notion of the world as a stage where being and acting are indivisible. In the process, I propose fresh insights to be gleaned if we approach Pessoa's art with Shakespeare's in mind, putting forward a new approach to the problem of his heteronymic *fingimento* [*feigning*] based on a reading by William Empson that forever changed the way we look at Shakespeare.

My central argument throughout this book, one I make explicit in the final chapter, is that Pessoa pitched himself against Shakespeare in the impersonal creation of dramatic others. Harold Bloom argues that Shakespeare invented the human; I wish to show how Shakespeare led Pessoa to invent the heteronyms.

Rather than infusing the pages that follow with qualifications like 'perhaps', 'maybe', 'it is likely that', or 'possibly', I offer this disclaimer from the outset: this is one reconstruction of how Pessoa read Shakespeare, responded to him, and appropriated him for the heart of his own creativity. Whether Pessoa's Shakespeare as the pervasive underlying framework of the heteronymic project is an interpretation as convincing and enlightening as the previous approaches to it, discussed in this Introduction, I defer to the better judgement of the reader.

EDITING PESSOA: EDITIONS USED AND PRESENTATION OF UNPUBLISHED TEXTS

The difficulties involved in editing Pessoa bear comparison to those in editing Shakespeare. In the case of the latter, for much of the past century there was a reigning consensus on what the final destination was supposed to be: a reconstruction, from the differing existing texts, of a 'Lost Archetype', the plays Shakespeare 'originally' wrote or, more problematically still, had in mind before their corruption in the printing house and/or the playhouse. This ideal produced conflated texts, a superimposition of conflicting printed sources from Shakespeare's time and immediately afterward, such as the 'good' and 'bad' Quartos and the 1623 Folio. Conflated texts obscure marked differences between the competing versions, and the rendered play becomes a patchwork threaded through with conjectures, guesses, and emendations from past editors like Harold Jenkins and Stanley Wells.

In 1986, the Oxford *Complete Works* printed two different versions of *King Lear* on the theory that they do not represent variations of a single 'Lost Archetype' but are, instead, texts that need to be treated as separate works of art, or as different stages of the same work. The move was controversial, but twelve years later *The Norton Shakespeare*, a leading American edition edited by Stephen Greenblatt, followed suit and published not two but three *Lears*, the two versions of the Oxford edition plus a third, traditional, conflated text. Ann Thompson and Neil Taylor, in the new Arden *Hamlet* (2006), continued the trend of refusing to decide between alternatives by publishing three versions of *Hamlet*, arguing that each one must be respected because Shakespeare's intentions are veiled beyond recovery with any degree of certainty.[1] This editorial trend has led to an ingenious solution in *The Enfolded Hamlets* (1996), an edition of the second Quarto and the Folio texts that contains bracketed within it all the variants from both, thus arguably coming the closest to the concept of a Shakespearean hypertext.[2] With the aid of new technology, such inclusive approaches promise new ways of editing open texts in the future.[3]

Pessoa's literary visions and revisions mean that, as is the case of Shakespeare, there is usually no consensual 'final' text to start from. A September 2009 conceptual exhibition at the *Casa Fernando Pessoa* focussed on a twelve-line ode attributed to Ricardo Reis containing twenty-five variant words or phrases. None of these are mutually exclusive, in the sense that they do not significantly alter the meaning of the poem. A mathematical computation came to the conclusion that, for this single ode, there are a dizzying 28,000 possible poems. The temporary nature of Pessoa's texts, their ultimate lack of final authority, is true even of the

---

[1] *Hamlet*, ed. Ann Thompson and Neil Taylor (3rd ed., London: Arden, 2006).
[2] *The Enfolded Hamlets: Parallel Texts of <F1> and {Q2} Each With Unique Elements Bracketed*, ed. Bernice W. Kliman (New York: AMS/London: Eurospan, 1996).
[3] For a pioneering work in progress on the simultaneous presentation of the variants in *Hamlet*, based on *The Enfolded Hamlets*, see *Hamlet Works* <www.hamletworks.org>.

writings he published in his lifetime: some contain, in his script, posterior modifications over the published text. The best example is Pessoa's handwritten modifications to the first edition of *Mensagem* (1934); the book's second edition, on which most modern ones are based, incorporated these alterations.[4] The result is that we are as far off from having definitive editions of Pessoa's writings as of Shakespeare's.[5]

The early editions of Pessoa's writings, such as those by the publisher Ática, were pioneering but are now largely discounted as full of obvious errors of transcription and comprehension, such as a consistent failure to pick up on his shorthand notation, in English, for the words 'therefore', 'because', and 'and'. Following the entry of Pessoa's archive into the public domain in 2005, there has been a proliferation of his writings, both of unpublished material and new editions of previously published texts.

Differences in editorial opinion concerning how Pessoa's writings should be presented have led to two principal contemporary schools of thought. The publisher Assírio e Alvim commissions prestigious Pessoa scholars with the task of performing the choices they (the editors) deem fit, or think Pessoa would have deemed fit had he adequately prepared his works for publication. Most modernise his spelling – Pessoa favoured old-fashioned Portuguese, archaic even at his time of writing – and silently amend glaring errors like typographical ones and inconsistent punctuation. They usually present, in the notes, Pessoa's most significant variants and hesitations. Critical editions, the academically-oriented 'Edição Crítica', published by Imprensa Nacional – Casa da Moeda (IN-CM), prefer not to tamper with Pessoa's texts, leaving them in their original spelling. They judiciously record each one of Pessoa's hesitations and variant phrasings, and aim not to impose any editorial organisation exterior to texts themselves.

In the case of Pessoa's published texts, wherever there is a choice between different renditions of the same text, ideally several editions should be used in conjunction. I have done so throughout this book: all editions of Pessoa's writings consulted are listed in the bibliography, and the footnotes make clear where cited pieces are taken from. The decision of what edition of Shakespeare's writings to favour, in contrast, could not have been easier: all excerpts, without exception, are taken from the edition of Shakespeare's *Complete Works* that Pessoa owned and used.

My transcriptions of Pessoa's unpublished texts on Shakespeare adhere to the more reader-friendly editions, like Assírio e Alvim's: although I have kept Pessoa's original spelling, I have corrected clear spelling errors and punctuation, and expanded shorthand notations for words like 'Shakespeare', 'Bacon', 'therefore', 'because' and 'and', as well as his abbreviated references to authors and titles of works. Where there are variants for any given word or passage, the one that

---

[4] *Mensagem* [*Message*] (Lisbon: Parceria António Maria Pereira, 1934). Pesosa's amended copy of this first edition is on display at the *Casa Fernando Pessoa*.
[5] Zenith published in 2010 his eighth edition of *Livro do Desassossego* for Assírio e Alvim. His first was published in 1998.

appears to be Pessoa's final thought, rather than his initial one, is preferred. Pessoa's crossed-out passages do not feature, nor do I indicate the few words he hesitated about keeping in the text, or where his posterior additions appear on the original manuscript; these additions are inserted in their relevant positions in the text, when Pessoa signals one, or in the position that seems most relevant to me, when he does not. Explanatory footnotes are limited to Pessoa's references and allusions. His underlinings are altered to italics, and all emphases are Pessoa's own. I have chosen not to modernise Pessoa's Portuguese.

The symbols used are the following:

☐   space left blank by Pessoa
†   illegible word
*   speculative reading

The above also applies to my transcriptions of Pessoa's marginalia.

All the unpublished texts cited in this book are transcribed in full in the Appendix; in total eighteen Pessoan texts are there presented for the first time, together with explanatory notes. They often reveal more about Pessoa, and his trademark concerns, than they do about Shakespeare.

SHAKESPEARE'S GENIUS

Shakespeare in Portugal

Pessoa encountered Shakespeare exclusively, it appears, as a reader, for he nowhere describes Shakespearean performances he might have seen. It is conceivable that he saw a production of *Hamlet* in Durban between 1898 and 1902, when the British Holloway Company toured South Africa, but there is no documentary evidence for it. [1] Nor is there any record that he attended productions of Shakespeare's plays in Portugal, even though they had been staged for over a century as foreign theatre companies periodically visited the country.[2] There was a taste for opera and concerts with Shakespearean themes as well as more conventional productions of his plays: since its opening in 1793, the Teatro S. Carlos [Lisbon Opera House] staged Rossini's *Othello*, Gounod and Bellini's *Romeo and Juliet*, Verdi's *Macbeth*, *Othello* and *Falstaff*, and Ambroise Thomas's *Hamlet*, among others.[3] Paganini took part in *Othello* at the S. Carlos in 1825, and Sarah Bernhard played a female Hamlet there in 1899. [4] By the early twentieth century, Shakespeare's major plays were sufficiently well-known to be parodied, as in Rafael Ferreira's farce *Omelette* (1905), published under the pseudonym 'Chá-que-inspira' [Inspiring Tea], and Francisco Rangel de Lima's pastiche aimed at children, *Othelosito* [*Little Othello*] (1906).[5]

To accompany the growing number of Shakespearean productions in Portugal over the course of the nineteenth century, newspaper articles commented on, and attempted to educate the public about, recent and forthcoming performances.[6] Prominent Portuguese writers Pessoa admired actively promoted Shakespeare, and eulogised him in their work. Almeida Garrett had attacked the Bard in his

---

[1] See P. B. Storrar, 'Leonard Rayne', in *Better Than They Knew*, ed. R. M. de Villiers (Cape Town: Purnell, 1972), pp. 124-135, p. 128.

[2] See Luiz Francisco Rebello, *Dicionário do teatro português* [*Dictionary of Portuguese Theatre*] (Lisbon: Prelo, 1978).

[3] See Maria de Lourdes Lima dos Santos, *Por uma sociologia da cultura burguesa em Portugal no século XIX* [*Towards a Sociological Study of Portuguese Cultural Middle-Class Life in the Twentieth Century*] (Lisbon: Presença, 1983).

[4] Cited in Estorninho, 'Shakespeare na Literatura Portuguesa', *Ocidente LXVII* (1964), p. 117. This might be the Portuguese tenor João Paganini rather than his more famous Italian counterpart, for the former features in Francisco da Fonseca Benevides's *O Real Theatro de S. Carlos de Lisboa desde a sua fundação em 1793 até à actualidade: estudo historico* [*The Royal Theatre of S. Carlos in Lisbon from its Foundation in 1793 to the Present: A Historical Study*] (Lisbon: Castro e Irmão, 1883), pp. 161, 180; though some descriptions of S. Carlos' performance history mention the Italian composer/violinist (such as 'Lisbon – Teatro Nacional de Sãoo Carlos', *Planetware* http://www.planetware.com/lisbon/teatro-nacional-de-sao-carlos-p-lisb-tnsc.htm), I have found no evidence to corroborate this.

[5] Cited in Estorninho, *op. cit.*, p. 119.

[6] Maria do Céu Saraiva Jorge, 'Shakespeare e a literatura oitocentista posterior a Garrett e Herculano', *Palestra* 23 (Lisbon: 1965), 56-58.

early poem 'Toucador' [Dressing Table] (1822), but his sojourn in England seems to have changed his mind completely, and he went on to organise the lecture tour of James Sheridan-Knowles in Lisbon, then Porto, in 1845, the first three of which were on Shakespeare. Garrett would later confess, in chapter 26 of *Viagens na Minha Terra* [*Travels in my Homeland*] (1846), 'Nunca tinha entendido Shakespeare, enquanto o não li em Warwick, ao pé do Avon, debaixo de um carvalho secular, à luz daquele sol baço e branco do nublado céu de Albion... ou à noite, com os pés no fender, a chaleira a ferver no fogão...' [I never understood Shakespeare until I read him in Warwick, near Avon, under a hundred-year-old oak tree, under the foggy white sun of Albion's cloudy skies... or at night, with my feet on the fender, the teapot boiling on the stove...] [7] Camilo Castelo Branco penned the poem 'A Shakespeare' [To Shakespeare] in 1878, and published the first Portuguese book-length study of one of his plays (Othello) in 1886. [8] Eça de Queirós lauded Shakespeare for his 'não sei quantos milhares, um número enorme de milhares de palavras. [Shakespeare] necessitou mesmo, para traduzir a sua emoção, de forjar por vezes o vocábulo' [I don't know how many thousands, a vast number of thousands, of words. Shakespeare even needed to invent new words in order to express his emotion]. [9] Teixeira de Pascoaes inserted Shakespeare's characters into two of his poems: Ophelia in 'A Sombra da Vida' [Life's Shadow], and both Hamlet and Ophelia in 'Londres' [London]. António Nobre's poem 'Males do Anto' [Anto's Ills] (*Só* [*Alone/Lonely*], 1892) features a book that has so powerful a hold over its protagonist, a thinly veiled portrait of the artist as a young man, that its effects on him are physical as well as psychological. The uncomprehending Sra. Carlota despairs of its impact on her feverish charge, mistaking his enthusiasm for its author as delirium:

Mas uma coisa que lhe faz ainda pior,
Que o faz saltar e lhe enche a testa de suor,
É um grande livro que ele traz sempre consigo
E nunca larga: diz que é o seu melhor amigo
E lê, lê, chama-me: 'Carlota, anda ouvir!'
Mas... nada ouço. Diz que é o Sr. Shakespeare.

---

[7] Cited in Estorninho, 'Shakespeare na Literatura Portuguesa', *Ocidente LXVII*, p. 115. For more on Garrett's reception of Shakespeare, see Flor, 'Para a imagem de Shakespeare em Garrett' [Towards an Image of Shakespeare in Garrett], and Helena Carvalhão Buescu, 'Tópicos para o debate' [Topics for Debate], both in *Garrett às portas do milénio* [*Garrett in the New Millenium*], ed. Fernando Mão de Ferro (Lisbon: Colibri, 2002), pp. 45-54 and 59-62 respectively.
[8] Camilo Castelo Branco, *Esboço de crítica. Othello, o Mouro de Veneza de William Shakespeare: tragédia traduzida para portuguez por D. Luiz de Bragança* [*A Study for A Critical Essay. Othello, the Moor of Venice by William Shakespeare, a Tragedy Translated into Portuguese by D. Luiz de Bragança*] (Porto: Chardron, 1886).
[9] Cited in Saraiva Jorge, 'Shakespeare e a literatura oitocentista posterior a Garrett e Herculano', *Palestra 23*, p. 65.

[But one thing that does him even greater harm
That makes him jump and fills his forehead with sweat
Is a large book he always carries with him
And never drops: he calls it his best friend
And reads, reads, calls me: 'Carlota, come hear!'
But... I hear nothing. He says it's Mr Shakespeare.]

In the same poem, the speaker alludes to 'Ó rainhas Macbeths / Da ambição! Ó Reis Lears da Loucura! Ó Hamlets / Da minha Vingança! / Ó Ofélias do Perdão!' [Oh Queen Macbeths / Of Ambition! Oh King Lears of Madness! / Oh Hamlets / Of my Vengeance! / Oh Ophelias of Forgiveness!][10]

The nineteenth century also saw the emergence of Portuguese translations of Shakespeare's plays. The first was *O Intrigante de Veneza, drama em 5 actos e 8 quadros* [*The Conniver of Venice, Drama in 5 Acts and 8 Scenes*], published in 1842 by José Maria da Silva Leal. This is a translation of *Othello*, but Leal's chosen title transposes the focus to Iago. Luís Augusto Rebelo da Silva's translation of *Othello*, with the more conventional title *O Mouro de Veneza* [*The Moor of Venice*], was published in 1856. D. Luís de Bragança's translations put Shakespeare firmly on the cultural map, as from 1877 onwards the reigning monarch embarked on Portuguese renditions based on the original text (many previous translations had been based on French ones), publishing his versions of *Hamlet* (1877), *O Mercador de Veneza* [*The Merchant of Venice*] (1879), *Ricardo III* [*Richard III*] (1880) and *Othello, O Mouro de Veneza* [*Othello, the Moor of Venice*] (1885), and leaving behind unpublished translations of *Romeu e Julieta* [*Romeo and Juliet*], *A Esquiva Donzela*, *Vénus e Adónis* [*Venus and Adonis*] and *O Estupro de Lucrécia* [*The Rape of Lucrece*]. There was a brief hiatus in new translations during the 1890s, which João Ferreira Duarte makes a convincing case is best explained by the political crisis of the 'Ultimatum' and a consequent Portuguese 'ideological embargo' on all things British.[11] In the 1890s, the staging of some Shakespearean plays was cancelled by popular demand.[12]

Of course, Pessoa did not have to read Shakespeare in translation, nor would he have wanted to. He was awarded his most important Shakespearean book, Shakespeare's *Complete Works*, as a school prize in Durban on 16 August 1905. It was a book Pessoa treasured, bringing it back to Portugal upon his definitive return in the same year. Almost exactly a year later he began to devour it, reading

---

[10] António Nobre, *Poesia completa* [*Complete Poetry*] (Lisbon: Dom Quixote, 2000), pp. 361, 351-52.

[11] João Ferreira Duarte, 'The Politics of Non-Translation: A Case Study in Anglo-Portuguese Relations', *Traduction, terminologie, rédaction* 13:1 (2000), 95-112.

[12] Flor, '*Hamlet* (1887): Tradução portuguesa de um caso patológico' [*Hamlet*: Portuguese Translation of a Pathological Case], in *Shakespeare entre nós* [*Shakespeare Amongst Us*], ed. Maria Helena Serôdio, João de Almeida Flor, Alexandra Assis Rosa, Rita Queiroz de Barros and Paulo Eduardo Carvalho (Ribeirão: Edições Húmus, 2009), pp. 184-200, p. 188.

The Tempest in one sitting on 17 August 1906, and the *Comedy of Errors* and *Much Ado About Nothing* over the following two days, according to his reading diary for that year.[13]

Pessoa's earliest recorded contact with Shakespeare had been three years earlier, for *The Life of King Henry V* was part of his Matriculation exam of 1903.[14] Writing of his literary development years later, he recognised his British education in the then British colony of Natal, of which Shakespeare was an integral part, as 'a factor of supreme importance in my life, and, whatever my fate be, indubitably shaping it.'[15]

Although Pessoa had no need to read Shakespeare in any language other than the original English, he kept abreast of Portuguese translations of the Bard's plays, which he invariably condemned as inadequate, and devised grandiose plans to publish his own in their stead.

In 1908, the Porto publishers Lello & Irmãos set out to produce Portuguese editions of Shakespeare's complete works, entrusting the translation to Domingos Ramos and Henrique Braga. By 1913, Ramos had translated a small number of plays, including *Hamlet*, *The Merchant of Venice*, and *Julius Caesar*. Pessoa reacted with aggressive derision to these efforts, writing a draft letter to the publishers lamenting their editorial decision to allow Ramos to perform prose translations of Shakespeare's dramatic poetry. He argued that one must, in the case of Shakespeare, always translate 'o verso para verso e a prosa para prosa, e que verso e que prosa têm de ser!' [verse into verse and prose into prose, and what verse and prose they must be!][16]

Pessoa declares in another piece that, of everyone familiar with Shakespeare in all Latin countries, only someone completely immersed in the spirit of the Shakespearean canon ('inteiramente penetrado do espírito da obra shakespeariana') is up to the Herculean task.[17] That this figure is Pessoa himself is, with characteristic immodestly, soon made explicit:

> O tradutor português que a fará, tendo publicado um livro de versos *em inglês*, foi, a propósito desse livro, mencionado em um artigo elogioso do *Times* como 'absolutamente penetrado do espírito shakespeariano', e o crítico manifestava o seu pasmo pelo facto, sobretudo tratando-se de um estrangeiro. Igual circunstância não consta, nem seria de esperar que constasse, de nenhum dos tradutores de Shakespeare em nenhum dos países de língua latina.[18]

---

[13] See *Cadernos I* [*Notebooks I*], ed. Jerónimo Pizarro (Lisbon: IN-CM, 2009), p. 210.

[14] See Alexandrino E. Severino, *Fernando Pessoa na África do Sul: a formação inglesa de Fernando Pessoa* [*Fernando Pessoa in South Africa: Fernando Pessoa's English Upbringing*] (Lisbon: Dom Quixote, 1983), pp. 158-161.

[15] Letter to the *British Journal of Astrology*, 8 February 1918, in *Corr I*, p. 258.

[16] Cited in Flor, 'Shakespeare em Pessoa', in *Shakespeare*, p. 59.

[17] Cited in António Mega Ferreira, *Fernando Pessoa – O Comércio e a Publicidade* [*Commerce and Advertising*] (Lisbon: Cinevoz-Lusomedia, 1968), p. 186.

[18] *Ibid.*

[The Portuguese translator who will do this, having published a book of poems *in English*, was, with reference to that book, mentioned in a complimentary article in the *Times*, as being 'absolutely penetrated by Shakespeare's spirit', and the critic expressed his wonder at the fact, above all because he was a foreigner. No other Shakespeare translator, in any Latin-language country, is in this position, nor would he be expected to be.]

This brisk movement, from an ostensibly objective discussion about how best to translate Shakespeare, to a personal identification with the Bard, is typical of Pessoa's engagement with him. So is the self-serving nature of the identification: 'penetrado do espírito shakespeariano' is a slight but significant alteration of the original phrasing of the *Times Literary Supplement*'s review of Pessoa's *35 Sonnets*, and 'pasmo' [wonder/awe] is too strong a word for the reviewer's praise. [19] Furthermore, the reviewer had described Pessoa's poems, not their author, as being 'steeped in Shakespeare', with no mention of shadowy spirits, whereas Pessoa's word 'espírito' [spirit] refers to a state of mind but has additional religious connotations pointing to the notion of souls and, by extension, soulmates. Pessoa would continue to employ the word 'soul' in his appreciations of Shakespeare's genius, and his explanations of his own.

Pessoa's ambition to translate Shakespeare was no passing fancy. In a plan for Íbis, the first publisher he set up, he proposed to produce, among a number of non-Shakespearean titles, 'Shakespeare: Obras: (1) Tragédias. (2) Comédias. (3) "Histórias"' [Shakespeare: Works: (1) Tragedies. (2) Comedies. (3) 'Histories'] (*PC I*, p. 185). There are similar projects for the later Olisipo. [20] In an unpublished manuscript, Pessoa declares his intention to 'translate Shakespeare's plays at the rate of one per year' (76A-10). In a letter of 20 June 1923 to João Castro Osório, he promises an even more furious rate of production:

> De Shakespeare, proponho-me a traduzir, por enquanto, as seguintes dez peças: *A Tormenta, Hamlet, Príncipe da Dinamarca, O Rei Lear, Macbeth, Otelo, António e Cleópatra, O Mercador de Veneza, Sonho de uma Noite de Verão,* e duas outras, sobre cuja escolha não estou ainda decidido, mas que serão provavelmente o *Coriolano* e a comédia *Como quiserdes*. [...] Das traduções de Shakespeare comprometo-me a entregar uma peça por trimestre. (*Corr II*, pp. 13-14.)

> [I propose to translate, for the time being, the following ten Shakespeare plays: *The Tempest, Hamlet, Prince of Denmark, King Lear, Macbeth, Othello, Anthony and Cleopatra, The Merchant of Venice, A Midsummer Nights' Dream,* and two others, which I have not yet decided, but which will probably be *Coriolanus* and the comedy *As You Like It*. [...] I commit to submitting one play

[19] *Times Literary Supplement* 870 (19 August 1918).
[20] For one of Pessoa's plans to translate *The Tempest, Hamlet* and *King Lear*, see *PPP II*, p. 195.

every four months.]

As late as 1930, Pessoa held fast to his ambition to translate Shakespeare's writings into Portuguese, in plans now extended to include the dramatist's *Sonnets* (1609) and other lyric poems (*Venus and Adonis*, 1593, and *The Rape of Lucrece*, 1594) in addition to his plays, and envisioned this project as a profitable commercial venture. [21] João Gaspar Simões asserts that Pessoa's intention to translate, publish and profit from Shakespeare's works was never carried further than abortive attempts. [22] Pessoa's marginalia in his three books by Shakespeare, the *Complete Works* and two separate editions of *The Tempest*, confirms this, as do the manuscripts in his archive; taken together, they reveal that Pessoa began by attempting to translate large sections of *Hamlet* and *The Tempest*. As representative examples, he translates Hamlet's 'Question it, Horatio', upon seeing his father's ghost, as 'Interroga-o', and 'How now, Horatio! You tremble and look pale' is rendered as 'Então... treme e está pálido' (*CW*, pp. 941, 943).

One of Pessoa's copies of *The Tempest* is littered with tentative translations, in different writing materials and with numerous variants and modifications. These reveal an attempt to render Shakespeare's poetry as poetry rather than prose, in keeping with his attack on those who did otherwise. The beginning of Ariel's famous song 'Full fathom five thy father lies' appears in Pessoa's 1908 copy of *The Tempest* thus:

> Full fathom five thy father lies
> Of his bones are coral made;
> Those are pearls that were his eyes:
> Nothing of him that doth fade,
> But doth suffer a sea-change
> Into something rich and strange. [23]

Pessoa translates these lines, in the spaces between them, as:

> A cinco braças jaz teu pae
> Os seus ossos coral são:
> Pérolas são seus olhos, ai!
> Nada d'elle *corre ou vai
> Mas, no mar *contudo, fica
> Qualquer c.[oisa] estranha e rica

Something is undeniably lost in Pessoa's attempt to maintain Shakespeare's original rhyme scheme, for it leads him to insert an otherwise redundant, jarring

---

[21] Pessoa outlines the business plan in some detail in his letter to Gaspar Simões of 10 January 1930 (*Corr II*, pp. 188-189).

[22] Gaspar Simões, *Vida e obra*, p. 497.

[23] *The Tempest* (London: Cassel & Co, 1908), p. 43.

'ai!' [Oh!] in the third line for this sole purpose. However, his translation is a valiant effort to remain faithful to Shakespeare's original lyricism, maintaining not only the original rhyme scheme but also the exact same number of syllables in each line; it even closely mirrors their scansion. Compare Pessoa's attempt to the following modern translation of Ariel's song into Portuguese, conducted by three translators working together:

> A cinco braças jaz morto o teu pai
> Já se tornaram seus ossos corais,
> Já foram olhos e pérolas são,
> Tudo em seu corpo teve alteração.
> Nada se perdeu, o mar o mudou,
> Em coisa mais rica ele o transformou.[24]

This translation alters the rhyme scheme from ABABACC to AABBCC, and even then makes the first a half-rhyme. Its lines are all ten syllables each, while Pessoa's translation reproduces Shakespeare's original eight.

Although the quality of Pessoa's translation is questionable – that grating 'ai' somewhat mars the whole – his attempt does corroborate his explicit intention to mirror Shakespeare's original text. In a wonderful piece titled 'Sobre traduzir Shakespeare' [On Translating Shakespeare], probably meant as a preface to his translations of the Bard's writings, Pessoa explains that what will distinguish them from all existing ones is precisely their 'exacto translado de Shakespeare para português' [exact transcription of Shakespeare into Portuguese]:

> Achei que a peor cousa que se podia obrigar a um portuguez era traduzir Shakespeare. Porisso – entenda-se bem – se traduzi Shakespeare foi para discordar do estado actual da mentalidade portugueza. Em Portugal nunca se traduziu acima de Castilho.[25] O vernaculo é a desculpa do stupido, como a fé é o fogão do pobre de spirito.
>
> Não devo àquelles a quem não devo explicações outra explicação por não seja esta. Fallo em Shakespeareano de proposito, e pressinto ao fallar que não me compreendem.
>
> Diz Sydney Smith que um escosez só percebia um dito de espirito mediante

24 *A Tempestade, seguido de 'O Mar e o espelho' de W. H. Auden* [*The Tempest, followed by W. H. Auden's 'The Sea and the Mirror'*], trans. José Manuel Mendes, Luís Lima Barreto and Luis Miguel Cintra (Lisbon: Cotovia, 2009), p. 45.
25 António Feliciano de Castilho (1800-1875) was a Portuguese writer whose poems *Amor de melancolia* [*Love of Melancholy*] (1828), *A primavera* [*Spring*] (1837), and *O Outono* [*Autumn*] (1863) paved the way for the Portuguese Romantic movement. Castilho was born in Lisbon and was blind from the age of six, but he gained a reputation for scholarship, translating Ovid's *Metamorphoses*, Virgil's *Georgics*, Goethe's *Faust*, and plays by Molière and Shakespeare (despite not knowing English).

intervenção cirurgica.[26] Só com a operação do timpano pode um portuguez perceber Shakespeare. É preciso pôr este commentario antes de esta tradução. O que o leitor vae ler é o exacto translado de Sh[akespeare] para portuguez. Vae o leitor não perceber nada. É que isto é Shakespeare. O resto é o rei D. Luiz e os outros.[27]

[I thought the worst thing one could force a Portuguese to do was to translate Shakespeare. Therefore, please note that if I translated Shakespeare, it was because I disagree with the current Portuguese mentality. In Portugal no one has ever translated better than Castilho. The language is the excuse of the stupid, like faith is the stove of the poor of spirit.

I don't owe those to whom I owe no explanation a better explanation than this. I speak like Shakespeare deliberately, and I suspect as I speak no one will understand me.

Sidney Smith says a Scotsman can only understand a witticism following a surgical intervention. Only following inner ear surgery can a Portuguese person understand Shakespeare. It is necessary to put this note before the translation. What the reader will read is the exact transcription of Shakespeare into Portuguese. The reader will not understand a thing. Because this is Shakespeare. Everything else is king D. Luiz and the others.]

This seems to have been Pessoa's universal ideal of translation, for his Portuguese rendition of Edgar Allan Poe's poem 'The Raven', first published, as 'O Corvo', in *Athena* 1 (1924), contains a note explaining it is 'ritmicamente conforme o original' [rhythmically in accordance with the original].[28] Pessoa's ideal of fidelity to Shakespeare's lyricism was to find its best outlet in his own sonnets in English.

Shakespeare in Pessoa's Poetry

Pessoa was fascinated by Shakespeare's *Sonnets*, more so than by any other Shakespearean text judging by the marginalia in his copy of the *Complete Works*. His chief interest in them resided in what they might reveal about the Bard's sexuality, a topic which merits separate treatment in Chapter 4. He was also drawn, however, to their technical virtuosity and rhetorical flourishes, which he took as a model for his own *35 Sonnets*, which he self-published in 1918. David

---

[26] Sydney Smith, an English cleric who worked in Edinburgh around 1800, famously commented: 'It requires a surgical operation to get a joke well into a Scotch understanding.' (Cited in *A Memoir of the Reverend Sydney Smith by his Daughter Lady Holland, with A Selection From His Letters*, ed. Sarah Austin, 2 vols. (London: Longman, Brown, Green, and Longmans, 1855) I, pp. 31-32.)

[27] *A Tormenta, de William Shakespeare*, série Pessoa Editor, ed. Mariana Gray de Castro (Lisbon: Guimarães Editores, 2011), with Introduction and Appendix 'Sobre traduzir Shakespeare', pp. 36-39.

[28] *Athena: edição facsimilada [Athena: Facsimile Edition]* (Lisbon: Contexto, 1994), p. 3.

Shepherd explores two further influences on the poems apart from Shakespeare: English Romantic poetry and metaphysical poetry, both of which informed Pessoa's use of symbol and metaphor. [29] But their greatest single influence remains, undeniably, Shakespeare.

Upon their publication, English reviewers immediately noticed their essential point of reference: *Graphic* wrote that they 'bear the traces of a great admiration of the Shakespearian.'[30] Pessoa was proud of his Shakespearean poems, and sent them to such disparate locations as the Advocates' Library in Edinburgh, the University Library in Cambridge and the British Museum in London. (This last copy, sent in 1922 with a dedication in Pessoa's hand, is today in the Rare Books section of the British Library.) He kept until his death newspaper cuttings of early reviews, from such diverse publications as the *Yorkshire Post* and the *Finance Chronicle*.[31]

The critical reception of *35 Sonnets*, however, has not always been as positive as Pessoa's estimation of their worth. While early reviews, like that in the *TLS*, praised their 'ultra-Shakespeareanisms, and their Tudor tricks of repetition, involution and antithesis', others, like that in the *Glasgow Herald*, were less charitable.[32] The debate over the quality of *35 Sonnets* continues: in 1982 John Pilling berated Pessoa for sounding, in the poems, 'like a lame contemporary of Shakespeare', while Philadelpho Menezes, six years later, praised the sequence as a linguistic *tour de force*.[33] Most modern editors relegate them to minor works of the Pessoan canon: Zenith, in a 2007 edition, subscribes to the prevalent notion that they are of greater interest for their embryonic expressions of ideas which find fuller expression in Pessoa's other writings than for their inherent quality.[34] One critic goes as far as to state that 'Todo o drama pessoano se encontra *in nuce* nos *35 Sonnets*' [The whole Pessoan theatre can be found *in nuce* in *35 Sonnets*].[35]

35 Sonnets comprises Pessoa's most direct, overt, and sustained poetic appropriation of Shakespeare. Although there are references to the Bard's life and work in *Livro do Desassossego* [*The Book of Disquiet*] (1982), Shakespeare is entirely absent from the poetry Pessoa signs under his own name in Portuguese,

---

[29] Shepherd, 'Os 35 Sonnets de Fernando Pessoa vistos por um inglês' [Pessoa's 35 Sonnets Viewed by an Englishman], Arquivos IV:1 (January 1982), 45-84.

[30] 'Books of General Interest', *Graphic* XCVII (17 August 1918).

[31] See *Fernando Pessoa: Imagens de uma vida* [*Images of a Life*], ed. Manuela Nogueira (Lisbon: Assírio e Alvim, 2005), pp. 90-98.

[32] *TLS* 870; 'The sonnets are well done, and but for a certain crabbedness of speech, due to an imitation of a Shakespearean trick, would be excellent.' (*Glasgow Herald*, 19 September 1918.)

[33] Pilling, 'Fernando Pessoa (1888-1935)', in *An Introduction to Fifty Modern European Poets*, p. 176; Philadelpho Menezes, *Fernando Pessoa: 35 Sonnets, Tradução* [*Translation*] (São Paulo: Arte Pau-Brasil, 1988), p. 11.

[34] Zenith, Preface to *Obra Essencial de Fernando Pessoa: Poesia Inglesa* [*Pessoa: English Poetry*], ed. Zenith, trans. Luísa Freire (Lisbon: Assírio e Alvim, 2007) p. 15.

[35] Esteban Torre, 'Fernando Pessoa, poeta metafísico' [Metaphysical Poet], *Revista do Ocidente* [*Western Magazine*] 94 (March 1989), 72.

as well as that he attributes to Alberto Caeiro and Ricardo Reis. This is initially surprising, for most lovers of Shakespeare, like Pessoa's contemporary Modernists T. S. Eliot and James Joyce, infuse their writings with Shakespearean references, echoes and allusions. But further to serving as a stylistic model underpinning *35 Sonnets*, Shakespeare only features in a handful of poems ascribed to Álvaro de Campos. Even in these, he is treated superficially and in passing: witness the throwaway reference to 'Shakespeare da sensação que começa a andar a vapor' [Shakespeare of sensation that starts to travel by steam] in Campos's 'Saudação a Walt Whitman' [Salutation to Walt Whitman], when Shakespeare is listed as one of several possible parallels to Whitman's genius, others including 'Jean-Jacques Rousseau do mundo que havia de produzir máquinas' [Jean-Jacques Rousseau of the world which would produce machines] and the compound ghost 'Milton-Shelley do horizonte da Electricidade futura!' [Milton-Shelley of the horizon of future Electricity!] (*AdC*, pp. 161-2)There is one notable exception.

It seems remarkable that no one has yet thought to confront Campos's poem that begins 'Se te queres matar, porque não te queres matar?' [If you want to kill yourself, why don't you want to kill yourself?] (1926) to what is arguably the best known speech in all of Shakespeare, Hamlet's 'To be, or not to be' soliloquy (3.1.64-98).[36] The opening line of Pessoa's poem immediately recalls the Dane's meditation on the positives and negatives of being alive, and it contains Pessoa's most prolonged literary dialogue with Shakespeare excluding *35 Sonnets*, so it is worth questioning the nature of Pessoa's reply to Hamlet.

The opening lines of 'To be, or not to be' could be a perfect summary of the theme of Pessoa's poem:

To be, or not to be: that is the question:
Whether 'tis nobler in the mind to suffer
The slings and arrows of outrageous fortune,
Or to take arms against a sea of troubles,
And by opposing end them?

In it, death – or, rather, the condition of not being alive – is envisioned as a highly desirable state:

To die: to sleep;
No more; and, by a sleep to say we end
The heart-ache and the thousand natural shocks
That flesh is heir to, 'tis a consummation
Devoutly to be wish'd.

---

[36] All citations from Hamlet's speech from *CW*, pp. 958-59; All citations from Campos's poems from *Álvaro de Campos: Poesia*, ed. Teresa Rita Lopes (Lisbon: Assírio e Alvim, 2002), pp. 304-06.

Hamlet had explicitly expressed a death-wish in his opening soliloquy in the play, 'O! that this too too solid flesh would melt' (1.2.136-61), but came to the deflating conclusion that committing suicide would be contrary to God's law:

O! that [...] the Everlasting had not fix'd
His canon 'gainst self-slaughter! O God! O God!

He had also already directed at Polonius the immensely memorable line: 'You cannot, sir, take from me anything that I would more willingly part withal – Except my life, except my life, except my life.' (2.2.215)

If his life is the thing Hamlet would most willingly part withal, and leaving aside the religious implications of the deed, why does he choose not to kill himself? The immediate answer is the one he offers in 'To be, or not to be', the fear of the undiscovered country that lies the other side of death:

Who would fardels bear,
To grunt and sweat under a weary life,
But that the dread of something after death,
The undiscover'd country from whose bourne
No traveller returns

One of the things Hamlet is in effect doing, in this speech, is talking himself out of committing suicide. Many of the most famous productions of the play treat 'To be, or not to be' as an unambiguous suicide speech: in his 1948 film, Laurence Olivier pulls out a dagger and holds it to his neck as he proclaims it.

In 'Se te queres matar, porque não te queres matar?', Pessoa deconstructs the logic of Hamlet's fear of the 'undiscover'd country' by arguing that, since nothing is known in any case (and this scepticism pervades Pessoa's entire literary output), any talk of the unknown is meaningless:

Tens, como Hamlet, o pavor do desconhecido?
Mas o que é conhecido? o que é que tu conheces,
Para que chames desconhecido a qualquer coisa em especial?

[Are you, like Hamlet, terrified of the unknown?
But what is known? What do you know,
That you should call anything in particular unknown?]

The poem's speaker then cites Falstaff as an example of the opposite world-view to Hamlet's. In Falstaff's case, it is his lust for life, rather than his attraction to death, that makes him fear an untimely demise:

Tens, como Falstaff, o amor gorduroso da vida?
Se assim a amas materialmente, ama-a ainda mais materialmente:
Torna-te parte carnal da terra e das coisas!

[Do you, like Falstaff, have a greedy lust for life?
If you love it so materially, love it even more materially:
Become a carnal part of the earth and of things!]

The inescapable argument of the poem 'Se te queres matar' is that, whether you hate or love life, like Hamlet and Falstaff, respectively, better to take arms against a sea of troubles, and by opposing end them. In other words, suicide is not only a valid, but a positively recommendable way out. The implicit flirtation of the poem's addressee with self-slaughter is thus praised, throughout the poem, as an act of bravery rather than one of spinelessness, a course of action the speaker declares he would also take had he only the necessary courage:

Se te queres matar, porque não te queres matar?
Ah, aproveita! que eu, que tanto amo a morte e a vida,
Se ousasse matar-me, também me mataria...
Ah, se ousares, ousa!

[If you want to kill yourself, why don't you want to kill yourself?
Oh, make the most of it! Because I, who so love death and life,
If I dared to kill myself, I would also kill myself...
Oh, if you dare, dare!]

Notice the speaker's subtle identification, in the second line, with Hamlet and Falstaff in turn, who are here alluded to by their presiding attitudes towards being alive: 'Eu, que tanto amo a morte e a vida' [I, who so love death (like Hamlet) and life (like Falstaff)].

Contrary to 'To be, or not to be', 'Se te queres matar' is not a dramatic monologue, in the style of almost all of Pessoa's heteronymic poems. We are faced, instead, with an implicit dialogue, in which we only have access to one side of the conversation. Who is the implicit addressee of the poem, its conspicuous absence, the 'tu' [you] in the line 'Se te queres matar, porque não te queres matar?', the conspicuously absent presence who, we learn, flirts with the idea of committing suicide and is spurred to do so by the speaker?

The clue is in the date Pessoa ascribes to the poem. He does not date the vast majority of his poetic output, particularly those poems that, like this one, he did not publish himself. The exceptions tend to carry fictional dates: 'Autopsicografia' [Autopsychography], which opens with the famous line 'O poeta é um fingidor' [the poet is a feigner], which was published in the magazine *Orpheu* in 1915, is dated April 1st, April Fool's Day. Another case in point is the poem 'Opiário' [Opiary], which was published in the second issue of *Orpheu* (1915), but backdated to March 1914. The reason for this is that the poem displays Campos's style before he supposedly met, and came under the influence of, Alberto Caeiro, which could only have happened after the Master's appearance on the supposed triumphal day, March 8th 1914 (this date is also, of course, fictional). Pessoa refers to his backdating of 'Opiário' in a letter of 1915 to Armando Côrtes-Rodrigues:

Ia-me esquecendo... com efeito, esqueci-me... Na lista da colaboração da revista [*Orpheu*], depois dos *Frisos* do Almada Negreiros vão duas poesias do meu *filho* Álvaro de Campos – o homem da ode de cuja terminação (descritiva da Noite) você tanto gostava. Umas das poesias é aquela *Ode Triunfal* (o canto das máquinas e da civilização moderna) que v[ocê] já conhece. A outra é uma poesia anterior (que é posterior) do mesmo cavalheiro. Depois, quando seguir para aí a revista, lhe falarei deste assunto mais detalhadamente.[37]

[I was about to forget... indeed, I forgot... On the list of the magazine's collaborations, after Almada Negreiros's *Friezes* there are two poems by my *son* Álvaro de Campos – the man who wrote the ode whose ending (describing the Night) you liked so much. One of the poems is the *Triumphal Ode* (the song about machines and modern civilisation) you already know. The other is an earlier poem (which is posterior), by the same gentleman. Later, when the magazine comes your way, I will speak to you about this subject in greater detail.]

With such chronological games in mind, let us turn to the date he deliberately gives the poem 'Se te queres matar, porque não te queres matar'. It is April 26th, 1926, the tenth-year anniversary of the self-inflicted death – the *suicide* – of his best friend, and fellow Modernist, Mário de Sá-Carneiro.[38]

As if to call our attention to the importance of the dates that circumscribe a life, Pessoa writes in the poem the following lines that visually recall the inscriptions on tombstones:

Só és lembrado em duas datas, aniversariamente:
Quando faz anos que nasceste, quando faz anos que morreste;
Mais nada, mais nada, absolutamente mais nada.

[You are only remembered on two dates, annually:
The anniversary of your birth, and the anniversary of your death;
Nothing more, nothing more, absolutely nothing more.]

In Sá-Carneiro's writings, suicide is a central obsession, and many of his poems and short stories foreshadow his own tragic demise: six out of the seven main characters in the collection *Princípio* [*Beginning*] (1912) kill themselves. One of Sá-Carneiro's poems, the one most editors retrospectively title 'Fim' [The End] (the title is made up by them) and place at the end of their anthologies, expresses a desire to die in circus-style fanfare:

– Quando eu morrer batam em latas,
Rompam aos saltos e aos pinotes –

---

[37] Pessoa, letter to Armando Côrtes-Rodrigues, 4 March 1915, in *Corr I*, p. 156.
[38] See 'Aparato Genético', in *AdC*, p. 429.

Façam estalar no ar chicotes,
Chamem palhaços e acrobatas![39]

[– When I die beat upon drums,
Burst into leaps and somersaults –
Crack the air with whips,
Summon clowns and acrobats!]

In high school, Sá-Carneiro had witnessed the suicide of Tomás Cabreira Júnior. His poem in memory of his dead friend, 'A um suicida' [To a suicide] (1911) concludes by praising the bravery of his deed. The act of taking one's life is, in this poem, lauded as an admirable accomplishment, vastly preferable to a passive life of little achievement:

Foi triste, muito triste, amigo a tua sorte –
Mais triste do que a minha e mal-aventurada
... Mas tu ainda alcançaste alguma coisa: a morte,
E há tantos como eu que não alcançam nada...[40]

[Your fate, my friend, was sad, very sad –
Sadder than mine and ill-fated
... But you still conquered something: death
And there are so many like me who conquer nothing...]

If Sá-Carneiro is, as I argue, the implicit addressee of Pessoa's poetic apology for suicide, 'Se te queres matar' takes on a darkly serious undertone that counteracts its superficial black humour. Hamlet is Pessoa's favourite Shakespearian character; 'Se te queres matar' is a dialogue with his most famous soliloquy. The poem's conclusion that, after all, Sá-Carneiro's action, in killing himself, was the noblest – nobler than that of Hamlet, one of the most beloved characters in Western literature – is a generous, moving tribute to a dear friend.

Why should Pessoa choose to make his oblique tribute to Sá-Carneiro via the intermediary of Álvaro de Campos, ascribing him the poem? It seems to me significant that Sá-Carneiro, who followed at first hand the genesis of the heteronyms, was immediately attracted by the immensely dramatic possibilities their universe offers. This would be an excellent reason for Pessoa to fashion, in his honour, a dramatic poem openly evoking Shakespeare, whom many readers hold to be the greatest dramatist of all time. Furthermore, Sá-Carneiro makes clear in a letter written to Pessoa a few months after the heteronym's appearance, in 1914, who his favourite is: 'Muito interessante o enredo Alberto Caeiro, Ricardo Reis e Álvaro de Campos. Fascinante o enredo.... Devo dizer-lhe que simpatizo

---

[39] Mário de Sá-Carneiro, *Poemas Completos* [*Complete Poems*], ed. Fernando Cabral Martins (Lisbon: Assírio e Alvim, 2001), p. 132.
[40] *Ibid.*, p. 234.

singularmente com este cavalheiro' [The Alberto Caeiro, Ricardo Reis and Álvaro de Campos plot is fascinating... I must say I am particularly fond of this last gentleman]. [41]

Another celebrated poem by Álvaro de Campos bears the exact same date as 'Se te queres matar, porque não te queres matar?': 'Lisbon Revisited (1926)'. The poem's tone is one of melancholy nostalgia for the past, which it revisits, recaptures, reconjures. It closes with the striking stanzas:

> Outra vez te revejo – Lisboa e Tejo e tudo -,
> Transeunte inútil de ti e de mim,
> Estrangeiro aqui como em toda a parte,
> Casual na vida como na alma
> Fantasma a errar em salas de recordações,
> Ao ruído dos ratos e das tábuas que rangem
> No castelo maldito de ter que viver...
>
> Outra vez te revejo,
> Sombra que passa através das sombras, e brilha
> Um momento a uma luz fúnebre desconhecida,
> E entra na noite como um rastro de barco se perde
> Na água que deixa de se ouvir...
>
> Outra vez te revejo,
> Mas, ai, a mim não me revejo!
> Partiu-se o espelho mágico em que me revia idêntico.
> E em cada fragmento fatídico vejo só um bocado de mim –
> Um bocado de ti e de mim!... (*AdC*, p. 131)
>
> [Once more I see you – Lisbon and Tagus and everything -,
> A useless onlooker of you and myself,
> A stranger here like everywhere,
> Incidental as much in life as in soul,
> A ghost wandering the rooms of memory,
> To the sound of rats and creaking floorboards
> In the damned castle of having to be alive...
>
> Once more I see you,
> A shadow passing into shadows, and shining
> An instant in an unknown funereal light
> And entering the night like the wake of a lost ship
> In the water that can no longer be heard...

---

[41] Pessoa, letter to Sá-Carneiro, 20 June 1914, in *Cartas a Fernando Pessoa* [*Letters to Fernando Pessoa*], 2 vols. (Lisbon: Ática, 1958), I, p. 161.

Once more I see you,
But, oh, myself I do not see!
The magic mirror where I saw myself the same has broken,
And in each fateful fragment I see but a piece of me -
A piece of you and of me!]

If we remember that this poem, like 'Se te queres matar, porque não te queres matar?', was either written on, or deliberately dated, the tenth-year anniversary of Sá-Carneiro's suicide, it becomes difficult to read these lines without thinking of him as the veritable ghost that wanders through the rooms of memory, the shadow passed into shadows, entering the endless night to shine in a funereal light, while Pessoa remains imprisoned in the castle of being alive. How much of his presence may also be felt in the collective 'tu' [you] ('Outra vez te revejo – Lisboa e Tejo e *tudo*' [Once more I see you – Lisbon and Tagus and *everything*]) in the phrase that is repeated no fewer than five times in the poem: 'Outra vez te revejo' [Once more I see you]?

Critical Appraisals: Shakespeare in Pessoa's Canon

In contrast to the relative scarcity of allusions to Shakespeare in Pessoa's poetry, his critical appraisals of the dramatist's work abound, characteristically fragmentary, dispersed and disjointed, and usually in the context of wider examinations on art and literature, authorship, genius and madness, and sexuality. Although Pessoa never published a full-length piece of criticism on Shakespeare – it appears he never completed one to his satisfaction – the latter features more prominently than any other writer in Pessoa's critical texts, as testified by the 'Índice de autores citados' [Index of Authors Cited] in Fernando Cabral Martins's edition of Pessoa's criticism.[42]

'Erostratus' (late 1920s) and 'Impermanence' (early 1930s), Pessoa's two most developed essays on the subject of artistic greatness and of what will survive into succeeding ages, evoke Shakespeare throughout.[43] In these and other critical texts, Pessoa often compares him to other canonical giants, as the ultimate benchmark against which artistic genius must be measured. As he declares at one point: 'whatever genius may be, it is certain that Shakespeare has it' (*GL*, p. 354). The main candidates for Shakespeare's equals are, apart from Pessoa himself, Milton, Homer, Dante, Whitman, Keats and Camões – probably in that order, judging from the number of times he twins the Bard with each.

Pessoa enjoys citing Shakespeare and Milton, in particular, in the same breath. In 'Erostratus', he declares that Shakespeare has great genius and great intelligence but little talent, and that Milton has great genius and great talent but little intelligence; the result of Shakespeare's comparative lack of talent is that he

---

[42] See *Crítica: ensaios, artigos e entrevistas* [*Criticism: Essays, Articles and Interviews*], ed. Fernando Cabral Martins (Lisbon: Assírio e Alvim, 2000), pp. 535-537.
[43] For the dating of these two essays see Zenith, 'Critérios e organização da presente edição' [Criteria and Organization of this Edition], in *H*, p. 38.

'does not accumulate in his time or in the next time the results of genius and the results of the other quality [i.e. intelligence]' (*H*, p. 130). Pessoa muses on the differences between these attributes in dozens of writings, and discovers Shakespeare's lack of talent to be particularly evident in his inability to successfully publish his brilliant works, as we shall see at the beginning of Chapter 3.[44] Here, his point is that Shakespeare did not have the necessary practical ability to promote himself as a writer and therefore reap, in his lifetime or the succeeding generation's, the fruit of his genius: celebrity, wealth, reputation.

Homer is another possible parallel to Shakespeare:

> Não sei se se tem reparado sufficientemente em [...] quam curiosamente similhantes são, pois, os dois maiores poetas do mundo. Num caso, o antigo, a fusão, por um indivíduo Homero (outra hypothese se não pode admittir) de um lyrismo epico disperso em uma epopeia fixa. No outro caso, o moderno, a sublimação, por um génio em comprehender e exprimir, de uma dramaturgia de enredo e acção em dramaturgia de almas e poesia.[45]

> [I don't know if it has been sufficiently noted [...] how similar the two greatest poets in the world are. In one case, the ancient one, the fusion, by an individual called Homer (we cannot allow for another hypothesis) of an epic lyricism dispersed into a fixed epic. In the other case, the modern one, the sublimation, by a genius of understanding and expression, of a theatre of plot and action into a theatre of souls and poetry.]

John Keats is also regularly pitted against Shakespeare:

> Keats probably – almost certainly – loved beauty more intensely than Shakespeare, for Keats was intense and one-souled, whereas Shakespeare was spasmodically intense and many-souled. (*GL*, p. 352)

In 'Erostratus', Pessoa writes that Whitman and Shakespeare both succeed in 'gathering in their individuality the totality of observation and experience which are traditions of results within the human soul' (*H*, p. 169).

Such schoolboy compare-and-contrast exercises, wherein Pessoa compares Shakespeare to the other writers he admires, may appear simplistic from a writer from whom we expect greater critical sophistication, but they represent more than easy references for the reader, or instances of name-dropping designed to showcase his wide reading, although they are both of these things. More significantly, they represent Pessoa's attempt to establish his literary canon, and forge for himself a place in that canon.

In the lengthy piece 'Milton maior do que Shakespeare' [Milton Greater Than

---

[44] For Pessoa's writings on genius, talent, intelligence, wit and related concepts, see *GL*.
[45] Mariana Gray de Castro, 'Shakespeare, dramaturgo invisível' [Shakespeare, Invisible Dramatist], *Jornal i* (30 December 2009), p. 42.

Shakespeare], attributed to Ricardo Reis, Pessoa writes:

> Uma epopéa é mais difficil de escrever – e portanto maior – do que um drama. Ninguém diz que o *Rei Lear* seja maior do que o *Paraiso Perdido*; o que se diz é que a somma da obra, e sobretudo das tragedias, de Shakespeare, é mais que aquella epopéa. (*RR*, p. 199)

> [An epic is more difficult to write – and therefore greater – than a drama. No one claims *King Lear* is greater than *Paradise Lost*; what is claimed is that the sum total of Shakespeare's work, and in particular of his tragedies, is greater than that epic.]

That Reis should idolise Milton's powerful, formally constructed poetry above the poetics of Shakespeare's plays is not surprising, even though he recognises that Shakespeare's output, taken as a whole, represents a greater achievement than *Paradise Lost*. In 'Impermanence', Pessoa similarly declares Keats to be a better poet than Shakespeare, although not a greater writer overall (*H*, p. 237). In *Livro do Desassossego*, he has Soares reiterate the insight that others were better constructors of poetry, notwithstanding Shakespeare's wider scope:

> Se eu tivesse escrito o *Rei Lear*, levaria com remorsos toda a minha vida de depois. Porque essa obra é tão grande, que enormes avultam os seus defeitos, os seus monstruosos defeitos, as coisas até mínimas que estão entre certas cenas e a perfeição possível delas.
>
> [...] Amo alguns poetas líricos porque não foram poetas épicos ou dramáticos, porque tiveram a justa intuição de nunca querer mais realização do que a de um momento de sentimento ou de sonho. [...] Nenhum drama de Shakespeare satisfaz como uma lírica de Heine. É perfeita a lírica de Heine, e todo o drama – de um Shakespeare ou de um outro, é imperfeito sempre. Poder construir, erguer um Todo, compor uma coisa que seja como um corpo humano, com perfeita correspondência nas suas partes, e com uma vida, uma vida de unidade e congruência, unificando a dispersão de feitios das suas partes! (*LD*, pp. 277-78)

> [Had I written *King Lear*, I would regret all my subsequent life. For that work is so great that its defects seem great, monstrous, even the tiny gap between certain scenes and their possible perfection.
>
> [...] I love some lyric poets for not having been epic or dramatic poets, for having the correct intuition of not wishing for greater success than a moment of feeling or dreaming. [...] Not one of Shakespeare's plays satisfies like a poem of Heine's. Heine's poetry is perfect, and all drama – by Shakespeare or anyone else – is always imperfect. To be able to construct, erect a whole, compose something akin to the human body, with a perfect connection between every part, and with life, a life of unity and congruence, unifying the dispersion of temperaments of each part!]

But Shakespeare's scope is precisely what redeems him. In Emerson's essay 'Shakespeare; or the Poet', an essay Pessoa read (see Introduction), Emerson's opening line focuses on this very aspect of the playwright's genius: 'Great men are more distinguished by range and extent, than by originality.'[46] Although Pessoa subscribes to this view, whenever he ponders whether Shakespeare is the greatest poet who ever lived, he concludes that he is not. He writes to an unnamed English publisher in 1916: 'Personally, I confess that I tend ever more and more to put Milton above Shakespeare as a poet' (*Corr I*, p. 235). The operative words in that sentence are 'as a poet'.

Beyond not standing alone as a poet, Pessoa considers Shakespeare to be even more deficient as a playwright, as he explains in a letter of 10 August 1925 to Francisco Costa:

> Um Homero, um Dante, um Milton, como, em porém menor grau, um Camões, são é certo mais *limitados* que Shakespeare no que exprimem; são, mais certamente ainda, menos profundos na expressão; são, porém, mais complexos, porque exprimem construindo, arquitectando, estruturando, e Shakespeare – patentemente um precipitado e um impaciente – é naturalmente falho de qualidades de complexidade construtiva. (*Corr II*, p. 85)

> [A Homer, a Dante, a Milton and, although to a lesser extent, a Camões, are certainly more *limited* than Shakespeare in what they express; they are, even more certainly, less profound in their expression; they are, however, more complex, because they express by construction, architecture, structure, and Shakespeare – patently impatient and hasty – is naturally lacking in the qualities of constructive complexity.]

The criticism that Shakespeare's plots can be careless, unbelievable, and badly constructed is an old one. It is one of the main arguments, for instance, in a book Pessoa owned by Georges Pellissier, *Shakespeare et La Supersition shakespearienne* [*Shakespeare and the Shakespearean Superstition*] (1914).[47] In it, Pessoa underlined such assertions as 'Ayons le courage de le dire, ce "dieu du théâtre" est un très mauvais dramatiste' [Let us have the courage to say that this 'god of the theatre' is a terrible dramatist]. [48] He also underlined the following statement to this effect in one of his books by J. M. Robertson: 'it is idle to pretend that Shakespeare was deeply concerned to secure perfect artistic consistency. As an adaptor and reconstructor he worked wonders.'[49] Robertson was the prolific author of formidably scholarly, albeit not particularly innovative or imaginative, books on Shakespeare, several of which are in Pessoa's library.

---

[46] Emerson, *Works*, p. 187.
[47] Georges Pellissier, *Shakespeare et La Superstion shakespearienne* (Paris: Hachette, 1914).
[48] *Ibid.*, p. 3.
[49] J. M. Robertson, *The Problem of "Hamlet"* (London: George Allen & Unwin, 1919), p. 86.

In one text, Pessoa returns to the problem of Shakespeare's inadequacies as a dramatist:

O poeta lyrico que seja tão grande lyrico que transborde para dramaturgo fica com pois as qualidades *psychologicas* do dramaturgo, mas não com as qualidades *constructivas*, que pertencem a uma outra categoria.

No dramaturgo, há porém, 3 ordens de qualidades:

1. *as qualidades psychologicas* – pelas quaes elle visiona por dentro as personagens. (São estas que o lyrico maximo pode ter)

2. *as qualidades equilibradas* – pelas quaes elle equilibra

(a) o assumpto geral com os episódios,

(b) os psychismos com a acção,

(c) os psychismos entre si. (São qualidades que elle tem de commum com o epico.)

3. *as qualidades constructivas* – pelas quaes constrói o drama propriamente dito – isto é, elabora a acção no grau propriamente e exclusivamente dramatico.

Shakespeare tem (1) em alto grau, (2) em um grau menos notavel; é falho em (3).[50]

[The lyrical poet who is such a great lyricist that he becomes a dramatist thus has the *psychological* qualities of a dramatist, but without the characteristics of *construction*, which belong to a different category.

In the dramatist, there are however 3 types of characteristics:

1. *the psychological characteristics* – through which he views the characters from within. (These are the characteristics the greatest lyricists can have)

2. *balance* – through which he balances

(a) the overall theme with each episode,

(b) the psychisms with the action,

(c) the psychisms with one another. (These characteristics are shared with the epic.)

3. *construction* – through which he constructs the drama itself – that is, develops the action in a proper and exclusively dramatic manner.

Shakespeare has (1) to a high degree, (2) to a lesser extent; he lacks (3).]

This is rather a long-winded way of saying that Shakespeare, although adroit at depicting his characters from the inside, with psychological depth, is not very adept at constructing good plots. It is possible that Pessoa held the two qualities to be mutually exclusive, for he scribbled an approving 'good' in the margin of a biography of Shakespeare he owned next to the sentence: 'When a plot engrosses

---

[50] *Apreciações Literárias de Fernando Pessoa* [*Literary Apreciations*], ed. Pauly Ellen Bothe (Critical Edition; Lisbon: IN-CM, 2013), p. 243. First transcribed and presented in my doctoral thesis *Fernando Pessoa's Shakespeare* (King's College London, April 2010).

the vitality of a dramatist's mind, his character-drawing dies.'[51] Pessoa's refusal to be impressed by Shakespeare as a dramatist explains why he does not use him as a model for his own plays. (The only play Pessoa ever published, *O Marinheiro* [*The Mariner*] (1913), is an entirely static one, and in this light more akin to dramatic poetry than 'pure' drama. The play was never staged during Pessoa's lifetime.)

In a text titled 'Shakespeare – his defects' (Pessoa wrote several texts with this heading), Pessoa explores Shakespeare's generic classification, exploring whether he is in essence a lyric poet, a dramatist, or a dramatic poet:

1. Is Shakespeare a great dramatist *and* a great poet; a great dramatist essentially; or a great poet essentially and a dramatist only secondarily or out of qualities coherent to being a great poet?

2. Not *essentially* a great dramatist, like Corneille, Molière and even Racine who are dramatists first and poets very secondarily. A man essentially a dramatist is essentially a constructive mind (and Shakespeare is the reverse: he has no notion of construction...) He proceeds by degrees of intuition.

3. Not equally a dramatist and a poet, as e.g. Ben Jonson. His power of expression far exceeds his power of construction; his great dramatic force is in the comprehension of character and the power to *express* mental states, qualities, conflicts which can exist outside drama (as in poems, novels, etc.) and therefore not fundamental to the 'dramatist' type of mind.

4. Shakespeare is therefore essentially a poet, but he is a poet of such force and power that he rises naturally to dramatic level.[52]

Pessoa's conclusion is that Shakespeare is not essentially a dramatist or a lyric poet: he is essentially a *dramatic poet*. This generic classification is central to our understanding of Shakespeare's place in Pessoa's canon. Rita Patrício suggests that Pessoa's negative comments about Shakespeare's art are explained by his attraction to imperfections.[53] They are better explained, however, by Pessoa's distinction between the poetic genres, for on inspection every single ambivalent, or downright derogatory, appraisal of the Bard's genius hinges on one of two aspects: his achievement as a poet, or his dexterity as a playwright. In both capacities Pessoa considers Shakespeare to have equals and, on occasion, betters. It is as a *dramatic poet* that Pessoa's Shakespeare reigns supreme.

Not incidentally, for Pessoa dramatic poetry represents the highest form of art. He writes in one text: 'We have proved that Shakespeare is a lyric poet of the very highest type, indeed the highest representation of that genius.'[54] The highest

---

[51] John Masefield, *William Shakespeare: His Life and Works* (London: Williams and Norgate/New York: Henry Holt, n.d.), p. 33.
[52] *Apreciações Literárias de Fernando Pessoa*, ed. Pauly Ellen Bothe, p. 247. First transcribed and presented in my doctoral thesis *Fernando Pessoa's Shakespeare*.
[53] See Patrício, *Episódios da teorização estética em Fernando Pessoa*, pp. 172-182.
[54] *Apreciações Literárias de Fernando Pessoa*, ed. Pauly Ellen Bothe, p. 249. First transcribed and presented in my doctoral thesis *Fernando Pessoa's Shakespeare*.

representation of that genius is, as he declares in 'Os graus da poesia' [The Levels of Poetry], dramatic poetry:

O primeiro grau da poesia lírica é aquele em que o poeta, concentrado no seu sentimento, exprime esse sentimento. Se ele, porém, for uma criatura de sentimentos variáveis e vários, exprimirá como que uma multiplicidade de personagens, unificadas somente pelo temperamento e o estilo. Um passo mais, na escala poética, e temos o poeta que é uma criatura de sentimentos vários e fictícios, mais imaginativo do que sentimental, e vivendo cada estado de alma antes pela inteligência que pela emoção. Este poeta exprimir-se-á como uma multiplicidade de personagens, unificadas, não já pelo temperamento e o estilo, pois que o temperamento está substituído pela imaginação, e o sentimento pela inteligência, mas tão somente pelo simples estilo. Outro passo, na mesma escala de despersonalização, ou seja de imaginação, e temos o poeta que em cada um dos seus estados mentais vários se integra de tal modo nele que de todo se despersonaliza, de sorte que, vivendo analiticamente esse estado de alma, faz dele como que a expressão de um outro personagem, e, sendo assim, o mesmo estilo tende a variar. Dê-se o passo final, e teremos um poeta que seja vários poetas, um poeta dramático escrevendo em poesia lírica. Cada grupo de estados de alma mais aproximados insensivelmente se tornará uma personagem, com estilo próprio, com sentimentos porventura diferentes, até opostos, aos típicos do poeta na sua pessoa viva. E assim se terá levado a poesia lírica — ou qualquer forma literária análoga em sua substância à poesia lírica — até à poesia dramática, sem, todavia, se lhe dar a forma do drama, nem explícita nem implicitamente. (*PETCL*, p. 106)

[The first level of lyric poetry is when the poet, focussed on his emotion, expresses that emotion. If, however, he is a creature of variable and various emotions, he will express what seems like a multiplicity of characters, unified solely by temperament and style. One step further along the poetic scale, and we have the poet who is a creature of various and fictional emotions, more imaginative and emotional, and living each state of mind through his intelligence rather than emotion. This poet will express himself as a multiplicity of characters, no longer unified by temperament and style, because imagination takes the place of temperament, and intelligence the place of emotion, but only by style itself. One more step along the same scale of depersonalization, or rather, of imagination, and we have the poet who embodies each of his various mental states so fully that he becomes completely impersonal, and thus the style itself will tend to vary. If the final step is taken, we will have a poet who is various poets, a dramatic poet writing lyric poetry. Each group of states of mind which are linked to one another will become a character, with his own style, with emotions perhaps different, even contrary to, those typical of the poet in real life. And so we will have turned lyric poetry – or any analogous literary form – into dramatic poetry, without, however, giving it the form of a drama, either explicitly or implicitly.]

The traditional contrast between lyric (passive, personal, subjective) and dramatic (active, impersonal, objective) poetry stems from Aristotle's *Poetics*, as Pessoa recognises in the introduction to this piece. But the distinction between drama and dramatic poetry did not arise until the early nineteenth century, when Victor Hugo and countless others enunciated the progress of poetry from the primitive to the modern as lyrical, epic, and dramatic.[55] The Greek tragedians were, of course, all poets, as Pessoa is well aware. However, as the author of a book he owned argues, the 'essential character' of Greek plays 'was lyrical, and not at all dramatic or tragic, in the modern sense of these words.'[56] Pessoa underlined this insight.

The Modernist generation to which Pessoa belongs, in revising the Romantic celebration of the lyric, firmly placed dramatic poetry at the apex of the generic hierarchy.[57] Joyce, in *A Portrait of the Artist as a Young Man* (1916) argues for the hierarchical progression of poetry from lyric to epic to dramatic.[58]

Pessoa's generic classification of Shakespeare is tendentious, for there is no denying that Shakespeare was both a dramatist and a lyric poet, and we have seen that Pessoa himself was attracted to his lyric poetry, especially his *Sonnets*. But it explains why, despite his negative appraisals of the Bard as both poet and dramatist – despite his belief that other writers, like Milton and Dante, surpass him on these two scores – Pessoa can place Shakespeare firmly at the centre of his canon, declaring that 'o nome maior de toda a literatura europeia é o de Shakespeare' [Shakespeare's is the greatest name of all European literature].[59]

In line with Pessoa's classification of Shakespeare as a dramatic poet, subsequent critics like Harold Bloom, Harry Berger and Lukas Erne have insisted that Shakespeare's plays are better read as poetry than seen as drama, that he is a man of the page rather than the stage, a dramatic poet rather than a poetic dramatist.[60]

[55] See Victor Hugo, *Cromwell* (Paris: Testard, 1827).

[56] John Stuart Blackie, 'Of the Greek Tragedy', in *The Lyrical Dramas of Aeschylus, translated into English Verse by John Stuart Blackie* (1906; London/Toronto: J. M. Dent & Sons; New York: E. P. Dutton & Co., 1917), pp. 12-13.

[57] See H. H. Anniah Gowda, *Dramatic Poetry from Mediaeval to Modern Times* (Madras, India: The Macmillan Company of India, 1972).

[58] James Joyce, *A Portrait of the Artist as a Young Man* (1916), ed. Seamus Deane (London: Penguin, 1992), pp. 232-233.

[59] *PPP II*, p. 185; first published in António Mega Ferreira, *Fernando Pessoa – O Comércio e a Publicidade* (Lisbon: Cinevoz – Lusomedia, 1968), p. 185; cited also in Pizarro, *Escritos sobre génio e loucura*, p. 345.

[60] See Ron Rosenbaum, *The Shakespeare Wars: Clashing Scholars, Public Fiascos, Palace Coups* (New York: Random House, 2006), pp. 34-37.

Shakespeare's Invention of the Human

For Pessoa, the distinguishing characteristic of the dramatic poet, that which sets him apart from the lyric poet and the dramatist, is his ability to construct psychologically credible stage characters, with discernable personalities different to his own, whom we can recognise as profoundly human. In 'Os graus da poesia', he defines dramatic poetry as being 'poesia lírica posta na boca de diversos personagens' [lyric poetry voiced by different characters] (*PETCL*, p. 106). Joyce defines dramatic poetry in similar terms in essay of 1900, describing it as 'literature in dialogue'. [61]

In one of the pieces in which Pessoa classifies Shakespeare as a dramatic poet, he writes:

> Distingamos, no typo do dramaturgo-poeta, o que é o apport do poeta e o que é o apport do dramaturgo. O dramaturgo-poeta differe do dramaturgo vulgar em que a sua arte é feita *mais fundo*; a acção do drama-em-verso passa-se mais perto das almas do que a do drama vulgar. O elemento lyrico, portanto, é aqui presente no *aprofundamento da vida psychica das personagens. O elemento dramático.*[62]

> [Let us distinguish, in the poet-dramatist type, what pertains to the poet and what pertains to the dramatist. The poet-dramatist differs from the ordinary dramatist in that his art is made *more profoundly*; the action of the drama-in-verse takes place closer to souls than the action of ordinary drama. The lyrical element, therefore, is present in the *depth of psychic life of the characters. The dramatic element.*]

In 'Impermanence', Pessoa twins Shakespeare with two other dramatic poets he admires, Browning and Whitman, on this very score:

> We see the same care for universal men in Shakespeare, who penetrates their natures and their waking souls, in Whitman, who penetrates their lives, and in Browning, who penetrates their *separate types* (the philosophical tendency obscure in their intuitions). All describe what man does not reveal. (*H*, p. 238)

As ever, Pessoa can disagree with himself in the space of a few pages; Browning is soon, in the same essay, dismissed as forgettable: 'Browning, Byron will disappear altogether, even, perhaps, to the very names' (*H*, p. 243). But Pessoa was not always a good judge of artistic longevity; he also predicted Rodin's statues

---

[61] Joyce, 'Drama and Life' (1900), in *Occasional, Critical, and Political Writings*, ed. Kevin Barry (Oxford: Oxford University Press, 2000), p. 23.

[62] *Apreciações Literárias de Fernando Pessoa*, ed. Pauly Ellen Bothe, p. 243. First transcribed and presented in my doctoral thesis *Fernando Pessoa's Shakespeare*. Bothe suggests 'opposto' [opposite] instead of 'apport' [purview].

would soon be forgotten.

In short, as Pessoa puts it most memorably, in reference to Shakespeare: 'a [dramatic] poet is selfish, he builds others from himself' ('Essay on Intuition', in *PC II*, p. 238).

The ability to build others from oneself is the prime quality Pessoa discovers in Shakespeare from the start. In a letter to the *Natal Mercury* newspaper of 7 July 1905, written before he received Shakespeare's *Complete Works*, there is the following revealing passage:

> To us, Englishmen [Pessoa is writing as Charles Robert Anon], of all men the most egotistic, the thought has never occurred that misery and greed ennoble, despicable and self-caused though they be. A drunken woman reeling through the streets is a pitiable sight. The same woman falling awkwardly in her drunkenness is, mayhap, an amusing spectacle. But this very same woman, drunken and awkward though she be, when weeping the death of her child is no contemptible nor ridiculous creature, but a tragic figure as great as your Hamlets and your King Lears. (*Corr I*, p. 14)

The parallel must work both ways: if the weeping woman's plight can be likened to the 'personal' tragedies of Hamlet and Lear, their fictional tragedies strike us as deeply 'human'. At the tender age of seventeen, Pessoa was already struck by the psychological core of Shakespeare's plays. The difficulty in capturing it precisely in words is reflected by Pessoa's recurrent use, in his appraisals of Shakespeare's genius, of that vague, metaphysical word with profound associations but ultimately indefinable contours, 'soul'. In one text, Pessoa eulogises Shakespeare as 'o maior intuitivo da alma humana' [the greatest diviner of the human soul].[63] What Pessoa most loves and admires in Shakespeare is the way he creates, displays and inhabits other souls, the souls of the dramatic characters he puts on stage.

In numerous texts, Pessoa emphasises the primacy of 'soul' in the age of Shakespeare: 'Qual é a atitude da Renascença perante o universo e a vida? Que é que para ela constitui essencialmente a Realidade? É a alma e só a alma' [What is the Renaissance's stance towards the universe and life? What essentially is Reality? The soul, and only the soul].[64] He often compares this attitude, favourably, to the Romantic era's lack of such psychological insight: 'Para os românticos a única verdadeira Realidade é a Natureza; da Alma conhecem só cada um a sua alma individual. Daí o carácter inteiramente diverso da poesia romântica em relação à da Renascença. [...] A sua fraqueza psicológica é conhecida: os únicos

---

[63] *Sensacionismo e Outros Ismos [Sensationism and Other Isms]*, ed. Jerónimo Pizarro (Lisbon: IN-CM, 2009), p. 94; first published, with modernised spelling, by Gianluca Miraglia, as 'Fernando Pessoa – Um texto inédito' [An Unpublished Text], *Colóquio-Letras* 125-126 (June-December 1992), 195-198, p. 198.

[64] *Textos de crítica e de intervenção [Critical and Interventionist Texts]* (Lisbon: Ática, 1980), p. 77.

românticos capazes de alguma intuição psicológica, Goethe e Shelley, apoiam-se no passado, à tradição da Renascença, na figura de Shakespeare, para beber psicologia [...] Para a Renascença a Realidade é a Alma, para o Romantismo a Realidade é a Natureza' [For the Romantics, the only true Reality is Nature; of the Soul each one knows only his individual soul. Thus the completely different character of Romantic poetry from Renaissance poetry. [...] Its psychological weakness is well known: the only Romantics capable of a little psychological intuition, Goethe and Shelley, drink their psychology from the past, from the Renaissance tradition, in the person of Shakespeare [...] For the Renaissance Reality is the Soul, for Romanticism Reality is Nature]. [65]

Pessoa rhetorically asks, in one piece: 'Afinal, o que é uma obra literária senão a projecção em linguagem de um estado de espírito, ou de uma alma humana?' [After all, what is a literature but the projection in language of a state of mind, or a human soul?] (*PC II*, p. 87). This is reminiscent of Harold Bloom's pronouncement, in *Shakespeare: The Invention of the Human* (1998) that 'the representation of human character and personality remains always the supreme literary value.' Bloom is as unequivocal as Pessoa in his appraisal as to where Shakespeare's 'eminence was located: in a diversity of persons. No one, before or since Shakespeare, made so many separate selves.' Bloom's preface and introduction are littered with remarks to this effect: '[Shakespeare] went beyond all precedents (even Chaucer) and invented the human as we continue to know it'; 'Shakespeare has taught us to understand human nature'; 'No world author rivals Shakespeare in the apparent creation of personality'. Bloom insists that the Bard's characters overflow the boundaries of representation and become self-authorising creations in their own right, 'larger and more detailed than any closest friends or lovers seem to be.'[66] Little wonder that Pessoa, who also seems to have become more fully himself by representing other selves, should be drawn to the exact same quality; he has Bernardo Soares declare, in strikingly similar terms: 'Tenho reparado, muitas vezes, que certas personagens [...] tomam para nós um relevo que nunca poderiam alcançar os que são nossos conhecidos e amigos' [I have often noticed that certain characters [...] assume for us a significance that our acquaintances and friends could never attain] (*LD*, p. 275).

Bloom's thesis that Shakespeare invented the human as we know it is controversial in critical circles, not least because it alternatively lambasts, dismisses, and ignores prevalent twentieth-century readings of Shakespeare, in particular the New Historicism which has dominated since the 1980s, unapologetically harking back to an earlier, nineteenth-century tradition long out of fashion. William Kerrigan explains that Bloom is 'attempting to bring back character criticism', the approach that 'assumed its enduring contours in the Romantic criticism of Samuel Taylor Coleridge and William Hazlitt.'[67] Pessoa was

---

[65] Letter to Boavida Portugal, n.d. [1912], in *Corr I*, pp. 49-50.
[66] Harold Bloom, *Shakespeare: The Invention of the Human* (New York: Riverhead Books [Penguin], 1998), pp. 4, 1, xx, 2, xix, xviii.
[67] William W. Kerrigan, 'The Case for Bardolatry: Harold Bloom Rescues Shakespeare

much closer in time to the tradition Bloom revives: it was still prevalent at his time of writing, and well represented in the books in his library.

Looking back over his school years in a letter of 1932 to José Osório de Oliveira, Pessoa cites his chief literary influences, at that time, as Shakespeare, Milton, and the English Romantic poets (*Corr II*, pp. 278-9). His allusion to the latter in the same breath as Shakespeare is revealing, for Romantic readers of Shakespeare, many of whom were major poets in their own right, pioneered the image of the Bard as a creator of souls.

Before the Romantic generation turned its attention to Shakespeare, earlier criticism had turned obsessively to the rules of the drama, judging Shakespeare's plays in relation to the classical unities of time, action and space. Samuel Johnson had in mind the concept of a correct and regular writer to pitch against the incorrect and irregular Shakespeare. Pessoa may or may not have been familiar with Johnson's view of Shakespeare; he owned a copy of his *Lives of the Poets* (1779-81), but this book of essays does not feature the Bard because Jonson, unlike Pessoa, classifies him as a dramatist rather than a dramatic poet.

The Romantic critics' single greatest contribution to Shakespeare studies was their shift in attention from Shakespeare's dramatic action to his dramatic characters. In the introduction to his 1768 edition of the plays, Edward Capell describes Shakespeare as 'this *Proteus*, who could put on any shape that either serv'd his interest or suited his inclination.'[68] Capell coined the metaphor while discussing Shakespeare's capacity to write in whatever genre the public demanded, but six years later William Richardson, in his *A Philosophical Analysis and Illustration of Some of Shakespeare's Remarkable Characters* (1774), one of the first pieces of what came to be known as character criticism, wrote that 'the Proteus of the drama' was able to change 'himself into every character, and [enter] easily into the condition of human nature.'[69] The image was subsequently used by the chief Romantic readers of Shakespeare in both England and Germany. [70] Pessoa's Shakespeare, a writer who 'viveu os tipos mais diferentes de humanidade com igual esplendor de imaginação e de inteligência' [lived the most diverse types of humanity with equal splendour of imagination and intelligence] is evocative of this Proteus ('Anatole France' [1914], in *PETCL*, p. 345).

In the second half of the eighteenth century, books began to appear to explain the workings of Shakespeare's characters in relation to the plays in which they featured. In his *Essay on the Dramatic Character of Sir John Falstaff* (1777), Maurice

---

From the Critics', in *Harold Bloom's Shakespeare*, ed. Christy Desmet and Robert Sawyer (New York: Palgrave, 2001), pp. 33-42, p. 33.

[68] Cited in *The Romantics on Shakespeare*, ed. Jonathan Bate (London: Penguin, 1992), p. 11.

[69] William Richardson, *A Philosophical Analysis and Illustration of Some of Shakespeare's Remarkable Characters* (Edinburgh: J. Murray/London: W. Creed, 1774), p. 17.

[70] See Brian Vickers, 'The Emergence of Character Criticism, 1774-1800, *Shakespeare Studies* XXXIV (1981), 11-21.

Morgann attempted to show that Falstaff was not a coward.[71] He gave him a complete life history, presenting the character as a real person whom we can know and love. Falstaff thus transcends the plays in which he appears and is seen instead as the archetype of a set of human characteristics. This treatment was subsequently wrought upon a whole range of Shakespearean characters. Eça de Queirós inaugurated the approach in Portugal with his detailed study of Lady Macbeth in a newspaper article of 1866, the first piece of character criticism in the country.[72]

In Johann Wolfgang von Goethe's *Wilhelm Meisters Lehrjahre* [*William Meister's Apprenticeship*] (1774), which Pessoa owned in a French translation, Wilhelm analyses the character of Hamlet as if he were a real person.[73] He begins, as the *Bildungsroman* novel typically does, with the character's childhood. He then reconstructs Hamlet's youth: a student and thinker, a good companion and conversationalist, a tender lover. He proceeds to the moment of crisis: the father's death, the uncle's succession to the throne, the mother's over-hasty remarriage. He concludes by finding the key to the tragedy in the disjunction between Hamlet's internal nature and the external task he is called upon to perform. The novel contains what became a standard Romantic metaphor for Hamlet's character: 'An oak tree planted in a precious pot which should only have held delicate flowers. The roots spread out, the vessel is shattered.'[74]

The actors in *Wilhelm Meister* involved in the production of *Hamlet* express doubt as to whether the play can be represented adequately on the stage. The conclusion is reached that it must be performed in adapted form, because *Hamlet* can only be read, for 'it has something of the breadth of a novel'.[75] With the Romantics, Shakespearean tragedies became, according to Hegel, the tracing of the 'progress and history of a great soul, its inner development, the picture of its self-destructive struggle against circumstances, events, and their consequences.'[76] The effect of character criticism was to transform Shakespeare's characters into novelistic rather than dramatic fictions. Sometimes overtly so, as in the appearance of prequels and sequels to Shakespeare's plays, which imagined events before and after those depicted on stage, filling in gaps in the offstage lives of the characters. Two examples that appeared in Pessoa's lifetime are the anonymous collection of stories *The True Ophelia and Other Studies of Shakespeare's Women* (1913) and Lilie Buffum Chace Wyman's novel *Gertrude of*

---

[71] Maurice Morgann, *An Essay on the Dramatic Character of Sir John Falstaff* (London: T. Davies, 1777).

[72] Eça de Queirós, 'Macbeth', *Gazeta de Portugal* (1866).

[73] Johann Wolfgang von Goethe, *Werther, Faust, Hermann et Dorothée* (Paris: Ernest Flammrion, n.d. [1832?]).

[74] Cited in Ann Thompson and Neil Taylor, 'Introduction', in *Hamlet*, ed. Ann Thompson and Neil Taylor, p. 124.

[75] *Ibid.*, p. 125.

[76] Georg Wilhelm Friedrick Hegel, *Aesthetics: Lectures on Fine Art*, trans. T. M. Knox (Oxford: Clarendon, 1975), p. 1231.

Denmark: An Interpretative Romance (1924). The novelistic approach to Shakespeare's characters reached its apogee when Hamlet was given an unconscious, in Freud's *The Interpretation of Dreams* (1899), in a reading that had a profound impact on the twentieth-century reception of the play. This is a book that Pessoa seems to have been completely unaware of (his knowledge of Freud will be explored in greater depth in Chapter 4). Freud relates Hamlet to Oedipus, the protagonist of a Greek tragedy, but his interest in his psychology is novelistic. Pessoa's approach to Shakespeare's characters is also inherently novelistic, notwithstanding his classification of their author as a dramatic poet. The two genres share affinities, as he has Bernardo Soares explain in *Desassossego*: 'Um romance é uma história do que nunca foi e um drama é um romance dado sem narrativa' [A novel is a story of what never was, and a drama is a novel without a narrative] (*LD*, p. 140).

Coleridge was arguably the most influential nineteenth-century critic of Shakespeare, and Pessoa owned a copy of his *Lectures on Shakspeare [sic] and Other Poets and Dramatists* (1907).[77] Unfortunately, the lack of marginalia in this book gives us no indication of the passages Pessoa was most drawn to, but it contains Coleridge's most significant reflections on the Bard. In them, Coleridge highlights the primacy of Shakespeare's characters above all else: 'The interest in the plot is always in fact on account of the characters, not *vice versa*, as in almost all other writers; the plot is a mere canvass and no more'; 'Shakespeare's characters are all *genera* intensely individualized.'[78] One of Coleridge's most famous pronouncements about Shakespeare is that he was '*myriad-minded*'.[79] The phrase is evocative of Pessoa's description of Shakespeare, in one of his critical appraisals cited above, as 'many-souled'. Camilo, in the first Portuguese study of a Shakespeare play, had celebrated the Bard in similar terms: 'Shakespeare, o colosso, ressalta, intérprete de todas as modalidades da complicada alma humana sob feições diversas, vibrando-a fibra por fibra' [Shakespeare, the colossus, expresses and interprets every type of complex human soul with its unique features, making every fibre vibrate].[80]

Pessoa's 'standard' books on Shakespeare (as opposed to those specifically on the Shakespearean authorship controversy, listed separately in Chapter 2) reveal that Romantic character criticism was alive and well during his lifetime. These are, in chronological order of publication:

---

[77] *Coleridge's Lectures on Shakspeare [sic] and other Poets and Dramatists* (1907; London: J. M. Dent & Sons/New York: E. P. Dutton & Co, 1914).

[78] *Ibid.*, pp. 33, 67.

[79] Coleridge, *Biographia Literaria or Biographical Sketches of My Literary Life, and Opinions* (1817; Whitefisth, Montana: Kessinger, 2005), chapter XV, p. 151.

[80] Cited in Flor, 'Camilo e a Tradução de Shakespeare' [Camilo and Shakespeare Translation], *Actas do XIII Encontro da Associação Portuguesa de Estudos Anglo-Americanos* [Papers form the XIII Conference of the Portuguese Anglo-American Studies Association] (Porto, 19-21 de Março de 1992), pp. 178-193, p. 184.

1. Coleridge, Samuel Taylor. *Coleridge's Essays and Lectures on Shakespeare and Some Other Old Poets and Dramatists* (London: J. M. Dent and Sons, New York: E. P. Dutton and Co., n.d. [1907])

2. Masefield, John. *William Shakespeare: His Life and Works* (London: Williams and Norgate, New York: Henry Holt, n.d. [1911])

3. Mathew, Frank. *An Image of Shakespeare* (London: Jonathan Cape, n.d. [1922])[81]

4. Pellissier, Georges. *Shakespeare et la Supersition Shakespearienne* (Paris: Hachette, 1914)

5. Robertson, J. M. *The Problem of 'Hamlet'* (London: George Allen & Unwin, 1919)

6. --- *'Hamlet' Once More* (London: Richard Dobden-Sanderson, 1923)

7. Seibel, George. *The Religion of Shakespeare* (London: Watts and Co., 1924)

8. Shaw, Bernard. *The Doctor's Dilemma; and the Dark Lady of the Sonnets* (Leipzig: Bernhard Tauchnitz, 1914)

9. Knight, G. Wilson. *Myth and Miracle: An Essay on the Mystic Symbolism of Shakespeare* (London: J Burrow and Co., 1929).[82]

The writings of Robertson, for instance, are fully in keeping with the Romantic tradition. As late as 1930, in *The Genuine in Shakespeare* (a book not included in the list above because it focuses primarily on the Shakespearean authorship problem), Robertson declares that Shakespeare's genius resides exclusively in his dramatic characters, who are akin to flesh-and-blood people:

Great genius for dramatic poetry [...] consists not in plot-making or plot-constructing; and the gift for these yields in the main immemorable [*sic*] work. The required genius consists, fundamentally, in the power to conceive or create what we feel to be living personalities; to enter into any kind of soul in any dramatic situation; to make us feel that in each we are listening to a real voice, even in verse, which actual people do speak.[83]

Pessoa wrote 'ex' (for 'excellent') in the margin next to the passage. He also underlined Robertson's assertion that 'Shakespeare's real interest is in persons,

---

[81] Pessoa sent out for this book in December 1924: see his letter to W. Heffer & Sons, in *Corr II*, pp. 62-63.

[82] There are numerous chapters or essays on Shakespeare in other books in Pessoa's library, such as James Russell Lowell's 'Shakespeare Once More' in *A Gallery of The English Poets: Lessing, Rousseau: Essays by James Russell Lowell, with "An Apology for a Preface"* (London: The Walter Scott Publishing Co, n.d.), pp. 81-148, and George Gilfillan's 'Shakespeare – A Lecture' in *Literary Portraits* (London: J. M. Dent & Co., New York: E. P. Dutton & Co., n.d. [Introduction dated 1909]), pp. 184-215.

[83] Robertson, *The Genuine in Shakespeare: A Conspectus* (London: George Routledge & Sons, 1930), p. 30.

not in plots', and his view that he was 'not an originator of plots and plays; he was the transformer and transfigurer of souls.'[84]

Pessoa was so embedded in Romantic Shakespearean criticism that he assimilated its methods as well as its ideas: the parallel between Shakespeare and Milton, for instance, was common practice in the period. Matthew Arnold, in an essay on the author of *Paradise Lost*, cites Shakespeare throughout; like Pessoa, Arnold concludes – 'this I take as requiring no discussion, this I take as certain' – that Milton was the greater poet. Pessoa underlined these words in his copy of the essay. [85] Coleridge was more charitable than Arnold or Pessoa regarding Shakespeare's poetic ability, placing him and Milton together, as 'compeers not rivals', on 'the two glory-smitten summits of the poetic mountain.'[86]

In the twentieth century, although periodically revived, character criticism has not enjoyed widespread favour among professional Shakespeareans, as illustrated by the critical backlash to Bloom's book on Shakespeare. But it continues to be the preferred attitude of general readers, as evidenced by the mainstream appeal of Bloom's thesis: few other books on Shakespeare have become bestsellers. The Shakespearean director Peter Brook argues that Shakespeare's magnificent characters also account for the enduring attraction of actors and directors to his plays:

> Shakespeare's sense of each character having *endless facets* so you can see, year after year after year, new interpretations can be given to any character and they're *always* based on truths which are *there* – that is what is unique and I think this is inseparable from Shakespeare being so anonymous. One thing everyone can agree about him is that he is the least known of any great writer.[87]

Shakespeare's perceived anonymity would lead some readers to question whether he in fact wrote the works that go under his name, as we shall see in the next chapter. But Brook's notion of the Bard's anonymity is not only due to the lack of surviving historical evidence about him; it is also a product of the strong association between drama and impersonality. As Jorge de Sena puts it in an essay on one of José Régio's plays: 'a verdade é que o teatro corresponde como criação poética [...] ao máximo de despersonalização de que é susceptível a humanidade criadora' [the truth is that theatre corresponds, as poetic creation [...] to the maximum degree of impersonality its human creators are capable of].[88]

---

[84] *Ibid.*, pp. 135, 102.

[85] Matthew Arnold, 'Milton', in *Essays in Criticism: Second Series* (London: Macmillan and Co., 1927) pp. 62-63. Arnold immediately qualifies this assessment, however, in terms of diction and rhythm, calling Milton 'the one great artist of the highest rank *in the great style.*' (My italics.)

[86] Cited in Jonathan Bate, *Shakespeare and the English Romantic Imagination* (Oxford: Clarendon, 1986), p. 2.

[87] Cited in Rosenbaum, *The Shakespeare Wars*, p. 367.

[88] Jorge de Sena, 'Sobre "Benilde ou a Virgem-Mãe" de José Régio' [On José Régio's 'Benilde

Dramatic Poetry and Impersonality: The Artist 'refined out of existence'.[89]
In a letter of 1802, Coleridge writes of Shakespeare's uncanny ability to imagine himself as someone else:

> It is easy to clothe Imaginary Beings with our own Thoughts and Feelings; but to send ourselves out of ourselves, to *think* ourselves in to the Thoughts and Feelings of Beings in circumstances wholly and strangely different from our own/hoc labor, hoc opus/and who has achieved it? Perhaps only Shakespeare.[90]

Hazlitt, in his essay 'On Shakespeare and Milton' (1818), compares this talent to that of the ventriloquist, going as far as to suggest that Shakespeare is a transmigrater of souls:

> Each of his characters is as much itself, and as absolutely independent of the rest, as well as of the author, as if they were living persons, not fictions of the mind. The poet may be said, for the time, to identity himself with the character he wishes to represent, and to pass from one to another, like the same soul successively animating different bodies. By an art like that of the ventriloquist, he throws his imagination out of himself, and makes every word appear to proceed from the mouth of the person in whose name it is given [...] His characters are real beings of flesh and blood; they speak like men, not like authors. One might suppose that he had stood by at the time, and overheard what passed.[91]

The notion of Shakespeare being a 'soul successively animating different bodies' is close to metempsychosis.

In his *Characters in Shakespeare's Plays* (1817), Hazlitt had ventured that Shakespeare's ability to travel through his dramatic characters at will left him with 'scarcely [...] an individual existence of his own'.[92] A year later, in the context of his thinking on Shakespeare, Keats would coin the memorable image of the 'chameleon poet' who was 'continually in for and filling [*sic*] some other Body', the effect of which was to leave him with 'none, no Identity' of his own.[93]

---

or the Virgin Mother], in *Régio, Casais, a "presença" e afins* [*Régio, Casais, Presença Magazine and Others*] (Porto: Brasileira Editora, 1977), pp. 104-109, p. 106.

[89] Joyce, *A Portrait*, p. 219.

[90] Coleridge, letter to William Sotheby, July 1802, in *Collected Letters of Samuel Taylor Coleridge*, ed. Earl Leslie Griggs, 6 vols. (Oxford: Clarendon, 1971), II (1801-1806), p. 810.

[91] Hazlitt, 'On Shakespeare and Milton', in *Lectures on the English Poets* (London: Taylor and Hessey, 1818); repr. in *The Romantics on Shakespeare*, ed. Jonathan Bate, p. 184.

[92] Cited in Bate, 'Introduction', in *The Romantics on Shakespeare*, p. 7.

[93] Keats, letter to Richard Woodhouse, 27 October 1818, in *Letters of John Keats 1814-1821*, ed. H. E. Rollins, 2 vols. (Cambridge, MA: Harvard University Press, 1958), I, pp. 386-7. This passage is sometimes rendered as either 'continually in, for, and filling' or as 'continually informing and filling'.

Such haunting words of authorial impersonality were instrumental in shaping the artistic ideals of the Modernist generation to which Pessoa belonged, both in terms of literary practice and critical theory. The Modernists came to regard impersonality as one of the hallmarks of artistic genius; Eliot's seminal essay 'Tradition and the Individual Talent' (1919) argues that the best part of a poet's work is 'a continual self-sacrifice, a continual extinction of personality'.[94] Joyce envisions the perfect author as being 'like the God of creation, [...] within or behind or beyond or above his handiwork, refined out of existence, indifferent, paring his fingernails.'[95] These words follow in a direct line from Flaubert's prescription that 'L'artiste, dans son oeuvre, doit être comme Dieu dans l'univers, présent partout et visible nulle part' [An author in his work must be like God in the universe, present everywhere and visible nowhere].[96] Pessoa marked out the following sentence in an essay on Shakespeare that he owned: 'This unconsciousness, or impersonality, I have always held to be the highest style of genius.'[97]

Keats viewed Shakespeare's impersonality in dramatic terms, writing in his letter to Woodhouse that 'the poetical character [...] is not itself – it has no self [...] it has no character [...] It has as much delight in conceiving an Iago as an Imogen.'[98] Joyce similarly asserts, in his 1900 essay 'Poetry and Drama', that 'In every other art personality, mannerism of touch, local sense, are held as adornments, as additional charms. But here [i.e. in drama] the artist forgoes his very self.'[99] In *A Portrait*, he has Stephen theorise that in the movement from lyric to epic to dramatic the personality of the poet, 'at first a cry or a cadence or a mood and then a fluid and lambent narrative, finally refines itself out of existence, impersonalises itself, so to speak.' Elsewhere in the same book, Joyce expands the idea in similar terms to Pessoa in 'Os graus da poesia':

> The lyrical form is in fact the simplest verbal vesture of an instant of emotion, a rhythmical cry such as ages ago cheered on the man who pulled at the oar or dragged stones up a slope. [...] The simplest epical form is seen emerging out of lyrical literature when the artist prolongs and broods upon himself as the centre of an epical event and this form progresses till the centre of emotional gravity is equidistant from the artist himself and from others. The narrative is no longer purely personal. The personality of the artist passes into the narration itself, flowing round and round the persons and the action like a vital sea. [...] The dramatic form is reached when the vitality which has flowed and eddied round each person fills every person with such vital force that he

---

[94] Eliot, *Selected Prose of T.S. Eliot*, ed. Frank Kermode (London: Faber and Faber, 1975), p. 40.
[95] Joyce, *A Portrait*, pp. 219, 233.
[96] Gustave Flaubert, letter to Louise Collet, 9 December 1852, in *Correspondance*, 4 vols. (Paris: Gallimard, 1973-1998), II, p. 204.
[97] Gilfillan, 'Shakespeare – A Lecture', in *A Gallery of Literary Portraits*, p. 190.
[98] Keats, letter to Woodhouse, 27 October 1818, in *Letters*, p. 386.
[99] Joyce, *Occasional, Critical, and Political Writings*, p. 26.

or she assumes a proper and intangible esthetic life.[100]

Pessoa, in 'Os graus da poesia', similarly explains that the ascending progression of poetry from lyric to dramatic is characterised by increasing degrees of impersonality. In a different version of the same piece, he cites Shakespeare as the maximum exponent of dramatic poetry precisely because of his 'espantoso grau de despersonalização' [astounding degree of depersonalization]:

> O quarto grau da poesia lírica é aquele, muito mais raro, em que o poeta, mais intelectual ainda mas igualmente imaginativo, entra em plena despersonalização. Não só sente, mas vive, os estados de alma que não tem directamente. Em grande número de casos, cairá na poesia dramática, propriamente dita, como fez Shakespeare, poeta substancialmente lírico erguido a dramático pelo espantoso grau de despersonalização que atingiu. (*PETCL*, p. 67)

> [The fourth level of lyric poetry, much rarer, is when the poet, more intellectual still but just as imaginative, becomes completely impersonal. He not only feels, but lives, the states of mind he does not directly possess. In a great number of instances, he will fall into dramatic poetry, strictly speaking, as did Shakespeare, who was a substantially lyric poet raised to the level of the dramatic by the astounding degree of impersonality he attained.]

Pessoa goes as far as to write, at one point, that Shakespeare's impersonality allows him to create a body of work that is, quite literally, out of this world: his 'poder de impersonalização, de se consubstanciar com a alma de qualquer personagem que inventasse ou adaptasse e a animar com uma vida íntima completa' [his power of impersonality, of consubstantiation with the soul of any character he invents or adapts and animates with a complete inner life] resulting in 'qualquer coisa de outro mundo e de um entendimento que não é o humano' [something out of this world and beyond human understanding].[101] 'Consubstantiation' is an unequivocally religious word, referring to the Christian doctrine that the substance of the bread and wine coexists with the body and blood of Christ in the Eucharist.

Such Bardolatry began with Ben Jonson's remark, in 'De Shakespeare Nostrat' [Of Our Shakespeare], that he loved him, and honoured his memory, 'on this side idolatry.' Pessoa drew a line next to this tribute in his copy of *The Works of Ben Jonson*. The passage begins with Jonson's famous assertion that Shakespeare never blotted a line, which contributed to the Romantic view of him as an inspired genius:

---

[100] *A Portrait*, p. 233.
[101] *Sensacionismo*, p. 93.

I remember, the players have often mentioned it as an honour to Shakespeare, that in his writing (whatsoever he penned) he never blotted a line. My answer hath been, Would he had blotted a thousand. Which they thought a malevolent speech. I had not told posterity this, but for their ignorance, who choose that circumstance to commend their friend by, wherein he most faulted; and to justify mine own candour: for I loved the man, and do honour his memory, on this side idolatry, as much as any.[102]

The application of religious terminology to the Bard gained critical currency in the eighteenth century: for Pope, Shakespeare was 'divine' (1737); for Johnson, he was 'immortal' (1747): his genius was 'divine emanation', therefore 'inexplicable' and 'incomprehensible'.[103] When Elizabeth Montagu maintained, in 1789, that Shakespeare 'was approved by his own age, admired by the next, and is revered, and almost adored by the present', she did not overstate the case.[104] The story of the forger William Henry Ireland, who in the late 1790s produced 'lost' manuscripts, supposedly in Shakespeare's hand, that fooled his father and many eminent personages of the day, shows how by that time there was an appetite for Shakespearean relics.

Thomas Carlyle's essay 'The Hero as Poet' evokes Goethe's fascination with Shakespeare's ability to create a vivid interior life for his characters: 'you may say what [Goethe] himself says of Shakespeare: "His characters are like watches with dial-plates of transparent crystal; they show you the hour like others, and the inward mechanism also is all visible."'[105] Pessoa drew a line next to these words, and underlined Carlyle's pronouncement that 'there is actually a kind of sacredness in the fact of such a man being sent into this Earth.'[106] Goethe's image of Shakespeare as a watchmaker, cited by Carlyle and annotated by Pessoa, is reminiscent of the teleological argument from design, the argument being that an intelligent creator must exist because the universe is as intelligently designed as the inward mechanism of a watch.

Writing in 1907, Walter Raleigh deplored the religious treatment of Shakespeare, arguing that it was high time to treat the playwright as a human being, a craftsman depicting dramatic characters rather than a deity creating

---

[102] Ben Jonson, *Discoveries*, *The Works of Ben Jonson*, 3 vols., (London: Chatto & Windus, 1897-1904), III, p. 393.

[103] Cited in Louis Marder, *His Exits and His Entrances: The Story of Shakespeare's Reputation* (Philadelphia: Lippincott, 1963), p. 18; see also Robert Witbeck Babcock, *The Genesis of Shakespeare Idolatry 1766-1799: A Study in English Criticism of the Late Eighteenth Century* (New York: Russel and Russel, 1964), pp. 121-5.

[104] Elizabeth Montagu, *An Essay on the Writings and Genius of Shakespear* [sic], *Compared with the Greek and French Dramatic Poets. With Some Remarks Upon the Misrepresentations of Mons. de Voltaire* (1789; New York: Augustus M. Kelley Publishers, 1970), p. 10.

[105] Thomas Carlyle, *Sartor Resartus; Heroes; Past and Present* (London: Chapman and Hall, 1903), p. 97.

[106] *Ibid.*, p. 103.

flesh-and-blood people.[107] But the cult of Shakespeare continued unabated into the twentieth century. Pessoa himself is wont to liken Shakespeare to a god in instances of sheer hero-worship: 'Shakespeare escreve como um anjo caído [...] Shakespeare escreve como um deus carnal (*a carnal god*)' [Shakespere writes like a fallen angel [...] Shakespeare writes like a carnal god] (*PI*, p. 384). In describing him in this way, Pessoa literalises the metaphor behind his continual use of the word 'souls' to describe the Bard's dramatic characters.

In the second half of the century, Jorge Luis Borges appropriated Keats's image of the 'chameleon poet' for his short story, in English, 'Everything and Nothing' (1961) – in the letter to Woodhouse Keats had written that the poetical character, having no self, is 'every thing and nothing' – to offer us an image of Shakespeare as God in no uncertain terms.[108] Borges writes that, to begin with, Shakespeare had no identity of his own: 'There was no one in him'. As an actor, he discovered that the best way to fill that void was to imagine and impersonate others: 'No one has ever been so many men as this man, who like the Egyptian Proteus [that recurring image again] could exhaust all the guises of reality.' After his death, Shakespeare confronted God:

> History adds that before or after dying he found himself in the presence of God and told Him: 'I who have been so many men in vain want to be one and myself.' The voice of the Lord answered from a whirlwind: 'Neither am I anyone; I have dreamt the world as you dreamt your work, my Shakespeare, and among the forms in my dream are you, who like myself are many and no one.'[109]

No better way to approximate Shakespeare to God than to have God voice the parallel himself.

The image of Shakespeare as the invisible (because completely impersonal) God of creation is usually taken figuratively, but the author of *The Romantic Cult of Shakespeare* (1998) argues that Bardolatry is 'a secular cult whose psychology, ritual and rhetoric reveal latent religious patterns.'[110] He further argues that 'the characteristic response that distinguishes the cultic attitude from the critical, however, is the unconditional readiness to acknowledge and defend Shakespeare's unfathomable perfection even when the plays happen to show features the admirer would deplore in some (or any) other work written by somebody else.'[111] If so, Pessoa's stance is more critical than cultic, for he is not blind to Shakespeare's faults as a poet and dramatist, even if he never says a word

---

[107] Walter Raleigh, *Shakespeare* (1907; London: Macmillan, 1965), p. 23.

[108] Keats, Letter to Richard Woodhouse, 27 October 1818, in *Letters*, p. 387.

[109] Jorge Luis Borges, *Labyrinths: Selected Stories and Other Writings*, trans. James Irby (New York: Penguin, 1964), pp. 248-9.

[110] Péter Dávidházi, *The Romantic Cult of Shakespeare: Literary Reception in Anthropological Perspective* (London: Macmillan, 1998), p. ix.

[111] *Ibid.*, p. 13.

against him as a dramatic poet.

Shakespeare's Genius and the Heteronymic Project

Pessoa's Shakespeare, whose genius resides in his impersonal creation of dramatic others, is a fusion of the Romantic conception of genius to which Pessoa ascribes and his Modernist ideal of invisible authorship.[112] He is also, however, a product of Pessoa's autobiographical self-projections, for Pessoa continually projects his insights into his own creativity on to the Bard. In an unpublished text (reproduced on the following page), he writes:

> Literature is the art of expressing artificially through words a feeling, or a number of feelings, which have undergone a process, conscious or unconscious, of analysis by thought. Until a feeling has been analysed by thought, and thus reduced to intelligibility to others, it has not reached the literary stage; for that analysis eliminates the element which is purely personal, which is the feeling itself, and consolidates by intellect the general and transmissible part. This intellectualized feeling is put into words because words are the material of literature. Finally, once put into words, it is so put artificially, such being the condition of all art. The very words art and artifice are related.
>
> The writing of literature involves three elements: (1) expression, which is the rendering in as highly intelligent a way as possible of what is felt; (2) verbalizing, which is the careful attention to the words which is used for that expression; (3) construction, which is the disposition of the whole thus produced into as artificially exact a way as possible. (76-20)

This reads as a straightforward exposition of Pessoa's goal of impersonality, in keeping with that expressed in the programmatic poem 'Autopsicografia' [Autopsychography] (1934) and elsewhere. The passage's most remarkable feature is its heading: '*Identity of Shakespeare*'. Another text, this time a projected preface for Pessoa's own work, similarly bears the sub-heading, in parenthesis: '(aproveitar para Shakespeare)' [(make use of this for Shakespeare)] (*PI*, p. 27). As a third example of self-projection, in the piece 'Sobre traduzir Shakespeare' [On Translating Shakespeare] Pessoa opens with the striking sentence: 'A infelicidade fundamental de cada individuo é não ser outro individuo' [Everyone's fundamental unhappiness is not being someone else].[113] This may well be a general truth, although it is of course debatable, and it may be doubly true of Pessoa, but the fact is that we simply cannot know whether or not it is true of Shakespeare. These are pertinent illustrations of the way in which Pessoa, in his readings of Shakespeare's genius, descends into the critic's favourite vice, that of refashioning the subject in his own image.

---

[112] For Pessoa's conception of genius and its Romantic sources see Maria Irene Ramalho de Sousa Santos, *Fernando Pessoa's Turn in Anglo-American Modernism* (Hanover/London: University Press of New England, 2003), pp. 35-47.
[113] In *A Tormenta, de William Shakespeare*, p. 36.

Identity of Shakespeare.
------------------- -------------

Literature is the art of expressing artificially through words a feeling, or a number of feelings, which have undergone the process, conscious or unconscious, of analysis by thought. Until a feeling has been analysed by thought, and thus reduced to intelligibility to others, it has not reached the literary stage; for that analysis eliminates the element which is purely personal, which is the feeling in itself, and consolidates the by intellect the general and transmissible part. This intellectualized feeling is put into words because words are the material of literature. Finally, once put into words, it is so put artificially, such being the condition of all art. The very words art and artifice are related.

The literary writing of literature involves thus three elements: (1) expression, which is the rendering in as highly intelligent a way as possible of what is felt; (2) verbalizing, which is the careful attention to the material (words) which is used for that expression; (3) construction, which is the disposition of the whole thus produced into as artificially exact a way as possible.

There are, thus, three literary types: (1) the expressionist, (2) the verbal, and (3) the constructive. The constructive type is known as the classical, and the result is logical, frigid and exact. The verbal type tends to the opposite. The expressionist type

The common example of expression is what is called wit. The common example of verbalism is what is called style. The common example of constructiveness is what is called logic.

In many of Pessoa's appraisals of the Bard's genius, he might as well be speaking of himself:

> Representativeness must be general to hope for survival *on that score*. An artist must *sum up a whole age* to live out of that [age]. All secondary and perishing artists represent certain currents, but the artist who survives on this score must represent the current at bottom of all those currents.

The common characteristic of all representative artists is that they include all sorts of tendencies and currents.

The highest type of this kind of artist is Shakespeare.[114]

In a letter of 15 February 1934 to Tomás Ribeiro Colaço, Pessoa writes that even his shortcomings are the same as the Bard's: 'verifiquei definidamente que estou totalmente desadaptado de escrever com simplicidade. Já do nosso confrade William Shakespeare dizia alguém [...] que conseguira escrever em todos os estilos, excepto o simples. Assim, ao menos, estou mal em boa companhia' [I have definitively verified that I am completely unable to write plainly. Someone said of our friend William Shakespeare [...] that he could write in every style, except the plain. Therefore, at least I am deficient in good company] (*Corr II*, p. 325).

Most significantly, in a piece outlining the aims of *Orpheu*, Pessoa declares that he and his friends are driven by the same desire he ascribes to Shakespeare, the invention of the human: 'Nós do Orpheu faziamos, em nossa literatura, a expressão de estados complexos e contraditorios de alma' [We of the Orpheu group, in our literature, expressed complex and contradictory states of soul].[115] In another text, he ostensibly turns his attention to the sheer scope of Shakespeare's artistic achievement:

> Variety is the only excuse for abundance. No man should leave twenty different books unless he can write like twenty different men.
> [...] If he can write like twenty different men, he is twenty different men, however that may be, and his twenty books are in order. (*H*, p. 179)

Pessoa could here be describing the heteronymic project. This brings us to the central site of identification he forges between the essence of his own genius and that of the writer he most admires.

It is common knowledge that Pessoa defines himself as being, like his Shakespeare, a dramatic poet. This generic self-classification is put most forcefully in his late letters to João Gaspar Simões and Adolfo Casais Monteiro, in which he begins to offer systematic explanations for his creativity. Pessoa writes in a letter of 11 December 1931 to Gaspar Simões:

> O ponto central da minha personalidade como artista é que sou um poeta dramático; tenho, continuamente, em tudo quanto escrevo, a exaltação íntima do poeta e a despersonalização do dramaturgo [...] Desde que o crítico fixe [...] que sou essencialmente poeta dramático, tem a chave da minha personalidade. (*Corr II*, p. 255)

> [The core point of my personality as an artist is that I am a dramatic poet; I have, continually, in everything I write, the personal exaltation of the poet and

---

[114] *Sensacionismo*, p. 236.
[115] *Ibid.*, p. 94.

the impersonality of the dramatist [...] As long as the critic remembers [...] that I am essentially a dramatic poet, he has the key to my personality.]

He goes on to make the same association between dramatic poetry and impersonality in his own case that he had made in reference to Shakespeare: 'como poeta dramático, sinto despegando-me de mim' [As a dramatic poet, I feel by getting away from myself] (*Corr II*, p. 256). In the same way, Pessoa informs Casais in a letter of 20 January 1935 that his instinctive 'despersonalização' [depersonalization] is essential to his self-classification as a dramatic poet: 'o fenómeno da minha despersonalização instintiva, a que aludi em minha carta anterior, para explicação da existência dos heterónimos, conduz naturalmente a essa definição' [the phenomenon of my instinctive impersonality, which I alluded to in my previous letter, in order to explain the existence of the heteronyms, leads naturally to this classification] (*Corr II*, p. 350). He then immediately explains that this impersonality is what allows him to inhabit dramatic personalities outside himself, in terms highly evocative of his descriptions of Shakespeare's art: 'Vou mudando de personalidade, vou [...] enriquecendo-me na capacidade de criar personalidades novas, novos tipos de fingir que compreendo o mundo, ou, antes, de fingir que se pode compreendê-lo' [I go on changing personalities, I go on [...] enriching myself in the ability to create new personalities, new ways of pretending to understand the world, or, rather, pretending we can understand it] (*Corr II*, p. 351).

In other words, the great impersonality Pessoa ascribes to Shakespeare and himself is what allows both men, he claims, to create dramatic characters who are just as real, and possibly more real, than their flesh-and-blood authors. As he explains in an unfinished projected preface to *Aspectos* [*Aspects*], a planned collection of heteronymic works:

> Afirmar que estes homens todos diferentes, todos bem definidos [i.e. the heteronyms], que lhe passaram pela alma incorporadamente, não existem – não pode fazê-lo o autor destes livros; porque não sabe o que é existir, nem qual, Hamlet ou Shakespeare, é que é mais real, ou real na verdade. (*PIAI*, p. 95)

> [The author of these books cannot assert that all these different men, all clearly defined, who passed bodily through his soul, don't exist; for he does not know what it means to exist, nor who, Hamlet or Shakespeare, is more real, or truly real.]

To strengthen the parallel between both men's genius, in a draft of the above letter to Casais, Pessoa writes that his dramatic impersonality in effect leaves him with no identity of his own:

> Hoje já não tenho personalidade: quanto em mim haja de humano, eu o dividi entre os autores vários de cuja obra tenho sido o executor. Sou hoje o ponto de reunião de uma pequena realidade só minha.

Trata-se, contudo, simplesmente do temperamento dramático elevado ao máximo; escrevendo, em vez de dramas em actos e acção, drama em almas. Tão simples é, na sua substância, este fenómeno aparentemente tão confuso. (*PIAI*, p. 101)

[Today I no longer have a personality: whatever within me is human, I have divided between the various authors whose works I execute. Today I am the meeting point of a small reality belonging only to me.

This is, however, merely the dramatic temperament elevated to its maximum degree; writing, instead of plays in acts and action, drama in souls. This apparently confusing phenomenon is, in essence, this straightforward.]

To drive the point home, one of the 'souls' of Pessoa's drama, Álvaro de Campos, helpfully informs us that 'Fernando Pessoa [...] não existe, propriamente falando' [Fernando Pessoa does not, strictly speaking, exist.] [116] With such a tenuous identity of his own, Pessoa becomes, like his Shakespeare, a fellow invisible God of artistic creation.

Pessoa's self-elevation to the realm of the divine finds its best expression in the orthonymous poem 'Deixo ao cego e ao surdo' [I leave to the blind and the deaf] (1930). Its opening stanza expresses his oft-quoted desire to 'sentir tudo/de todas as maneiras' [feel everything/in every possible way] and the poem contains a programme for how this is to be achieved: 'Quebro a alma em pedaços/E em pessoas diversas' [I break my soul into pieces/And into various people]; 'Sou vário e não sou eu' [I'm various and not myself].[117] The poem continues:

Assim eu me acomodo
Com o que Deus criou,
Deus tem diverso modo,
Diversos modos sou.

Assim a Deus imito.
Que quando fez o que é
Tirou-lhe o infinito
E a unidade até.[118]

[I've learnt to adapt my self
To the world God has made.
His mode of being is different;
My being has different modes.

---

[116] *Notas para a recordação do meu Mestre Caeiro* [*Notes for the Memory of My Master Caeiro*], ed. Teresa Rita Lopes (Lisbon: Estampa, 1997), p. 75.
[117] *Poesia do Eu* [*Poetry of the Self*], ed. Richard Zenith (Lisbon: Assíro e Alvim, 2006), pp. 213-214.
[118] *Ibid.*, p. 214.

Thus I imitate God,
Who, when he made what is,
Took from it the infinite
And even its unity.][119]

A poem Pessoa attributes to Álvaro de Campos, which begins 'Afinal, a melhor maneira de viajar é sentir', puts even more explicitly the quasi-divine aspect of impersonally creating other souls:

Quanto mais eu sinta, quanto mais eu sinta como várias pessoas,
Quantas mais personalidades eu tiver,
Quanto mais intensamente, estridentemente as tiver,
[...]
Mais análogo serei a Deus, seja ele quem for
[...]
Cada alma é uma escada para Deus,
Cada alma é um corredor-Universo para Deus (*AdC*, pp. 151-252)

[The more I feel myself to be several people
The more personalities I have,
The more I have them intensely, stridently,
[...]
The closer I will be to God, whoever He may be
[...]
Each soul is a stairway to God
Each soul is a Universe-corridor to God]

Pessoa's creation of the heteronyms is thus granted a metaphysical justification. This is pertinent to his sense of himself as a missionary, which becomes in this context more than an instance of megalomania. As Zenith points out, in one of his manuscripts Pessoa copied out a verse from St. Paul's First Epistle to the Corinthians: 'I became all things to all men, that I might save all.'[120] Pessoa's sense of himself as a missionary is directly applicable to *Mensagem*, a project similar in intent to Stephen Dedalus's desire, at the end of *A Portrait*, to 'forge [...] the uncreated conscience of my race', but it is equally applicable to his heteronymic project, for his fragmentation into other souls makes him, like Shakespeare and God, both everything and nothing.[121]

If Pessoa is, as he asserts, a quasi-divine impersonal dramatic poet in the style

---

[119] *Fernando Pessoa & Co.*, ed. and trans. Richard Zenith, (New York: Grove Press, 1998), p. 245.
[120] Zenith, 'Introductory Note', in *Forever Someone Else: Selected Poems*, ed. and trans. Zenith (Lisbon: Assíro e Alvim, 2009), pp. 13-22, p. 15.
[121] Joyce, *A Portrait*, pp. 275-276.

of Shakespeare, it logically follows that his heteronyms are akin to characters in a play. The analogy is proposed by Pessoa himself: 'Álvaro de Campos', he writes, 'é o personagem de uma peça; o que falta é a peça' [is the character in a play; what is missing is the play itself] (*AdC*, p. 15).

There is much more to say about Pessoa's approximation between Shakespeare's genius and his own. In the final chapter of this book, 'Shakespeare and the Invention of the Heteronyms', we shall explore in greater depth Pessoa's continual evocation of the Bard in the context of his heteronymic project, and his appropriation of his key insights into the Bard's dramatic art for his own drama in people. Before then, let us turn to Pessoa's readings of Shakespeare's invisibility, madness, and sexuality, all three of which reinforce his alignment of Shakespeare's genius with his own.

SHAKESPEARE'S INVISIBILITY

The Shakespearean Authorship Controversy

In his appraisals of Shakespeare's genius, Pessoa upholds the Bard as the supreme dramatic poet, with all the impersonality this entails. Such impersonality, he claims, echoing the sentiments of Keats and other Romantics, and with an eye on the Modernist vision of impersonal authorship, has the effect of leaving the Bard with a tenuous identity of his own, akin to the invisible God of creation. But what if Shakespeare was so invisible that he did not exist outside his writings: what if he did not author the works that go under his name? The question is absurd, yet it was precisely this sort of thinking that generated one of the greatest conspiracy theories of the late-nineteenth century, the Shakespearean authorship controversy, or the debate over whether the works attributed to the actor of Stratford-upon-Avon were in fact produced by another writer, or group of writers.

It is not incidental that the rise of the authorship controversy should coincide with the nineteenth-century Bardolatry that elevated Shakespeare into a God, as Pessoa recognises: 'Shakespeare is posited as a god; it is not strange that Shakespeare of Stratford should fail in the part' (*GL*, p. 352). Furthermore, as Jonathan Bate puts it, 'The moment a faith takes hold, heretics emerge.'[1] Heretics, or anti-Stratfordians, are misled by Shakespeare's seeming invisibility – as one of the characters in Joyce's *Ulysses* puts it, 'of all great men he is the most enigmatic. We know nothing but that he lived and suffered. Not even so much'[2] – into a search for a concealed author who penned the Works in his stead. Interestingly, anti-Stratfordians intent on dethroning Shakespeare tend to do so only in order to replace him on the divine throne with their own candidate for authorship. William Smedley provides a good example of the treatment in a passage Pessoa marked out in his copy of *The Mystery of Francis Bacon* (1912): 'At a very early age, probably before [Bacon] was twelve, he had conceived the idea that he would imitate God, that he would hide his works in order that they might be found out – that he would be seen only by his mind and that his image should be concealed.'[3]

Pessoa read and wrote extensively on the Shakespearean authorship debate, so much so that it constitutes the most significant part, in quantitative terms, of his writings on Shakespeare. Indeed, it is in the context of the authorship controversy that he embarks on many of the analyses of Shakespeare's genius discussed in the previous chapter. Despite this, Pessoa's fascination with Shakespeare's invisibility has generated few studies to date. The most developed is João Almeida Flor's pioneering article of 1984, in which he argues that Pessoa's intention was to pragmatically reconcile Stratfordian and anti-Stratfordian views.[4] That this was Pessoa's aim is unlikely, because such a project is doomed to

[1] Bate, *The Genius of Shakespeare* (London: Macmillan, 1997), p. 74.
[2] Joyce, *Ulysses* (1922; London: Penguin, 2000), p. 186.
[3] William Smedley, *The Mystery of Francis Bacon* (London: Robert Banks & Son, 1912), p. 105.
[4] Flor, 'Fernando Pessoa e a questão shakespeariana' [Fernando Pessoa and the

failure from the outset. Either you believe that Shakespeare the actor wrote the works ascribed to him, or you believe that someone else did; between these positions there is no middle ground.

Those who claim the actor they dismissively call 'the Stratford man' to be an unlikely author of the Shakespearean canon posit that its true author was someone who could not, or would not, reveal himself; this is usually imagined to be an aristocrat unwilling to stigmatise his name by attaching it to something so undignified as a play. Among the most heavily backed alternative candidates for the authorship of Shakespeare's works are Francis Bacon, Edward de Vere (17th Earl of Oxford), William Stanley (6th Earl of Derby) and, more recently, Christopher Marlowe. In *Ulysses*, Stephen Dedalus groups such worthies together, humorously dismissing them as 'Rutlandbaconsouthampton-shakespeare or another poet of the same name in the comedy of errors [who] wrote *Hamlet*.'[5]

Since the early decades of the twentieth century, the authorship controversy has largely fallen out of favour, at least in academic circles, although there was until recently a Master's degree in 'Shakespeare Authorship Studies' at Brunel University. In Pessoa's day, in contrast, interest in it was at its peak. Famous figures of the late-nineteenth and early-twentieth centuries, including prominent writers like Walt Whitman, Henry James, Ralph Waldo Emerson and Mark Twain, came to be famous doubters.

Whitman was convinced that 'only one of the "wolfish earls" so plenteous in the plays themselves, or some born descendent and knower, might seem to be the true author of those amazing works'; Henry James wrote to a friend in 1903 that he was 'haunted by the conviction that the divine William is the biggest and most successful fraud ever practiced on a patient world'; Mark Twain dryly remarked, in a book Pessoa owned, that 'So far as anybody actually knows and can prove, Shakespeare of Stratford-on-Avon never wrote a play in his life.'[6] Sigmund Freud's belief that the true author of the Shakespearean canon was Edward de Vere, a belief he made public in the 1930 edition of *The Interpretation of Dreams*, proved an embarrassment to his first biographer Ernest Jones, and has remained an embarrassment ever since. Freud's footnote reads: 'I no longer believe that William Shakespeare, the actor from Stratford, was the author of the works that have so long been ascribed to him. Since the publication of *Shakespeare Identified* [1920] I am almost convinced that the assumed name conceals the personality of Edward de Vere, Earl of Oxford. The man from Stratford seems to have nothing at all to justify his claim, whereas Oxford has almost everything.'[7] Ernest Jones

---

Shakespeare Question], in *Afecto às letras*, pp. 276-283.

[5] Joyce, *Ulysses*, p. 199.

[6] Whitman, 'What lurks behind Shakespeare's historical plays?', in *November Boughs* (London: Alexander Gardner, 1889), pp. 50-53, p. 52; James, *Letters of Henry James* (New York: Scribner, 1929), p. 254); Twain, *Extract from Captain Stormfield's Visit to Heaven; and Is Shakespeare Dead?* (Leipzig: Bernhard Tauchnitz, n.d. [1909]), p. 13.

[7] Cited in Norman Holland, *Psychoanalysis and Shakespeare* (Michigan: MacGraw-Hill, 1966), p. 57.

typifies the usual response: 'I recall some faddist ideas he had about Shakespeare's personality. He [...] pooh-poohed the Baconian theories, but in later life he was greatly taken with the idea of the Earl of Oxford being the author of the plays and was rather disappointed at my scepticism.'[8]

Authorship obsessives, of whom Pessoa was one, gravitate to the so-called 'biographical problem', or the difficulty in reconciling what is known of the historical Shakespeare with the brilliant consciousness implicit behind his works. Investigations of the biographical problem focus on the perceived discrepancies between Shakespeare's life and his writings; for example, the fact that at least one of Shakespeare's daughters could neither read nor write, or even sign her name, is unnerving to Pessoa. He sarcastically remarks:

> Seu pae não soubéra escrever; de suas trez filhas, duas tambem não sabiam. D'onde parece dever-se concluir que o melhor modo de ser analphabeto podendo não o ter ficado, é ter por pae o maior poeta do mundo. (*GL*, pp. 345-6).

> [Her father could not write; two out of her three daughters could not either. From which it seems reasonable to conclude that the best way to be illiterate, without needing to be, is to have the greatest poet in the world for a father.]

Through an analysis of the plays, key contributors to the debate have discovered fields of expert knowledge they claim Shakespeare must have mastered, such as an intimate familiarity with aristocratic manners and pursuits, a technical knowledge of seamanship, military and medical terminology, country sports such as hawking and falconry, and the law. In a manner representative of this approach, the lawyer George Greenwood comes to the conclusion that Shakespeare's plays can only have been penned by a lawyer (self-projection is endemic in the controversy).[9] Shakespeare's allegedly superhuman vocabulary, said to be far greater than that of any other English writer, is another key piece of 'evidence' often cited by anti-Stratfordians. Max Muller writes on this score:

> We are told on good authority by a country clergyman that some of the labourers in his parish had not 300 words in their vocabulary [...] A well-educated person in England who had been at a public school, and at the university, who reads his Bible, his Shakespeare, *The Times*, and all the books of Mudie's Library, seldom uses more than about 3,000 or 4,000 words in actual conversation. Accurate thinkers and close reasoners, who avoid vague and general expressions, and wait till they find the word that exactly fits their meaning, employ a larger stock, and eloquent speakers may rise to a command of 10,000. The Hebrew Testament says all that it has to say with 5,642 words;

---

[8] Ernest Jones, *The Life and Times of Sigmund Freud*, 3 vols. (London: Hogarth, 1957), I, p. 22.

[9] George Greenwood, *The Shakespeare Problem Restated* (London: John Lane, 1908).

Milton's works are built up with 8,000, and Shakespeare, who probably displayed a greater variety of expression than any writer in any language, produced all his plays with about 15,000 words. [10]

Shakespeare's enormous vocabulary is one of the strongest arguments of groupists, those who favour a group authorship theory, possibly led by a master writer or plotter. Most groupists consider Shakespeare to be one of several authors working in collaboration: this is what H. T. S. Forrest proposes in *The Five Authors of Shakespeare's Sonnets* (1923), a book Pessoa owned, in which he imagines a sonnet tournament with Shakespeare, Barnes, Donne and Daniel fighting it out for a prize offered by the *Sonnets'* dedicatee, the Earl of Southampton.[11]

Authorship doubters argue that there is no surviving document linking Shakespeare to any form of literary activity. Indeed, no literary manuscript in Shakespeare's hand exists unless we count 'Hand D', the disembodied phrase for the author of a handwritten section of the manuscript play *Sir Thomas More* (c.1591-3), which most Shakespeareans do not. [12] Shakespeare's detailed will, leaving his wife what is probably the most cryptic bequest in history, his 'second-best bed', might have been drawn up, and signed on his behalf, by lawyers. Stephen Dedalus, in his lecture on Shakespeare in *Ulysses*, wonderfully counters the idea that this was a valuable bequest: 'She [Ann Hathaway] lies out in start stiffness in that secondbest bed, the mobled queen, even though you prove that a bed was as rare as a motorcar is now and that its carvings were the wonder of seven parishes.'[13]

Furthermore, the only time Shakespeare unequivocally speaks in his own voice, save perhaps for the dedicatory epistles to *Venus and Adonis* and *The Rape of Lucrece*, is as a witness in the Wigmaker's case, the legal action of Belott versus Mountjoy in the Court of Requests at Westminster.[14] James Shapiro argues that Shakespeare speaks 'for and as himself' on a single occasion in the plays, namely in his revised epilogue to *The Second Part of Henry the Fourth*, modified for performance at court.[15] However, it is problematic to attribute any sentiments of

---

[10] Max Muller, *Lectures on the Science of Language* (London: Longmans, 1871) p. 41. Estimates of Shakespeare's vocabulary vary wildly, depending on who is doing the counting.

[11] H. T. S. Forest, *The Five Authors of Shakespeare's Sonnets* (London: Chapman and Dodd, 1923).

[12] For a summary of the case for and against the identification of Shakespeare with 'Hand D' see Rosenbaum, 'The Indian, the Judean and Hand D', in *The Shakespeare Wars*, pp. 196-220.

[13] *Ulysses*, p. 198.

[14] The trial documents were first published by Charles Wallace in 1910, and are cited in most subsequent biographies of Shakespeare; one modern account of the episode is Charles Nicholl's *The Lodger: Shakespeare on Silver Street* (Michigan: Allen Lane, 2007).

[15] James Shapiro, *1599: A Year in the Life of William Shakespeare* (London: Faber and Faber, 2005), p. 39.

an impersonal dramatic poet to an unmediated authorial voice.

In his copy of Mark Twain's piece on the controversy, Pessoa underlined the assertion, echoed by almost all anti-Stratfordians, that Shakespeare's 'eminent literary contemporaries [...] *did not regard him as the author of his Works.*'[16] This is simply untrue, for several of Shakespeare's contemporaries refer to him as a playwright: witness Ben Jonson's celebratory poem in the First Folio. There is also the famous allusion to the 'upstart crow' in the pamphlet *Greene's Groatsworth of Wit, Bought with a Million of Repentance* (1592). Appearing less that a month after Robert Greene's death, *Greene's Groatsworth* was printed by Henry Chettle, who probably wrote large parts of it himself. It attacked many of the leading playwrights of the day (accusing Marlowe, for instance, of atheism, a serious charge[17]) and contained the following reference to another dramatist:

> there is an upstart Crow beautified with our feathers, that with his *Tygers hart wrapt in a Players hyde*, supposes he is as well able to bombast out a blanke verse as the best of you: and beeing an absolute *Iohannes fac totum*, is in his owne conceit the onely Shake-scene in a countrey.[18]

Most readers interpret this as an unmistakable, albeit slightly veiled, reference to Shakespeare. Halliwell Phillips argues that it was composed 'under the influence of a profound jealousy of Shakespeare'; E. K. Chambers asserts that 'We have no certainty of Shakespeare's presence in London before 1592, when a scoffing notice by Robert Greene shows that he was already an actor and had already begun to write plays'; Samuel Schoenbaum writes: 'That Greene has singled out Shakespeare for attack is evident from the punning reference to a Shake-scene, and confirmed by a parodic allusion to one of Shakespeare's earliest plays.' Bate believes that 'There can be no doubt that this refers to Shakespeare, the player turned 'maker' who is here accused of borrowing the stylistic plumage of university-educated playwrights such as Greene himself.'[19]

The 'upstart crow' reference to is an important one because it is the earliest surviving record of Shakespeare in the London theatre world following the 'lost years' of scant documentation, and it therefore features in almost every account of Shakespeare's life. The italicised phrase 'Tyger's hart wrapt in a Players hyde' appears to be a deliberate travesty of a line in *Henry VI*: 'O tiger's heart wrapped in a woman's hide!' That the 'upstart crow' was offended by these lines, and took

---

[16] Twain, *Is Shakespeare Dead?*, pp. 248-9. Twain's emphasis.

[17] See Greenblatt, *Will in the World: How Shakespeare Became Shakespeare* (London: Random House, 2004), p. 212.

[18] *Greene's Groatsworth of Wit* (1592; New York: Barnes & Noble, 1966), pp. 45-6.

[19] Halliwell Phillips, 'Shakespeare' (*Outlines of the Life of Shakespeare* (London: Longmans, 1881), p. 100; E. K. Chambers, *William Shakespeare – A Study of Facts and Problems*, 2 vols. (Oxford: Clarendon, 1930) I, p. 22; Samuel Schoenbaum, *William Shakespeare: A Compact Documentary Life* (Oxford: Clarendon, 1977), p. 151; Bate, *The Genius of Shakespeare*, p. 213.

action to remedy the insult, is suggested by Chettle's denial, less than three months after the pamphlet's appearance, that he had a hand in it, and his subsequent apology to him in print. Chettle explained in a twisted and unctuous apology that he should have blocked the printing of Greene's unwarranted remarks about this playwright: 'That I did not, I am as sorry as if the original fault had been my own, because myself have seen his demeanour no less civil than he excellent in the quality he professes.' [20] Anti-Stratfordians must tackle the problem of the reference to the 'upstart crow' and Chettle's about-turn. They do so by arguing that it is by no means an unambiguous allusion to Shakespeare, and may better refer to someone else. Joseph Sobran, author of *Alias Shakespeare: Solving the Greatest Mystery of All Time* (1997) describes the allusion to the 'upstart crow' thus: 'This supposed swipe at Shakespeare is mentioned in every biography, and appears even in the shortest biographical sketches. It has been quoted so often that most readers, including most English professors, have formed the mistaken impression that not only this sentence but the whole pamphlet is directed at Shakespeare [...]. Yet there are problems with this interpretation, apart from its assumption of a rather poor and awkward pun. For one thing, *Henry VI, Part 3*, was not yet publicly known to be Shakespeare's in 1592.'[21]

However, further evidence that the 'upstart crow' is Shakespeare is what many readers interpret as a direct reference to the incident in *Hamlet*. When Polonius begins to read out a letter from Hamlet addressed to 'the celestial, and my soul's idol, the most beautified Ophelia', he interrupts himself to exclaim: 'That's an ill phrase, a vile phrase; "beautified" is a vile phrase' (*CW*, p. 953). Shakespeare does not use the vile phrase on any other occasion. Pessoa was drawn to Polonius's condemnation of the word 'beautified', and appropriated the passage in which it appears during his courtship of Ophélia Queiroz, as we shall see in Chapter 5. His familiarity with the 'upstart crow' incident points to his wide reading on the Shakespearean authorship debate, and his intimate knowledge of its principal sites of contention.

'All my books are books of reference. I read Shakespeare only in relation to the "Shakespeare Problem". The rest I know already.'[22]

Pessoa's statement, although characteristically irreverent and self-aggrandising, is not as outrageous as it first appears, for he did seek out, read, annotate, and respond to an enormous number of books on the Shakespearean authorship debate. The books we know Pessoa read on the topic are worth listing in full, since this has not yet been attempted. [23] Of the twenty-five books directly on Shakespeare that survive in Pessoa's library, fifteen, well over half of the total, are specifically on the authorship controversy. Most are weighty, scholarly tomes;

---

[20] Cited in Greenblatt, *Will in the World*, p. 214.
[21] New York: Free/London: Simon and Schuster, 1997, pp. 33-34.
[22] Pessoa, *in GL*, p. 341.
[23] Pizarro's list in *GL* (p. 341), which contains six entries, is the most complete to date, but it aims to be representative rather than exhaustive.

Walter Begley's *Bacon's Nova Resuscitatio* (1905) alone is in three volumes. They are here listed in chronological order, for reasons that will become apparent when we come to relate Pessoa's thinking on the Shakespearean authorship back to his own artistic enterprise:

1. Woodward, Parker. *The Early Life of Lord Bacon* (London: Gay & Bird, 1902)
2. A Graduate of Cambridge [Begley, Walter]. *Is it Shakespeare? The Great Question of Elizabethan Literature Answered in the Light of New Revelations and Important Contemporary Evidence* (London: John Murray, 1903)
3. Bacon, Francis. *The Philosophical Works of Francis Bacon*, ed. John M. Robertson (London: George Routledge and Sons, 1905)
4. Begley, Walter. *Bacon's Nova Resuscitatio, or the Unveiling of his Concealed Works and Travels*, 3 vols. (London: Gay and Bird, 1905)
5. Greenwood, George. *The Shakespeare Problem Restated* (London: John Lane, 1908)
6. Beeching H. C. *William Shakespeare Player, Playmaker and Poet: a Reply to Mr. George Greenwood* (2nd ed., London: Smith, Elder & Co., 1908)
7. Greenwood, George. *In Re Shakespeare: Beeching v. Greenwood; A Rejoinder on Behalf of the Defendant* (London/New York: John Lane, 1909)
8. Twain, Mark. *Extract from Captain Stormfield's Visit to Heaven; and Is Shakespeare Dead?* (Leipzig: Bernhard Tauchnitz, n.d. [1909])
9. Smedley, William. *The Mystery of Francis Bacon* (London: Robert Banks and Son, 1912)
10. Demblon, Célestin. *Lord Rutland Est Shakespeare: Le Plus Grand des Mistéres Dévoilé Shaxper de Stratford Hors Cause* (Paris: Paul Ferdinand, 1913)
11. Robertson, J. M. *The Baconian Heresy: A Confutation* (London: Herbert Jenkins, 1913)
12. Frades Rosa-Cruz. *Secret Shakespearean Seals: Revelations of Rosicrucian Arcana: Discoveries in the Shakespeare Plays, Sonnets and Works Printed Circa 1586-1740* (Nottingham: Jenkins, 1916)
13. Lefranc, Abel. *Sous le masque de 'William Shakespeare': William Stanley VIe Comte de Derby*, 2 vols. (Paris: Payot & Cie, 1919)
14. Forrest, H. T. S. *The Five Authors of Shakespeare's Sonnets* (London: Chapman and Dodd, 1923)
15. Robertson, J. M. *The Genuine in Shakespeare: A Conspectus* (London: George Routledge and Sons, 1930)

The marginalia in the books above shows that Pessoa read most with great attention and, in many cases, more than once: most contain annotations in two different writing instruments, while Twain's *Is Shakespeare Dead?*, Greenwood's *In Re. Shakespeare* and Walter Begley's *Bacon's Nova Rescuscitatio* show evidence of at least three readings. Pessoa even perused nominally 'neutral' books in his library with an eye on the authorship controversy, the most significant being the following two:

1. Jonson, Ben. *The Works of Ben Jonson*, 3 vols. (London: Chatto & Windus, 1897-1904)
2. Bacon, Francis. *The Philosophical Works of Francis Bacon*, ed. J. M. Robertson (London: Routledge and Sons, 1905)

Bacon's book contains an introduction by Robertson, a staunch Stratfordian; in this introduction, one of the few passages Pessoa annotated is an attack on Baconianism.[24] As further evidence of his interest in these books in the context of the authorship problem, in the first volume of Jonson's *Works*, awarded to Pessoa as a school prize in 1903, two years before he received Shakespeare's *Collected Works*, he marked a passage referring to problematic Shakespearean apocrypha.[25] In the second volume, he scribbled page references on the back cover, one of which relates to Jonson's notorious remark that Shakespeare had 'small Latin and less Greek'.[26] In the third, he wrote 'Bacon?' next to a supposed hidden cipher, in one of Jonson's poems, that Baconians make much of. This supposed cipher is cited by many heretics, and appears in Jonson's poem 'On Cheveril the Lawyer'. The letters Pessoa circled – an anagram for 'F Bacon' – are rendered in bold:

No cause, no client fat, will CHEVERIL leese,
But as they come, on both sides he takes fees,
And pleaseth both: for while he melts his grease
For this; that wins, for whom he hold his peace.'[27]

Pessoa even ploughed his copy of Shakespeare's *Complete Works* for Stratfordian or anti-Stratfordian claims. Next to a passage in *Hamlet*, for example, he scribbled 'Baconian phrasing' (*CW* p. 954). He also annotated passages referring to the Shakespearean authorship controversy in the Introduction to his 1921 edition of *The Tempest*.

In his writings on the controversy, Pessoa mentions a further twenty-nine books not today extant in his library, often accompanied by brief reading notes, references to specific pages, and even prices. The most complete bibliography in

---

[24] See Robertson, 'Editor's Introduction', in *The Philosophical Works of Francis Bacon*, p. xiv.
[25] The bookplate inside each one reads: 'University of the Cape of Good Hope/Matriculation Examination/1903/Queen Victoria Memorial Prize/Awarded to/Fernando A. N. Pessôa/A. A. Eliott, M. A., acting Registrar'; see William Gifford, 'Memoir of Ben Jonson', in *The Works of Ben Jonson*, I, p. viii, footnote.
[26] Pessoa scribbled 'First Folio – 324'; 'Ref. to Sh. 519 (a)/p. 525 (b)'. The second page reference is to H. Ramsey's allusion to Jonson's famous dictum that Shakespeare had 'small Latin and less Greek' (in Jonson's First Folio tribute to Shakespeare), a phrase often cited by anti-Stratfordians. Ramsey writes of Jonson: 'That Latin he reduced, and could command/That which your Shakespeare scarce could understand.' Pessoa drew a line next to these words (*The Works of Ben Jonson*, II, back cover and p. 525).
[27] *The Collected Works of Ben Jonson*, III, p. 231. For another example in the same book, see p. 25.

his archive is a three-page list of books titled 'Questão Shakespeare-Bacon' [Shakespeare-Bacon Question] (144D2–16, 144D2–16v and 144D2-17). Although he probably did not read them all, for his archive is replete with ambitious reading lists, Pessoa was at least aware of the following titles (again listed in chronological order):

1. Bacon, Delia. *The Philosophy of the Plays of Shakspere [sic] Unfolded* (London: Groombridge and Sons, 1857)
2. Smith, William Henry. *Bacon and Shakespeare: an Inquiry Touching Players, Playhouses, and Play-Writers in the Days of Elizabeth* (London: John Russell Smith, 1857)[28]
3. Spedding, James. *The Letters and the Life of Francis Bacon, Including all his Occasional Works, Namely Letters Speeches Tracts State Papers Memorials Devices and all Authentic Writings not Already Printed Among his Philosophical Literary or Professional Works*, 7 vols. (London: Longmans, Green, Reader, and Dyer, 1862-74)
4. Green, Henry. *Shakespeare and the Emblem Writers* (London: Truber, 1870)
5. Spedding, James. *Evenings with a Reviewer: or, A Free and Particular Examination of Mr. Macaulay's article on Lord Bacon, in a Series of Dialogues* (London: Kegan Paul, Trench & Co., 1881)
6. Emerson, Ralph Waldo. *Works*, 12 vols. (London: Routledge, 1883) IV
7. White, Richard Grant. *Riverside Shakespeare* (London: Sampson Low & Co., 1883)
8. Donnelly, Ignatius. *The Great Cryptogram: Francis Bacon's Cipher in the So-called Shakespeare Plays*, 2 vols. (London: Sampson Low & Co., 1887)
9. Owen, Orville Ward. *Sir Francis Bacon's Cypher Story*, 5 vols. (New York: Howard Publishing Company, 1895)
10. Donnelly, Ignatius. *The Cipher in the Plays, and on the Tombstone* (London: Sampson, Lowe, & Co., 1899)
11. Bompas, George Cox. *Problem of the Shakespeare Plays* (London: Sampson Low & Co., 1902)
12. Calvert, Albert F. *Bacon and Shakespeare* (New York: Dean & Son, 1902)[29]
13. Reed, Edwin. *Francis Bacon our Shakes-speare* (London: Gay & Bird, 1902)
14. Webb, Thomas Ebenezer. *The Mystery of William Shakespeare: A Summary of Evidence* (London: Longmans & Co., 1902)
15. Acheson, Arthur. *Shakespeare and the Rival Poet* (London: John Lane, 1903)
16. Corbin, John. *A New Portrait of Shakespeare* (London: John Lane, 1903)
17. Sutton, William. *The Shakespeare Enigma: Assessing the Baconian Authorship of Shakespeare's Works* (Dublin: Sealy, Bryers & Co., 1903)
18. Pitt-Lewis. *The Shakespeare Story* (London: Swan Sonnenschein & Co., 1904)

[28] Pessoa writes 'enquiry' instead of 'inquiry' (see *GL*, p. 355).
[29] Speculative; Pessoa leaves a blank after this author's name (see 144D2-16v).

19. Stotsenbury, John, H. *Impartial Study of the Shakespeare Title* (Kentucky: John P. Morton & Co., 1904)
20. Davis, Latham. *Shakespeare Shake-speare England's Ulysses, the Masque of Love's Labor's Won or the Enacted Will. Dramatized from the Sonnets of 1609* (Delaware: M. N. Willey, 1905)
21. Robertson, J. M. *Did Shakespeare Write 'Titus Andronicus'?* (London: Watts & Co., 1905)
22. *Baconiana* (July 1906-Jan 1907)[30]
23. Gollancz, Israel (ed.). *The Shakespeare Classics: Being the Sources and Originals of Shakespeare's Plays* (London: Chatto & Windus, 1907)
24. Munro, John James, Clement Mansfield Ingleby, Lucy Toulmin Smith and Frederick James Furnivall. *The Shakespeare Allusion Book*, 2 vols. (London: Chatto & Windus, 1909)
25. Durning-Lawrence, Edwin. *Bacon Is Shake-Speare* (London: Gay and Hancock, 1910)
26. Roe, John Elisha. *Sir Francis Bacon's Own Story* (New York: Roycrafters, 1911)[31]
27. Lang, Andrew. *Shakespeare, Bacon and the Great Unknown* (London: Longmans, Green & Co., 1912)
28. Bleibtreu, Karl. *Der Wahre Shakespeare* (Munich: G. Mueller, 1907)
29. Lee, Sidney, Walter Alexander Raleigh and Charles Talbut Onions. *Shakespeare's England: An Account of the Life & Manners of His Age*, 6 vols. (London: Chatto & Windus, 1916)

This is an impressive bibliography on a single topic, all the more so when we consider that such books were not readily available in Portugal in Pessoa's day (or, for that matter, at any time since). Pessoa had to order many from abroad.[32] And since the list only includes the books either present in Pessoa's library or directly referred to in his manuscripts, it is conceivable that he read more. In one piece on the authorship problem, Pessoa cites Whitman, Emerson and Twain in the same breath (*GL*, p. 346). It is possible that he was as familiar with Whitman's and Emerson's anti-Stratfordian essays on the authorship problem as he was with Twain's *Is Shakespeare Dead?*, which he annotated at length, yet it is equally plausible that he knew about Whitman's and Emerson's objections second-hand, as they are two famous doubters often cited by anti-Stratfordians.

Pessoa's wide reading on the Shakespearean authorship controversy prompted him to write over two hundred pages on it, about ninety per cent of which are unpublished. In these he responds to, refutes, and examines the major battlefields of the debate, as outlined in the books he read. A comparison of

---

[30] Journal of the Bacon Society in London.
[31] Pessoa refers to this as '*The Own Story of Francis Bacon* (American pamphlet)' in 144D2-16v.
[32] See, for example, his efforts to obtain a copy of *Secret Shakespearean Seals* (*Corr I*, pp. 282, 292).

Pessoa's reading and writing on the authorship controversy offers us a fascinating glimpse of the poet as magpie, creatively appropriating, or downright misappropriating, his Shakespearean sources.

The Poet as Magpie: Appropriations and Misappropriations of Authorship Sources

Misappropriations can be genuine errors, but Pessoa's are sometimes wilfully misleading. A good example features in an unpublished piece, when Pessoa introduces the authorship problem thus:

> The primary argument on which the one-time Shakespeare-Bacon question – now more fitly to be called the Shakespeare-everyone question – was and is based is that there is such a disparity between the life and the work of the man that he can hardly be conceived to be its real author. 'I cannot marry the man to his verse' was Coleridge's expression of this doubt. (74A-26)

He goes on to declare:

> The argument as to the disparity between the man and the work falls under two heads: (1) the one Coleridge presumably alluded to, that between Shakespeare's life and character, so far as we know them, and the works under his name there is no psychological consonance; (2) the one that the works show several special sorts of learning – classical, legal and others – which Shakespeare would not have had. (74A-26)

Coleridge alluded to no such thing, nor did he ever express the slightest doubt that the historical Shakespeare was the true author of the Works. But Pessoa refers to him as an exponent of the biographical problem in several pieces, writing in another that

> The primary argument put forth in doubt of the identity of William Shakespeare of Stratford and the Shakespeare of literature is that there is no conformity between his genius, as shown in this works, and his life, in so far as it is known to us. Coleridge's 'I cannot marry his life to his verse' is the typical, and the often cited, statement in this respect. (*GL*, p. 353)

Coleridge's statement is *not* often cited in this respect, because it was Emerson, not Coleridge, who wrote the words Pessoa cites. Pessoa renders the sentiment as a direct quotation but it is instead a paraphrase, as hinted by the fact that it is slightly different in each instance. Neither is completely correct, for what Emerson wrote is that Shakespeare 'was a jovial actor and manager. *I cannot marry this fact to his verse.* Other admirable men had led lives in some sort of keeping with their thought; but this man, in wide contrast.'[33] Pessoa owned Emerson's essay in which

---

[33] Emerson, *Works*, pp. 193-194. My italics.

these words appear, so there is no good reason why he should not be able to faithfully reproduce them, or attribute them to the right man. He even refers, in an unpublished manuscript, to the very page on which they appear in the 1883 edition of Emerson's *Works* (76-83).

To quibble over the misattribution of Emerson's phrase to Coleridge may seem petty, but it reveals that Pessoa is here more interested in his chosen line of argument – namely, that a famous Shakespearean critic should call the attribution of Shakespeare's writings into question – than in fidelity to its source. It is an ironic coincidence, if Pessoa is not aware of the fact, that Emerson should be one of the chief proponents of reading as a creative activity (see Introduction).

Further to misquoting and misattributing his sources, Pessoa is prone to occulting them altogether. In one piece on the Shakespearean authorship, he writes that the inadequacy of the Bard's known biography

> torna obrigatório concordar com as frias palavras syntheticas de um critico recente e imparcial: 'Se não soubessemos nada, podiamos imaginar tudo.' O que realmente sabemos é fatal para a hypothese. Dá azo á mais fundada das suspeitas contra a identidade de Shakespeare o actor com Shakespeare o poeta. Explica inteiramente como é que Whittier poude escrever, *Não sei se Bacon escreveu ou não os assombrosos dramas; do que estou certo é de que o homem Shakespeare nem os escreveu nem os podia ter escripto*, e como John Bright poude dizer, no seu habitual estylo incisivo, *Quem acredita que Shakespeare de Stratford escreveu o* Hamlet *ou o* Lear *é uma besta* (*GL*, p. 346).

These words are an almost direct translation of a passage in Greenwood's anti-Stratfordian book *The Shakespeare Problem Restated* (1907), which Pessoa singled out as he was reading by drawing a line in the margin:

> *If we knew nothing, we might imagine anything.* What we do know is fatal to the case. It gives rise to the strongest possible presumption against the identity of Shakspeare the player with Shakespeare the poet. It fully explains how Whittier came to write 'Whether Bacon wrote the wonderful plays or not, I am quite sure the man Shakspere neither did nor could', and how John Bright came to say, in the vigorous style that was usual in him, 'Any man who believes that William Shakspere of Stratford wrote "Hamlet" or "Lear" is a fool.'[34]

Pessoa either had Greenwood's book open at this excerpt as he composed, or he later reconstructed it from his reading notes. Either way, Greenwood is an anti-Stratfordian, therefore hardly the impartial critic Pessoa claims he is. Further to being ungenerous, Pessoa's appropriation is tendentious in that 'besta' [beast/donkey] has more negative connotations than Greenwood's original 'fool'. This points to Pessoa's intentionally combative mode of expression in many of his writings on the authorship controversy.

---

[34] Greenwood, *The Shakespeare Problem Restated*, p. 203. Greenwood's emphasis.

At one point, Pessoa was intent on producing a sustained piece of writing on the topic, meant for publication in Portugal: in a letter of 22 March 1913 to Álvaro Pinho, he optimistically mentions an imminent 'folheto [...] sobre a questão da autoria da obra Shakespeareana' [pamphlet about the authorship of the Shakespearean works] (*Corr I*, pp. 91-2). The projected pamphlet appears in numerous lists in his archive but, like so many of Pessoa's plans, it failed to materialise. [35] A text titled 'William Shakespeare, Pseudonymo' [William Shakespeare, Pseudonym], which is, unusually in the case of Pessoa's writings on the controversy, typed and in Portuguese, is its most concrete incarnation, even though it lacks an ending. There are numerous preparatory drafts for this piece, and fragmentary writings which were the necessary groundwork for it. 'William Shakespeare, Pseudonymo' was published, together with a few of Pessoa's other texts on the authorship controversy, in Pizarro's edition of Pessoa's writings on genius and madness (*GL*, pp. 344-9). Since it comprises Pessoa's most developed piece on the matter, it seems a good place to begin our investigation into his engagement with the problem of Shakespeare's invisibility.

'William Shakespeare, Pseudonymo'

In 'William Shakespeare, Pseudonymo', Pessoa begins by outlining the case against the orthodox attribution of Shakespeare's writings in the standard anti-Stratfordian manner, by exposing the existence of a biographical problem. More unusual is his repeated use of the word 'pseudonym' in this context: '"William Shakespeare" será, literariamente, puro pseudonymo? Será parcialmente pseudonymo [...]? A interrogação é n'este sentido' [Is 'William Shakespeare', in literary terms, a simple pseudonym? Is it partially a pseudonym? The investigation lies in this direction] (*GL*, pp. 344-5). If 'Shakespeare' is a pseudonym, either wholly or partially – in the latter case presumably meaning that the actor penned some of the writings attributed to him, at least in collaboration – we are dealing with more than one author. Pessoa says as much when he goes on to declare: 'ha duas coisas possiveis: ou "William Shakespeare" é autonymo, e ha dois William-Shakespeares, um actor e outro poeta; ou "William Shakespeare" é pseudonymo' [there are two possibilities: either 'William Shakespeare' is an autonym, and there are two William-Shakespeares, one an actor and the other a poet; or 'William Shakespeare' is a pseudonym] (*GL*, p. 348). Incidentally, Pessoa seems not to have agreed with Greenwood and others who felt that '"Shakespeare", and, more particularly, "Shake-spear" makes a very good pseudonym', for he underlined these words and wrote 'why?' in the margin next to them in Greenwood's *In Re Shakespeare*. Pessoa marked out numerous assertions to this effect in his authorship books, such as Greenwood's pronouncement, in *The Shakespeare Problem Restated*, that 'the name "Shakespeare" [...] in this form, and more especially with a hyphen, "Shake-speare", [...] makes an excellent nom de plume.'[36]

Pessoa's stance in 'William Shakespeare, Pseudonymo' is anti-Stratfordian

---

[35] See, for example, *Sensacionismo*, pp. 436, 609.
[36] Greenwood, *In re Shakespeare.*, pp. 7, 36.

from the outset, for he takes the existence of a biographical problem as a given. As he puts it, in a sensationalist crescendo:

> A investigação biographica *nada tem revelado* (medite-se bem isto!) sobre um autor William Shakespeare como pessoa, como ente. [...] O que os biographos apuraram de illuminador do caracter do actor Shakespeare contradiz a tal ponto tudo quanto se pode ter como coexistente com uma alta actividade imaginativa que se tem immediatamente a noção de que ha, n'este problema, um erro qualquér, de qualquér especie. É que, ao que se descobre, William Shakespeare, actor, tinha apparentemente, como elementos basilares do caracter, todos aquelles traços que se reconhecem como caracteristicos do arranjista estupido – mercantilismo absoluto, indifferença por tudo quanto fosse intellectual, habilidade mesquinha e cauta em valer-se das circunstancias e dos homens, mas sem outro fito que o do ganho puro e simples. (*GL*, p. 345)

> [Biographical research *has revealed nothing* (ponder this!) about an actor William Shakespeare as a person, as a human being. [...] What biographers point to as being revealing about the character of the actor Shakespeare contradicts everything consistent with his profound imaginative activity to such an extent that one immediately thinks that there is, in this problem, a mistake of some sort. For, so far as we know, the actor William Shakespeare apparently had, as the cornerstones of his character, all the traits of a simple-minded arranger – a purely commercial mind, an indifference towards anything intellectual, a petty talent for taking advantage of circumstances and people, but with no other goal than pure and simple gain.]

This tone is reminiscent of Mark Twain's exposition of the biographical problem in *Is Shakespeare Dead?*, and it is no coincidence that Pessoa should have annotated the following passage in his copy of Twain's book:

> About him you can find out *nothing*. Nothing that even remotely indicates that he was ever anything more than a distinctly commonplace person – a manager, an actor of inferior grade, a small trader in a small village that did not regard him as a person of any consequence, and had forgotten all about him before he was fairly cold in his grave. We can go to the records and find out the life-history of every renowned *race-horse* of modern times – but not Shakespeare's![37]

The documentary evidence available on Shakespeare's life is indeed disappointing, for it tells us little about his genius, but it is in the nature of surviving documents that they should be mostly legal ones.

Pessoa then draws on the commonplace legal argument, the argument being that only a trained lawyer could have written Shakespeare's plays:

---

[37] Twain, *Is Shakespeare Dead?*, pp. 248-9. Original emphasis.

o uso tão constante, tão complexo, tão seguro, tão consubstanciado com o psychismo do poeta, de *termos de jurisprudencia*, para similes, para metaphoras, para simples acasos inconscientes de phrase, e o tão completo conhecimento dos usos e costumes do foro que é dificil, se não impossivel considerar tudo isso como trahindo outra cousa que não seja uma erudição preeminentemente de advogado ou jurisculto [*sic*]. (*GL*, p. 347)[38]

[the constant, highly complex and confident use of legal terms so infused the mind of the poet for similes, metaphors, chance spontaneous phrases, and the profound knowledge of legal language and custom makes it difficult, if not impossible, to consider all this as revealing anything other than the erudition, preeminently, of a lawyer or jurist.]

The legal case against the traditional attribution of Shakespeare's works is a strong one because Bacon and other candidates for authorship were lawyers, while the historical record makes it unlikely that Shakespeare from Stratford had any legal training. In his writings on the controversy, Pessoa cites formidable authorities as proponents for Shakespeare as lawyer, such as Lord Campbell, Chief-Justice of England at the time, Lord Penzance, and Richard Grant White. John Campbell, in *Shakespeare's Legal Acquirements Considered*, wrote that the legal knowledge present in the plays was instinctive and infallible: 'He uniformly lays down good law. While novelists and dramatists are constantly making mistakes as to the law of marriage, of wills and inheritance, to Shakespeare's law, lavishly as he propounds it, there can be neither demurrer, bill of exception, or writ of error.'[39] Campbell inclined towards the Baconians, but White was a Stratfordian who was just as struck by Shakespeare's legal mind.

The legal argument was particularly well catered for in Pessoa's library: it is expounded at length in Greenwood's *The Shakespeare Problem Restated* (1908); Robertson took issue with Greenwood in *The Baconian Heresy: A Confutation* (1913), claiming Shakespeare's law was faulty. Such confrontations are typical of the controversy: the apparent discrepancy between Shakespeare's life and the specialist knowledge patent in the works is emphasised by anti-Stratfordians, while those who favour the orthodox attribution counter that this knowledge is not, on inspection, overly impressive, or beyond the range of an intelligent Elizabethan.

The second argument Pessoa chooses to draw on is the much more controversial, and infinitely less widespread, in his day or since, sexual argument, the argument being that the writer of Shakespeare's works was evidently homosexual, whereas the actor Shakespeare was evidently not. Pessoa's paragraph on the disparity between the sexuality he discovers in the writer of Shakespeare's *Sonnets*, and that of the historical man, the married actor from

---

[38] Pessoa employs 'jurisculto' and 'jurisconsulto' [jurist] interchangeably in many texts.
[39] *Shakespeare's Legal Acquirements Considered* (London: John Murray, 1859), p. 74.

Stratford, is worth citing in full, as a prime example of his manipulative style in 'William Shakespeare, Pseudonymo':

> O outro ponto [...] é inútil querer considerar como não assente, farta-se d'elle o inquieto pasmo do leitor imparcial dos assombrosos sonetos. É a inversão sexual do poeta. O mysterioso inspirador da mais intensa e complexa poesia amorosa que se tem escripto seria tudo, mas não era mulher, como n'um momento de horrorosa, posto que moralissima, alienação mental de crítico, o poeta Coleridge quiz, desculpando, persuadir os outros que se tinha persuadido a si que acreditava. Pouco importa que o "sr. W. H." fosse William Herbert, Conde de Pembroke, como querem muitos, um actor William Hughes (cuja existência, aliás, por emquanto não consta de documento algum), como outros, e em especial Oscar Wilde, opinam, ou um individuo cujas iniciaes não sejam senão literariamente W. H. O caso é o sexo d'esse individuo. (*GL*, p. 347)

[It is pointless to consider the second point ambiguous, as it is plainly clear to the uneasy, impartial reader of the haunting sonnets. It is the poet's sexual inversion. The mysterious inspirer of the most intense, complex love poetry ever written might have been anything, but he was not a woman, as in a moment of horrible, albeit extremely moral, critial mental alienation, the poet Coleridge wished, apologetically, to persuade others that he had persuaded himself he believed. It matters little whether 'Mr. W. H.' was William Herbert, Earl of Pembroke, as many would have it, an actor called William Hughes (whose existence, incidentally, is so far not proved by any document), as others, particularly Oscar Wilde, speculate, or a person whose initials are only literarily W. H. What matters is the sex of that person.]

Pessoa's reading of Shakespeare's *Sonnets*, and its implications, will be discussed at length in Chapter 4, 'Shakespeare's Sexuality'. The point to make here is that the above words are infused with rhetorical tricks to forcefully put across as plain fact a highly tendentious reading of the *Sonnets*. Their author's sexual 'inversion' is presented to us as the only possible conclusion to an honest reading of the problematic compositions, when of course they can be approached as impersonal works of art rather than autobiographical confessions. Resounding names, those of Coleridge and Wilde, are cited for support, despite the fact, as Pessoa concedes, that Coleridge was one of few nineteenth-century readers of the *Sonnets* who refused to find in them, in his own words, 'even an allusion to that very worst of all possible vices'; writing to his son Hartley, Coleridge urged: 'I pray fervently that thou may'st know inwardly how impossible it was for a Shakespeare not to have been in his heart's heart chaste.'[40] He cannot possibly have been in his right mind, Pessoa suggests ('n'um momento de horrorosa [...] alienação mental'); nor could he have meant it: he merely wished to convince others that he had

---

[40] Coleridge, *Marginalia*, in *The Collected Works of Samuel Taylor Coleridge*, ed. Kathleen Coburn (London: Routledge and Kegan Paul,1969-), XII, p. 42.

convinced himself that he believed it. Notice, too, Pessoa's substitution of 'quiz' [wished] for the expected 'diz' [said]: Coleridge wanted, or *wished*, rather than proclaimed, the addressee of the *Sonnets* to be a woman, when he was anything but: 'seria tudo, mas não era mulher'.

Having posited as unequivocal fact that in his *Sonnets* Shakespeare addresses, in his own voice, a male lover, Pessoa immediately dismisses any speculation concerning the identity of this supposedly historical figure as unimportant. He evokes, as if in passing, Wilde's theory in *The Portrait of Mr W. H.* (1891), a story he owned in two different editions, that the 'fair youth' of the *Sonnets* was a boy actor in Shakespeare's company by the name of Willie Hughes. (In one of his bibliographies on the authorship controversy (144D2-16v), Pessoa lists Wilde's book among titles more obviously devoted to the subject, evidence that he was primarily interested in it in this context.) Pessoa's reference to Wilde has the effect of forging an immediate link, in the reader's mind, between Wilde's sexuality and that of the writer of the *Sonnets*.

Following his argument that the writer of the homoerotic *Sonnets* must have been homosexual, Pessoa then claims that the actor from Stratford was not, thus implying that they cannot have been the same man:

> o que consta da vida sexual de Shakespeare – uma anecdota quasi-indecente e o facto de que o seu primeiro filho nasceu cinco mezes apenas após a data de um casamento que parece ter sido forçado – não impugna a sua normalidade de macho. Tal é a desgraça do candidato tradicional a poeta que até o que não tem de vergonhoso lhe é prejudicial à candidatura. (*GL.*, p. 348)

> [what is known of Shakespeare's sex life – an almost obscene anecdote and the fact that his first son was born five months after what appears to have been a shotgun wedding – does not impugn his normality as a male. Such is the disgrace of the traditional candidate that even his non-shameful qualities hinder his candidacy.]

The anecdote in question can only be the famous passage in John Manningham's diary referring to a tryst between Shakespeare and one of his female admirers. Manningham was a law student at Middle Temple in the years 1601-1602, and kept a notebook of events and observations, including two references to Shakespeare. The second, helping to date the play, is a reference to a performance of *Twelfth Night*. His report is one of the few surviving contemporary anecdotes about Shakespeare the man, and probably the only one relating to his sexual behaviour, and consequently it is often cited. Many scholars, however, are sceptical of its truth, suspecting it to be too elaborate and humorous, and its final punch line altogether too tidy, to be a realistic description of an actual event and conversation:

March 1601
Vpon a tyme when Burbidge played Richard III there was a citizen gone soe

farr in liking with him, that before shee went from the play shee appointed him to come that night vnto hir by the name of Richard the Third. Shakespeare ouerhearing their conclusion went before, was intertained and at his game ere Burbidge came. Then message being brought that Richard the Third was at the dore, Shakespeare caused returne to be made that William the Conqueror was before Richard the Third. Shakespeare's name William.[41]

Pessoa's use of the sexual argument in 'William Shakespeare, Pseudonymo', a vastly less deployed anti-Stratfordian line of attack than the legal case against Shakespeare, is highly reminiscent of the thesis in one of the Baconian books he owned. *Is It Shakespeare?* (1903), bearing the sensationalist sub-heading *The Great Question of Elizabethan Literature Answered in the Light of New Revelations and Important Contemporary Evidence*, was shocking enough to be published anonymously, attributed to a nameless 'Graduate of Cambridge'; even today it is relegated to the Rare Books section of the Folger Library.[42] It is a book Pessoa studied closely, in at least three different sittings.[43] The Cambridge graduate was Walter Begley, who two years later would publish his three-volume *Bacon's Nova Resuscitatio*, another book Pessoa owned.

In *Is It Shakespeare?*, Begley begins by accumulating evidence for Francis Bacon's homosexuality, gathering inferences from the veiled references of his contemporaries, including his mother's letters and anecdotes of attempted blackmail by male lovers. Begley cites as evidence passages in the letters of Lady Anne Bacon to her elder son Anthony, complaining of Francis's unsuitable companions and servants. 'I pity your brother', writes Lady Anne, 'yet so long as he pities not himself, but keepeth that bloody Perez, yea a costly fellow, whose being about him, I verily fear, the Lord God doth mislike.' (Perez was a protégé of the Earl of Essex, who stayed with Bacon in his house near Twickenham Park.) Pessoa drew a line in the margin next to these words, and wrote an 'N' (for 'note') next to them. He also marked out Begley's statements that 'there are letters [...] very compromising for Francis Bacon, and have a worse appearance in regard to the scandal than his familiar acquaintance with Perez', and that 'it appears Bacon used to sleep with one of his men-servants and take him out with him in his coach.'[44]

Begley was not pioneering in his suggestion that Bacon was homosexual; John Aubrey in his *Brief Lives*, penned in the late sixteenth century but only published in the early-nineteenth, had referred to Bacon as *paiderastes*.[45] But Begley was the

[41] *Diary of John Manningham, of the Middle Temple, and of Bradbourne, Kent, Barrister-at-Law, 1602-1603*, ed. John Bruce (London: J. B. Nichols and Sons, 1868), p. 39.

[42] A Graduate of Cambridge [Walter Begley], *Is it Shakespeare?* (London: John Murray, 1903).

[43] Pessoa's marginalia in *Is it Shakespeare?* is in purple pencil, normal pencil, and black ink.

[44] *Is It Shakespeare?*, pp. 44. 48, 50.

[45] John Aubrey, *Lives of Eminent Men* (Oxford: Muday and Slatter, 1813). A near-complete

first to argue that Bacon's homosexuality made him a more likely candidate for the authorship of the Shakespearean canon than the Stratford man who could not have been so disgraced, for by the age of nineteen he was a married man and a father, and according to Manningham's diary he was a keen pursuer of women. Pessoa appropriates Begley's argument championing Bacon wholesale for 'William Shakespeare, Pseudonymo', and for once openly acknowledges the debt:

> Do poeta sabe-se alguma coisa. Sabe-se que é jurisconsulto, sabe-se que é invertido. [...] Basta que o problema se ponha assim, com o que cremos ser lucidez, para se tornar impossivel desviar a vista da figura que, sobre ser, parallelamente á de "Shakespeare", uma das maiores da sua epoca, accumula precisamente as trez qualidades que a analyse e a investigação arrancaram para a indubitabilidade. Trata-se do philosopho e estadista Francis Bacon. Era, como se sabe, advogado e jurisconsulto; era, como tambem se sabe, tido por a figura mais eminente e brilhante d'aquella sociedade; e era, como se pode ficar sabendo desde que se leia os dois documentados volumes do Rev. Walter Begley, conhecido como pederasta. (*GL*, p. 349)

> [We know a little about the poet. We know he was a lawyer, we know he was inverted. [...] We need only put the problem thus, with what we believe to be lucidity, to make it impossible to turn our gaze away from the person who, being together with 'Shakespeare' one of the greatest men of his age, has precisely the three qualities that analysis and research have made clear. I refer to the philosopher and statesman Francis Bacon. We know Bacon was a lawyer and a jurist; we further know he was the most eminent and brilliant figure of that society; and he was also, as we can discover reading the two well documented volumes by Reverent Walter Begley, known to be a pederast.]

Pessoa then considers a standard rebuttal to Baconianism. Robertson had raised the Stratfordian objection, in his introduction to *The Philosophical Works of Francis Bacon*, that because Bacon was so ambitious, hardworking and prolific under his own name that he did not complete his own philosophical writings, he could hardly have had the time and energy to produce the entire works of Shakespeare as well:

> it must be reckoned one of the supreme flights of human perversity to surmise that the man so immeasurably preoccupied with the two orbs of natural and civil lore actually wrought, in addition to what he vainly sought to do, the stupendous imaginative performance of Shakespeare. [46]

---

transcript, *Brief Lives Chiefly of Contemporaries set down John Aubrey between the Years 1669 and 1696*, ed. Andrew Clark (Oxford: Clarendon, 1898), remains the best edition available, despite a number of abridgements.

[46] *The Philosophical Works of Francis Bacon*, p. xiv.

Pessoa drew a line in the margin next to these words. In 'William Shakespeare, Pseudonymo', he dismisses the objection in no uncertain terms:

> Responda-se, de chapeu na mão, que a observação é idiota. Quando a formulou, o erudito e arguto racionalista vinha sem duvida de soffrer a passageira bestialisação de uma conferencia politica com o seu charlatanesco co-partidário, o sr. Lloyd George. Esta generosa hypothese nossa pode servir, até, para lhe desculpar mais peccados intellectuaes do que o de considerar vida cheia de trabalho publica uma que só o foi dos cincoenta annos em deante. (*GL*, p. 349)

> [Let us humbly reply, cap in hand, that the observation is idiotic. The erudite, shrewd rationalist clearly formulated it following the temporary bestialisation caused by a political meeting with his charlatan party colleage, Sr. Lloyd George. Our generous hypothesis can even serve to forgive greater intellectual sins than considering a busy public life a life that was only busy after the age of fifty.]

This is little more than character-assassination, aimed gratuitously at more than one character. Furthermore, Pessoa's knowledge of Bacon's public office is defective, for Bacon entered parliament as an MP in 1584, at the age of twenty-three, and from then on until granted his peerage in 1618 he served in successive parliaments, representing various constituencies including Taunton, Southampton, Liverpool, Ipswich and St Albans. Pessoa is on slightly firmer ground when he refers to Bacon's 'lost years':

> Entre o muito que se sabe da vida do philosopho, e que inclue constatar-se, os indubitaveis testemunhos, a sua precocidade intellectual e a sua capacidade e rapidez de trabalho, mesmo o seu não saber estar desoccupado, ha uma cousa que se não sabe, e que é o que esse genio infatigavel e precoce, que a si proprio se classificava de literato por natureza, fez entre os dezoito e os trinta e oito annos (de 1579 a 1599), approximadamente. (*GL*, p. 349)

> [Among the many things we know about the philosopher's life, which include unquestionable testimonies and stories of his intellectual precocity and the speed at which he worked, even his not knowing how to take time off, there remains something we don't know, which is what this tireless, precocious genius, who defined himself as a naturally literary man, did between the ages of about eighteen and thirty-eight.]

Pessoa's implication here, his answer to Robertson, is that Bacon might have penned the writings attributed to Shakespeare during this twenty-year span. And here Pessoa's most complete, coherent text on the Shakespearean authorship controversy abruptly ends. It is possible that an ending exists, lost in the depths of his archive, but it is equally likely that he never concluded the piece. As it stands,

'William Shakespeare, Pseudonymo' is a dazzling showcase of his wide reading and detailed knowledge of the authorship controversy. It is undeniably anti-Stratfordian, tending towards Baconianism.

Pessoa an Anti-Stratfordian?

There is further evidence which, misleadingly, suggests Pessoa may have flirted with Baconianism. Pessoa headed many of his texts on the authorship controversy 'Shakespeare-Bacon' or *vice versa*, and placed most of them in an envelope with the same heading.[47] Several of his unpublished fragments probe the possible parallels between Bacon's writings and those ascribed to Shakespeare. In one he writes: 'eu phantasio e faço-me um passatempo deleitoso no mero ponderar do quanto, na essencia reflectiva e □ do magno prosador de Inglaterra, faz pensar no poeta da anterior geração que escreveu o discurso idealisante de Prospero' [I fantasise and make a delicious pastime of pondering how far, in the reflective and □ essence of the great English prose writer, calls to mind the poet of the previous generation who wrote the idealising speech of Prospero] (76A-50).

In 1915 Pessoa wrote in a letter to Alfred Barley, author of an article on Bacon in *Modern Astrology*, requesting Bacon's detailed horoscope:

> I take the liberty of writing to you without being able to invoke any other excuse, except that I am a student of astrology. My purpose in writing is to request you to send me, if possible, Francis Bacon's horoscope.
>
> In your book *1001 Notable Nativities* you refer twice to Bacon's horoscope (in the notes), but you have omitted it from the nativities given. I am intensely interested in that figure, and should be much obliged if you could send me, if only in a post-card, the note of cusps and planets, as by the system adopted in your book, but including, if possible, the positions of Dragon's Head, Isis and Osiris, and giving, if you have them, the cusps and planet's places with the minutes.[48]

Barley replied that he did not posses it, but gave Pessoa speculative astrological pointers grounded in his belief that Bacon was the true author of the Shakespearean canon: 'I think Bacon (especially as Shakespeare) plainly shows the influence either of Gemini, or Mercury *in the ascendant* (love of *playing on words* for example).'[49]

Four years following this exchange, Pessoa attempted to obtain a further book

---

[47] Today catalogued as two envelopes in Pessoa's archive, 76 and 76A.

[48] Letter to Alfred Barley, 24 June 1915, in *Corr I*, p. 168. Barley was sub-editor of *Modern Astrology*, a 'Journal devoted to search for Truth concerning Astrology'. It is possible that Pessoa's letter was never sent, for Barley's reply of 24 January 1916 refers to a second letter of Pessoa's, dated 10 January of that year, now lost.

[49] Letter from Alfred Barley, 24 January 1916, in *Correspondência inédita* [*Unpublished Correspondence*], ed. Manuela Parreira da Silva (Lisbon: Horizonte, 1996), p. 95.) Original emphasis.

on the authorship controversy, this time from a Rosicrucian perspective; *Secret Shakespearian Seals* was penned by the mysterious Frades Rosa-Cruz.[50] To this end he composed two letters: the first to its publisher in England, Herbert Jenkins, inquiring whether the book was still available.[51] Impatient with either no reply or an unfavourable one, a month later he decided to approach one of its co-authors, Frank Woodward, directly: 'Should you publish a second edition of *Secret Shakespearean Seals*, I would be much obliged if you would instruct the publisher of it (Mr Jenkins or another) to notify me on its appearance.'[52] Woodward wrote to Pessoa that 'of this we [the two authors, presumably] feel sure – Francis Bacon was [...] the real Author of the "Shakespeare Plays" & the Author of many of the works of the period ascribed to other writers'.[53] Pessoa certainly enjoyed reading Baconian books, and corresponding with their authors. It is unclear who finally sent him the book, but *Secret Shakespearean Seals* made its way into Pessoa's library.

Ana Maria Freitas, in her entry on 'Shakespeare-Bacon' in the *Dicionário de Fernando Pessoa e do Modernismo Português*, concludes from such evidence that Pessoa was indeed a Baconian: 'Defensor da hipótese Francis Bacon' [A proponent of the Francis Bacon hypothesis]. [54] However, Pessoa's continual references to Bacon in the context of the Shakespearean authorship controversy merely reflect the fact that, in his day, Bacon was by far the leading candidate championed by anti-Stratfordians, as a cursory glance at the titles in his library will testify. By the end of the 1880s, the Baconian case had been debated in thousands of books, pamphlets, and newspaper and magazine articles: an 1883 article by Richard Grant White bore the apt title 'The Bacon-Shakespeare Craze'.[55] By 1885, support for the Baconian movement had warranted the establishment of The Bacon Society, which seven years later began regular publication of a journal, *Baconiana*, an issue of which is in Pessoa's library. Countless conspiracy theorists continued to descend into what Samuel Schoenbaum wonderfully calls 'the bog of Baconianism' until the Oxfordian faction began to gain adherents in the 1920s; Oxford was first proposed as a candidate in 1920, by the unfortunately named Thomas Looney, in the book that convinced Freud. [56] There are over three thousand full-length books on the case for Bacon in the section of the Folger Shakespeare Library devoted to the authorship controversy.[57]

---

[50] Frades Rosa-Cruz, *Secret Shakespearean Seals: Revelations of Rosicrucian Arcana: Discoveries in the Shakespeare Plays, Sonnets and Works Printed Circa 1586-1740* (Nottingham: Jenkins, 1916).

[51] Letter to Herbert Jenkins, 26 May 1919, in *Corr I*, p. 282. The reply is unknown.

[52] Letter to Frank Woodward, 20 June 1919, in *GL*, p. 292.

[53] Letter from Frank Woodward, 7 July 1919, in *Corr I*, p. 450.

[54] Ana Maria Freitas, 'Shakespeare-Bacon', in *Dicionário de Fernando Pessoa*, p. 800.

[55] Richard Grant White, 'The Bacon-Shakespeare Craze', *Atlantic Monthly* (April 1883).

[56] Thomas J. Looney, *"Shakespeare" Identified in Edward de Vere* (New York: Frederick A. Stokes Company, 1920).

[57] Schoenbaum, *Shakespeare's Lives* (Oxford: Clarendon; New York: Oxford University Press, 1970), p. 316.

Pessoa's alignment with the discourse of the day does not prove he was a Baconian. Moreover, despite his interest in Bacon as the best alternative candidate for the Shakespearean authorship, he was ultimately unconvinced by the Baconian case, declaring in one unpublished piece: 'we are *not* led to the conclusion that the poet Bacon was "Shakespeare"' (76-34; Pessoa's emphasis). He was equally unswayed by the case for any other candidate: judging from the marginalia in his copy of Abel Lefranc's books championing Rutland, Pessoa lost interest in the Rutland hypothesis before he reached the second volume.[58]

Freitas's conclusion must be further based on the evidence of 'William Shakespeare, Pseudonymo', one of Pessoa's few published texts on the controversy, which as it stands appears to be Baconian in sympathy. But 'William Shakespeare, Pseudonymo' is hardly representative of Pessoa's thinking on the Shakespearean authorship controversy. Indeed, it is something of an oddity in the context of his other writings on it: it is typewritten and in Portuguese, whereas most are handwritten and in English; it has a beginning and a middle, if not an end, and it is logically structured, whereas most other writings are fragmentary and disjointed; it is aggressively manipulative, whereas most others adopt a more neutral tone. This suggests that Pessoa's intention, in writing 'William Shakespeare, Pseudonymo', was to expose the existence of the Shakespearean authorship controversy to a Portuguese audience with little or no awareness of it.

By 1884, there were a hundred and sixty-one books on the Shakespeare authorship controversy published in America, sixty-nine in England, ten in Scotland, three in Canada, two in Germany, two in France, and one in each of the following counties: Italy, Holland, Ireland and India. There were none in Portugal.[59] In Pessoa's lifetime, no book on the Shakespearean authorship issue appeared in the country, and no book on it exists to this day. Had Pessoa published his projected pamphlet, as part of his ambition to establish the Bard more prominently in Portuguese culture (further represented by his intention to translate Shakespeare's writings into Portuguese, as described in Chapter 1), it is likely that this would have sparked an interest in Shakespeare's life and work, as happened in other countries.

Consider the very act of describing the Shakespearean authorship controversy to an audience for the first time. You might begin by explaining that there survives no literary document in Shakespeare's hand, and that his plays display specialised knowledge that a lowly actor could not have had, going on to point out that Bacon did, for he was a lawyer and a nobleman. At this point, you would sound as if you were a Baconian.

The clinching evidence that Pessoa was not an anti-Stratfordian is the

---

[58] Abel Lefranc, *Sous le masque de "William Shakespeare": William Stanley VI Comte de Derby* [*Under the Mask of 'William Shakespeare': William Stanley VI Earl of Derby*] (Paris: Payot, 1919). The first volume contains copious marginal notes by Pessoa; the second has a total absence of marginalia.

[59] W. H. Wyman, *Bibliography of the Bacon-Shakespeare Controversy* (Cincinnati: Thomson, 1884), p. 5.

following unpublished introduction and structure plan for 'William Shakespeare, Pseudonymo':

> Tencionamos, n'este opusculo, versar este problema, e apontar qual nos parece ser o seu estado actual. Como o candidato mais votado para autor da obra Shakespeareana é Francis Bacon, e como, por certo – pelas razões que no decurso da nossa exposição serão apontadas – este é quem mais argumentos tem em seu favor, o nosso exame da questão recahirá sobre a controversia Shakespeare-Bacon, propriamente dita. Buscaremos expôr qual nos pareça o estado actual d'ella.
>
> Como o que especialmente queremos é tornar o problema lúcido para o leitor, não o encararemos chronologicamente, mas seguindo o methodo que mais logicamente concatene os seus elementos componentes. Assim ser-nos-ha possivel dar aos interessados que o ignorem, uma noção concreta e completa de até onde chegou, hoje, o problema Shakespeare-Bacon.
>
> 1. Duvidas com respeito a Shakespeare.
> 2. Argumentos a favôr de Bacon (e Rutland).
> 3. Contra-argumentação Shakespeareana.
> 4. □   (76-31)

> [In this booklet I propose to explore the problem, describing what seems to me to be its current state. Since the most popular candidate for the authorship of the Shakespearean works is Francis Bacon, and since he is certainly – for reasons I will give during the exposition – the one with the most arguments in his favour, my examination of the controversy will probe the so-called Shakespeare-Bacon question. I will attempt to describe what seems to me to be its current state.
>
> Since what I most wish is to make the problem intelligible to the reader, I will not approach it chronologically, but rather following the method which links its component parts in the most logical manner. Thus, I will be able to give those who are interested but know nothing about the Shakespeare-Bacon problem a concrete and complete idea of where it is at today.
>
> 1. Doubts concerning Shakespeare.
> 2. Arguments in favour of Bacon (and Rutland).
> 3. Shakespearean counter-argument.
> 4. □

This plan suggests that Pessoa meant to continue the unfinished 'William Shakespeare, Pseudonymo' by outlining the case for other candidates further to Bacon, and that he would have concluded it by responding to the anti-Stratfordian stance with a 'Shakespearean', meaning Stratfordian, refutation.

In short, Pessoa was no Baconian, nor did he ever seriously entertain the notion that Shakespeare did not pen the works that go under his name. For a more balanced picture of the reasons behind his profound engagement with the

Shakespearean authorship controversy to emerge, his many unpublished writings on it must be taken into account.

Some are straightforward reading notes on the books he read.[60] Others are lists of dates alluding to biographical details for Bacon, Shakespeare, and alternative candidates.[61] Several, in contrast to 'William Shakespeare, Pseudonymo', refute anti-Stratfordian claims. In one Pessoa ridicules the notion, repeated by legions of heretics, that only a nobleman could have penned Shakespeare's plays, by taking this position to its *reductio ad absurdum*:

> It has been claimed that Shakespeare of Stratford, being a not very well educated man, could not write works which no one has ever shown to be the product of learning or culture. It has been claimed that Shakespeare of Stratford, being a middle class man, cannot have written works which show a familiarity with the inner life of princes and nobles which, in any case, no sort of work, short of a rhymed Debrett, can show. It has been claimed that Shakespeare of Stratford, being involved in sordid litigation, cannot be the author of works which show a great power of expression and a great sensibility to intuition.
>
> From this primary attitude [62] it is but a step to that which makes it compulsory that the author of the Shakespeare plays be a son of Queen Elizabeth, for it is a known fact that the greatest geniuses have been princes. (*GL*, p. 352-353)

In *Livro do Desassossego*, Pessoa has Soares declare that 'A *reductio ad absurdum* é uma das minhas bebidas predilectas' [*Reductio ad absurdum* is one of my favourite drinks], an attraction perfectly exemplified by the excerpt above (*LD*, p. 282). He also enjoys exploring all sides of the issue: in some unpublished pieces he counters the objection that there is an unbridgeable divide between the historical actor and the writer of the plays, while in others he appears to take the biographical problem for granted. Pessoa's interest in probing the key sites of

---

[60] See, for example, 76-57 and 76-58 in the Appendix.

[61] Shakespeare's words, in the dedication of his poem *Venus and Adonis*, about the poem being the 'the first heir of my invention', are often cited. Anti-Stratfordians call the dating of *Venus and Adonis* into question when arguing that someone else authored the poem, and at a different date to the accepted one. In one text Pessoa explores the issue:
'*Venus and Adonis*: "first heir of my invention." Is this to be taken as strict truth? Or not? And, if not, can "invention" have the Latin meaning, "find"? – "The first heir of my find?" What evidence is there of the Shakespearean *touch* before *Venus and Adonis*? Probably *none*. The Shakespearean *hand* in plays is *later*.
Then, it being natural that the "first heir" phrase is correct, what age was Shakespeare when *Venus and Adonis* was written?
But what of the 12 plays cited by Meres? Since *Titus* is cited, and this is not Shakespearean, what can be understood?' (76-14)

[62] This seems to be a direct translation of the Portuguese phrase 'atitude primária', meaning simple-minded (rather than initial).

contention from every angle is borne out by the marginalia inside the books he read: on the title page of *Richard III* in the *Complete Works*, for instance, Pessoa attempts to chart the play's publication history and refers to Stratfordian claims that its expansions display Shakespeare's own revisions:

> Published anonymously in 1597; in 1598 again ('by William Shake-speare'); then in 1602, 1605, 1612 (with unimportant changes in these cases); finally in Folio 1623, with marked improvements and revisions, but with 12 printers' errors peculiar to the Quarto of 1622. The expansions are 'quite in the manner of Shakespeare' (Cambridge editors), 'evidently from the perfecting hand of the author in the maturity of his powers' (Richard Grant White). (*CW*, p. 644)

Some of Pessoa's marginal annotations (ticks in the margin, for instance) reveal that he accepted certain arguments, while on other occasions he was clearly critical: next to Edwin Bormann's assertion in his Baconian pamphlet *The Quintessence of the Shakespeare Secret* (1905) that 'Ben Jonson, on Bacon's sixtieth birthday, praises him as *his* king, therefore as *king of poets*', Pessoa writes a sneering 'the "King" is James I!'[63]

Taken as a whole, Pessoa's writings on the authorship controversy do not represent a championing of any alternative candidate for the authorship of Shakespeare's works. This is unusual, because most writers who engage in the debate either forcefully put across their chosen candidate(s) for authorship – witness the tentative titles in Pessoa's library: *Lord Rutland Est Shakespeare* [*Lord Rutland Is Shakespeare*], *Francis Bacon our Shakes-speare*, *The Five Authors of Shakespeare's Sonnets* – or else they embark on Stratfordian refutations defending Shakespeare from the conspiracy theorists. Many, like Begley and Looney, are at least original in the arguments they employ, or can be credited with being the first to propose a given candidate or theory, however unlikely. Pessoa, in contrast, seems little interested in making any unique contribution to the Shakespearean authorship debate (there is one notable exception, as we shall see at the beginning of the following chapter). If he is not dealing with the problem of Shakespeare's invisibility in the standard way, it is worth probing the reasons behind his profound engagement with it. Pessoa's fascination with the subject, interesting enough in itself, as one major writer's immersion in a pressing topical debate, becomes exponentially more so when we relate it back to his own work.

Detective Stories, Men Who Never Were, and 'Transpersonalization'

The Shakespearean authorship controversy came of age during the heyday of British detective fiction. Since the 1890s, anti-Stratfordian books have almost invariably been structured like detective stories, with their unfoldings of the mystery and deductions of the solution. Looney begins by drawing up a list of the

---

63 Edwin Bormann, *The Quintessence of the Shakespeare Secret* (London: A. Siegle, 1905), p. 16.

characteristics of the plays, and then examines every possible 'suspect' to come up with the name of the perpetrator. In the authorship story, however, the perpetrator of the 'crime' is not the villain but the unfairly maligned and neglected hero.

The Baconian case, in particular, hinges on supposed hidden ciphers in the works. By selecting individual letters and words from Shakespeare's poems and plays, Baconians claim to have discovered hidden messages from Francis Bacon announcing himself as their true author. Ignatius Donnelly's *The Great Cryptogram: Francis Bacon's Cipher in the So-Called Shakespeare Plays* (1888), a book Pessoa mentions in his reading lists on the controversy, revisits the Shakespearean canon with the sole aim of finding such a cipher; Donnelly eventually discovers it embedded in the two parts of *Henry IV*: This narrative, 'always growing out of the same numbers, employed in the same way, and counting from the same, or similar, starting-points, cannot be otherwise than a prearranged arithmetical cipher.'[64]

In an unpublished manuscript, Pessoa refers to a 'biliteral cipher' that might be hidden in Shakespeare's First Folio (76A-54); Baconians have been drawn to the possibility because Bacon himself devised a biliteral cipher which he published as an illustrated plate in *De Augmentis Scientiarum* (*The Advancement of Learning*, 1605), by arranging the letters A and B in five-letter combinations, each representing a letter of the alphabet. They are also drawn to the Clown's nonsense word in *Love's Labour's Lost*, 'Honorificabilitudinitatibus'. The unusual word appears among scribbled notes in the Northumberland Manuscripts (found in 1867 in Northumberland House in the Strand), which contain copies of some of Bacon's writings; it also features, diagrammed, in the Bacon papers in the British Museum. Of the various messages produced by rearranging its letters, none was more positively announced than that of Sir Edwin Durning-Lawrence in *Bacon is Shake-speare* (1910):

> the true solution of the meaning of the long word 'Honorificabilitudinitatibus', about which so much nonsense has been written, is without possibility of doubt or question to be found by arranging the letters to form the Latin hexameter.
> HI LUDI F. BACONIS NATI TUITI ORBI
> These plays F. Bacon's offspring are preserved for the world.
> It is not possible to afford a clearer mechanical proof that THE SHAKESPEARE PLAYS ARE BACON'S OFFSPRING...
> It is not possible that any doubt can any longer be entertained respecting the manifest fact that BACON IS SHAKESPEARE. [65]

So sure was Durning-Lawrence that he had found the only correct solution that

---

[64] Ignatius Donnelly, *Diary*, cited by Martin Ridge, in *Ignatius Donnelly: The Portrait of a Politician* (Chicago/London: University of Chicago Press, 1962), p. 243.
[65] Durning-Lawrence, *Bacon is Shake-speare*, p. 102.

on 11 November 1910 he offered a reward to any reader of the *Pall Mall Gazette* who could invent 'another sensible anagram'. This challenge was accepted by one Ralph J. Beevor of St. Albans, who offered 'Abi inivit F. Bacon Histrio ludit' ('Be off, F. Bacon, the actor has entered and is playing'). Sportingly, Durning-Lawrence produced his cheque for one hundred guineas.

Pessoa cites Durning-Lawrence's book in his notes on the authorship controversy, and goes through its central Baconian arguments, including 'Honorificabilitudinitatibus and adjunct crypters [*sic*]' in an unpublished manuscript (76A-46). His marginalia reveals that he enjoyed trying his hand at the hidden codes proposed by various authors. In his copy of *The Collected Works of Ben Jonson* (III, p. 330), for example, Pessoa circles Bacon's name in Jonson's poem 'An Execration Upon Vulcan':

> **B**ut, on thy malice, tell me didst thou spy
> **A**ny least loose or scurrile paper lie
> **Con**cealed or kept there, that was fit to be,
> By thy own vote, a sacrifice to thee?

His experiments with possible titles for pieces of writing on the Shakespearean authorship, or for the piece that eventually became 'William Shakespeare, Pseudonymo', also point to his attraction to the controversy's detective-story nature:

> The Person of Shakespeare
> A Study in Transcendental Detection
> A Detective Study. (76-13)

In this unpublished manuscript (partly reproduced on the following page), Pessoa writes of the Shakespearean authorship controversy: 'This is therefore a "detective" criticism.' Furthermore, Pessoa's interest in the authorship mystery neatly coincides with his projects for his own detective stories featuring the super-sleuth Quaresma, as the following list of projected writings demonstrates:

> 14. Small book on Shakespeare-Bacon
> Longer book on Shakespeare-Bacon
> [...] 17. Contos Quaresma – em livro ou folhetos [Quaresma Short Stories – in book or pamphlet form].[66]

---

[66] *Sensacionismo*, p. 436.

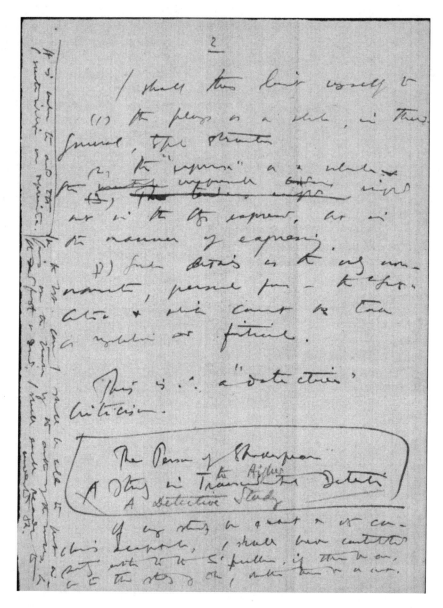

In another list of 'Obras, [...] ditas em 12-1-1914' [Works, [...] listed on 12-1-1914], 'Quaresma, Decifrador' [Quaresma, Decipherer] features alongside 'O Mito de William Shakespeare' [The William Shakespeare Myth].[67] There is even a direct reference to Shakespeare in one of Quaresma's stories, one that appears oddly out

[67] See *Fausto: Tragédia Subjectiva* [*Faust: A Subjective Tragedy*], ed. Teresa Sobral Cunha (Lisbon: Presença, 1988), pp. 200-201.

of place – a total *non sequitur* – unless we allow that the Shakespearean authorship controversy was at the forefront of Pessoa's mind when he came to craft his own detective fiction:

> o raciocinador nunca crê que a razão possa ser substancialmente irracional, que o raciocinador não admite o irracional como elemento positivo, e não simplesmente negativo. Olha lá, tu já leste Shakespeare?
> – Li em francês – respondeu Quaresma.
> O Tio Porco teve um gesto de impaciência.
> – É pior que não ter lido – disse. – Bem não é de Shakespeare que se trata. Há uma peça dele – continuou, virando-se para nós outros –, no *All's Well that Ends Well*, uma menina chamada Beatriz, que quando o tio lhe pergunta se vê bem, ou coisa parecida, responde: "Sim, tio, vejo uma igreja ao meio-dia."
> – Que diabo quer isso dizer? – perguntou o Guedes.
> – Não quer dizer nada, e aí é que está o caso – respondeu o Tio Porco sorrindo. [68]

> [The rational man never believes that reason may be substantially irrational, nor believes that the irrational may be a positive, rather than purely negative, element. Look here, have you ever read Shakespeare?'
> 'I read him in French', replied Quaresma.
> Uncle Pig gestured impatiently.
> 'That's worse than not having read him', he said. 'Well, the matter is not about Shakespeare. In one of his plays', he continued, turning to face the rest of us, '*All's Well that Ends Well*, there is a girl called Beatrice, who in response to her uncle's question of whether she sees well, or something like that, replies, "Yes, uncle, I see a church at noon."'
> 'What the devil does that mean?' asked Guedes.
> 'It doesn't mean anything, and that's the point', replied Uncle Pig with a smile.]

More significantly, Pessoa's fascination with the authorship controversy stems from the perceived biographical problem, grounded in the belief that Shakespeare's commonplace life is irreconcilable with the genius implicit in his works. As he explains:

> The assumption, from which this problem took its birth, seems to be that Shakespeare of Stratford lived a life considered incompatible with the life which is to be expected, by the expectors [sic], from a man of genius. (*GL*, p. 352)

Pessoa was drawn to passages, in his books on Shakespeare, that emphasised

---

[68] *Ficção e Teatro* [*Fiction and Theatre*], ed. António Quadros (Mem Martins: Europa-América, 1986), p. 105.

the disparity between the Bard's life and his work: he wrote an approving 'good', for instance, next to Gilfillan's assertion, in an essay on Shakespeare, that 'His external history is, in his own language, a blank; his internal, a puzzle, save as we may dubiously gather it from the escapes of his sonnets, and the masquerade of his plays.'[69]

Interestingly, Pessoa was also interested in the perceived invisibility of two other historical figures whose existence has been called into question, Homer and Christ. In one text, Pessoa declares: 'Não sei se se tem reparado sufficientemente em como o caso Shakespeare é similhante ao caso Homero' [I do not know whether it has been sufficiently noticed how similar the Shakespeare case is to the Homer case].[70] In *Desassossego*, he has Soares refer to 'aquele Jesus Cristo que não foi nada no mundo, tanto que se duvida dele pela história' [that Jesus Christ who was nothing in the world, so much so that history doubts his existence] (*LD*, p. 166). He brings the three examples of invisibility together in his previously cited introduction and structure plan for 'William Shakespeare, Pseudonymo':

> Entre os varios problemas historicos que teem erguido atraz de si uma poeira de interesse, ha trez que, quer em virtude da sua importancia historica, quer por via da sua importancia literaria, teem, mais do que os outros, conseguido apaixonar e prender.
>
> O primeiro – e sem duvida o mais importante, quer porque pertence ao mais importante e intimo de todos os phenomenos sociaes, porque seja o de, por isso, interesse mais geral, – é o problema da historicidade da figura de Jesus Christo.
>
> O segundo – de interesse mais limitado, porque corra num campo de erudição fatalmente restricta – é o chamado 'problema' ou 'questão' 'de Homero.'
>
> O terceiro – de um interesse mais geral, porque os livros que o tratam são mais acessiveis a um largo publico, e porque as obras discutidas são das mais conhecidas em toda a Europa – é o problema da autoria da obra Shakespeareana, ou, pelo menos, parte d'ella, para os que não admittem S[hakespeare] como autor. (76-31)

> [Of the several historical problems which have sparked a sprinkling of interest, three, by virtue of their historic, as well as literary, significance, have attracted greater fascination and passion than the rest.
>
> The first – and undoubtedly the most important, because it belongs to the most important and personal of all social phenomena and has, therefore, greater general interest – is the problem of the historical existence of Jesus Christ.
>
> The second – of more limited interest, being in a narrower field of erudition – is the so-called Homer 'problem' or 'question'

---

[69] Gilfillan, 'Shakespeare – A Lecture', in *A Gallery of Literary Portraits*, p. 188.
[70] Castro, 'Shakespeare, dramaturgo invisível', *Jornal i* (30 December 2009), p. 42.

The third – of wider interest, because the books about it are more accessible to a wide readership, and because the works in question are among the best known in Europe – is the problem of the authorship of Shakespeare's works, or, at least, part of them, for those who do not allow that Shakespeare was the their author.]

Pessoa himself lived a life considered incompatible with the life which is to be expected of a man of genius, and he is just as elusive as Shakespeare, Homer and Christ in his writings, so much so that his own invisibility has become a critical commonplace. Octávio Paz asserts that Pessoa's 'history could be reduced to the passage between the unreality of his daily life and the reality of his fictions.'[71] Jorge de Sena goes as far as to claim that Pessoa sacrificed his real existence, like a Christ, 'on the cross of being words, words, words'; his epithet 'the man who never was' has proved enduring.[72]

Some readers have even questioned, albeit firmly tongue-in-cheek, whether Pessoa might have been invented as a pseudonymous cover for other identities. Aurea Bueno published an ingenious article in 1984 putting forward the theory that the writings we think of as Pessoa's were in fact written by Campos, Caeiro and Reis, the authors of different poems published in literary magazines. To make matters more complicated, these three authors were themselves fictions, their poems having been penned by Casais, José Régio and Miguel Torga, respectively. Carlos Queiroz crafted the poetry of the orthonym and Gaspar Simões wrote his biography of Pessoa as a deflection for these machinations; David Mourão-Ferreira penned the love letters to Ophélia, and *Livro do Desassossego* was written by all of these authors in collaboration, right up to its publication in 1982. Sena was initially sceptical when he was let in on the secret, but he finally agreed to write all of the critical and theoretical texts ascribed to Pessoa.[73]

It is not difficult to see why, for Pessoans as well as for Pessoa, the image of a master-writer, who is also a master-plotter, working with a secret society of authors under his guidance to pen some of the finest literature of any age, at the same time working to conceal his identity, should be so appealing. In one of his previously cited letters to Woodward, one of his Baconian correspondents and the author of *The Early Life of Lord Bacon* (1902), a book Pessoa refers to, he declares:

I am most interested in the controversy round the identity of the author of the Shakespearean works, and in the curious arguments put forth in favour of

---

[71] *A Centenary Pessoa*, ed. Eugénio Lisboa and L.C. Taylor (Manchester: Carcanet, 1995), p. 3.
[72] Sena, 'The Man Who Never Was', in *The Man Who Never Was: Essays on Fernando Pessoa*, ed. George Monteiro (Rhode Island: Gávea-Brown, 1982), p. 31.
[73] Aurea Bueno, 'A verdade sobre a trama heteronímica: o Poeta português Fernando Pessoa não é menos fictício do que o Rei Artur' [The Truth About the Heteronymic Plot: The Portuguese Poet Fernando Pessoa is as Ficticious as King Arthur], *Diário de Avisos* (1 November 1984).

those works having been written by Francis Bacon, or by a society of dramatists or of authors under his guidance, or (as in the latest, and French, attribution) by Lord Derby. The attribution to the Earl of Rutland (by Celestin Demblon) seems to me unacceptable. (*GL*, p. 292)

Even as Pessoa examines Bacon as the putative author of Shakespeare's works, he is as drawn to the possible affinities between Bacon and himself as between the two Elizabethans. In his letter to Barley requesting a copy of Bacon's horoscope he admits as much, asserting that his interest in Bacon is fuelled by an interest in his own creative process:

My interest in Francis Bacon's horoscope is due to several circumstances, of which the Shakespeare-Bacon controversy is only one. The chief interest arises from a desire to see what in Bacon's horoscope registers his peculiar characteristic of being able to write in different styles (a fact even non-Baconians admit) and his general faculty of transpersonalization.

I possess (in what degree, or with what quality, it is not for me to say) the characteristic to which I am alluding. I am an author, and have always found it impossible to write in my own personality; I have always found myself, consciously or unconsciously[,] assuming the character of someone who does not exist, and through whose imagined agency I write. I wish to study to what this may be due by position or aspect and am therefore interested in the horoscope of a man who is known to have possessed this faculty in an extraordinary degree. (*Corr I*, pp. 168-9)

Pessoa's wish to obtain Bacon's horoscope is driven by the desire to gain an insight into possible astrologically-determined characteristics that allow him, like Pessoa himself, to write under different dramatic personalities. 'Transpersonalization' is a wonderfully expressive word, and we should probably credit Pessoa with its invention. The word does not feature in the *OED*, although presumably the prefix 'trans-' might be added to 'personal' and derivatives, thus creating the meaning 'to make trans-personal'. It is an apt description of what he considers to be the essence of his own genius, as well as Shakespeare's: the ability to create impersonal others.

In a previously cited unpublished text, Pessoa claims that it is Shakespeare's dramatic impersonality which leads him to be able to simulate, in his plays, the learning he might not have had in real life:

He could derive from one of his conversations with Ben Jonson as much simulation of learning – involuntarily intermingled with his rapid inspiration – as could, to a shallow psychologist, give proof of scholarship. He could turn the results of an hour's talk with a lawyer into an exuberance of natural legal expressions that an innocent critic would easily take for a trained lawyer's production. Even for a prehensile mind of no very high quality the simulation of learning, voluntary or involuntary, is extremely easy: a dictionary of quotations is *matter enough. I know a man (here in Portugal) whose knowledge of contemporary French literature is extensive, exact and vivid; so much so that we can hardly imagine that he has never read any at all of the books which, *with their authors, he so brilliantly and exactly explains and discusses. He simply buys and reads carefully every week the Nouvelles Littéraires[74], which is a kind of French John O'London.[75] If to this man this is possible, why not to Shakespeare? (74A-26)

What matters to an impersonal poet is not the life but the work, as a means to achieve immortality in the shape of posthumous glory, the subject of Pessoa's long essays 'Erostratus' and 'Impermanence'. As he has Soares write in *Desassossego*:

A literatura [...] parece-me ser o fim para que deveria tender todo o esforço humano. [...] dizer-se é sobreviver.
[...] Mais vale escrever do que ousar viver, ainda que viver não seja mais que comprar bananas ao sol, enquanto o sol dura e há bananas que vender. (*LD*, pp. 63, 183)

[Literature [...], it seems to me, should to be the goal of all human effort. [...] to speak oneself is to survive.
[...] It is better to write than to dare to live, even if living be no more than buying bananas in the sunshine, while the sun shines and there are bananas to sell.]

Invisible Authorship and the Heteronymic Project
That Pessoa's engagement with the Shakespearean authorship controversy was, in no small part, his way of meditating on his own brand of impersonal dramatic poetry, the heteronymic project – as Pizarro puts it, 'uma ante-câmara importante da criação dos heterónimos' [an important antechamber for the creation of the heteronyms] (*GL*, p. 341) – is a fact borne out by the chronology of his interest in it.

In one of the unpublished pieces in which Pessoa misattributes Empson's words to Coleridge, he goes on to counter the common charge that the man from Stratford could not have had the legal knowledge displayed in the plays by arguing that it was nothing exceptional for the period, and might easily have been tapped from the general *Zeitgeist*. The legal argument, he writes,

has been pulverized in abundant detail by the late J. M. Robertson in his book *The Baconian Heresy*. Robertson proved (1) that there was no particular learning, classic, legal, or otherwise, in the works, (2) that Elizabethan authors, not particularly learned themselves, show generally more learning, of all kinds,

---

[74] French literary review 1922-1985.
[75] *John O'London's Weekly* was a weekly literary magazine published by George Newnes of London between 1919 and 1954. At its height it had a circulation of 80,000.

than Shakespeare of the Works, (3) that, in particular reference to the legal point, the age was an age of litigation and interest in litigation and that for that reason legal expressions came readily to anyone at the time. (74A-26)

Pessoa's argument is here standard enough, and the excerpt above is of interest chiefly for its revelation of the length of time that he reflected on the Shakespearean authorship controversy. The clue is in Pessoa's reference to 'the late J. M. Robertson': Robertson died in 1933, and to address a living author as deceased is hardly appropriate. Pizarro argues, based on material evidence and identifiable references, that Pessoa penned 'William Shakespeare, Pseudonymo' in either 1912 or 1913 (see *GL II*, pp. 856-7). This means that Pessoa wrestled with the problem of Shakespeare's invisibility for over twenty years. It is possible to narrow the timescale of his most intense engagement with it, however.

The majority of Pessoa's writings on the controversy, as previously mentioned, display the heading 'Shakespeare-Bacon' or similar, which immediately suggests that they were penned before 1920, until which date Bacon was the most heavily backed alternative Shakespeare. Looney's pioneering book championing Oxford was published in 1920, but Pessoa makes few references to Oxford as a possible candidate, although he mentions many others. (One notable exception is an unpublished text in which he refers to Bacon, Derby, Rutland and de Vere [76-19, cited in Chapter 3]). If he were writing on the subject primarily after 1920, this would be an incongruous omission from one so well versed in the competing theories of the day.

Furthermore, Pessoa signed his name inside the overwhelming majority of the authorship books in his library 'Fernando Pessôa': six of the fourteen books bear this signature, while only one 'Pessoa', without the circumflex (the remainder are unsigned). Since Pessoa only dropped the circumflex in 1916, when he intended to publish *English Poems* in England, this further condenses the period of his keenest interest in the Shakespearean authorship to before 1916. There are various theories concerning why Pessoa altered his name thus, including a desire to metaphorically kill his father, but there is no reason to doubt that his immediate consideration was the one he put forward in a letter of 4 September 1916 to Armando Côrtes-Rodrigues: 'Como [...] vou publicar umas coisas em inglês, acho melhor desadaptar-me do inútil ^, que prejudica o nome cosmopolitamente' [Since [...] I will publish some things in English, I think it best to rid myself of the useless ^, which harms the name internationally] (*Corr I*, p. 220).

Look again at the list of books on the Shakespearean authorship controversy in Pessoa's library. Their dates of publication confirm that Pessoa was interested in the subject until at least 1930, and his knowledge of Robertson's death reveals he was still writing about it until at least 1933. However, eleven of Pessoa's fourteen books on the Shakespearean authorship debate, the staggering majority, were published before 1914 (compare this figure to two out of the eight books he owned of 'standard' Shakespeare criticism, listed in Chapter 1). Of the twenty-nine further authorship titles Pessoa mentions in his writings on the controversy, all but one were published before 1914. This means, although it does not prove, that

Pessoa could have read them before that date, which would correlate perfectly with the period in which he wrote his most developed text on the topic, 'William Shakespeare, Pseudonymo' (1912 or 1913). Pessoa's projected pamphlet features on two separate lists of 1912 and, most tellingly of all, on one dated 12 January 1914.[76]

This cumulative evidence suggests that the two years leading up to Pessoa's heteronymic explosion of 1914 were the pivotal ones of his engagement with Shakespeare's invisibility. During these two years, in particular, Pessoa was voraciously reading competing theories on the Shakespearean authorship controversy, working through its chief sites of contention in minute detail, responding to Stratfordian and anti-Stratfordian arguments in over two hundred texts, and working on a pamphlet designed to expose the controversy to a Portuguese audience.

This is not to suggest that Pessoa's engagement with the Shakespearean authorship was the single, or the most significant, influence on the creation of the heteronyms. To posit a straightforward chain of cause and effect would be misleading, for hundreds of other writers grappled with the controversy and not one of them, so far as we know, exploded into anything like heteronyms as a result, or attempted to become invisible authors. Pessoa had invested in dramatic persons not his, to borrow a phrase from Robert Browning, another dramatic poet he admired, from an early age. Rather, the Shakespearean authorship debate provided him with a valuable testing-ground for his reflections on invisible authorship, of the type he ascribed to Shakespeare's genius and his own (see Chapter 1). Like all of the major Shakespearean themes that attracted Pessoa's close attention, it offered him valuable sites of self-reflection, both in the sense of holding up a mirror to his own mode of invisible authorship, the heteronymic project, and in the sense of offering him a valuable conceptual space in which to ponder it.

---

[76] See *GL* II, 856-7 and *Fausto*, p. 201.

Shakespeare's Madness

Pessoa's Unique Contribution to the Authorship Controversy

Pessoa's engagement with the Shakespearean authorship controversy is of interest to us because of the issues it raises in relation to his own work, particularly in the context of the heteronymic project. Otherwise, his writings on it are not very original, grounded as they are in exploring his trademark concerns and points where he sees himself reflected. There is one site of contention in the debate, however, to which Pessoa makes an unprecedented contribution.

In several of his writings on the authorship controversy, Pessoa wrestles with the problem of Shakespeare's seeming unconcern with posterity, revealed by his apparent carelessness over the fate of his brilliant writings. That the greatest literary genius of all time should have left the publication of his plays up to the actors in his company, after his death, and that these writings should have appeared full of inconsistencies, and in different versions to that of the Quarto texts circulating during his lifetime, is an incongruity that has troubled generations of Shakespeare scholars, and one that plays into the hands of confirmed anti-Stratfordians. As Pessoa himself puts it:

> The common illusion is that a man of genius, be that genius small or great (minor or major), must necessarily have a concern for that genius and for its works in the future, and a respect for it, is one of the factors that has contributed to the disbelief in Shakespeare's authorship of the works which pass under his name. (*GL*, p. 350)

Pessoa's attraction to the problem of Shakespeare's perceived inability or unwillingness to publish is in keeping with his balanced attempt to explore all aspects of the authorship debate, and his particular attraction to those which mirror his own predicament. Despite having over 27,000 manuscripts to draw on, Pessoa too published little in his lifetime, relative to the ambitious plans to organise, revise, edit and present his works that are littered throughout his archive. The most notable exception is *Mensagem* (1934), and in that case the monetary prize he and his friends vied for was the immediate incentive.[1] The publication of *English Poems* and *35 Sonnets*, in 1917 and 1918 respectively, represents a different struggle: to establish himself as a worthy successor of English literary traditions, not least, that of Shakespeare's *Sonnets*.

It must be conceded, however, that Pessoa did publish numerous important poems in journals and little magazines; as Eduardo Lourenço argues: 'Pessoa só publicara um único livro em língua portuguesa, *Mensagem*, mas a quase totalidade dos seus mais belos poemas já tinha sido publicada nas diversas revistas ligadas ao nosso Modernismo' [Pessoa only published a single book in Portuguese,

---

[1] See Blanco, 'A Verdade sobre a *Mensagem*' [The Truth about *Message*], in *A Arca de Pessoa* [*Fernando Pessoa's Arc*], ed. Jerónimo Pizarro and Steffen Dix (Lisbon: Imprensa de Ciências Sociais, 2007), pp. 147-161.

Message, but almost all of his most beautiful poems had already been published in many Modernist magazines.][2]

In an unpublished text, Pessoa offers a possible rebuttal to the argument that a genius like Shakespeare must necessarily be concerned with the posthumous fate of his artistic output:

> It is one of the strangest logical positions in this unfortunate case that the real or apparent indifference of Shakespeare for his own works – neither publishing them, nor collating them, nor caring what works were published under his name – should be cited as an anti-Stratfordian argument. If this indifference be a fact, it is a fact, and it affects the author, whomsoever he may be. Indeed, it is a stronger argument for the authorship of a man like Shakespeare of Stratford than for any Bacon, Derby, Rutland or de Vere. A spontaneous, precipitate and headlong genius, not trained by position to give himself importance nor educated by learning to give importance to his works, will more readily be careless about those works than the other men who are assumed to have written these works. (76-19)

In other words, Shakespeare's lack of self-promotion does not strengthen the case for any alternative candidate for authorship, and his modesty might in any case be a sign of good breeding. Perhaps not himself quite convinced by this strange explanation, which is only put forward in this single manuscript, in other pieces Pessoa offers us a competing solution to the problem. In a detailed, unpublished list, he analyses the 'absolute carelessness of Shakespeare, whoever he was, about his works and their publication, except in a few cases, such as the two poems [*Venus and Adonis* and *The Rape of Lucrece*]' (76A-85). It 'means', he posits, 'one of the following things':

> (1) that he did not give his own works that importance which we give them,
> (2) that he was mentally diseased in some respect of the will and had no artistic scruple, not owing to absence of artistic qualities but owing to lack of will to put them into action except under a sudden and compelling inspiration,
> (3) that he simply arranged and altered other men's works and therefore cared little for the fate of the resultant work, which was never wholly his – as the Sonnets and the Poems were
> (4) that he was away from England,
> (5) that he had no power to interfere, either through fear or simply through having no power. The last is the least probable hypothesis. (76A-85)

Most of these speculations are standard enough, and have been posited by anti-Stratfordians over the years. Item two on the list, however, is unique to Pessoa. In another text he argues that even though Shakespeare 'no doubt [...] knew his genius' and 'no doubt [...] felt that he owed something to posterity, the more he

---

[2] *Fernando, Rei da nossa baviera*, p. 24.

thought of it the less fit he was to carry it out' (*GL*, p. 351).

What, specifically, did Pessoa think was the 'mental disease' that prevented Shakespeare from adequately publishing his brilliant writings? In one piece, he asserts that 'Shakespeare shows:

(1) *always* the characteristic of hysteria,
(2) in the beginning the consciousness of a neurasthenic so
(3) finally, a predominance of the neurasthenic over the hysterical characteristics. (*GL*, p. 363)

In a piece under the heading 'O Problema de Shakespeare psychologicamente considerado' [The Shakespeare Problem Considered Psychologically], Pessoa similarly declares: 'a analyse da ind[ividualidade] mental [de Shakespeare] leva à conclusão da base do caracter – a hystero-neurasthenia (N.B. A hystero-neurasthenia é sempre constitucional e innata)' [the analysis of Shakespeare's mental particularity leads us to conclude hystero-neurasthenia is at the base of his character (N.B. Hystero-neurasthenia is always constitutional and innate)] (*GL*, p. 357). A loose sentence, in Portuguese, on a page of unpublished notes, in English, on Shakespeare's 'constitutional mental disease' repeats his unmistakable 'Conclusão: hystero-neurasthenia de Shakespeare' [Conclusion: Shakespeare's hystero-neurasthenia] (76A-4).

Another text states Pessoa's diagnosis of Shakespeare's perceived madness twice: 'conclusion – *neurasthenia*. Therefore final conclusion: Shakespeare was a *hystero-neurasthenic.*' [3] Pessoa's conclusion that the Bard was a hystero-neurasthenic is unequivocal and unshakable, and it is echoed in numerous other pieces.

In proposing the 'madness' he discovers in the Bard, namely hystero-neurasthenia, as a solution to his seeming indifference to posterity, Pessoa alights on his unique contribution to the Shakespearean authorship controversy, one never proposed before or since. Although a strikingly original contribution, it must be conceded that it is a product of Pessoa's interest in Shakespeare as a dramatic poet rather than a poetic dramatist (see Chapter 1). Pessoa bypasses the practical considerations of an Elizabethan playwright entirely, but these would explain, for most readers, Shakespeare's interest in producing scripts and staging plays rather than publishing them.

Pessoa's proposed solution to the problem of Shakespeare's lack of concern with posterity points to his profound interest in the Bard's possible madness, another issue close to his own heart. As a young man, Pessoa would write letters to old schoolmasters in Durban posing as a psychiatrist, asking if they could shed any light on the psychological state of one of his patients, a certain Fernando Pessoa, who according to the letter had either recently committed suicide or was

---

[3] *Apreciações Literárias de Fernando Pessoa*, ed. Pauly Ellen Bothe, p. 249. First transcribed and presented in my doctoral thesis *Fernando Pessoa's Shakespeare*.

in a lunatic asylum.[4] On 31 August 1925 he drafted a letter to an unknown correspondent in which he claimed to consider checking himself into an asylum (*Corr II*, p. 87).

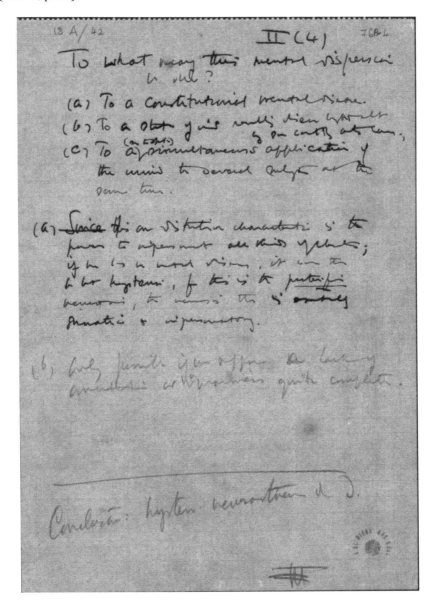

[4] *The Selected Prose of Fernando Pessoa*, ed. and trans. Zenith (New York: Grove Press, 2001), pp. 120-125.

Pessoa discovered in himself the exact same 'madness' he attributed to Shakespeare. He cites his 'histero-neurastenia fundamental' [fundamental hystero-neurasthenia] in a letter of 1916 to Sá-Carneiro.[5] In a letter to Hector and Henri Durville of 1919 he asserts, 'je suis un hystéroneurasthénique' [I am a hystero-neurasthenic], before embarking on a detailed exposition of his perceived neurosis. [6] The self-diagnosis would be repeated in copious self-referential writings over the years.

Pessoa's dual diagnosis, of himself and Shakespeare as fellow hystero-neurasthenics, is consistent with his attempt to forge firm sites of affinity between himself and the Bard. As in the case of his thinking on both men's genius and invisibility, it is useful to bear in mind that Pessoa's thoughts on their 'madness' are *sui generis* rather than objective. 'Madness' is too strong a term for the condition he ascribes to Shakespeare and himself, for hysteria and neurasthenia were regarded, in his day, as neuroses, and therefore fell under the milder clinical category of mental illness or disturbance rather than insanity.[7] In referring to the diagnosis, Pessoa employs words like 'madness', 'mental disease', 'mental condition', 'illness', 'insanity', and 'neurosis' almost interchangeably, but in the pages that follow I sometimes favour 'madness' (henceforth without quotation marks) because the designation points to its firm association, as we shall see, with the genius Pessoa ascribes to both men's art.

Pessoa's understanding of hysteria and neurasthenia and, more significantly, the uses he put them to, has a pervasive impact on his own work: he masterfully appropriates the madness he discovers in Shakespeare and his dramatic characters, especially Hamlet, for his heteronymic output, in particular the poetry of Álvaro de Campos. Furthermore, he offers his own Shakespearean madness as the psychological explanation for the heteronymic project.

The 'two Grand Neuroses of the Late Nineteenth Century'[8]

In Pessoa's day, hysteria was already an old disease, possibly the oldest category of neurosis in recorded medical history, with a colourful and chequered past.[9] Ancient Egyptian, Greek and Roman sources reveal the belief that the wandering womb could migrate around the body, creating all manner of curious physical and mental symptoms in women: it could 'make skin go numb (anaesthesia), engender fits, muteness, paralysis and [...] that choking breathlessness of "globus

---

[5] Letter to Sá-Carneiro, 14 March 1916, in *Cartas a Fernando Pessoa*, II, p. 221.
[6] Letter to Hector and Henri Durville, 10 June 1919, in *Corr I*, pp. 285-286. Hector Durville was the author of several works on therapeutic magnetism and Professor at the *École Pratique de Magnétisme et Massage* [Practicle School of Magnetism and Massage]. He was also the editor of *Journal du Magnétisme* [Magnetism Review].
[7] See Roy Porter and G. E. Berrios, *A History of Clinical Psychiatry: The Origin and History of Psychiatric Disorders* (London: Athlone Press, 1995).
[8] Petteri Pietikainen, *Neurosis and Modernity: The Age of Nervousness in Sweden* (Leiden/Boston: Brill, 2007), p. 2.
[9] For a history of hysteria, see Mark S. Micale, *Approaching Hysteria: Disease and Its Interpretations* (Princeton: Princeton University Press, 1996).

hystericus" when it lodged in the throat.' [10] The condition made a diagnostic comeback at the *fin de siècle* (c. 1880-1914), becoming an extremely popular diagnosis after it entered the mainstream of public awareness through the work of the renowned French clinical neurologist Jean-Martin Charcot. [11] Sigmund Freud was not alone in attributing the rediscovery of hysteria to Charcot, in an article of 1893[12]; over ten years earlier, the French journalist Jules Claretie had proclaimed that

> the illness of our age is hysteria. One encounters it everywhere. Everywhere one rubs elbows with it... Studying hysteria, [...] Monsieur Charcot [has] put [his] finger on the wound of the day. It is not only enclosed within the gray walls of the Salpêtrière; this singular neurosis with its astonishing effects; it travels the streets and the world.
> [...] Hystériques! Hystériques! Tous hystériques![13]

By 1882, the diagnosis was so widespread in France that Guy de Maupassant could parody its pervasive presence thus:

> Hysteria, Madame, now there is the word of the day. Are you in love? You are a hysteric. Are you indifferent to the passions that arouse other people? You are a hysteric, but a chaste hysteric. Do you cheat on your husband? You're a hysteric, but a sensual hysteric. Do you steal pieces of silk in a shop? Hysterical. You lie at every occasion? Hysterical! (Lying is even the distinguishing characteristic of hysteria.) Are you a glutton? Hysterical! Are you prone to nervousness? Hysterical! You are this, you are that, you are finally what all women have been since the world began? Hysterical! Hysterical, I tell you![14]

Charcot maintained that hysteria was also present in men, but his spectacular public demonstrations of female patients and the condition's very etymology, via

---

[10] Lisa Appingnanesi, *Mad, Bad and Sad: A History of Women and the Mind Doctors from 1800 to the Present* (London: Virago, 2008), p. 143.

[11] In this book, *fin-de-siècle* refers to the period between around 1880 and 1914, following the example, and the reasoning, of the editor of a 1996 book of essays on the literature of the period. See Lyn Pykett, 'Introduction', in *Reading* Fin-de-siècle *Fictions*, ed. Lyn Pykett (London/New York: Longman, 1996), pp. 1-15.

[12] Freud, *Collected Papers* (London: Basic Books, 1959), p. 20); first published as 'Charcot', *Weiner Medizinishe Wochenscrift* 37 (1893).

[13] Jules Claretie, *La vie à Paris: 1881* [*Life in Paris*] (Paris: Victor Harvard, n.d.), pp. 126, 135; cited and trans. Micale, 'Discourses of Hysteria in fin-de-siècle France, in *The Mind of Modernism: Medicine, Psychology, and the Cultural Arts in Europe and America, 1880-1940*, ed. Micale (Stanford: Stanford University Press, 2004), p. 84.

[14] Maupassant, 'Une femme' [A Woman], *Gil Blas* (16 August 1882), repr. in *Chroniques* [*Chronicles*], ed. Hubert Juin, 3 vols. (Paris: Union Générale d'Éditions, 1980), II, pp. 104-113; cited and trans. in Micale, *Approaching Hysteria*, p. 220.

Latin from Greek *husterikos* ('of the womb'), derived from *hustera* ('womb'), meant that it was largely perceived as being specific to women.

Neurasthenia, literally 'weakness' or 'debility' of the nerves, derived from *neuro* for nerve and *asthenia* for weakness, was, in contrast, a comparatively recent diagnostic category, and one more commonly applied to men. It was typically associated with upper-class, intellectual or artistic individuals in sedentary employment. The condition descended in a direct line from Renaissance ideas of melancholy, the classic description of which is in Robert Burton's *The Anatomy of Melancholy* (1621), a popular book that went through hundreds of editions in Europe and America, and articulated the polymorphous nature of the malady:

> The melancholic constitution manifested itself in anxiety, insomnia, irritability, and a variety of other complaints that fell into the category of neurosis. Doctors considered the neurotic manifestations of this humour difficult to treat, let alone cure, with many of its stages degenerating into deep depression and sometimes even madness. Thomas Willis, for example, believed that madness and melancholy were 'so-much akin, that these Distempers often change, and pass from one into the other'.[15]

Following Burton's intellectual odyssey, melancholy became a fashionable state of mind among young men, a psychological and medical condition attractive to status-conscious neurotics.[16] Melancholy in women, on the other hand, had more negative connotations, being viewed as biological and emotional in origin.[17]

The term neurasthenia was popularised as 'nervous exhaustion' by the American neurologist George Beard, in a series of books and articles he published from 1868 onwards, although even before Beard people had noted the 'constant correlation of certain symptoms and had grouped these together as marks of a definitive disorder.'[18] Beard's steady stream of writings on the subject, including the seminal *A Practical Treatise on Nervous Exhaustion (Neurasthenia), Its Symptoms, Nature, Sequences and Treatment* (1880), fired the medical and public imaginations.[19] Like melancholy before it, neurasthenia became the most

---

[15] Cited in J. S. Madden, 'Melancholy in Medicine and Literature: Some Historical Considerations', in *British Journal of Medical Psychology*, 72 vols. (London: British Psychological Society (1923-2001), XXXIX (1966), 116-131, pp. 127.

[16] See Charles Haventhal Jr, 'Robert Burton's *Anatomy of Melancholy* in Early America', *Papers of the Bibliographical Society of America* LXIII (1969), 157-175.

[17] Elaine Showalter, 'Representing Ophelia: women, madness, and the responsibilities of feminist criticism', in *Shakespeare and the Question of Theory*, ed. Patricia Parker and Geoffrey Hartman (London: Methuen, 1985), pp. 76-92, p. 81. See also Juliana Schiesari, *The Gendering of Melancholia* (Ithaca: Cornell University Press, 1992).

[18] Ivo Geikie Cobb, *A Manual of Neurasthenia (Nervous Exhaustion)* (London: Baillière, Tindall and Cox, 1920), p. 5.

[19] George Miller Beard, *A Practical Treatise on Nervous Exhaustion (Neurasthenia), Its Symptoms, Nature, Sequences and Treatment* (New York: Wood and Company, 1880).

fashionable neurosis in the Western world, the *fin-de-siècle* 'cultural illness *par excellence*'.[20] The diagnosis was applied to almost any psychoneurosis in the period.

Of the thousand natural shocks that flesh is heir to, hysteria and neurasthenia have today been struck off the list by the medical profession, having been either absorbed into other diagnoses or rationalised out of existence. Other once-popular maladies have suffered the same fate: Craig Raine humorously discusses the disappearance of 'brain fever', a mysterious ailment that undid many a nineteenth-century heroine, from modern fiction – in Dostoevsky's *The Brothers Karamazov* (1880), Madam Hohlakov fears Katerina Ivanova's hysteria might cause brain fever, and the death of Luísa, in Eça de Queirós's *O Primo Basílio [Cousin Basílio]* (1878), is induced by the condition.[21] Most modern psychiatrists view hysteria as a legacy diagnosis, an obsolete catch-all term for a long list of possible manifestations: one Victorian physician catalogued seventy-five pages of symptoms and called the list incomplete.[22] Neurasthenia is still diagnosed in Hong Kong and Taiwan, but elsewhere fatigue is now considered to be a symptom of some other disorder rather than a disease in its own right. What is currently known as Chronic Fatigue Syndrome bears a strong resemblance to what the Victorians thought of as neurasthenia.[23]

Although hysteria and neurasthenia are today obsolete diagnoses, in Pessoa's day they were the two most widespread mental disorders in the Western world. He was well versed in the clinical literature of both neuroses: he owned, among many others, Arthur Lovell's *Volo or the Will: What it is; How to Strengthen, and How to Use it* (1900), Charles Godfrey Leland's *Have you a strong will?: or how to develope [sic] and strengthen will-power, memory, or any other faculty or attribute of the mind, by the easy process of self-hypnotism* (1912) and David Fraser Harris's *Nerves* (1913).[24] He also owned José de Lacerda's *Os Neurasthenicos: esboço d'um estudo medico e philosophico* (1895) [*Neurasthenics: A Medical and Philosophical Study*] with a preface by Sousa Martins.[25] Sousa Martins had been Cesário Verde's

---

[20] Pietikainen, *Neurosis and Modernity*, p. 38.

[21] Craig Raine, 'Whatever Became of Brain Fever?', in *Haydn and the Valve Trumpet* (1990; London: Picador, 2000), pp. 12-21; Fydor Dostoevsky, *The Brothers Karamazov* (1880), trans. Constance Garnett (New York: Barnes and Noble, 2004), p. 199.

[22] See Micale, 'On the "Disappearance" of Hysteria: A Study in the Clinical Deconstruction of a Diagnosis', *Isis* 84 (1993), 496–526; on the Victorian enthusiasm for hysteria, see Laura Briggs, 'The Race of Hysteria: '"Overcivilization" and the "Savage" Woman in Late Nineteenth-Century Obstetrics and Gynaecology', *American Quarterly* 52 (2000), 246–73.

[23] The entry for 'neurasthenia' in Roberto Patarca-Montero's *Concise Encyclopaedia of Chronic Fatigue Syndrome* (London: Routledge, 2000) tells users to 'See Chronic Fatigue Syndrome, Definition' (p. 58).

[24] Charles Godfrey Leland, *Have you a strong will?: or how to develope [sic] and strengthen will-power, memory, or any other faculty or attribute of the mind, by the easy process of self-hypnotism* (1912; 2nd ed., London: Nichols and Co., 1900); David Fraser Harris, *Nerves* (London: Williams and Norgate, New York: Henry Holt and Co., n.d. [1913]).

[25] José de Lacerda, *Os Neurasthenicos: Esboço d'um estudo medico e philosophico* (Lisbon:

doctor, and would go on to diagnose Antero de Quental as neurasthenic, as we shall see. Little wonder that the *fin-de-siècle* neuroses came to be an integral part of Pessoa's self-analysis, as exemplified in a letter of 10 October 1935 to Tomás Ribeiro Colaço:

> O facto é que, desde o ano passado, tenho estado sob o influxo de estados nervosos de diversas formas e feitios, que por um longo período me arrancaram da vontade até o desejo de não fazer nada. Tenho-me sentido uma espécie de filme psíquico de um manual de psiquiatria, secção psiconevroses. (*Corr II*, p. 354)

> [The fact of the matter is that, since last year, I have been under the influence of nervous conditions of different shapes and styles, which for a long while forcibly removed from my will even the desire to do nothing. I have felt like a sort of psychic film of the psychoneuroses section of a psychiatry textbook.]

There were medical distinctions, as Pessoa recognised better than most non-specialists, between hysteria and neurasthenia, but his application of the compound word 'hystero-neurasthenia' to himself and Shakespeare, as an umbrella classification for a prevalent state of mind, is in keeping with the fluid, nebulous boundary between the two neuroses, particularly when they migrated to art. Pessoa's usage is uncommon, but not unprecedented: hystero-neurasthenia appears in the index of a 1905 clinical handbook, and in a number of case histories of the period.[26]

Erudite Neuroses and their Critics: '*Fin-de-siècle! Fin-de-siècle!* Literature is a thing of [...] nerves'[27]

Hysteria and neurasthenia became 'contagious diagnostics' at the *fin de siècle*, that is, 'medical diagnoses that become relatively popular within a fairly short period of time (c. 10 years), and which are also accepted or even embraced by (certain sections) of the general population.'[28] One section of the general population to embrace them with open arms was its artists, and in particular its creative writers, many of whom drew directly on the medical theories of the day in their fiction. Paris was the leading centre of *avant-garde* psychological medicine, and French

---

M. Gomes, 1895).

[26] J. Michell Clarke, *Hysteria & Neurasthenia: The Practitioner's Handbook* (London/New York: The Bodley Head, 1905), p. 238; F. G. Gosling, *Before Freud: Neurasthenia and the American Medical Community, 1870-1910* (Urbana, Chicago: University of Illinois Press, 1987), p. 38.

[27] Lionel Johnson, untitled article, *Anti-Jacobin* (1891); cited in Hurb Hermans, W. E. Krul and Hans van Maanen, *1894: European Theatre in Turmoil: Meaning and Significance of the Theatre a Hundred Years Ago* (Amsterdam: Rodopi, 1996), p. 20.

[28] Pietikainen, *Neurosis and Modernity*, p. 6.

writers were therefore the first to make use of the madness of the age in their art. Other writers, of different cultures, soon followed suit.

Gustave Flaubert's *Madame Bovary* (1857) is the watershed novel dealing directly with hysteria as its central subject-matter. The novel was first serialised in *La Revue de Paris* [*Paris Review*] in 1856, resulting in a trial in January 1857, on charges of obscenity, that made the story notorious. It soon became a bestseller in book form, hailed as a seminal work of psychological realism.

Flaubert's father was a physician, as was his brother, and he himself was a serious if unsystematic reader of medical literature, probably inspired by his own epileptic seizures. Symptoms which would have been recognised by contemporary readers as those of a hysteric – dizziness, weak spells, heart palpitations, and bouts of nerves – abound in the novel's protagonist, Emma Bovary. Flaubert himself never labelled Emma Bovary a hysteric, but others did, and he did not openly contradict them. Charles Baudelaire was the first, in a famous early review of 1857 which Flaubert praised for its insightful criticism of his book. In this review, Baudelaire hailed the groundbreaking transposition of hysteria from medicine to literature:

L'hystérie! Pourquoi ce mystère physiologique ne ferait-il pas le fond et le tuf d'une oeuvre littéraire, ce mystère que l'Académie de médecine n'a pas encore résolu, et qui, s'exprimant dans les femmes par la sensation d'une boule ascendante et asphyxiante (je ne parle que du symptôme principal), se traduit chez les hommes nerveux par toutes les impuissances et aussi par l'aptitude à tous les excès?[29]

[Hysteria! Why would this physiological mystery not serve as the backdrop for a literary work, this mystery the Academy of Medicine has not yet resolved and which, manifesting itself in women by the sensation of a rising and asphyxiating lump in the throat (I am speaking only of the principal symptom), reveals itself in nervous men by all manner of impotence and also by an aptitude for every excess?]

Émile Zola's epic cycle of novels depicting the national decline of France, the twenty-volume *Rougon-Macquart* series (1870-93), traces the spread of neurotic pathologies through six generations of two French families, back to the original neurological defect, or 'tare nerveuse', of Tante Dide, the progenitor of both the Rougon and Macquart lines, who suffered from semi-imbecility, nervous attacks, and convulsions. In these novels, hysteria operates as a pathology that can generate other vices in offspring, including alcoholism, prostitution, sexual perversion, criminality, and suicide. Joris-Karl Huysman's *À Rebours* [*Against the Grain*] (1884) is another major work to cast literary hysterics. Des Esseintes, its

---

[29] Charles Baudelaire, 'Madame Bovary', in *Oeuvres complètes* [*Complete Works*], 2 vols., ed. Claude Pichois (Paris: Gallimard, 1975), II, p. 83; first published in *L'artiste* [*The Artist*] (18 October 1857).

protagonist, craves artistic novelties and 'a few suggestive books [...] to shake up his nervous system with erudite hysterias', as well as innovative musical harmonies to leave him 'choked by the suffocating *boule* of hysteria.'[30] A cultural historian has discovered that Huysmans drew directly on two medical texts, both recently out in new editions, as guides to the depiction of Des Esseintes's nervousness.[31]

Literary hysteria soon made its way outside France's borders. In Robert Louis Stevenson's *The Strange Case of Dr Jekyll and Mr Hyde* (1886) Jekyll's housemaid breaks into 'hysterical whimpering.'[32] Doctors are central to the story, which is presented as a clinical case. In Bram Stoker's *Dracula* (1897), almost everyone in the novel falls prey to hysteria: Mina Murray is forced to 'suppose' she is 'hysterical'; Lord Godalming 'grew quite hysterical'; even Van Helsing, the seemingly secure bastion of masculine reason and wisdom, 'one of the most advanced scientists of the day', collapses, faced with Lucy's death, into 'a regular fit of hysterics.'[33] Such neurotic fictional characters of the *fin-de-siècle* are the artistic siblings of Freud's Dora and other hysterics.[34]

Emma Bovary, Des Esseintes, and the characters in *Dracula* are more hysterical than neurasthenic, but in most cases artists assimilated and appropriated the two *fin-de-siècle* neuroses as a more or less vague language of nerves and nervousness, rather than as definitive diagnostic categories. Baudelaire's *spleen*, typical of the perceived *mal du siècle*, is a shadowy nervousness which its sufferers, in his stories, are unable to precisely define: 'Mes nerfs trop tendus ne donnent plus que des vibrations criardes et douloureuses' ['My overly tense nerves produce only garish, painful vibrations'], a typical protagonist declares.[35] 'Spleen' has stronger links to neurasthenia than to hysteria, for it was thought to produce black bile, the overproduction of which was one of the hallmarks of the melancholy temperament from which neurasthenia derived.

Not concerned with a precise transposition of *fin-de-siècle* psychology to literature, however, writers of fiction alternately applied, parodied, plagiarised,

---

[30] Cited in Alfred Edward Carter, *The Idea of Decadence in French Literature 1830-1900*, (Toronto: University of Toronto Press, 1958), p. 83.

[31] Specifically, he drew on *Traité des névroses* and *Nouveaux éléments de pathologie générale* [*Treatise on Neuroses and New Aspects of General Pathology*]. See Debora Leah Silverman, *Art Nouveau in Fin-de Siècle France: Politics, Psychology, and Style* (Los Angeles: University of California Press, 1989), pp. 13-17.

[32] Robert Louis Stevenson, *The Strange Case of Dr Jekyll and Mr Hyde*, ed. Jenni Calder (Harmondsworth: Penguin, 1979), p. 64.

[33] Bram Stoker, *Dracula: A Tale* (1897; Oxford: Oxford University Press, 1983), pp. 184, 230, 112, 174.

[34] See Nina Auerbach, *Woman and Demon* (Cambridge, M.A.: Harvard University Press, 1982), pp. 22-24.

[35] Baudelaire, 'Le Confiteor de l'artiste' [The Artist's Confiteor], in *Oeuvres complètes* [*Complete Works*], I, p. 278. *Les Fleurs du Mal* [*The Flowers of Evil*], which Pessoa owned, contains a number of poems under the heading 'Spleen et Idéal'. See Charles Baudelaire, *Les Fleurs du Mal* (Paris: Ernest Flammarion, n.d.).

appropriated and misappropriated the new mental sciences.[36] Machado de Assis's short story 'O Alienista' [The Alienist] (1882) features a mind doctor intent on furthering the scientific study of the neuroses. Implicit in Machado's story, which expertly transforms metonymy into metaphor, is the conviction that madness is partly a social construct, and that no complete dividing line lies between sanity and insanity, but rather a vast and shadowy borderland, as Maupassant had suggested in the very same year. The protagonist of Machado's story ends up admitting that four-fifths of the population of his local town are, in one way or another, mad – and therefore releases them back into society because their madness must be normal. He then imprisons himself, taking to its logical conclusion the belief that, since he is the only 'normal' one left, normality must be madness.[37]

Portuguese writers of the period also explore the two grand neuroses in their work. In Cesário's 'Esplêndida' [Splendid], the poem's speaker accompanies the *femme fatale* 'como um doido, em convulsões,/Febril, de colarinho amarrotado' [like a madman, in convulsions/Feverish, with a wrinkled collar].[38] The poem that most readers know as 'Contrariedades' [Difficulties], the heading under which it appeared in *O Livro de Cesário Verde* [*The Book of Cesário Verde*] (1887), was initially titled 'Nevroses' [Neuroses] (1876).[39] Nervous episodes are also common in Nobre's poems, such as 'Lusitânia no Bairro Latino' [Lusitania in the Latin Neighbourhood], a poem written, not incidentally, while Nobre was in Paris, the heartland of hysterics and neurasthenics, in 1891-1892, the heyday of Parisian neurotics:

Tísicos! Doidos! Nus! Velhos a ler a sina!
[...] Reumáticos! Anões! Delirium tremens! Quistos![40]

[Consumptives! Madmen! Naked men! Old men reading their fortune!
[...] Rheumatics! Dwarves! Delirium tremens! Cysts!]

'Delirium tremens' was one of the long list of symptoms associated with hysteria, and Nobre's poetry is infused with the nervous *mal du siècle*; in 'Males do Anto' [*Anto's Ills*], the speaker declares:

Nem mesmo sei dizer que doença era a minha,
Porque eram todas, eu sei lá!

---

[36] See Judith Ryan, *Vanishing Subject: Early Psychology and Literary Modernism* (Chicago: University of Chicago Press, 1991).
[37] Joaquim Maria Machado de Assis, *O Alienista e O Espelho* [*The Alienist and The Mirror*] (Rio de Janeiro: Ediouro, 1996).
[38] Cesário Verde, *Obra Completa* [*Complete Works*], ed. Joel Serrão (Lisbon: Horizonte, 1988), p. 74; first published in *Diário de Notícias* [newspaper] (22 March 1874).
[39] *Ibid.*, p. 107.
[40] Nobre, *Poesia completa* [*Complete Poetry*], p. 193.

[...] os meus nervos gastos, velhos,
Convulsionavam-nos relâmpagos vermelhos[41]

[I cannot even say which illness I suffered from,
Because it was all of them, I don't know!
[...] my spent, old nerves,
Were convulsed by red lightening bolts]

Pessoa was a keen reader of *fin-de-siècle* literary, as well as medical, treatments of neurosis. In the 'Notas' [Notes] that Armando Côrtes-Rodrigues compiled of Pessoa's influences between 1905 and 1908, Baudelaire and Cesário both feature, which indicates that Pessoa encountered several of the above literary appropriations of the neuroses at the same time.[42] No copy of *Madame Bovary* is today extant in his library, but we know he first read it in 1907, for an entry in his reading diary for that year reads: 'July 14: Flaubert: "Madame Bovary"' (*GL II*, p. 624). The novel was one he greatly admired: in 'Impermanence' Pessoa posits that of the nineteenth-century novelists, it is 'probable' that 'only Flaubert' will survive into succeeding ages (*H*, p. 243). We do not know when Pessoa read *Dracula*, but a copy of the book can be found in his library, and his enthusiasm for Nobre's poetry is well documented.

There is also an allusion to *Madame Bovary* in *Desassossego*. The relevant passage reads:

As misérias de um homem que sente o tédio da vida do terraço da sua vila rica são uma coisa; são outra coisa as misérias de quem, como eu, tem que contemplar a paisagem do meu quarto num 4º andar da Baixa, e sem poder esquecer que é ajudante de guarda-livros.
'Tout notaire a rêvé des sultanes'... (*LD*, p. 492)

[The anguish of a man afflicted by life's tedium on the terrace of his opulent villa is one thing; quite another is the anguish of someone like me, who must contemplate the scenery from my fourth-floor rented room in downtown Lisbon, unable to forget that I'm an assistant bookkeeper.
'Tout notaire a rêvé des sultanes'...][43]

Incidentally, this is a further instance of Pessoa citing from memory, for the quotation is slightly off. Zenith's note for this passage reads: '*Tout notaire a rêvé des sultanes*': This is a condensed paraphrase of a sentence found in Flaubert's *Madame Bovary*: 'Le plus médiocre libertin a rêvé des sultanes; chaque notaire porte en soi les débris d'un poète' [The most mediocre libertine has dreamed of

[41] *Ibid.*, p. 349.
[42] *Cartas a Armando Côrtes-Rodrigues* [*Letters to Armando Côrtes-Rodrigues*] (Lisbon: Horizonte, 1985), p. 76.
[43] Trans. Richard Zenith, in *Book of Disquiet* (London: Penguin, 2002), p. 466.

oriental princesses; every notary bears within him the debris of a poet].

The artistic appropriation of the neuroses of the age did not go unnoticed by contemporary cultural critics, particularly in France and Germany. Côrtes-Rodrigues concludes his notes of Pessoa's influences between 1905 and 1908 with the entry: 'Livro capital que destrói parte de toda esta influência: *A Degenerescência*, de Max Nordau. [Pessoa] Lê então vários livros sobre psiquiatria' [The book which destroys part of all this influence: Max Nordau's *Degeneration*. Pessoa goes on to read several books about psychiatry].[44] There is evidence that Pessoa read *Madame Bovary* and *Degeneration* (1892) in the very same year, 1907.[45] The simultaneity of his contact with two important treatments of neuroses, one literary and the other pseudo-clinical, is significant, for in *Degeneration* Nordau takes as an established fact 'the enormous increase in hysteria in our day', a fact he sees reflected in the features of *fin-de-siècle* Europe as a whole, especially those of its art scene.[46] *Degeneration*, for reasons difficult for modern readers to fathom – it being so contrary to our current sensibility – was 'easily the most widely-read piece of cultural criticism in central Europe between Friedrich Wilhelm Nietzsche's *Thus Spoke Zarathustra* (1883-84) and Oswald Spengler's *The Decline of the West* (1918)'.[47] Theories of degeneration had first been aired in specialist scientific journals in the 1860s, but it was only following Nordau's book that the concept became one of the great organising principles of the late-nineteenth century, a heuristic fiction which stemmed from, and in turn influenced, literary fictions.[48]

Nordau and his circle, in their antimodernist diatribes, probed the mental condition of *fin-de-siècle* artists on the strength of the perceived neurotic elements in their work. Huysmans, Nordau charges, is 'the classical type of the hysterical mind without originality who is the predestined victim of every suggestion.'[49] In another instance, Nordau explains that because the Germans lack the native artistic sensibility of the French, in Germany hysteria was expressing itself through other channels, most notably rampant anti-Semitism and 'the Wagner fashion'.[50] Nietzsche, in 'The Wagner Case', would agree with him, stating that 'Wagner's art is sick. The problems he brings onto the stage [are] nothing but the problems of hysterics – the convulsive nature of his emotion, his overexcited sensibility, his taste for sharper and sharper spices [...] *Wagner est une névrose.*'[51]

[44] *Cartas a Armando Côrtes-Rodrigues*, p. 76.
[45] In a reading list of 1907, Pessoa writes, 'Max Nordau: *Dégénérescence* [*Degeneration*] (trad. A. Dietrich). I. 120 pages./May 29th: Max Nordau: *Deg.* I. 255 p./[...] June 8: Nordau: Vol II up to p. 100' (*GL*, p. 624).
[46] Max Nordau, *Degeneration*, trans. George L. Mosse (New York: Howard Fertig, 1968), p. 36.
[47] Micale, *Approaching Hysteria*, p. 207
[48] See Lyn Pykett, Introduction, in *Reading* Fin-de-siècle *Fictions* (London/New York: Longman, 1996), pp. 12-14.
[49] Nordau, *Degeneration*, p. 103.
[50] *Ibid.*, pp. 171-213.
[51] Nietzsche, *The Nietzsche Reader,* ed. R. J. Hollingdale (Harmondsworth, Middlesex:

No copy of *Degeneration* is to be found in Pessoa's library, but it contains five other books by Nordau, all of which Pessoa annotated.[52] (His marginalia in these books shows that he did not accept many of Nordau's arguments uncritically, and he also owned a scathing attack on Nordau, the anonymous *Regeneration: A Reply to Max Nordau*.)[53] Further to these, Pessoa possessed four books on Charles Darwin's theory of evolution and various books referring to Césare Lombroso. He seems to have been unconvinced by Lombroso's ideas, writing in one text that the link of genius and madness 'teve interpretações extremas e absurdas, como em Lombroso' [had extreme and absurd interpretations, as in Lombroso] (*PETCL*, p. 87). Darwin had emphasised the difference between the sexes to women's detriment, often basing himself on pioneering criminologists like Lombroso and the cranial measurements they had taken. In *Dracula*, Van Helsing explains to the other characters in the novel that the fearful enigma of the vampire has to be approached not through a popular physiognomy but through the insights of the craniometry currently being developed in Lombroso's criminal anthropology: 'The Count is a criminal and a criminal type. Nordau and Lombroso would so classify him, and *qua* criminal he is of imperfectly formed mind.'[54] Darwinian theories of evolution were appropriated by some *fin-de-siècle* psychologists to further the therapeutic pessimism of Nordau and Lombroso; biological inheritance, it was thought, could pave the way for madness and criminality. The existence of a Portuguese book called *Degenerescência* [*Degeneration*] (1901) in Pessoa's library, based on what is probably the earliest PhD dissertation on the topic in the country, shows that the ideas associated with neurosis and degeneration had penetrated Portuguese culture by the new century: *Degenerescência* contains separate chapters dedicated to Lombroso, Darwin, criminology, evolution, degeneration, hysteria and neurasthenia.[55]

The fashion for diagnosing artists and artistic movements as neurotic and degenerate quickly caught on, sparking a new genre of literary and cultural criticism that flourished before the advent of psychoanalysis. Countless personages, dead or alive, were subjected to the new psychological scrutiny – Rousseau, the Marquis de Sade, Byron, Poe, Dostoevsky, Nietzsche, Napoleon –

Viking, 1981), pp. 142-43.

[52] Nordau, *Vue du dehors: essai de critique scientifique et philosophique sur quelques auteurs français contemporains*. Trad. *Auguste Dietrich [Seen From Without: An Essay of Scientific and Philosophical Criticism of Some Contemporary French Authors]* (Paris: Félix Alcan, 1903), *Paradoxes sociologiques [Sociological Paradoxes]*, trans. August Dietrich (Paris: Félix Alcan, 1907), *On art and artists*, trans. W. F. Harvey (London: T. Fisher Unwin, 1907), *Paradoxes psychologiques [Psychological Paradoxes]*, trans. Dietrich (Paris: Félix Alcan, 1911) and *Psycho-physiologie du génie et du talent [Psycho-phisiology of Genius and Talent]*, trans. Dietrich (Paris: Félix Alcan, 1911).

[53] Anon. [Alfred Egmont Hake and Nicholas Murray Butler], *Regeneration: A Reply to Max Nordau* (Westminster: Archibald Constable and Co., 1895).

[54] Stoker, *Dracula*, p. 342.

[55] Albino Pacheco, *Degenerescência [Degeneration]* (Coimbra: Imprensa da Universidade, 1901).

and there appeared medical-psychological analyses of wider movements like Romanticism and Decadentism. An early critic of *À Rebours* lamented: 'The hero of Monsieur Huysmans [...] is sick, like all the heroes of the novels of this sick era [...] He is prey to the *neurosis of the age* ['*la névrose du siècle*']. He is from Charcot's Hospital.'[56] The *London World* ran its review of Thomas Hardy's *Jude the Obscure* (1895) under the title 'Hardy the Degenerate.'[57] Doctoral theses were conducted in this vein: representative titles include *La Folie de Maupassant* [*Maupassant's Madness*] (1907), *Dégénérescence et dispsomanie d'Edgar Poe* [*Edgar Poe's Degeneration and Dipsomania*] (1907) and *Essai sur la psychologie morbide de Huysmans* [*An Essay on Huysman's Morbid Psychology*] (1917).[58] As Chris Baldick observes, this line of criticism is 'not only judicial in tone but positively inquisitorial, indulging in a kind of perversion-hunting' rooted in 'a simple model of [pre– or anti-Freudian] normality and mental consistency.'[59]

Flaubert was inevitably branded a neurotic post-mortem. Doctors had assumed that the novelist suffered from periodic seizures, but when it was revealed that these had been accompanied by depressions, neuralgias, crying spells, and sexual frigidity, speculation arose that the writer's nervous attacks may have been hysterical. The controversy culminated in the medical thesis *Flaubert et la médecine* [*Flaubert and Medicine*] in 1905.[60] Its author, who subsequently became a Flaubert scholar, exhaustively reviewed the available documentation about the writer's life, alongside the latest medical research on neurotic disorders, to confidently proclaim Flaubert's a case of hystero-neurasthenia. This sets a notable precedent for Pessoa's diagnosis of Shakespeare, and himself, as suffering from the same malaise.

The Madness of Modernism: 'o facto essencial é que estou doente' [the essential fact is I am ill][61]

Despite the vehement attack of Nordau and others, the generation of Modernist writers who succeeded Flaubert's continued to incorporate the neuroses into their art. In their Surrealist manifestos, Louis Aragon and André Breton, both of whom had attended medical school as young men, branded hysteria 'the greatest

---

[56] Barbey d'Aurevilly, cited in Carter, *Idea of Decadence*, p. 86. Original emphasis.

[57] Cited in Richard Dellamora, 'Homosexual Scandal and Compulsory Heterosexuality in the 1890s', in *Masculine Desire: The Sexual Politics of Victorian Aestheticism* (Chapel Hill/London: University of North Carolina Press, 1990), pp. 189-212, p. 201.

[58] Zacharie Lacassagne, *La Folie de Maupassant* (unpublished doctoral dissertation, University of Toulouse, 1907); B. Carrère, *Dégénérescence et dispsomanie d'Edgar Poe* (unpublished dissertation, University of Toulouse, 1907); G. Lavalée, *Essai sur la psychologie morbide de Huysmans* (unpublished doctoral dissertation, University of Paris, 1917).

[59] Chris Baldick, *The Social Mission of English Criticism 1848-1932* (Oxford: Clarendon, 1983), p. 217.

[60] René Dumesnil, *Flaubert et la médecine* (Paris: Societé francaise d'imprimerie et de librairie, 1905).

[61] *AdC*, 'Opiário' [Opiary], p. 64.

poetic discovery of the end of the nineteenth century', hailing it as not merely 'a pathological phenomenon', but of great usefulness for art, 'in every way [...] a supreme mode of expression.'[62]

Eliot draws extensively on the language of nerves in his early poetry. *Prufrock and Other Observations* (1917) is steeped in the discourse: an exasperated Prufrock draws on it when he finds it impossible to communicate his mental state: 'It is impossible to say just what I mean!/But as if a magic lantern threw the nerves in patterns on a screen', and his hesitations, visions and revisions are a prime example of the paralysis of the will associated with neurasthenia.[63] Eliot's prose poem 'Hysteria', in the same collection, depicts a hysterical attack.

Eliot remarked in a letter of 1921 that English doctors all seemed to specialise in 'nerves'.[64] The second part of *The Waste Land*, a poem published a year later, is infused with nervous conversation and nervous silences:

My nerves are bad to-night. Yes, bad. Stay with me.
Speak to me. Why do you never speak? Speak.
What are you thinking of? What thinking? What?
I never know what you are thinking. Think.[65]

Ezra Pound, judging from his notes on the manuscript draft of the poem, did not like this nervous dialogue. He found it too realistic, and wrote a disapproving 'photographic' next to it. Eliot's first wife Vivien, on the contrary, whom Eliot described as suffering from 'nerves' herself (she was permanently admitted to an asylum in 1938), praised it for this very quality.[66] In an attempt to override Pound's remark, she wrote next to it in large, capital letters: 'WONDERFUL'.[67] Eliot kept the passage in the poem.

Why this continued artistic interest in hysteria and neurasthenia in the early decades of the new century? The most plausible explanation is that both conditions were connected, in the minds of doctors, patients and artists, with the strains of modernity. Beard argued that neurasthenia was caused by the stresses of modern civilisation, and physicians in the Beard school of thought linked it to growing urbanisation. It was, as Robert Musil notes in *The Man Without Qualities* (1930-42), 'a nerve-racked age', one of 'restlessness and constant change, of speed

---

[62] 'Le cinquantenaire de l'hysterie (1878-1928)' [50 Years of Hysteria], in *Histoire du surréalisme: Doc`uments surréalistes* [*History of Surrealism: Surrealist Documents*], ed. Maurice Nadeau (Paris: Seuil, 1948), pp. 125, 127.

[63] Eliot, 'The Love Song of J. Alfred Prufrock', in *Collected Poems 1909-1962* (London: Faber and Faber, 1963), p. 17.

[64] Eliot, letter to Julian Hurley, 31 October 1921; cited in *The Waste Land: A Facsimile and Transcripts of the Original Drafts*, ed. Valerie Eliot (London: Faber and Faber, 1971), p. xxii.

[65] Eliot, *The Waste Land*, in *Collected Poems*, p. 67.

[66] Eliot, letter to Conrad Aiken, 21 August 1916, cited in *The Waste Land: A Facsimile*, pp. x-xi.

[67] *The Waste Land: A Facsimile*, pp. 10-11.

and shifting perspectives, in which something was definitely amiss.'[68] The two grand neuroses mirrored the furious pace of modernity, which acted as a shock on the nervous system.[69] In the postscript to the 1912 edition of *Jude the Obscure*, Hardy suggests that Sue should be regarded as a type of 'the intellectualized, emancipated bundle of nerves that modern conditions were producing, mainly in cities as yet.'[70] Another bundle of nerves – a man with 'toda a sensibilidade dos meus nervos' [all the sensibility of my nerves], with his 'nervos postos à superfície' [nerves skin deep] – is Bernardo Soares, who complains of the city's 'horrorosa histeria dos comboios, dos automóveis, dos navios' [horrible hysteria of trains, automobiles, ships], which does not allow its inhabitants to sleep (*LD*, pp. 203, 263, 143).

Writing as late as in 1922, a clinician concluded that neurasthenia was still 'rampant in all large cities, often undistinguished from its near-neighbour hysteria, and its chief symptoms are headache, gastro-intestinal disturbances, and subjective sensations of all kinds.'[71] It is no coincidence that subjective sensations of all kinds became the cornerstone of the experimental currents pervading Europe, as an array of Modernist -*isms* vied to best capture the spirit of the day. In Italy there was Marinetti's aggressive futurism; in France, painters were exploding traditional perspectives with cubism; Germany had expressionism; Britain Ezra Pound and Wyndham Lewis's dizzying vorticism. In Portugal, Pessoa and the other Modernists linked to the review *Orpheu* (1915) were synthesizing these different currents to usher a cosmopolitan Modernism into the country. The *Orpheu* artists enjoyed being labelled mad ('os doidos do *Orpheu*'); one of their number, Ângelo de Lima, was 'objectively' mad, sending in his contributions from an asylum.

One of their longer-lived experiments was with 'sensacionismo' [sensationism] (derived from '*sensação*', [sensation]), a mutilated version of futurism adapted by Pessoa and Sá-Carneiro for the home market. As an aesthetic stance, 'sensacionismo' corresponds closely to Eliot's assertion that, for artists of his generation, it was no longer enough to 'look into our hearts and write'; they must instead examine 'the cerebral cortex, the nervous system, and the digestive tracts.'[72] This notion informs numerous Modernist masterpieces: *Ulysses* springs immediately to mind. Joyce recognised that modern man was a bundle of nerves: 'one might say of modern man that he has an epidermis.'[73] Pessoa describes *Ulysses*, in his only surviving text on Joyce, as 'o delírio [...] dos psiquiatras, exposto como fim' [the delirum [...] of psychiatrists, exposed as an end in itself.] [74]

Álvaro de Campos, the most Modernist of the heteronyms, whom Pessoa at one

[68] Cited in Lisa Appignnanesi, *Mad, Bad and Sad*, p. 100.
[69] See Louis A. Sass, *Madness and Modernism: Insanity in the Light of Modern Art, Literature, and Thought* (Cambridge, Mass.: Harvard University Press, 1994).
[70] Thomas Hardy, *Jude the Obscure* (Toronto: Macmillan, 1969), p. viii.
[71] Cobb, *A Manual of Neurasthenia*, p. 14.
[72] Eliot, *Selected Prose*, p. 66.
[73] Joyce, *Occasional, Critical and Political Writings*, p. 188.
[74] Cited in Zenith, 'Joyce, James', in *Dicionário de Fernando Pessoa*, p. 369.

point describes as 'the undisciplined child of sensation', is the heteronym who suffers the most acutely from the nervousness triggered by modernity.[75] In the final stanza of 'Passagem das Horas' [Time's Passage], Pessoa makes the link between madness and sensationism explicit when he has Campos describe himself as 'Absolutamente doido só por sentir' [Absolutely mad solely through feeling].[76]

The terminology of nerves infuses Campos's poetry to a remarkable degree. His early, more sensationist poems are full of allusions to the *fin-de-siècle* neuroses. In 'Ode Triunfal' [Triumphal Ode] (1914) he speaks of 'todos os meus nervos dissecados fora' [all my dissected nerves], and hails electricity as 'nervos doentes da Matéria!' [nerves sick of Matter!] (*AdC*, pp. 81, 89). In 'Ode Marítima' [Maritime Ode] (1915) he feels weighing on his nerves 'o facto de que [o Pacífico] é o maior dos oceanos' [the fact that [the Pacific] is the largest of all oceans] and deplores his 'nervos postos como enxárcias' [nerves worn like shrouds]; in the same poem, he collectively refers to 'Os nossos nervos femininos e delicados' [Our feminine, delicate nerves] and mentions the age's 'Histeria de sensações' [Hysteria of sensations] (*AdC*, pp. 112, 120, 127, 132). In his sprawling, unfinished 'Saudação a Walt Whitman' [Salutation to Walt Whitman] (1915), Campos writes of 'Os meus versos-ataques-histéricos,/Os meus versos que arrastam o carro dos meus nervos' [My hysterical-attack-verses,/My nerves that drag the carriage of my nerves], and speaks of a 'Megalomania dos nervos' [Megalomania of nerves] (*AdC*, p. 169). There is a lengthy passage about nerves in 'Passagem das Horas':

> nos meus nervos todas as machinas, todos os systemas de engrenagem,
> Nos meus nervos locomotiva, carro-electrico, automovel, debulhadora a vapor,
> Nos meus nervos machina maritima, Diesel, semi-Diesel, Campbell,
> Nos meus nervos installação absoluta a vapor, a gaz, a oleo e a electricidade[77]

> [my combustion-engine nerves that run on heavy or light oil,
> My all-machine, all-gear-system nerves,
> My train, tram, car, steam-thresther nerves,
> Ship-engine, diesel-engine, semidiesel, Campbell nerves,
> 100 percent steam-run, gas-run, oil-run, and electric-run nerves][78]

There are even references to the two grand neuroses in Campos's less sensationist poems. In the opening line of the more decadent 'Opiário' [Opiary] (1914), Pessoa has Campos assert: 'minh'alma é doente' [my soul is ill]. Campos goes on to describe himself as a typical product of *fin-de-siècle* neurosis: 'São dias só de febre na minha cabeça' [These are days full of fever in my head], 'Tenho os nervos na forca, vinte a vinte' [My nerves are on the hangman's noose, score by

---

[75] Cited in L. C. Taylor, 'Life and Times', in *A Centenary Pessoa*, p. 220.
[76] *Álvaro de Campos: A Passagem das Horas*, ed. Cleonice Berardinelli (Lisbon: IN-CM, 1988), p. 33.
[77] *Ibid.*, p. 26.
[78] *Fernando Pessoa and Co.*, ed. and trans. Richard Zenith, pp. 151-2.

score], 'sou um convalescente do Momento' [I'm a convalescent of the Age], 'Sou doente e fraco' [I'm ill and weak]; 'estes nervos são a minha morte' [these nerves will be the death of me] (*AdC*, pp. 59, 60, 61, 62). In an early sonnet, he writes: 'Sonho, histérico oculto, um vão recanto...' [I dream, an occult hysteric, in a vain corner...] (*AdC*, p. 78). Even once his futurist energy has been spent, in 'Tabacaria' (1928) he is still suffering from nerves, as he vividly captures in the image of himself as a departing train, with

uma partida apitada
De dentro da minha cabeça
E uma sacudidela dos meus nervos e um ranger de ossos na ida. (*AdC*, p. 320)

[a whistle of departure
Inside my head
And a shaking of my nerves and a creaking of my bones on the way.]

In another late Campos poem, of 1930, we read: 'Hoje tenho uma alma parecida com a morte dos nervos' [Today my soul seems like the death of my nerves] (*AdC*, p. 398).

In an untitled poem, Campos sees himself as a reflection for the madness of his generation, 'Ah, com os nervos de toda a gente, os meus nervos vibram...' [Oh, my nerves vibrate with everyone's nerves], and despairs of his condition: 'Ó doença humanitária dos meus nervos vibrando cheios de outras pessoas' [Oh humanitarian disease of my nerves vibrating full of other people] (*AdC*, pp. 240, 241). In another, he admits: 'Eu [...] tenho vivido através do meu sangue e dos meus nervos' [I have lived by my blood and by my nerves] (*AdC*, p. 219). Campos's poetic nervousness reflects Nordau's thinking on the negative symbiosis between art and neurosis: a couplet in 'Saudação a Walt Whitman' reads 'Raios partam a mandriice que nos faz poetas,/A degenerescência que nos engana artistas' [Damn the laziness that makes us poets,/The degeneration that makes us think we're artists]; in 'Passagem das Horas', he describes himself as 'este degenerado superior sem arquivos na alma' [this superior degenerate with no archives in his soul] (*AdC*, p. 176, 192).

Pizarro, who has worked extensively on Pessoa's reading and writing on genius and madness, argues in an article that 'Pessoa seria um histero-neurasténico, mas ao escrever enquanto Campos potenciaria só o seu histerismo. [...] Campos seria uma "subpersonalidade", precisamente por não ter um traço neurasténico...' [Pessoa is a hystero-neurasthenic, but writing as Campos he draws only on his hysteria. [...] Campos is a 'subpersonality', precisely because he has no trace of neurasthenia...].[79] It was Pessoa himself who first posited that Campos represented the hysterical side of his own hystero-neurasthenia, being an artistic embodiment of 'o mais histericamente histérico de mim' [the most hysterically

---

[79] Pizarro, 'Da Histeria à Neurastenia (Quental e Pessoa)' [From Hysteria to Neurasthenia], *Conceito* 1 ('Loucura & Desrazão') (Autumn 2005), 168-178, p. 173.

hysterical part of me].[80] Pessoa goes as far as to declare, a touch hyperbolically in light of other Modernist treatments of madness, that 'none has ever approached him in the [...] hysteria of our age' (*PC II*, pp. 236-7).

It is simply not true, however, that the poetry of Campos displays exclusively hysterical, rather than neurasthenic, tendencies. In the early poems there are more references to hysteria than neurasthenia, but even in these Campos is prone to shifting between hysteric and neurasthenic postures, often within the same poem. In 'Passagem das Horas', which exuberantly opens with the sensationist motto 'Sentir tudo de todas as maneiras' [To feel everything in every possible way], Campos confesses that he prefers thinking about smoking opium to smoking it, and enjoys looking at absinthe more than drinking it (*AdC*, p. 196). In the scientific language of today, such poetic mood swings might best be described as bipolarity, or swings between euphoria and depression. In Pessoa's day, they would have been regarded as alternations between hysteria and neurasthenia. Furthermore, if we look at Campos's poems chronologically, there is a progression from the early hysteria of his futurist odes (in 'Ode Marítima' [Maritime Ode] he denounces those around him as neurasthenic weaklings rather than hysterical energisers like himself: 'Estupores de tísicos, de neurasténicos, de linfáticos' [Consumptive, neurasthenic, limphatic bastards]) to a later neurasthenia, epitomised by the speaker's stance in 'Tabacaria'.

The neurasthenia Pessoa ascribes to Campos is related to an omnipresent theme in Pessoa's orthonymic poetry, the 'dor de pensar' [pain of (over)thinking]. Pessoa hints at the suffering caused by the neurosis when he speaks of Campos's 'terrible self-analysis' (*PC II*, pp. 236-237). Campos's poem that begins 'Que noite serena!' [What a peaceful night!] describes the 'dor de pensar' in almost literal terms: 'dói, dói, dói.../Por amor de Deus, párem com isso dentro da minha cabeça' [it hurts, it hurts, it hurts.../For heaven's sake, stop that inside my head] (*AdC*, p. 477). Neurasthenia, it was believed, was caused by excessive intellectual introspection, which had the effect of leaving its sufferer paralysed, unable to act and to feel. This is the predicament of the protagonist of Pessoa's play *Faust*, who answers Maria's moving speech beginning 'Amo como o amor ama./Não sei razão p'ra amar-te mais que amar-te' [I love like love loves./I know no reason to love you beyond loving you] with a cold: 'compreendo-te tanto que não sinto' [I understand you so well I feel nothing.][81]

By 'Tabacaria', Campos's poetic neurasthenia has left him incapable of all physical action, perfectly encapsulated in the near-nonsense phrase 'Semiergo-me' [I half rise] (*AdC*, p. 325). The non-introspective, therefore non-neurasthenic, Esteves 'sem metafísica' [with no metaphysics] provides a healthy antithesis to Campos in this poem. Not incidentally, Esteves is characterised exclusively by his physical actions rather than his thoughts: he walks into the tobacco shop, buys cigarettes, walks out, puts the change in his pocket, waves and smiles.

Soares's stance is also that of the neurasthenic: 'não tenho vontade nos nervos'

---

[80] Letter to Casais, 13 October 1935, in *Corr II*, p. 341.
[81] *Fausto*, pp. 83-84.

[my nerves have no will]; 'Nunca encontrei argumentos senão para a inércia' [I have never discovered any arguments, except for inertia] (*LD*, pp. 99, 246). *Desassossego* is rife with comparisons between its protagonist's mental condition, essentially introspective, and the healthy activity of those around him. Patrão Vasques serves exactly the same function in Soares's book as Esteves does in 'Tabacaria'. Soares grasps the intended symbolism in a flash of insight: 'Ah, compreendo! O patrão Vasques é a Vida. A Vida, monótona e necessária, mandante e desconhecida. Este homem banal representa a banalidade da Vida' [Oh, I see! Boss Vasques is Life. Life, monotonous and necessary, bossy and unknown. That banal man represents the banality of Life] (*LD*, p. 53). A further symbolic representative of the non-neurotic, active life embodied by Esteves and Patrão Vasques is the unnamed reaper in Pessoa's orthonymic poem 'Ela canta, pobre ceifeira' [She sings, poor reaper].[82] In this poem, infused with the anguishing 'dor de pensar' ('O que em mim sente 'stá pensando' [What in me feels is thinking]) the speaker expresses an explicit wish to be the unthinking, all-feeling other ('canta, canta sem razão' [sing, sing without reason]), embodied in the image of the reaper who is able to burst into spontaneous song, rather than shackled to his own neurasthenic self.[83]

Pessoa's most powerful image of what a life free from the madness of Modernism, which the orthonym, Campos and Soares all suffer from, might look like is arguably the heteronym Alberto Caeiro. In 'Mestre, meu mestre querido' [Master, my dear master], Campos openly envies Caeiro's escape from the 'dor de pensar', for in his case 'nenhuma coisa feriu, nem doeu, nem perturbou' [nothing ever wounded, hurt, or perturbed] (*AdC*, p. 337). The poem offers us a vision of the potential cure for neurosis in Caeiro's passive acceptance of life, and his rejection of introspection or metaphysical speculation. 'Pensar incomoda como andar à chuva' [Thinking is as uncomfortable as walking in the rain], Pessoa has Caeiro declare in the opening poem of *O Guardador de Rebanhos* [*The Keeper of Sheep*] (*AC*, p. 22), implying that over-thinking, beyond being unpleasant, can lead to illness, as can being caught in the rain. That Pessoa intended Caeiro to represent a non-neurotic counterpart to Campos is suggested by a text in which he writes that Caeiro holds thought to be a 'disease'.[84] He has Campos himself concede, in 'Tabacaria', that metaphysical thought is the result of feeling slightly ill – 'uma consequência de estar mal disposto' [a consequence of feeling out of sorts] – and Soares likens it even more explicitly to a type of madness in *Desassossego*: 'A metafísica pareceu-me sempre uma forma prolongada da loucura latente.' [Metaphysics has always seemed to me a prolongued type of latent madness] (*AdC*, p. 326; *LD*, p. 116).

Pessoa's heteronymic experiments with hysteria are indebted to the tradition pioneered by Flaubert and developed by his fellow Modernists, as we have seen. It is likely that those with neurasthenia derive largely from his reading of *Hamlet*.

---

82 *Poesia do eu*, p. 171.
83 *Ibid.*
84 Cited in L. C. Taylor, 'Life and Times', in *A Centenary Pessoa*, p. 220.

The Madness of Shakespeare's Characters

Shakespeare's dramatic creations, already treated as if they were real people in the period's character criticism (see Chapter 1), became a prime target for *fin-de-siècle* neurosis-hunting. Doctors pointed to Hamlet and Lear as examples of neurotic constitutions and temperaments.[85] Two years before offering his Oedipal explanation for Hamlet's character, Freud referred to 'Hamlet the hysteric' in a letter of 1897.[86] A book titled *The Hysteria of Lady Macbeth* was published in 1912.[87]

Pellissier's *Shakespeare et La Supersition Shakespearienne* [*Shakespeare and the Shakespearean Superstition*] (1914), a book Pessoa owned, contains a chapter devoted to 'La Psychologie dans les Grands Personnages: Macbeth et Othello; Hamlet' [The Psychology of the Great Characters: Macbeth and Othello; Hamlet]. Pessoa did not agree with Pellisier that 'Coriolan, Timon, Roméo, Lear, excluent toute étude psychologique' [Coriolanous, Timon, Romeo, Lear exclude all psychological study], for he underlined the reference to 'Lear' and scribbled a question mark next to it. He wrote 'all wrong' next to Pellissier's assertion, in another chapter: 'Évidemment Shakespeare n'a vu dans ce rôle [Lear] qu'une admirable matière à déployer toute sa rhétorique' [Clearly Shakespeare did not see in this role [Lear] anything beyond an admirable subject-matter in which to deploy his rhetoric.][88] Instead, Pessoa eulogises Shakespeare for his ability to explore, through his dramatic characters,

> abnormal mental states, in which the opinion of modern psychiatricians [*sic*] has given him a distinct preeminence. The senile dementia of Lear, the hysteria of Lady Macbeth, Macbeth's epileptoid character, the hystero-neurasthenia of Hamlet. (*GL*, p. 354)

In a publishing plan for Olisipo, Pessoa mentions the plays *The Tempest*, *Hamlet*, and *King Lear* (*PPP II*, p. 195). This is representative of the Shakespearean plays he was most drawn to, and it is no coincidence that their protagonists should all be, to a greater or lesser extent, mad. Like his contemporaries, Pessoa delights in discovering in Shakespeare's characters symptoms of *fin-de-siècle* psychiatric conditions:

> a ciência moderna pasma da perfeição sintomatologia com que são delineadas, vivas e concretas, com os traços físicos como os psíquicos, a

---

[85] See John S. Haller, *American Medicine in Transition 1840-1910* (Chicago: University of Illinois Press, 1981), pp. 9-14.

[86] Freud, letter to Fliess, 15 October 1897, in *The Complete Letters of Sigmund Freud to Wilhelm Fliess, 1887-1904*, trans. Jeffrey Moussaieff Masson (Cambridge, M. A.: University of Harvard Press, 1985), p. 272.

[87] Isador H. Coriat, *The Hysteria of Lady Macbeth* (New York: Moffat, Yard, 1912).

[88] Georges Pellisier, *Shakespeare et La Superstion Shakespearienne* (Paris: Hachette, 1914), p. 288.

histero-neurastenia de Hamlet, a demência senil de Lear, a histero-epilepsia de Lady Macbeth. [...] Ibsen, que quis fazer drama psiquiátrico, não conseguiu, nem sequer de longe, criar personagens tão inteiramente verdadeiras, perante a própria psiquiatria, como Shakespeare. (*PETCL*, p. 87)

[modern science is dumbfounded by the symptomalogical perfection with which the physical and mental characteristics are described, vividly and concretely: Hamlet's hystero-neurasthenia, Lear's senile dementia, Lady Macbeth's hystero-epilepsy. [...] Ibsen, who wished to write psychiatric drama, did not come close to Shakespeare's ability to create characters so entirely real, according to the tenets of psychiatry.]

Pessoa's classification of Campos and Hamlet as neurotic personalities is a further point of contact he forges between the two. But although Pessoa describes Hamlet, on these two occasions, as hystero-neurasthenic, he is chiefly drawn to the Prince's neurasthenic postures, as suggested by his poetic response to his melancholy 'To be or not to be' soliloquy (see Chapter 1). In one text, he declares

A tragedia de Hamlet não é, como quiz Goethe, a de uma vontade incompetente para arcar com uma tarefa, ou liberdade, que lhe é imposta. Nem mesmo é, como outros, mais complexamente, quereriam, a de uma vontade doente em lucta com o pensamento. A tragedia é, com effeito, d'esta especie, porém mais complexa, e, ao mesmo tempo, mais humana. É a de uma vontade doente incapaz de arcar com uma tarefa, ou responsabilidade, *com a qual reconhece que pode arcar, dadas que* fossem certas condições, dado certo amparo à volição, mantidas certas circunstâncias que permittisem uma organização de impulsos esporadicos em determinação concatenada. Um isolamento que, em parte, temperamento de pensador causa, interiormente porque quebra a vontade e a embota, exteriormente porque torna difficil a ligação com os outros e fugitiva a influenciação pelos acontecimentos que seguem no sentido de desigual tendência.[89]

[Hamlet's tragedy is not, as Goethe posited, that of a will incapable of performing the task, or freedom, imposed upon him. Neither is it, as others, more complexly, posited, that of an ill will at odds with his thought. His tragedy is, in fact, of this nature, but it is more complex and, at the same time, more human. It is that of an ill will incapable of performing a task, or responsibility, *which he knows he could perform, given* the right circumstances, if his will were stronger, if he were able to organise his sporadic impulses into determined effort. His isolation is caused partly by his being a thinker, internally because this breaks his will, externally because it makes his connection to others difficult, and the impact of the chaotic events outside his control fleeting.]

---

[89] *Apreciações Literárias de Fernando Pessoa*, ed. Pauly Ellen Bothe, p. 251. First transcribed and presented in my doctoral thesis *Fernando Pessoa's Shakespeare*.

Pessoa's reference to Hamlet's 'vontade doente incapaz de acção', although he does not say so in so many words, smacks of neurasthenia. Significantly, Goethe is usually credited with pioneering the image of Hamlet as a neurasthenic personality with his description of the melancholy Prince, in *Wilhelm Meister*, as a man paralysed by excessive intellectual introspection, 'Sicklie'd o'er with the pale cast of thought': 'To me it is clear that Shakespeare meant, in the present case, to represent the effects of a great action laid upon a soul unfit for the performance of it. In this view the whole piece seems to me to be composed.' Hamlet's first soliloquy ('O, that this too too solid flesh should melt') prompts Wilhelm to develop the idea of Hamlet's melancholy: 'This *taedium vitae* is a common oppression on minds cast in the Hamlet mould, and is caused by disproportionate mental exertion, which necessitates exhaustion of bodily feeling. Where there is a just coincidence of external and internal action, pleasure is always the result; but where the former is deficient, and the mind's appetency of the ideal is unchecked, realities will seem cold and unmoving.' [90] Countless subsequent interpreters echoed Goethe's interpretation of Hamlet's character. For example, Dyson Wood writes in 1870 that that Hamlet is the

> prey of most painful mental conflicts, the intensity of which occasionally almost drives him to desperation. The sad result of this state of things on a sensitive nature is too often the setting up of a condition of chronic and habitual irritability, which may end either in actual insanity, or in such a weakening of the brain's power, that the individual, unless invigorated by an entire change of scene and occupation, becomes utterly unfit for anything like sustained mental effort.[91]

Coleridge, in particular, did much to popularise such a view, famously postulating, in his *Lectures on Shakspeare*, which Pessoa owned, that Hamlet 'is a man living in meditation, called upon to act by every motive human and divine, but the great object of his life is defeated by continually resolving to do, yet doing nothing but resolve.' In the same book, he writes: 'we see a great, an almost enormous, intellectual activity, and a proportionate aversion to real action'; 'this *taedium vitae* is a common oppression on minds cast in the Hamlet mould, and is caused by disproportionate mental exertion, which necessitates exhaustion of bodily feeling.' [92]

A few Portuguese artists agreed that Shakespeare had created Hamlet as a neurotic character. For his 1887 production of *Hamlet*, the actor Eduardo Brazão, who wished to penetrate the problematic character's innermost psychology, asked José António de Freitas to produce a new translation of the play. Freitas's translation, and its accompanying study, discovered in the Prince degeneration

---

[90] Goethe, *Wilhelm Meister*; cited in Bate, *The Romantics on Shakespeare*, pp. 306-307, 316.
[91] Dyson Wood, *Hamlet: A Psychological Point of View* (London: Longmans, Green, Reader, and Dyer, 1870), p. 22.
[92] *Coleridge's Lectures on Shakspeare*, pp. 479, 136, 477.

and neurosis, in an analysis grounded in topical French psychological theories and their echoes in Portugal. [93] In his study, Freitas approaches Hamlet as a pathological case, and concludes: 'Em nossa opinião Hamlet é um histérico [...] a personagem shakesperiana pode ser apresentada como um exemplar perfeitíssimo da histeria masculina' [In my opinion Hamlet is a hysteric [...] this Shakespearean character can be played as a perfect example of male hysteria.] In describing Hamlet as irresolute and lacking in willpower, however, Freitas alights on the typical description of the neurasthenic temperament: 'Enfermou da doença a que os gregos davam o nome de melancolia, *bílis negra*; doença que invade os ânimos acossados de aflições, fustigados por horríveis catástrofes, cruelmente desenganados, nas suas ilusões' [He suffered from the disease the Greeks called melancholy, black bile; the disease which invades spirits who are afflicted, beset by terrible catastrophes, cruelly deceived in their illusions].

Eduardo Brazão's performance of Freitas's vision of *Hamlet* was influential, as was the latter's published translation of the play. Its second edition of 1912 contained an expanded introduction in which Freitas extended his pathological study to other Shakespearean characters:

> Está Othello, de quem Iago diz que é um epiléptico; está Romeu, que é um erotómano; está Timon, que é um misantropo; está Macbeth, que é um criminoso-nato; está Lady Macbeth, que é uma sonâmbula; está o Rei Lear, que é um demente senil; está Falstaff, que é não só um belo exemplo mas um acabado exemplar de alcoólico.[94]

> [We have Othello, whom Iago says is an epileptic; we have Romeo, who is an erotomaniac; we have Timon, who is a misantrope; we have Macbeth, who is a born criminal; we have Lady Macbeth, who is a sleepwalker; we have King Lear, who suffers from senile dementia; we have Falstaff, who is not merely a good example but an archetype of a washed-up alcoholic.]

In Robertson's *'Hamlet' Once More* (1923), Pessoa underlined Robertson's conclusion that the play represented 'a re-writing without a reconstruction of Kyd's [play], with the old action and a new psychosis.'[95] More like a neurosis, perhaps, but Robertson's words reveal that the tendency to diagnose Hamlet continued well into the 1920s. It offered an attractive, understandable interpretation for one of the greatest problems in the play, that of Hamlet's preference for indulgent soliloquies and his inability to actively avenge his father's murder, and it continued to hold sway many years after Freud offered a competing interpretation of Hamlet's inability to act, with his formulation of the Oedipus Complex, in *The Interpretation of Dreams* (1901).

---

[93] See Flor, '*Hamlet* (1887): Tradução portuguesa de um caso patológico', in *Shakespeare entre nós*, pp. 184-200.

[94] Cited in *Ibid.*, pp. 194-96.

[95] Robertson, *'Hamlet' Once More*, pp. 118, 162.

In recent years, there have been sporadic revivals of the type of psychological criticism Pessoa and his contemporaries performed on Shakespeare and his dramatic characters, not least aimed at Pessoa himself. The Portuguese physician Mário Saraiva attempts to diagnose Pessoa's own madness in the books *O caso clínico de Fernando Pessoa* [*Fernando Pessoa's Clinical Condition*] (1990) and *Pessoa ele próprio. Novo estudo nosológico e patográfico* [*Pessoa Himself: A New Nosological and Pathological Study*] (1992).[96] In the first, he concludes that Pessoa was a veritable psychopath. Discovering in the poet also traces of schizophrenia, a word coined in 1908 but scarcely used in Pessoa's day, Saraiva urges researchers of his archive to enlist the services of specialist psychiatrists.[97] It is questionable how helpful such retrospective diagnoses are; all we can know for sure is that Pessoa, like countess other writers of the period, expertly appropriates the madness of the age for his art.

While Pessoa views Hamlet as essentially neurasthenic, however, we have seen that he places Campos at a different point on the sliding scale between hysteria and neurasthenia, describing this heteronym as essentially hysterical, and himself as a hystero-neurasthenic, like Shakespeare. This points to Pessoa's understandable anxiety concerning the topical thinking on neurosis, gender, and sexuality.

Neurosis, Gender, and Sexuality

There is a common assumption that artists have a female as well as a male sensibility. As Mario Praz argues, in *The Romantic Agony* (1956): 'feminine minds are those to which psychologists give the name "schizoid"; and it is questionable whether the minds of all artists are not, in a greater or lesser degree, of this kind.'[98] Pessoa accepts his feminine side when he writes in a letter of self-analysis:

> Não encontro dificuldade em definir-me: sou um temperamento feminino com uma inteligência masculina. A minha sensibilidade e os movimentos que dela procedem, e é nisso que consistem o temperamento e a sua expressão, são de mulher. As minhas faculdades de relação – a inteligência, e a vontade, que é a inteligência do impulso – são de homem. (*PIAI*, p. 27)

> [I have no difficulty in defining myself: I am a feminine temperament with a masculine intelligence. My sensibility and the resulting actions, which are my temperament and its expression, are those of a woman. My relationship traits – intelligence, and will, which is the intelligence of impulse – are those of a man.]

[96] Mário Saraiva, *O caso clínico de Fernando Pessoa* (Lisbon: Referendo, 1990); *Pessoa ele próprio. Novo estudo nosológico e patográfico* (Lisbon: Clássica Editora, 1992).
[97] For the emergence of schizophrenia as a diagnosis, see Roy Porter and G. E. Berrios, *A History of Clinical Psychiatry*, pp. 38-39.
[98] Mario Praz, 'Foreword', in *The Romantic Agony*, trans. Angus Davidson (New York: Meridian, 1956), p. xii.

This explanation is grounded in the topical dichotomy between hysteria/femininity ('temperament', 'sensibility') and neurasthenia/masculinity ('intelligence', 'will'). The diagnosis of male hysteria brought with it implications of femininity and gender inversion.

The gender inversion associated with male hysteria pervades the literature of the period. Sá-Carneiro's poem 'Feminina' [Feminine] expresses a wish to become the other sex:

Eu queria ser mulher para excitar quem me olhasse,
Eu queria ser mulher pra me poder recusar...[99]

[I wish I were a woman so I could excite those who looked at me,
I wish I were a woman so I could refuse them myself...]

Nobre, in one poem, writes of having, in the dual sense of owning and possessing, a 'torre de leite' [tower of milk], symbol of both the phallus and the breast.[100] His poetry led Teixeira de Pascoaes to quip that Nobre was a great poetess. Campos flirts with gender inversion in several of his poems, most openly in 'Ode Marítima':

Ser o meu corpo passivo a mulher-todas-as-mulheres
Que foram violadas, mortas, feridas, rasgadas pelos piratas!
Ser no meu ser subjugado a fêmea que tem de ser deles!
[...] Ser-vos a fêmea, ser-vos as femêas, ser-vos as vítimas. (*AdC*, p. 125)

[For my passive body to be the woman who is all women
Ever raped, killed, hurt, mauled by pirates!
To be in my subjugated self the female who must be theirs!
[...] To be your woman, your women, your victims.]

Pessoa's heteronymic universe is on the surface a male-dominated world, from which the female has been conspicuously excluded; the similar homoerotic atmosphere of *Jekyll and Hyde* prompted Henry James to declare: 'There is something almost impertinent in the way [...] in which Mr Stevenson achieves his best effects without the aid of the ladies, and "Dr. Jekyll" is a capital example of his heartless independence.'[101] The heteronymic project only features, among its dozens of dramatic voices, a solitary female author, Maria José, the putative author of a single, pathetic love letter. Maria José, whose very name flirts with gender ambiguity, is ill and a hunchback – hardly a thriving example of femininity. Campos, with his hysteria and his gender inversion, is arguably more feminine.

---

[99] Sá-Carneiro, 'Feminina', in *Poemas Completos*, p. 144.
[100] Nobre, 'Lusitânia no Bairro Latino', in *Poesia Completa*, p. 181.
[101] Henry James, 'Robert Louis Stevenson', *The Century Magazine* 35:4 (April 1888), 869-79, p. 878.

Campos's poetic acceptance of the opposite gender, rooted in the hysteria Pessoa explicitly bestows upon him, is part of Pessoa's desire to achieve, with his heteronyms, full self-expression, in line with his vision of the ideal artist as the God of creation, capable of fragmenting into other selves. Hélène Cixous posits that 'Accepting the other sex as a component makes [poetic persons] much richer, more various, stronger, and – to the extent that they are mobile – very fragile.'[102] Very fragile: 'Coitado do Álvaro de Campos!' [Poor Álvaro de Campos!]. She and Julie Kristeva, in their gender theories, advocate 'feminine writing' as a new style of expression that can give voice to all that Western rationalism has repressed, arguing that it is a is a practice that both men and women can engage in; one of Cixous's most famous analyses is of Molly's monologue in *Ulysses*.[103]

The problem with accepting the opposite gender too openly, however, is that individuals who resisted conventional gender expectations were often labelled as abnormal, or even perverse.[104] For Freud, perversion and neurosis stand in a relation of positive to negative, since neurotics, faced with cultural requirements, have only succeeded in an apparent and increasingly unsuccessful suppression of their instincts:

I have described the neuroses as the 'negative' of the perversions because in the neuroses the perverse impulses, after being repressed, manifest themselves from the unconscious part of the mind – because the neuroses contain the same tendencies, though in a state of 'repression', as do the positive perversions.

Crucially, this positive/negative relation is immediately taken over into an observation of gender difference:

The discovery that perversions and neuroses stand in the relation of positive and negative is often unmistakeably confirmed by observations made on the members of one generation of a family. Quite frequently a brother is a sexual pervert, while his sister, who, being a woman, possesses a weaker sexual instinct, is a neurotic whose symptoms express the same inclinations as the perversions of her sexually more active brother. And correspondingly, in many families the men are healthy, but from a social point of view immoral to an undesirable degree, while the women are high-minded and over-refined, but severely neurotic.[105]

---

[102] Hélène Cixous, *Sorties: Attacks/Ways Out/Forays*, in *Literary Theory: An Anthology*, ed. Julie Rivkin and Michal Ryan (London: Blackwell, 2004), pp. 351.

[103] See *ibid.*, p. 349-352.

[104] See Elaine Showalter, 'Syphilis, Sexuality and Fiction in the *Fin-de-siècle*', in *Sex Politics and Science in the Nineteenth Century Novel*, ed. Ruth Bernard Yeazell (Baltimore: Johns Hopkins University Press, 1986), pp. 76-92.

[105] Freud, '"Civilized" sexual morality and modern nervous illness', in *The Standard Edition of the Complete Psychological Works of Sigmund Freud*, 24 vols. (London: Hogarth Press,

The case of Antero de Quental correlates perfectly with this male/female divide. Antero had been clinically diagnosed as hysterical by the great Charcot in 1877, but upon his return to Portugal Sousa Martins gave him the milder, more masculine diagnosis of neurasthenia. (Pizarro points out that Sousa Martins showed no reticence in diagnosing Antero's mother and sisters as hysterical.[106]) Pessoa knew of Antero's story: he read Sousa Martins's 'Nosografia' [Nosography], which contains the clinician's diagnosis of Antero, and a 1929 book by António Sérgio on the same topic. [107] Incidentally or otherwise, Campos's poetic development from hysteria to neurasthenia mirrors the change in Antero's diagnosis.

Antero's case illustrates how, despite the growing application of hysteria to artistic and literary men in the early twentieth-century, neurasthenia was a vastly more desirable, or at least less undesirable, condition for a male intellectual. Most alleged male neurotics who had the opportunity to answer back their doctors or critics, by virtue of being alive (many were diagnosed only after their death), vastly preferred the label of neurasthenic. Flaubert is one of very few men to have put forward the view of himself as hysterical, by fully identifying with his hysterical protagonist when he famously declared that 'Madame Bovary, c'est moi' [I am Madame Bovary], and also in his personal letters, which contain numerous declarations of his hysterical pathology, including descriptions of some of hysteria's most stylised symptoms. Baudelaire considered that part of the genius of *Madame Bovary* lay in the fact that Flaubert, 'poète hystérique' [hysterical poet], had successfully transformed himself into a woman: 'Il ne restait plus à l'auteur, pour accomplir le tour de force dans son entier, que de se dépouiller (autant que possible) de son sexe et de se faire femme' [It only remained for the author to accomplish the feat in its entirety by ridding himself of his gender (whenever possible) and become a woman].[108]

When Baudelaire himself was clinically diagnosed as hysterical in the final year of his life, however, he wrote to a friend disapprovingly of his doctors' verdict: '[They] told me for my only consolation that I am *hysterical!*'[109]

At worst, male hysteria was thought to imply an enjoyment of what was considered to be the worst of all possible vices, homosexuality, for there was much confusion, in the period, between gender inversion (femininity, effeminacy, effeteness) and sexual inversion. The pioneering sexologist Havelock Ellis, in his 1897 book *Sexual Inversion*, distinguishes lesbian behaviour on the basis of gender

---

1953-1974), X, pp. 190, 191.

106 Pizarro, 'Antero de Quental, entre contradições e esquecimentos' [Antero de Quental, Between Contradiction and Forgetfulness], *Estudos Anterianos* [*Antero* Studies] 11-12 (April-October 2003), 57-65, p. 60.

107 Cited in Pizarro, 'Da Histeria à Neurastenia (Quental e Pessoa)', *Conceito* 1, pp. 175-176.

108 'Madame Bovary', in *Oeuvres complètes*, II, pp. 83, 81.

109 *Baudelaire: Correspondance* [*Correspondence*], ed. Claude Pichois and Jean Ziegler, 2 vols. (Paris: Gallimard, 1973), II, p. 583. Baudelaire's emphasis.

inversion alone.[110] The charge of 'effeminacy' as a term of personal abuse often connoted male-male desire; Wilde's *The Picture of Dorian Gray* (1890) was attacked for its effeminacy as well as its homoeroticism. The *Athenaeum* went as far as to refer to it as 'unmanly, sickening, vicious', and the *Scotts Observer* remarked that 'its interest is medico-legal'.[111]

Pessoa has Campos describe Whitman, with his 'atitude de mulher' [female atitude], as a 'grande pederasta' [great pederast] (*AdC*, pp. 163, 161). He displays anxiety about the implications of male hysteria when he informs Casais, in his letter on the genesis of the heteronyms of 13 January 1935, that if he were a woman the poetry of Campos would alarm the neighbourhood (*AdC*, p. 341).

Pessoa would have known, being so familiar with the nuances of both neurotic disorders, that his self-diagnosis of choice automatically emphasises the neurasthenic rather than the hysteric grounding of the dual neurosis: in the medical texts in which it features, hystero-neurasthenia refers specifically to a variety of neurasthenia, rather than the other way around.[112] The effect of Pessoa's claim to have channelled all of his hysteria into Campos is to further the view of him, Pessoa, as more neurasthenic than hysterical, following the reasoning that hystero-neurasthenia minus hysteria equals neurasthenia. (Soares, as a semi-heteronym whose personality is close to Pessoa's own, is more neurasthenic than hysterical.)

Furthermore, Pessoa cites his perceived neurasthenic characteristics much more often than his perceived hysterical ones, even if he classifies himself as a hystero-neurasthenic. This is particularly apparent in his correspondence. On 22 October 1932, for instance, he informs Gaspar Simões:

> Não sei se lhe disse: tive uma espécie de intoxicação geral, à qual se sobrepunha e sobrepõe, *ante e post* (pois que em parte provocou a intensidade da intoxicação, e em parte se agravou com essa intensidade), o que, se não é uma neurastenia aguda, lhe copiou com êxito as feições e as maneiras. Tem sido, mais particularmente, a acção desta última inacção que me tem tido preso – já de mim tão naturalmente idóneo para as clausuras da vontade! (*Corr II*, p. 275)

> [I'm not sure I told you: I had a sort of all-encompassing food poisoning, which further caused (and still does), before and after (for it partly provoked the intensity of the food poisoning, and partly increased due to its intensity), if

---

[110] Havelock Ellis, *Sexual Inversion*, in *Studies in the Psychology of Sex*, 8 vols. (London: Watford, 1897), I.

[111] See David Hilliard, 'Unenglish and Unmanly: Anglo-Catholicism and Homosexuality', *Victorian Studies* 25 (1982), 181-210; Cited in Ed Cohen, 'Writing Gone Wilde: Homoerotic Desire in the Closet of Representation', *Publications of the Modern Languages Association of America* 102 (1987), pp. 798-823, pp. 803, 805.

[112] See, for example, Clarke's 1905 *Hysteria & Neurasthenia: The Practitioner's Handbook*, p. 238.

not an acute neurasthenia, something which successfully copied its traits and ways. It has been, more specifically, the action of this final inaction which has kept me prisoner – I, who am already so naturally prone to being held prisoner to my will!]

In a fascinating corollary, Pessoa often cites his neurasthenia as an excuse for not promptly answering his correspondents. In a letter of 8 April 1913 to Mário Beirão, he declares: 'Escrevo à pressa, e logo sobre a recepção do postal. Assim não me foge a energia para responder. Estou altamente neurastenizado' [I write in a hurry, and as soon as I received your card. This way the energy to reply will not escape me. I am profoundly neurathenised] (*Corr I*, p. 92). In 1929, he employs the same reasoning in a letter to Gaspar Simões: 'Aquela minha leve alienação mental, que é um dos meus privilégios mais Campos, tem estado permanentemente à minha cabeceira, ainda nas horas em que não estou deitado. Não tenho feito nada, e não tenho escrito nada, nem (a prova existe na ausência da prova) a ninguém' [The slight mental alienation, which is one of my most Campos priviledges, has been always at my bedside, even when I am not lying down. I have done nothing, written nothing, nor even to anyone (the proof is in the absence of proof)].[113] In 1933, and again to Gaspar Simões, he repeats his evocation of his neurasthenic condition as an excuse for not writing. A year later he tells Casais the same: 'Recebi o seu livro *Poemas do Tempo Incerto*, que achei, francamente, admirável. Conto passar parte do mês próximo no Estoril, com a minha família (tenho estado só, há meses, em Lisboa, a não ser que uma crise neurasténica constitua acompanhamento); então lhe escreverei longamente' [I received your book *Poems of an Uncertain Time*, which I found, quite frankly, admirable. I hope to spend part of next month in Estoril, with my family (I have been on my own, for months, in Lisbon, unless a neurasthenic crisis constitutes company); I will write you at length then].[114] Pessoa's lifelong strategy of evoking his neurosis as an explanation for his inaction – as early as 1912 he had promised Álvaro Pinho: 'Escrevo para participar que, não havendo catástrofe nevrose, lhe enviarei de aqui amanhã o meu fim de artigo!' [I write to tell you that, barring a nervous catastrophe, I will send you the end of my article tomorrow from here!] – is driven by the exact same logic he employs to 'solve' the problem of Shakespeare's inability to publish (*Corr I*, p. 53).

In the case of both men, he also cites their madness as the necessary counterpart to their genius.

The Madness of the Heteronymic Project: 'Genius is a disease, a glorious disease, but a great one.'[115]

Pessoa marked out the following passage in Nisbet's *Marriage and Heredity* (1908), in which the psychiatrist Henry Maudsley urges men to examine potential

---

[113] Letter to Gaspar Simões, 6 December 1929, in *Corr II*, p. 177.
[114] Letter to Casais, 24 December 1934, in *Corr II*, p. 330.
[115] Pessoa (Charles Robert Anon), in *PI*, p. 159.

wives carefully for physical signs of degeneracy:

'In families where there is a strong disposition to insanity', writes Maudsley, 'one member may sometimes suffer from one form of nervous disease, another from another form; one perhaps has epilepsy, another severe neuralgia or hysteria, a third may commit suicide, a fourth may become maniacal or melancholic, and it sometimes happens that the fifth *evinces remarkable artistic talent*.'[116]

The chapter in which these words appear is titled 'The Procreation of Genius'.[117] Pessoa's hope was that his touch of madness, a tangible genetic threat running in his family (his grandmother Dionísia died mad), would result in a remarkable artistic talent rather than a more serious pathological condition.

In *Faust*, Pessoa has Goethe explain that from his soberly mad soul was born the genius of his art:

Goethe: Do fundo da inconsciência
Da alma sobriamente louca
Tirei poesia e ciência
E não pouca.

[From the depths of my subconscious
And my soberly mad soul
I plucked poetry and science
And much of it.]

Following this speech, Shakespeare, whom Pessoa also transforms into a dramatic character in his play, makes explicit the underlying conceit: 'é loucura a inspiração!' [inspiration is madness!][118]

Pessoa was fascinated by the relationship between genius and madness, which he largely explored, in the age-old tradition, as being two sides of the same coin. Theories on the madness of genius, informed by the topical clinical discourse on the neuroses, were widespread at the *fin de siècle*; Havelock Ellis writes that 'I ever more realize how great a part is played in the lives of men and women by some little concealed germ of abnormality'; he postulates that such an abnormality is the very mark of genius.[119] Pessoa, on the back page of his copy of Carlyle's critical essays, writes the similar assertion: 'Le génie est une névrose' [Genius is a

---

[116] J. F. Nisbet, *Marriage and Heredity: A View of Psychological Evolution*. (Edinburgh: John Grant, 1908), p. 149. Original emphasis.
[117] Pessoa also owned Nisbet's *The Insanity of Genius and the General Inequality of Human Faculty, Physiologically Considered* (3rd ed., London: Ward and Downey, 1893).
[118] *Fausto*, p. 69.
[119] Ellis, *Selected Essays*, ed. J. S. Collis (London: Dent, 1943), p. 301.

neurosis.] It is a book that dates back to Pessoa's high school years. [120] He reiterates the insight elsewhere: 'Genius is a neurosis' (*GL*, p. 128). Pessoa could be less categorical on the matter, for in another text he concedes: 'Genius is not a neurosis. But it is accompanied by one' (*PETCL*, p. 56). Whatever the case, he holds genius and madness to be inextricably linked; as he declares in a letter of 1916 to an unidentified correspondent:

> a teoria, hoje um pouco desleixada, [...] de que o génio é uma nevrose – a tese que Lombroso estragou, mas que existe soberbamente defendida na *Insanity of Genius* de Nisbet – tem só o defeito de ser axiomática. (*Corr II*, pp. 226-227)

> [the theory, today a little sloppy, [...] that genius is a neurosis – the thesis Lombroso ruined, but which is brilliantly defended in Nisbet's *Insanity of Genius* – has the single defect of being axiomatic.]

Consequently, many of Pessoa's appreciations of Shakespeare's genius mention the inevitable madness he believes such genius entails. In one, he writes: 'He stands forth as the greatest example of genius, pure genius, genius immortal and unavailing.' A few sentences later he declares, with the air of stating an obvious fact: 'He stands before us, melancholy, witty, at times half insane' (*PETCL*, p. 303).

That Pessoa believed hystero-neurasthenia, the specific madness he diagnosed in Shakespeare, to be a necessary element of the Bard's genius, impersonal dramatic poetry (see Chapter 1), is evident from the following plan for a study of his work:

> Sendo Shakespeare um poeta-dramaturgo vejamos se elle é um hystero-neurasthenico, atravez da sua obra.
> (a) o temperamento hystero-neurasthenico
> (b) o que deve dar como apontando-se na obra de um poeta
> (c) exame da obra de Shakespeare sob este ponto de vista. Coincidencia absoluta. (*GL*, p. 371)

> [Seeing as Shakespeare is a poet-dramatist, let us examine whether is a hystero-neurasthenic, via an analysis of his works.
> a) the hystero-neurasthenic temperament
> b) that which must make itself apparent in a poet's work
> c) analysis of Shakespeare's work under this light. Absolute correlation.]

Pessoa applies the formula to dramatic poetry in general, writing in one piece that if we encounter in an artist hystero-neurasthenia, that is, 'hysteria

---

[120] Carlyle, *Sartor Resartus*, front and back covers. Pessoa dated this book 1904 beneath his signature.

subtilizando-se em neurasthenia, temos o temperamento do poeta-dramaturgo' [hysteria subtilizing itself in neurasthenia, we have the poet-dramatist's temperament] (*GL*, p. 376). Since the condition is necessary to the making of the highest type of art, it may be a blessing instead of a curse, as he implies in the projected preface to an edition of his own heteronymic poetry:

> A obra completa, cujo primeiro volume é este, é de substância dramática, embora de forma vária – aqui de trechos em prosa, em outros livros de poemas ou de filosofias.
>
> É, não sei se um privilégio se uma doença, a constituição mental que a produz. (*PIAI*, p. 95)

> [The complete works, of which this is the first volume, are dramatic in nature, although they vary in form – here in excerpts of prose, in other books in poems or philosophies.
>
> I don't know whether the mental condition which produces it is a blessing or a disease.]

It is only logical that Pessoa should therefore offer his own perceived madness as the psychological explanation for his own brand of dramatic poetry, the heteronymic project. In his letter of 11 December 1931 to Gaspar Simões cited in Chapter 1, he declares:

> Do ponto de vista humano – em que o crítico não compete tocar, pois de nada lhe serve que toque – sou um histeroneurasténico com a predominância do elemento histérico na emoção e do elemento neurasténico na inteligência e na vontade. (*Corr II*, p. 255)

> [From the human point of view – which the critic is not qualified to probe, for it will do no good – I am a hysteroneurasthenic with a predominance of the hysteric element in the emotion and the neurasthenic element in the intelligence and the will.]

Gaspar Simões accepted Pessoa's self-diagnosis without question, but he did not accept it as the key to Pessoa's creativity, writing in a biographical sketch of 1936: 'Não creio que ninguém tenha penetrado ainda na *explicação central* desta personalidade, que, sendo genial, era, no entanto, capaz de nos dar de si própria esta síntese simplista: – "sou um hystero-neurasthenico."' [I do not believe anyone has so far penetrated into the *key explanation* of this personality, who, although brilliant, was however capable of giving this simplistic account of himself: 'I am a hystero-neurasthenic'].[121] He would instead find the key in Pessoa's repressed

---

[121] Gaspar Simões, 'Notas à margem duma carta de Fernando Pessoa' [Notes on One of Pessoa's Letters], in *Novos Temas* [*New Themes*] (Lisbon: Inquérito, 1938) pp. 156-157. See also his essay 'Fernando Pessoa', in *Retratos de poetas que conheci: autobiografia*

sexuality, as we shall see in the following chapter, via Freudian interpretations that Pessoa would vehemently reject.

In his letter to Casais on the genesis of the heteronyms, Pessoa links his madness to his genius more explicitly:

> Começo pela parte psiquiátrica. A origem dos meus heterónimos é o fundo traço de histeria que existe em mim. Não sei se sou simplesmente histérico, se sou, mais propriamente, um histero-neurasténico. Tendo para a segunda hipótese, porque há em mim fenómenos de abulia que a histeria, propriamente dita, não enquadra no registo dos seus sintomas. Seja como for, a origem mental dos meus heterónimos está na minha tendência orgânica e constante para a despersonalização e para a simulação. (*Corr II*, p. 340)

> [I will begin with psychiatry. The origin of my heteronyms is my deep streak of hysteria. I don't know if I am merely hysterical, or if I am, more specifically, a hystero-neurasthenic. I lean towards the second possibility, for I suffer apathy, which does not, strictly speaking, belong to hysteria's list of symptoms. Whatever the case, the mental origin of my heteronyms is my organic and continual tendency for depersonalization and simulation.]

A penchant for depersonalization and simulation was thought to be one of the chief characteristics of hysteria. Emma Bovary gave her name to a condition called *Bovarysme*, which signified illusions about the self, dissatisfactions, and the desire to be another. Jules de Gaultier, who coined the term in the 1890s, described it as 'le pouvoir départi à l'homme de se concevoir autre qu'il n'est' [man's ability to conceive himself as another]. [122] This sounds suspiciously like the ability to impersonally create dramatic characters, the essential quality Pessoa ascribes to Shakespeare's genius and his own. One of Pessoa's attempted definitions of hysteria alludes precisely to the condition's *Bovarysme*:

> The psychic symptoms of *hysteria are – extreme oscillation of mood,* depression alternating with elation with no apparent, or no sufficient cause; *simulation and depersonalization,* whether in the form of common lying, of practical acting, or of auto-suggestion of false emotions, fictitious purposes and unnatural ideas; *day-dreaming* and all its forms, from a love of artificiality, decoration and scenario in preference to life (this being the objective form), to the ache for the unseen, for the remote, for that which is not here nor even anywhere. (*GL*, p. 375)

In one of his unpublished texts on Shakespeare, he makes the link between the

---

[*Portraits of Poets I Have Known: An Autobiography*] (Lisbon: Brasília Editora, 1974), pp. 43-49.

[122] Jules de Gaultier, *Le Bovarysme, la psychologie dans l'oeuvre de Flaubert* [*Bovarysme: Psychology in Flaubert's Works*] (Paris: L. Cerf, 1898), p. 4.

Bard's tendency for impersonation and the symptoms of hysteria explicit:

> His one distinctive characteristic is the power to impersonate all kinds of characters; if he has a mental disease, it can thus be but hysteria, for this is the neurosis that is essentially dramatic and impersonatory. (76A-4)

We have seen that Pessoa was as seduced by Shakespeare's *Bovarysme* as was Eliot, who claimed: 'I do not believe that any writer has ever exposed this *Bovarysme*, the human will to things as they are not, more clearly than Shakespeare.'[123]

It is somewhat surprising that Pessoa should conceive of the heteronymic project, in psychological terms, purely based on *fin-de-siècle* notions of hysteria and neurasthenia. These were largely outdated by the time of the heteronyms' appearance in 1914, and competing psychological theories dealing with multiple, or dissociative, personality would supersede them entirely in Pessoa's lifetime.

Psychologists of the late-nineteenth century spoke of secondary personalities dissociated from the primary one. In 1892, Binet published a book on alterations in personality in which he writes: 'One observes in a large number of people, placed in the most diverse conditions, the normal unity of consciousness is disintegrated. Several distinct consciousnesses arise, each of which may have perceptions, a memory, and even a moral character, of its own.'[124] Ribot published a book in 1895 which denied the existence of a superordinate self and instead postulated the existence of multiple selves.[125] Janet found that by hypnotizing a hysterical patient named Lucie, she became 'a different person in short' and he began to think of her in her different states as Lucie 1, Lucie 2, and Lucie 3.[126]

The American psychologist William James heard Janet speak at the first International Congress of Physiological Psychology, held in Paris in August 1889. He later wrote that the 'simultaneous co-existence of the different personages into which one human being may be split is the great thesis of M. Janet's book', but he cautioned that 'a self presided' over the other personalities: 'a split-off, limited, and buried, but yet a fully conscious self.'[127] James's article 'The Hidden Self' was published in March 1890, and it influenced his brother Henry James's short story 'The Jolly Corner' (1908) in which the narrator encounters his own hidden self.[128] In a chapter in his influential *Principles of Psychology* (1890), published two years

[123] Eliot, *Selected Essays* (New York: Harcourt, Brace and World, 1960), p. 111.
[124] Cited in John Rowan, *Subpersonalities: The People Inside Us* (London: Routledge, 1990), p. 243.
[125] *Ibid.*
[126] Cited in Robert D. Richardson, *William James: In the Maelstrom of American Modernism. A Biography* (Boston/New York: Mariner Books, 2007), p. 296.
[127] William James, *Essays in Psychology* (Cambridge, M.A.: Harvard University Press, 1983), pp. 258, 259, 263.
[128] William James, 'The Hidden Self', *Scribner's Magazine* 7 (1890), 361-73; Henry James, 'The Jolly Corner', *The English Review* (December 1908), 5-35.

later in an abridged version as *Psychology: The Briefer Course*, William James declares that '*a man has as many social selves as there are individuals who recognise him* and carry an image of him in their mind.'[129] He explains that 'From this there results what practically is a division of the man into several selves; and this may be a discordant splitting'.[130] He speaks of a 'Hierarchy of the Mes'.[131] Modernist writers of Pessoa's generation would leave behind the stark *fin-de-siècle* dichotomies of aware versus hypnotized, or of doubles (expressed in *fin-de-siècle* fiction like *Jekyll and Hyde, The Picture of Dorian Gray*, and *A Confissão de Lúcio*) to deal instead with the ideas of James and his circle about *multiplicity* of personality. (James's description of the mind-world connection, which he described in terms of a 'stream of consciousness', would also have a direct and significant impact on Modernist art.)

Another influential psychologist was the American Morton Prince, who like James helped to disseminate European ideas about psychopathology, especially in understanding dissociative phenomena. Prince drew around him all the important practitioners in the burgeoning field of abnormal psychology at that time, including James – who ranked Prince among the major investigators of the unconscious, along with Janet, Binet, Breuer and Freud – and became the American expert in dissociative disorders, which he also labelled multiple personality disorder. From 1898 to 1911, he made intensive studies of multiple personality, and published numerous accounts of these in the academic and popular press, a representative title of one of his fourteen books being *The Dissociation of a Personality* (1906). Multiple personality, Prince formulated, depended upon dissociation and reassociation, or depersonalization and repersonalization, as he then termed them.[132] His theories, appropriated by Henry Head and others in Britain, gained widespread recognition and acceptance: the third edition of the *Diagnostic and Statistical Manual of Mental Disorders* (DSM III, 1980) has a section devoted to Dissociative Disorders, which includes multiple personality and 'depersonalization disorder (or neurosis)'. It defines 'depersonalization disorder' as:

> a dissociative disorder in which the sufferer is affected by persistent or recurrent feelings of depersonalization and / or derealization. Symptoms include a sense of automation, going through the motions of life but not experiencing it, feeling as though one is in a movie, feeling as though one is in a dream, feeling a disconnection from one's body; out-of-body experience, a detachment from one's body, environment and difficulty relating oneself to

---

[129] William James, *Psychology: The Briefer Course* (1892; Toronto: General Publishing Company, 2001), p. 46. Original emphasis.

[130] *Ibid.*, p. 47.

[131] *Ibid.*, p. 57.

[132] See Nathan G. Hale, 'Introduction', in Morton Prince, *Psychotherapy and Multiple Personality: Selected Essays*, ed. Nathan G. Hale, Jr. (Cambridge, M.A.: Harvard University Press, 1975), p. 9.

reality. It is by no means related to psychosis as sufferers maintain the ability to distinguish between their own internal experiences and the objective reality of the outside world.[133]

Henri Ellenberger, in *The Discovery of the Unconscious* (1970), argues that while subpersonalities could develop spontaneously, they could also be influenced by suggestion, exaggerated by investigators, and established more firmly through personification.[134] Multiple personality theory, in its insistence upon depersonalization, hierarchical selves, and personification, would appear to offer a better clinical analogy for Pessoa's heteronymic project than the neurotic model he proposes. Yet there are no books by William James or Morton Prince in Pessoa's library, and no evidence that he was directly familiar with their ideas. Neither figure in Pizarro's edition of Pessoa writings on genius and madness, although, as Pizarro points out in *Entre génio e loucura*, Pessoa and James shared a number of influences, including Nisbet.[135]

However, in conceiving and explaining his heteronymic project, in psychological terms, exclusively in light of *fin-de-siècle* notions of hysteria and neurasthenia, Pessoa places himself in illustrious company. Although hysteria and neurasthenia were viewed by doctors, their suffering patients, and cultural critics like Nordau as an undesirable condition, their presence in artistic and literary men was largely construed positively, as impressive, even ennobling attributes. Lombroso, who viewed the female hysteric with contempt, linked male hysteria to genius in his book *L'homme de génie* [*The Man of Genius*] (1889).[136] Maupassant, with characteristic overstatement, pronounced that 'all great men were hysterical', explaining that 'Napoleon I was (but not the other one), [and] Marat, Robespierre and Danton were.'[137] Pessoa has Soares align himself with the great neurasthenic figures: 'os grandes homens de inacção, a cujo número humildemente pertenço' [the great men of inaction, to whose number I humbly belong]; 'hei-de sempre sentir, como os grandes malditos, que mais vale pensar que viver' [I will always feel, like the great tragic heroes, that it is better to think than to live] (*LD*, pp. 170, 207). Both of these statements are very possibly veiled references to Hamlet, and in any case refer to personalities such as his. In reference to himself, Pessoa writes in the draft of a letter to Casais cited in the previous chapter:

---

[133] Cited in Rowan, *Subpersonalities*, pp. 13-14.
[134] Ellenberger, *The Discovery of the Unconscious* (New York: Basic Books, 1970), pp. 126-147.
[135] Pessoa annotates some of the same passages, in his copy of Nisbit's *The Insanity of Genius*, that James cites in his writings (see *Entre génio e loucura*, pp. 100, 102.) Another shared influence is Binet-Sanglé's book *La Folie de Jesus* [*Jesus's Madness*], which directly informed a piece Pessoa projected for Alexander Search, *The Mental Disorder(s) of Jesus*. Binet-Sanglé is cited by James as a prime example of clinical materialism. (*Ibid*, p. 111.)
[136] Lombroso, *L'homme de génie* [*The Man of Genius*] (Paris: Félix Alcan, 1889), pp. 465-85.
[137] Cited in Micale, *Approaching Hysteria*, p. 248.

Não me custa admitir que eu seja louco, mas exijo que se compreenda que não sou louco diferentemente de Shakespeare, qualquer que seja o valor relativo dos produtos do lado são da nossa loucura. (*PIAI*, p. 101)

[I don't mind admitting that I am mad, but I demand it be understood that I am mad in the same way that Shakespeare is mad, whatever may be the relative value of the sane byproducts of our madness.]

The sane byproducts of both men's madness are Shakespeare's dramatic characters and Pessoa's heteronyms: the essence of their literary genius.

SHAKESPEARE'S SEXUALITY

'Abnormal Inclinations' (76A-75)

Pessoa was as fascinated by the subject of sexuality as he was by genius and madness, notwithstanding his continual disclaimers to the contrary, such as the statement in his letter of 11 December 1931 to Gaspar Simões: 'Pouco [...] me interessou a sexualidade, própria ou alheia' [I have never been much interested in sexuality, either my own or other people's] (*Corr II*, p. 252).

Pessoa's interest in his own sexuality is particularly evident in his automatic writing, a practice that became fashionable during the second half of the nineteenth century as a way of communicating with departed spirits. In the 1920s automatic writing was adopted by the French Surrealists, who saw in it the opportunity for creating art that sprang directly from the unconscious. It was so widespread in Pessoa's day that it was practised by the most unlikely Modernists: by the rational Eliot as well as the esoteric Yeats. Pessoa became interested in spiritualist sessions through his aunt Anica, and he received most of his astral communications between 1916 and 1917. The spirits he most frequently communed with were the poet and philosopher Henry More (1614-1687), More's colleague Wardour, and the obscure 'Voodooist'. They urged the twenty-six year old Pessoa to solve the problem of his virginity by having sex with a woman.[1] A typical excerpt reads:

> You must not maintain your chastity more. You are so misogynous that you will find yourself morally impotent, and in that way will not produce any complete work in literature. You must abandon your monastic life and *now*.
>
> Make up your mind to do your duty by Nature, not in a manner so insane as now. Make up your mind to go to bed with the girl who is coming in to your life.[2]

Pessoa later dismissed his sessions of automatic writing as the result of his hystero-neurasthenia, mingled with self-suggestion.[3] This explanation is evocative of Eliot's argument that a spontaneous 'efflux of poetry' may be produced by 'some forms of ill-health, debility or anaemia' rather than 'being a present form of a friendly or impertinent demon', and it points to the *fin-de-siècle* association between neurosis and 'perverse' sexuality.[4]

The founding texts of sexology, the scientific study of the human sexual which emerged at in the closing decades of the nineteenth century, tended to pathologise the sexual, associating it with topical notions of neurosis, perversion, and degeneration. Richard von Krafft-Ebing's *Psychopathia Sexualis* (1869), which set

---

[1] *Escritos autobiográficos, automáticos e de reflexão pessoal* [*Autobiographical, Automatic and Personal Writings*], ed. Zenith (Lisbon: Assírio e Alvim, 2003), p. 209.
[2] *Ibid.*, p. 224.
[3] 'Um Caso de Mediunidade' [A Case of Mediundity], in *ibid.* p. 333.
[4] Eliot, 'The Use of Poetry and the Use of Criticism', in *Selected Prose*, p. 89.

out with the objective of furthering 'our knowledge concerning the *pathology* of the sexual life', became a reference book for doctors and judges.[5] Pessoa was familiar with the *fin-de-siècle* clinical discourse on sexuality. One of the representative clinical books he owned was *Walt Whitman's Anomaly* (1913), with a note on the cover stating that 'The sale of this book is restricted to Members of the Legal and Medical professions.'[6] Whitman's 'anomaly', according to this book, is homosexuality.

The term 'homosexual' was coined by the Swiss physician Karoly Benkert in 1869, and entered English usage when *Psychopathia Sexualis* was translated during the 1890s. No one in Shakespeare's day would have thought of themselves as homosexual or, indeed, sought to define their identity by their sexual activity.[7] However, the engagement of the desires of a predominantly male audience for boys who took women's parts in the plays of the period suggests that one of the pleasures of theatre-going was to test cultural expectations about whom one should desire.[8]

In *The History of Sexuality* (1978-1984), Michel Foucault argues that the modern conception of homosexuality is a nineteenth-century invention. Sodomy had previously been conceived judicially as a series of forbidden acts which anyone might commit. The sodomite had previously been regarded as an aberration, but the nineteenth-century homosexual became a personage, a past, a case history.[9] 'The homosexual' became a category for organising sexuality alongside other newly recognisable neurotic and degenerate types, as Eve Sedgwick explains:

> a rich stew of male algolagnia, child-love, and autoeroticism, to mention no more of its components, seemed to have as indicative a relation as did homosexuality to the whole, obsessively entertained problematic of sexual 'perversion' or, more broadly, 'decadence'. Foucault, for instance, mentions the hysterical woman and the masturbating child, along with 'entomologized' sexological categories such as zoophiles, zooerasts, auto-monosexualists, and gynecomasts, as typifying the new sexual taxonomies.[10]

Teleny (1893) is the seminal *fin-de-siècle* novel dealing directly with a homosexual relationship. Set in *fin-de-siècle* Paris, it relates the magnetic

---

[5] Richard von Krafft-Ebing, *Psychopathia Sexualis*, 5th ed., trans. C. G. Chaddock (Philadelphia/London: F. A. Davis, 1892), p. iv. My italics.

[6] W. C. Rivers, *Walt Whitman's Anomaly* (London: George Allen and Company, 1913).

[7] Alan Bray, *Homosexuality in Renaissance England* (New York: Columbia University Press 1995), p. 16.

[8] See Stephen Orgel, *Impersonations: The Performance of Gender in Shakespeare's England* (Cambridge: Cambridge University Press, 1996), pp. 53-82.

[9] Michel Foucault, *The History of Sexuality: An Introduction*, trans. Robert Hurley (New York: Pantheon, 1978), p. 43.

[10] Sedgwick, *Epistemology of the Closet* (1990), in *Literary Theory: An Anthology*, ed. Julie Rivkin and Michael Ryan (London: Blackwell, 2004), p. 912.

attraction and passionate though ultimately tragic affair between a young Frenchman, Camille des Grieux, and the Hungarian pianist René Teleny, who narrates the story. Its authorship is unknown, but it has long been attributed to Oscar Wilde, possibly in collaboration or in an editorial capacity. Wilde's involvement is supported by the Parisian erotic bookseller Charles Hirsh, whose memoir describes how Wilde himself brought the manuscript to Hirsch's Librairie Parisienne in 1890, instructing that it be held until a friend, who would be carrying Wilde's card, came to retrieve it. By 1893, the manuscript made its way into the hands of Leonard Smithers, a liaison between authors, publishers, and distributors. He was in a small and tightly interwoven group of publishers involved in the production and distribution of pornography in London and Paris. From 1892 to 1894 the group released a series of pornographic novels under the imprint Erotika Biblion Society. *Teleny* was published 1893 as part of this series in a limited edition of 200 volumes, with significant edits by Smithers, including the omission of an Introduction and a change in the setting from London to Paris.[11]

Teleny perfectly captures the *fin-de-siècle* association between neurosis and homosexuality: Des Grieux suffers a 'fit of nervousness' when his passion is first aroused; his nerves are 'utterly unstrung' by his homosexual longing for Teleny.[12] His immersion in the illicit romance is accompanied by fears of encroaching madness, informed by his knowledge of topical notions of heredity and degeneration: 'You know, my father died mad.'[13] A medical book he encounters adds to his concern.

In his writings on Shakespeare's sexuality, Pessoa concludes that Shakespeare's 'abnormal inclinations', as he puts it in an unpublished list titled 'Psychology of the author of *Shakespeare's* works', were the same as Whitman's, namely homosexuality (76A-75). He says as much in 'Erostratus' when he declares that Shakespeare and Whitman were both 'paederasts, by the bye' (*H*, p. 169). In the piece titled 'Sobre traduzir Shakespeare' (see Chapter 1), Pessoa refers to the Bard as the 'Chefe dos pederastas' [Chief of the pederasts]. Another representative piece on Shakespeare's sexuality reads: 'Do poeta sabe-se alguma cousa. Sabe-se que é jurisconsulto, sabe-se que é invertido'. [We know a little about the poet. We know he was a lawyer, we know he was inverted] (*GL*, p. 34). In an unpublished text, Pessoa lists Shakespeare's 'sexual inversion' as one of the Bard's three 'characteristic peculiarities' (76A-3). That 'homosexuality' stood in a negative relation to 'heterosexuality' is metaphorically indicated by the word that historically preceded it, and Pessoa's word of choice, 'inversion'.[14] *Teleny*'s subtitle

---

[11] See James Nelson, *Publisher to the Decadents: Leonard Smithers in the Careers of Beardsley, Wilde, Dowson* (Philadelphia: Pennsylvania State University Press, 2000) and Lisa Sigel, *Governing Pleasures: Pornography and Social Change in England, 1815-1914* (Piscataway: Rutgers University Press, 2002).

[12] Anon. (attributed to Wilde et al), *Teleny, or The Reverse of the Medal* (New York: Mondial, 2006), pp. 7, 6.

[13] *Ibid.*, p. 85.

[14] See George Chancey, 'From Sexual Inversion to Homosexuality', *Salmagundi* 58-59.

is 'The Reverse of the Medal'.

Before examining the impact of the sexuality Pessoa discovers in Shakespeare on his own work, it is worth questioning how and why he deduces the Bard's 'abnormal inclinations'.

Pessoa's Reading of Shakespeare's *Sonnets*

We saw in Chapter 2 how much Pessoa enjoyed corresponding with Baconians. In an undated letter of 1912 to William Smedley, the author of one of the Baconian books he owned, he declares:

> Incidentally I may state that – in disagreement with the idealizing tendency shown by you in your attitude towards the *Sonnets* – I will prove that Bacon and Shakespeare were fatally sexual inverts. (*GL*, p. 342)

Pessoa's reference to Shakespeare's *Sonnets* in the same breath as his perceived 'inversion' is key, for the poems have generated, since the dawn of the Romantic era, this very type of speculation. Biographical readings[15] of the *Sonnets*, concluding that their author must have been homosexual, feature in many of the anti-Stratfordian books Pessoa read, including Smedley's *The Mystery of Francis Bacon*. Pessoa was fascinated by the problematic compositions, and he annotated more passages in the *Sonnets* than in any other piece in his copy of Shakespeare's *Complete Works*.

The dedication of Shakespeare's *Sonnets* is tantalisingly ambiguous. It is possible that, as the 'onlie begetter of these ensuing sonnets', W. H. could be a misprint for Shakespeare's initials, 'W. S.', or, less conceivably, 'W. SH.' (In an interesting coincidence, most of Pessoa's manuscripts on Shakespeare bear the initials 'W.Sh.') If 'W. H.' refers to Shakespeare, then 'our ever-living poet' is presumably God, who promises him eternity. Other candidates include the person who obtained the manuscript for the publisher or, more plausibly, the inspirer and dedicatee of the *Sonnets*, the 'Fair Youth' addressed in several of the poems. If 'Mr. W. H.' is the Fair Youth, then the 'ever-living poet' must be Shakespeare himself,

---

(1982-1983), 114-146. John Addington Symonds collaborated with Havelock Ellis on the first volume, on 'Inversion', of the latter's *Studies in the Psychology of Sex* (1897). Cited in Stephen Heath, 'Psychopathia Sexualis: Stevenson's *Strange Case* (*Critical Quarterly* 28 (1986), 69-79, p. 73).

[15] I refer to Romantic readings of Shakespeare as 'biographical' because the term 'psychological' was new to criticism in the period, so much so that Coleridge apologised for using it in his 1818 *Treatise on Method*. For a definition of 'biographical criticism', see X. J. Kennedy and Dana Gioia's *Literature: An Introduction to Fiction, Poetry, and Drama*, (6th ed., New York: HarperCollins, 1995), pp. 1798-1802. Pessoa's readings of Shakespeare, on the other hand, when they are not purely 'biographical', in the sense of being concerned with incidents in Shakespeare's real life, are more commonly referred to as 'psychological' (for example, his interest in Shakespeare's madness, Chapter 3). As I will show in this chapter, they are not psychoanalytical. 'Impersonal readings' are opposed to both biographical and psychological ones.

who promises him 'eternity' by immortalising him in verse.

Pessoa aligns himself with those who identify the 'Mr. W. H.' of the *Sonnets*' dedication with the Fair Youth, for next to his copy of the dedication, he drew a vertical line following 'Mr. W. H.', in effect splitting it into two clauses, the first of which thus becomes: 'To the onlie begetter of these insuing sonnets Mr. W. H.' (*CW*, p. 1198). The identity of this cryptic character became one of the most vexed biblio-biographical mysteries of the nineteenth century.

The first time the *Sonnets* were reprinted, in 1640, thirty-one years after they had first appeared, John Benson altered the pronouns in three of them from male to female, and omitted eight of the poems explicitly addressed to a man. He ran together several of the remainder to form seventy-two poems in all, and gave them titles suggestive of heterosexual romance, naming sonnet 113 ('Since I left you, mine eye is in my mind'), for instance, 'Self-flattery of her Beauty'. Benson's text was the basis of most seventeenth-century editions, for the original Quarto text of the *Sonnets* was only reprinted in a responsibly edited version in 1709. Other, more scholarly editions followed, but not for half a century: George Steevens' in 1766, Edward Capell's in the same year, and the influential annotated edition by Edmond Malone in 1790.[16]

When the *Sonnets* became widely available in a form that made apparent their autobiographical nature, the desire to embed them in a story about Shakespeare's love life became endemic in their reception. Six years after Malone's edition was published, August Wilhelm Schlegel announced that the *Sonnets*' chief value lay in their inspiration in an actual friendship and love, an idea he allowed full rein in his well-attended lectures in Vienna about ten years later. Schlegel claimed that he was the first commentator to ever read the sequence as evidence of Shakespeare's life story, and concluded that the sequence depicted 'most unequivocally the actual situation and sentiments of the poet; they make us acquainted with the passions of the man; they even contain remarkable confessions of his youthful errors. [...] It betrays more than ordinary deficiency of critical acumen in Shakespeare's commentators, that none of them, so far as we know, have ever thought of availing themselves of his Sonnets for tracing the circumstances of his life.'[17] William Wordsworth agreed with him, writing in the 'Essay Supplementary to the Preface' to his *Poems* of 1815, the same year Schlegel's lectures first appeared in English translation, that in the *Sonnets* Shakespeare 'expresses his own feelings in his own person.'[18] In 'Scorn not the Sonnet' (1827), Wordsworth reiterated the insight by formulating the phrase that would reverberate through the ages: 'With this key, Shakespeare unlocked his heart.' 'Did he?' retorted Robert

---

[16] See Stephen Booth, 'Facts and Theories about Shakespeare's Sonnets', in *Shakespeare's Sonnets*, ed. Stephen Booth (1977; New Haven: Yale University Press, 2000), pp. 543-544.
[17] Schlegel, article in Schiller's *Horen*, 1796; repr. in *A Course of Lectures on Dramatic Art and Literature*, trans. John Black (London: A. J. W. Morrison, 1846), p. 352.
[18] Wordsworth, *The Poetical Works of William Wordsworth* (1815; London: Edward Moxon, 1849), p. 583.

Browning in 'House', forty years later. 'If so, the less Shakespeare he!'[19] Many nineteenth-century readers of the sequence considered that the nature of the vice depicted in the *Sonnets* made an 'honest' biography of the Bard impossible. An article in the *Monthly Review* CV (1824) by an anonymous critic implied that the poet was homosexual: 'The age of James the First', he lamented, 'was an age of impurity; and the manners of the sovereign, and the consent of Catholic Europe, had given a license to practices which may not in these happier days be tolerated, but of which then a sonneteer could boast.' He went on to lament that an honest biography of Shakespeare could not be written.[20]

There is, of course, no evidence that Shakespeare speaks in his own voice, as opposed to that of a dramatic *persona*, in the *Sonnets*. Their speaker may be as much literary convention as personal-confessional. Consequently, not all nineteenth-century readers accepted Wordsworth's 'key' and its imputation of Shakespeare's homosexuality: we have seen that Samuel Taylor Coleridge, on the contrary, discovered in the dramatist not pederasty but rather 'all the feelings, the sensibility, the purity, innocence, and delicacy of an affectionate girl of eighteen.'[21] Alexander Dyce declared, in 1832, that the poems were composed in an assumed character, because they were penned at different times and in different styles.[22] A similar view was expressed by H. N. Hudson: 'these poems were intended mainly as flights or exercises of fancy, thrown in to the form of a personal address, and written, it may be, in some cases at the instance or in compliment of the Poet's personal friends.'[23] Bolton Corney expressed the same view thirty years later, claiming the *Sonnets* to be '*poetical exercises*.'[24] Thomas Kenny, in his *Life and Genius of Shakespeare* (1864), erroneously claimed that most of his contemporaries agreed the compositions to have been produced by the poet in a 'purely fanciful and fictitious character.'[25]

Other readers were in two minds about the story the *Sonnets* tell. Nathan Drake, the first Shakespearean biographer to take the poems seriously as a source of personal revelation, declared in 1817 that the Fair Youth was Henry Wriothesley, Earl of Southampton, the patron to whom Shakespeare had dedicated *Venus and Adonis* and *The Rape of Lucrece*. (The other major candidate is William Herbert, third Earl of Pembroke, to whom the first Folio of Shakespeare's dramatic works is dedicated.) However, Drake considered that the 'Dark Lady' was not an autobiographical figure, concluding with '*the most entire conviction*' (Drake's italics), that the temptress was an imaginary creation

---

[19] Both cited in Schoenbaum, *Shakespeare's Lives*, pp. 253-254.

[20] Anon., *Monthly Review* CV (1824) 398-412, p. 412.

[21] Coleridge, *Coleridge's Shakespearean Criticism*, 2 vols., ed. Thomas Middleton Raysor (London: Constable & Co., 1930), II, p. 119.

[22] Alexander Dyce, 'Memoir of Shakespeare', in *William Shakespeare: Poems* (London: AMS Press, 1832), p. lxxvi.

[23] *Works*, ed. H. N. Hudson (Boston: 1856), p. 118.

[24] Bolton Corney, *The Sonnets of William Shakespeare* (New York: J. Miller, 1862).

[25] Thomas Kenny, *The Life and Genius of Shakespeare* (London: Longman, 1864) pp. 53-54.

introduced solely to express the feelings associated with illicit love.[26] Sidney Lee made a critical about-turn at the close of the century. In his 1897 article on Shakespeare in the *Dictionary of National Biography*, he had categorically declared that the poems were personal confessions rather than impersonal poems: 'Attempts have been made to represent them as purely literary exercises, mainly on the ground that a personal interpretation seriously reflects on Shakespeare's moral character. But only the two concluding sonnets (153 and 154) can be regarded by the unbiased reader as the artificial products of a poet's fancy.'[27] Readers of the New York edition of the *Dictionary*, published a few months later, were on the contrary informed that the *Sonnets* were 'to a large extent undertaken as literary exercises' and that it was only Shakespeare's dramatic instinct which misled readers into the illusion that they were confessional.[28] Lee went on to devote a substantial section of his 1898 *Life* to the anti-biographical theory, and declared that their subject-matter was nothing unusual for the period.[29]

Despite a few detractors and equivocators, however, by the mid-nineteenth century biographical readings of the *Sonnets* were so pervasive that David Masson could declare that

> criticism seems now pretty conclusively to have determined, what it ought to have determined long ago, that the *Sonnets* of Shakespeare are, and can possibly be, nothing else than a poetical record of his own feelings and experience – a connected series of entries, in his own diary – during a certain period of his London life.

It was a 'fact', Masson concluded, that 'these *Sonnets* of Shakespeare *are* autobiographic – distinctly, intensely, painfully autobiographic.'[30]

Since Romantic writers wrote for and about themselves in a manner 'unprecedented in literary history', as Wordsworth remarks, they read in the same way.[31] Theirs was the heyday of biographical criticism, an epoch when it was felt that a writer's 'opinions, character, personality [...] with whatever difficulty, are and must be decipherable in his writings', according to Thomas Carlyle.[32] In 'The Hero as Poet' (1903) Carlyle ventured that Shakespeare's works were 'so many

---

[26] Nathan Drake, *Shakespeare and His Times: including the biography of the poet, a new chronology of his plays, and a history of the manners, customs, amusements, superstitions, poetry and elegant literature of his age*, 2 vols. (London: Longman, 1817), II, p. 73.

[27] *Dictionary of National Biography*, LI (London: Macmillan, 1897), p. 363.

[28] *Dictionary of National Biography*, LI (New York: Macmillan 1897), p. 363.

[29] See *A Life of William Shakespeare* (London: Smith Elder & Co., 1898).

[30] David Masson, 'Shakespeare and Goethe', in *Essays Biographical and Critical, Chiefly on English Poets* (Cambridge: Macmillan, 1856), p. 79.

[31] Cited in John Buxton, *Sir Philip Sidney and the English Renaissance* (London: Macmillan, 1987), p. 22.

[32] Carlyle, 'Goethe', in *Critical and Miscellaneous Essays*, in *Works*, 18 vols. (London: Chapman and Hall, 1898-1901), XVI, pp. 245-246.

windows, though which we see a glimpse of the world that was in him.'[33] Pessoa underlined these words in his copy of Carlyle's essay. In 'Shakespeare; or the Poet', another essay Pessoa read attentively, Ralph Waldo Emerson rhetorically asked:

> Who ever read the volume of the Sonnets, without finding that the poet had there revealed, under masks that are no masks to the intelligent, the lore of friendship and of love; the confusion of sentiments in the most susceptible, and, at the same time, the most intellectual of men?[34]

Pessoa was familiar, too, with Coleridge's resistance to a biographical reading of the *Sonnets* (see Chapter 2), and with Browning's reply to Wordsworth's 'key', for he cites it verbatim in his letter of 11 December 1931 to Gaspar Simões.

> A Robert Browning [...] referiram uma vez o que havia de indiscutível quanto à pederastia de Shakespeare, tão clara e constantemente afirmada nos *Sonetos*. Sabe o que Browning respondeu? "Então ele é menos Shakespeare." ("If so the lesse [*sic*] Shakespeare he.") (*Corr II*, p. 253)

> [Someone once showed Robert Browning the undisputable facts pointing to Shakespeare's pederasty, which is so clearly and continually affirmed in the *Sonnets*. Do you know what Browning replied? 'If so, the less Shakespeare he.']

But the single most profound influence on Pessoa's reading of Shakespeare's *Sonnets* was Wilde's intriguing thesis on them, as put forward in *The Portrait of Mr. W. H* (1889).

The original version of *Mr W. H.* was published as an article in 1889, but Wilde became more and more obsessed with the subject of Shakespeare's *Sonnets*, and during the next four years he revised and augmented the story, in the process more than doubling its length. The manuscript of the revised story was thought to have been lost in the chaos that accompanied the sale of Wilde's property after his arrest; many years later, it was discovered in the offices of Wilde's publisher, John Lane, and the revised version was finally printed in 1921. Pessoa had access to the original text, which he owned in two different editions: *Lord Arthur Savile's Crime and Other Prose Pieces* (Leipzig: Bernhard Tauchnitz, 1909) and *Le Portrait de Monsieur W.H.* (Paris: Bibliothèque Cosmopolite, 1906).

In Wilde's story, the portrait of Mr. W. H., a beautiful youth, is kept in a locked cabinet in the home of Erksine, who is a good deal older than the unnamed narrator. It depicts a youth, about seventeen years old. (The age that Wilde attributes to Mr. W. H. holds a minor biographical interest in itself, for Wilde was first seduced to homosexual practices by the seventeen-year-old Robert Ross.[35]

---

[33] Carlyle, 'The Hero as Poet. Dante, Shakespeare', in *Sartor Resartus*, p. 102.

[34] Emerson, *Works*, p. 191.

[35] Richard Ellmann, 'Introduction', in *The Artist as Critic: Critical Writings of Oscar Wilde* (New York: Random House, 1969), p. xix.

Pessoa was aware of the fact, on the evidence of a biographical list he drew up to accompany his astrological chart for Wilde.[36]) Erskine reveals that the portrait belonged to his friend Cyril Graham, who had developed an original theory about Shakespeare's *Sonnets*: Graham believed that Mr. W. H. was an effeminate boy actor in Shakespeare's company by the name of Willie Hughes, the *Hews*-Hughes of sonnet 20 ('A woman's face with nature's own hand painted'). Unfortunately, the list of actors prefacing the First Folio contains no mention of Willie Hughes, so demonstration of the theory must depend exclusively upon a biographical reading of the *Sonnets*. After Graham's death, the unnamed narrator takes it upon himself to construct a convincing case for Shakespeare's passion for the young actor, based on an accumulation of internal poetic evidence.

Comparing Pessoa's marginalia, in his copy of the *Sonnets* (*CW*), to the chief pieces of poetic evidence cited in Wilde's story reveals the direct nature of the latter's impact on Pessoa's conclusion about Shakespeare's sexuality. This is even more apparent if we use the copy of Wilde's story that Pessoa annotated; significantly, it is the only piece in Pessoa's English-language collection of Wilde's essays to display his marginalia.

Next to the dedication of the *Sonnets*, Pessoa scribbled three numbers. The first, '20' appears next to the line 'To the only begetter of'. Sonnet 20 is the one where Graham discovers the identity of the *Sonnets*' dedicatee, and it is the pivotal one in discussions about the nature of the relationship depicted in the sequence. On the surface, it offers an explicit denial of any sexual element to the friendship between the speaker and the Fair Youth: ostensibly, the sonnet argues that the speaker has no use for the other man's sexual parts, and this explanation is sometimes accepted. Michael Spiller, for instance, writes: 'Shakespeare's love for the young man was not physically homosexual, as Sonnet 20 makes quite clear.'[37] Others argue, on the contrary, that sonnet 20 'reveals a man who is nearly obsessed by the fact that his lover has a penis.'[38] Since the 1960s, however, many have argued that the sonnet does not deny the possibility of a sexual relationship between the two men, for the earlier part of the poem shows that the speaker finds the rest of the young man as attractive as he might expect himself to find a female object of desire. As Stanley Wells puts it in *Looking for Sex in Shakespeare* (2004), 'It would be a naïve young man who, addressed in these terms, did not regard himself as the object of desire.'[39]

Graham discovers the surname of the Fair Youth in the line 'A man in hew, all

---

[36] I first published this list in 'Oscar Wilde, Fernando Pessoa, and the Art of Lying', *Portuguese Studies* 22 (2006), 219-249, p. 235.

[37] *Development of the Sonnet: An Introduction* (London/New York: Routledge, 1992), p. 155.

[38] Rictor Norton, *The Homosexual Literary Tradition: An Interpretation* (New York: Revisionist Press, 1974), p. 250.

[39] Stanley Wells, *Looking for Sex in Shakespeare* (Cambridge: Cambridge University Press, 2004), p. 65.

Hews in his controwling'.[40] He argues that, because 'in the original edition of the Sonnets "Hews" is printed with a capital letter and in italics', this clearly indicates an intentional play on words. Pessoa underlined this assertion in his copy of Wilde's story. He was also drawn to the so-called 'punning sonnets' (135, 'Whoever hath her wish, thou hast thy *Will*', and 136, 'If thy soul check thee that I come so near') cited to claim that the Christian name of Mr. W. H. was the same as Shakespeare's own, Will (*CW*, p. 1218).

Pessoa wrote 'O. W.' (for 'Oscar Wilde') next to sonnet 78 ('So oft have I invok'ed thee for my Muse') (*CW*, p. 1210).

This is one of only three sonnets that feature in *Mr W. H.* more than once, and it is instrumental to the case. He introduces it to explain that

the art of which Shakespeare talks in the *Sonnets* is not the art of the *Sonnets* themselves, which indeed were to him but slight and secret things – it is the art of the dramatist to which he is always alluding; and he to whom Shakespeare said [in the last two lines of sonnet 78] -
Thou art all my art, and dost advance
As high as learning my rude ignorance.[41]

Pessoa's 'O.W.' appears next to the third line: 'As every alien pen has got my use'. Wilde's protagonist argues that this sonnet's 'play on words (use=Hughes) is of course obvious'.[42] Pessoa underlined the words 'my use' in sonnet 78, and several other puns on 'use' in other poems. Stephen Booth, in his wonderful annotated edition of Shakespeare's *Sonnets* (1977), explains that in them the word 'use' 'carries suggestions of "right of possession" [...] and "privilege of using" – in a sexual sense.'[43]

There are numerous other instances of Pessoa testing out Wilde's reading of the *Sonnets*, as expressed in *The Portrait of Mr W. H.*, for himself. As an example, Graham interprets sonnet 53 ('What is your substance, whereof are you made') as a compliment by Shakespeare to Willie Hughes on the versatility of his acting, positing that the lines 'would be unintelligible if they were not addressed to an actor, for the word "shadow" had in Shakespeare's day a technical meaning connected with the stage.'[44] Pessoa drew a line, in his copy of the *Sonnets*, next to the line Graham cites. (*CW*, p. 1209).

---

[40] Wilde, 'The Portrait of Mr. W. H.', in *Lord Author Savile's Crime*, p. 170.
[41] Ibid., pp. 167-8.
[42] *Ibid.*, p. 171.
[43] *Shakespeare's Sonnets*, ed. Stephen Booth, p. 269.
[44] *Lord Arthur Savile's Crime*, p. 170.

1210   Sonnets.

LXXVII.

Thy glass will show thee how thy beauties wear,
Thy dial how thy precious minutes waste;
The vacant leaves thy mind's imprint will bear,
And of this book this learning mayst thou taste.
The wrinkles which thy glass will truly show
Of mouthed graves will give thee memory;
Thou by thy dial's shady stealth mayst know
Time's thievish progress to eternity.
Look! what thy memory cannot contain,
Commit to these waste blanks, and thou shalt find
Those children nursed, deliver'd from thy brain,
To take a new acquaintance of thy mind.
    These offices, so oft as thou wilt look,
    Shall profit thee and much enrich thy book.

LXXVIII.

So oft have I invok'd thee for my Muse
And found such fair assistance in my verse
As every alien pen hath got my use
And under thee their poesy disperse.
Thine eyes, that taught the dumb on high to sing
And heavy ignorance aloft to fly,
Have added feathers to the learned's wing
And given grace a double majesty.
Yet be most proud of that which I compile,
Whose influence is thine, and born of thee:
In others' works thou dost but mend the style,
And arts with thy sweet graces graced be;
    But thou art all my art, and dost advance
    As high as learning my rude ignorance.

LXXIX.

Whilst I alone did call upon thy aid,
My verse alone had all thy gentle grace;
But now my gracious numbers are decay'd,
And my sick muse doth give another place.
I grant, sweet love, thy lovely argument
Deserves the travail of a worthier pen;
Yet what of thee thy poet doth invent
He robs thee of, and pays it thee again.
He lends thee virtue, and he stole that word
From thy behaviour; beauty doth he give,
And found it in thy cheek: he can afford
No praise to thee but what in thee doth live.
    Then thank him not for that which he doth say,
    Since what he owes thee thou thyself dost pay.

LXXX.

O! how I faint when I of you do write,
Knowing a better spirit doth use your name,
And in the praise thereof spends all his might,
To make me tongue-tied, speaking of your fame!
But since your worth—wide as the ocean is,—
The humble as the proudest sail doth bear,
My saucy bark, inferior far to his,
On your broad main doth wilfully appear.
Your shallowest help will hold me up afloat,
Whilst he upon your soundless deep doth ride;
Or, being wrack'd, I am a worthless boat,
He of tall building and of goodly pride:
    Then if he thrive and I be cast away,
    The worst was this;—my love was my decay.

LXXXI.

Or I shall live your epitaph to make,
Or you survive when I in earth am rotten;
From hence your memory death cannot take,
Although in me each part will be forgotten.
Your name from hence immortal life shall have,
Though I, once gone, to all the world must die:
The earth can yield me but a common grave,
When you entombed in men's eyes shall lie.
Your monument shall be my gentle verse,
Which eyes not yet created shall o'er-read;
And tongues to be your being shall rehearse,
When all the breathers of this world are dead;
    You still shall live,—such virtue hath my pen,—
    Where breath most breathes,—even in the mouths of men.

LXXXII.

I grant thou wert not married to my Muse,
And therefore mayst without attaint o'erlook
The dedicated words which writers use
Of their fair subject, blessing every book.
Thou art as fair in knowledge as in hue,
Finding thy worth a limit past my praise;
And therefore art enforc'd to seek anew
Some fresher stamp of the time-bettering days.
And do so, love; yet when they have devis'd
What strained touches rhetoric can lend,
Thou truly fair wert truly sympathized
In true plain words by thy true-telling friend;
    And their gross painting might be better used
    Where cheeks need blood; in thee it is abus'd.

LXXXIII.

I never saw that you did painting need,
And therefore to your fair no painting set;
I found, or thought I found, you did exceed
The barren tender of a poet's debt:
And therefore have I slept in your report,
That you yourself, being extant, well might show
How far a modern quill doth come too short,
Speaking of worth, what worth in you doth grow.
This silence for my sin you did impute,
Which shall be most my glory, being dumb;
For I impair not beauty being mute,
When others would give life, and bring a tomb.
    There lives more life in one of your fair eyes
    Than both your poets can in praise devise.

Whether or not Pessoa was ultimately convinced by Wilde's story about the *Sonnets* – perhaps, as Wilde is anecdotally claimed to have said of himself, he *almost* believed in Willie Hughes – it directly informed his belief that Shakespeare was homosexual. Another direct source for this belief was Begley's *Is It Shakespeare? The Great Question of Elizabethan Literature Answered in the Light of*

New Revelations and Important Contemporary Evidence, the book Pessoa drew on for his most developed piece of writing on the Shakespearean authorship controversy, 'William Shakespeare, Pseudonymo' (see Chapter 2). Begley admitted in this book that a biographical reading of the *Sonnets* was crucial to his theory: 'I cannot help feeling that the Sonnets refer more than once to a real scandal in the background.'[45] Pessoa underlined this sentence, and he scribbled 'W. Begley' next to sonnet 40 ('Take all my loves, my love, yea, take them all') in the *Complete Works*. It is the only name to feature in his marginalia on Shakespeare's *Sonnets* apart from Wilde's.

New Revelations from Pessoa's Reading of the *Sonnets*

Pessoa's conviction that Shakespeare was homosexual is based upon the *Sonnets* alone, even though material in Shakespeare's plays has caused several readers to reach the same conclusion. When the matter was being widely discussed due to biographical interpretations of the *Sonnets*, the plays were also ploughed for evidence of homosexuality, but Pessoa himself nowhere discusses Shakespeare's sexuality in the context of his plays. [46]

Further to being based exclusively on his reading of the *Sonnets*, Pessoa's conviction about Shakespeare's homosexuality is grounded in an unabashedly biographical approach to them. That Pessoa should be drawn to biography in general, and to the life of Shakespeare in particular, is problematic because it contradicts his ideal of impersonality, but it is nevertheless the case. He drew an approving line in the margin next to Carlyle's pronouncement, in *Sartor Resartus*, that 'Biography is by nature the most universally profitable, universally pleasant of all things: especially Biography of distinguished individuals.' [47] Ferrari has demonstrated that Pessoa acquired separate biographies of the distinguished individuals Byron, Carlyle, Keats and Shelley during a short period of time when he was living in Durban. [48] Furthermore, Pessoa was attracted enough to the central tenet of biographical criticism, the principle that an author's life informs his work, to craft sophisticated life stories for the heteronyms.

In his defence, Pessoa is hardly the only writer in history whose penchant for biography and biographical readings goes against his insistence on impersonality, as both aesthetic theory and poetic ideal. Eliot's poetic self-effacement is so successful that Hugh Kenner titled his biography of him *The Invisible Poet* (1959), but Eliot admitted in later life: 'my own theorizing has been epiphenomenal to my

---

[45] Begley, *Is It Shakespeare?* p. 213.
[46] For an overview of this material, and for passages in the plays that have been interpreted as pointing to Shakespeare's homosexuality, see Stanley Wells, '"I think he loves the world only for him": Men loving men in Shakespeare's plays', in *Looking for Sex in Shakespeare*, pp. 66-97.
[47] Carlyle, *Sartor Resartus*, pp. 51, 1.
[48] Ferrari, 'A biblioteca de Fernando Pessoa na génese dos heterónimos', in *Fernando Pessoa: O Guardador de papéis*, p. 182.

tastes.'[49] Cixous's *L'Exil de James Joyce* (1968) is also strangely out of keeping with her otherwise impersonal criticism, its central thesis being that 'la vie et l'oeuvre de Joyce sont consubstantielles' [Joyce's life and work are of a piece].[50] In an interview she admitted that she had wanted to use a somewhat experimental and unconventional approach, but wound up working within the traditional, 'constraining' mode of the standard 'academic type of production'.[51] Joyce himself, the supreme champion of impersonality, has Stephen voice an outrageously biographical reading of Shakespeare in *Ulysses* (section nine, 'Scylla and Charybadis'). In it, Stephen argues that by writing *Hamlet* Shakespeare attempted to compensate for a sexual cuckolding perpetrated by his older and more experienced wife, and that Shakespeare's son, Hamnet, who died young, was possibly conceived adulterously by one of Shakespeare's brothers, either Richard or Edmund, who are always depicted as villains in Shakespeare's plays. From tendentious pieces of literary evidence, Stephen concludes that Shakespeare's art stemmed directly from the circumstances of his life – 'He drew Shylock out of his own long pocket' – and goes on to apply this idea to all literature:

> Maeterlinck says: *If Socrates leave his house today he will find the sage seated on his doorstep, If Judas go forth tonight it is to Judas his steps will tend*. Every life is many days, day after day. We walk through ourselves, meeting robbers, ghosts, giants, old men, young men, wives, widows, brothers-in-love. But always meeting ourselves.[52]

Of course, Stephen is a dramatic character not to be confused with his author, and it is likely that in this lecture scene Joyce is mocking his earlier aesthetic theorising, for he has all the other characters present laugh at, or otherwise dismiss, Stephen's biographical reading of Shakespeare, and the passage ends by Stephen conceding, Wilde-like, that he does not believe his own theory:

> – You are a delusion, said roundly John Eglinton to Stephen. You have brought us all this way to show us a French triangle. Do you believe your own theory?
> – No, Stephen said promptly.[53]

But whether or not Joyce agrees with Stephen's approach to Shakespeare, in order to write it he had to read numerous biographies of the Bard, and his knowledge of the disputed 'facts' of his life, such as the episode of the 'upstart

---

[49] Hugh Kenner, *The Invisible Poet*, (London: Methuen & Co Ltd, 1959); Eliot, *To Criticize the Critic* (New York: Farrar, Straus and Giroux, 1965), p. 20.
[50] Hélène Cixous, *L'Exil de James Joyce* [*James Joyce's Exile*] (Paris: Grasset, 1968) p. 19.
[51] Cited in *The Reception of James Joyce in Europe*, 2 vols., ed. G. Geert Lernout and Wim Van Mierlo (London: Thoemess Contiuum, 2004), II, p. 376.
[52] Joyce, *Ulysses*, pp. 197, 204.
[53] *Ibid.*, p. 205.

crow', the authorship controversy, and countless others, was profound.[54]

In addition to being at odds with his ideal of impersonality, Pessoa's reading of Shakespeare's *Sonnets* goes against his appraisal of Shakespeare as an impersonal dramatic poet, as invisible as the God of creation (see Chapter 1). Numerous nineteenth-century readers of the *Sonnets* are caught in exactly the same contradiction. Keats and others celebrated Shakespeare's lack of identity, and the difficulty in relating his commonplace life to the genius of his works led to the authorship controversy (see Chapter 2), but the same readers often approached the *Sonnets* as coded autobiography. Neither they, nor Pessoa, ever set this up as a problem. Of course, the Romantic poets did not view impersonality as an aim in itself, as Pessoa did. However, even in the case of those who do, a biographical approach to the *Sonnets* has often proved irresistible.

Since Wilde, the preferred critical stance towards the *Sonnets* has been an impersonal one; resistance to the biographical approach has even led modern commentators to suggest that the sequence is a parody of soneteering.[55] This stance culminated in Booth's 1977 edition of the *Sonnets*, in which he categorically dismisses any biographical speculation about Shakespeare's sexuality as irrelevant: 'William Shakespeare was almost certainly homosexual, bisexual, or heterosexual. The sonnets provide no evidence on the matter.'[56] Booth laments the fact that sonnet 20 is so often cited as evidence of Shakespeare's homosexuality.[57] But even the most extreme advocate for an impersonal reading of the *Sonnets* can be seen to allow that they probably have some biographical basis, even if it is now lost to us, when he writes in an Appendix that 'The sexual undercurrents of the sonnets are of the sonnets; *they probably reflect a lot that is true about their author*, but I do not know what that is.'[58]

In the same way, Jonathan Bate, in a chapter titled 'Shakespeare's Autobiographical Poems?' in his book *The Genius of Shakespeare* (1997), sets out by arguing that the compositions are impersonal: 'Shakespeare was not a Romantic poet like Wordsworth who just sat down and wrote a sonnet when he felt one coming on, or like Keats for whom the sonnet was above all a way of expressing his own intense feelings.'[59] He denounces what he calls the 'Romantic biographical fallacy'. A few pages later, however, he puts forward Southampton as both the addressee of the *Sonnets*' dedication ('Mr W. H.') and the Fair Youth of the poems: 'Once all the facts are collected, the case for Southampton as the original

---

[54] Specifically, Joyce draws on George Brandes's *William Shakespeare* (London: Kessinger, 1898), Frank Harris's *The Man Shakespeare and his Tragic Life-Story* (New York: M. Kennerly, 1909) and Sidney Lee's *A Life of William Shakespeare* (London: Smith Elder, 1898).

[55] See, for example, Katharine Wilson, *Shakespeare's Sugared Sonnets* (New York: Barnes and Noble, 1974).

[56] *Shakespeare's Sonnets*, ed. Stephen Booth, p. 548.

[57] *Ibid.*, p. 163.

[58] *Ibid.*, p. 549. My italics.

[59] Bate, *The Genius of Shakespeare*, p. 38.

patron/youth looks irrefutable. To regard the Sonnets as parody, exercise, or pure play is to forget the economic urge which drove Shakespeare to write.' To strengthen this attribution, he proposes a new biographical reading of the sequence:

> our understanding of the sonnets will be assisted if we *suppose* – not if we confidently assert – that they are tied to some rather sordid intrigue in the Southampton household around 1593-4.'[60]

Bate puts forward the nature of this supposed intrigue in a highly tendentious biographical reading:

> It seems to me that an Elizabethan earl of possibly homosexual orientation would be more likely to sleep with a married woman of lower social status because he wanted to score off her husband than because he desired her himself. Suppose that the young Earl's guardian, who wishes to marry him off against his will, places an agent in his household in order to report back on the progress of the marriage suit and related affairs. Suppose that the agent is married. To sleep with his wife would be the most delicious revenge for the man's presumption in reporting intimate matters back to Burghley.

As he finally concedes, 'I began to work on the sonnets with a determination to adhere to an agnostic position on the question of their autobiographical elements. But, like Sidney Lee, I have been unable to hold fast to my unbelief.'[61]

The final revelation from Pessoa's reading of Shakespeare's *Sonnets* is that it owes nothing to Freudian thinking. Siegbert Solomon Prawer's chapter on Freud's readings of Shakespeare in *A Cultural Citizen of the World: Sigmund Freud's Knowledge and Use of British and American Writings* (2009), shows Freud's approach to Shakespeare, unsurprisingly, to be psychoanalytical: when Freud became convinced that the real author of Shakespeare's works was Oxford, he looked for events in the Earl's life which mirrored the incidents depicted in the *Sonnets*.[62] But Pessoa does not appropriate psychoanalytical readings of the *Sonnets*; his conclusion about Shakespeare's sexuality stems instead from the nineteenth-century sources charted above. In other words, Pessoa's approach to Shakespeare is biographical and psychological, but it is not psychoanalytical.

This is also evident in his approach to Shakespeare's madness (Chapter 3): Pessoa's diagnosis of the Bard as hystero-neurasthenic is completely non-Freudian, even though Freud and Breuer published *Studies in Hysteria*, the founding book of psychoanalysis, in 1895. However, when *Studies in Hysteria*

---

[60] *Ibid.*, p. 54.
[61] *Ibid.*, pp. 45, 49, 55, 58.
[62] Siegbert Solomon Prawer, *A Cultural Citizen of the World: Sigmund Freud's Knowledge and Use of British and American Writings* (London: Legenda, 2009), pp. 6-10.

appeared, it was one of dozens of books on the fashionable neurosis. Competing books on hysteria and neurasthenia, like Maurice Craig's handbook on *Nerve Exhaustion* (1922) were still being published in the 1920s. Pessoa's lack of interest in psychoanalysis, relative to competing *fin-de-siècle* psychological theories, is further evidenced by the books in his personal library (one by Freud; dozens by other psychologists and pseudo-psychologists) and by the manuscripts in his archive (few references to Freud; hundreds to other theorists; see *GL*). Pessoa's few writings that mention Freud tend to focus on alternative theories of neurosis and sexuality. For example:

> A psiquiatria nota, com efeito, que a desagregação psíquica é quase sempre acompanhada pelo desvio sexual. Quase sempre? A mais recente das teorias psiquiátricas diz que sempre. Freud e os seus discípulos, através da "psico-análise", afirmam a origem sexual de todas as psicoses. Justa ou não esta doutrina extrema, o certo é que a sexualidade domina os factos psíquicos tanto, se não mais, que os físicos; e que a sua importância notavelmente se vê quando se analisam as manifestações mentais de um louco ou de um degenerado. (*PETCL*, p. 87)

> [Psychiatry notes, certainly, that mental confusion is almost always accompanied by sexual deviance. Almost always? The most recent psychiatric theory says always. Freud and his disciples, through psychoanalyses, maintain that all psychoses have a sexual origin. Whether or not this extreme doctrine be correct, what's certain is its remarkable importance can be seen when we analyse the mental manifestations of a madman or a degenerate.]

I have argued that Pessoa's readings of Shakespeare show him to have encountered psychoanalysis later than is supposed, and that its impact on him was less influential than is commonly held.[63] If it is true that, contrary to popular belief, Pessoa largely either ignored, or was largely uninterested in, Freudian thinking until the late 1920s, he would not be the only Modernist of his generation to do so. Gertrude Stein's psychology was wholly non-Freudian. When Aragon and Breton praised hysteria as a great poetic discovery in 1928, they saluted Charcot rather than Freud. Marcel Proust's *À la recherche du temps perdu* [*In Search of Lost Time*] (1913-1927) draws directly on contemporary medical sources, such as Bergson on time and memory, Janet on psychological automatisms, Alfred Binet on fetishism, Théodule Ribot on maladies of the will, and Émile Egger on the stream of consciousness – but not on Freud's theories.[64] Eliot, in an essay of 1919, either ignored Freud's Oedipal interpretation of *Hamlet* completely or rejected it

---

[63] Castro, 'Pessoa, Shakespeare's *Sonnets*, and the Problem of Gaspar Simões', in *Fernando Pessoa's Modernity Without Frontiers: Influences, Dialogues and Responses*, ed. Mariana Gray de Castro (Woodbridge: Tamesis, 2013), pp. 143-56.
[64] See Michael R. Finn, *Proust, the Body and Literary Form* (Cambridge: Cambridge University Press, 1999).

outright, even though it had been published in *The Interpretation of Dreams* twenty years earlier. Since Eliot could find in the play no suitable 'objective correlative' for Hamlet's inaction, which means that he accepted neither the neurotic nor the Oedipal explanation of his character, he reached the startling conclusion that the play was an artistic failure:

> The only way of expressing emotion in the form of art is by finding an 'objective correlative'; in other words, a set of objects, a situation, a chain of events which shall be the formula of that *particular* emotion; such that when the external facts, which must terminate in sensory experience, are given, the emotion is immediately evoked. If you examine any of Shakespeare's most successful tragedies, you will find this exact equivalence [...] Hamlet (the man) is dominated by an emotion which is inexpressible, because it is in *excess* of the facts as they appear. [...] We must simply admit that here Shakespeare tackled a problem which proved too much for him. Why he attempted it at all is an insoluble puzzle.[65]

However, Eliot leans towards a neurotic, rather than Oedipal, explanation for Hamlet's character when he asserts in this essay that 'The intense feeling, ecstatic or terrible, without an object or exceeding its object, is something which every person of sensibility has known; it is doubtless a subject of study for pathologists.' [66] In the long run, Freud became the single most influential psychological theorist of the twentieth century, but 'Until as late as 1920, many [alternative psychological thinkers] were in fact much better known than Freud in the world of science, ideas, and culture.'[67] Pessoa means what he says when he writes, in his letter of 11 December 1931 to Gaspar Simões, that he never needed Freud to 'distinguir, pelo simples estilo literário, o pederasta e o onanista' [distinguish the pederast from the onanist, solely by their literary style] (*Corr II*, p. 254), for he confidently deduces Shakespeare's sexuality from the *Sonnets* without Freud's help.

This is not to suggest that Pessoa's encounter with psychoanalytic criticism, in the shape of his inquisitive future biographer João Gaspar Simões, was uneventful. It was instrumental in shaping his posterior explanations for his art, in particular his homoerotic output, and it caused him to quietly tone down his homoerotic poetry from then on. Like Joyce, Pessoa soon recognised that psychoanalysis was 'neither more nor less than blackmail.'[68] Pessoa displays much anxiety that critics like Gaspar Simões might reach, on the evidence of his own homoerotic writings, the same conclusion about his sexuality that he had reached about Shakespeare's based on the *Sonnets*, but now with a more scientific backing. Before exploring the

---

[65] Eliot, 'Hamlet and His Problems', in *Selected Prose*, pp. 48-49:
[66] *Ibid.*
[67] Micale, 'The Modernist Mind: A Map', in *The Mind of Modernism*, p. 9.
[68] Cited in Maud Ellmann, 'Introduction', in *Psychoanalytic Literary Criticism*, ed. Maud Ellmann (London: Longman, 1994), p. 1.

aftermath of Pessoa's encounter with Freud, it is worth questioning what Pessoa's homoerotic writings might owe to his reading of Shakespeare's.

Shakespeare's *Sonnets* and Pessoa's Homoeroticism

'Antinous' (1918) is the most homoerotic poem Pessoa signed under his own name.[69] João Manuel Gomes argues that the poem marks the symbolic suicide of the young Pessoa, to pave the way for the heteronyms who would reign 'em impérios totalmente castos e puros' [in completely chaste, pure empires]. [70] But Álvaro de Campos, in his poems ('Ode Marítima', 'Passagem das Horas', 'Soneto Já Antigo' [Old Sonnet] and others) as well as numerous prose pieces, displays the kind of sexual behaviour that landed Wilde in prison with two years' hard labour. Pessoa's homoerotic writings, particularly those of Campos, some of whose poems were included in a French anthology of gay literature in 1984, have been the focus of numerous studies.[71] Rather than present a summary of these, what follows is a tentative suggestion of something that has not yet been considered: the ways in which Pessoa's homoerotic writings may have been influenced by his reading of Shakespeare's.

Most readers intent on ploughing the *Sonnets* for evidence of Shakespeare's homosexuality, like Wilde and Begley, bypass the sonnets dealing with the Dark Lady entirely, but Pessoa was interested in these, for he annotated 144 ('Two loves I have of comfort and despair') and 127 ('In the old age black was not counted fair') in his copy of the *Complete Works* (*CW*, pp. 1217, 1219). Katherine Duncan-Jones and Eve Sedgwick both argue that the Dark Lady functions, in these sonnets, as a point of triangulation for homosexual desire: she is a necessary intermediary

---

[69] See Édouard Roditi, 'Fernando Pessoa, Outsider Among English Poets', in *The Literary Review*, VI:3 (Spring 1963), 372-391; Yara Frateschi Vieira, 'O discuro erótico nos poemas "Antinous" e "Epithalamium"' [Erotic Discourse in the poems 'Antinous' and 'Epithalamium'], in *Número especial do Boletim Informativo do C.E.P, consagrado a Fernando Pessoa* [*Special Issue Dedicated to Fernando Pessoa*] (1985), pp. 67-75 and Jorge de Sena, 'Fernando Pessoa e a literatura inglesa' [Fernando Pessoa and English Literature], *Comércio* ('*Cultura e Arte*' supplement, 8 November 1953; repr. in *Estrada Larga* (Porto: Porto Editora, n.d. (1958), pp. 192-7).

[70] João Manuel Gomes, 'Para acabar de vez com a obscenidade' [To End Obscenity Once and For All], *Jornal de Letras* [*Literary Review*] (14 June 1988).

[71] 'Fernando Pessoa *(1888-1935)*', in *Les amours masculines: Anthologie de l'homosexualité dans la littérature* [*Male Loves: An Anthology of Homossexuality in Literature*], ed. Michel Larivière (Paris: Lieu Commun, 1984), pp. 351-362. Representative studies of Campos's homoeroticism include Armando Ventura Ferreira, 'Sequência para Fernando Pessoa' [Sequence for Fernando Pessoa], *Contravento: Letras e Artes* 3 (April 1970) 8-13; repr. in *Memória dos mitos* [*Memory of Myths*] (Lisbon: Arcádia, 1971), pp. 175-204; Zenith, 'Pessoa's Gay Heteronym?', *Lusosex: Gender and Sexuality in the Portuguese-Speaking World*, ed. Susan Canty Quinlan and Fernando Arenas (Minneapolis/London: University of Minnesota Press, 2002) pp. 35-46, and longer passages in such books as Sousa Santos's *Atlantic Poets*, and *Embodying Pessoa: Corporeality, Gender, Sexuality*, ed. Anna M. Klobucka and Mark Sabine (Toronto/London: University of Toronto Press, 2007).

that enables the physical relationship between the speaker and the Fair Youth.[72] The exact same concept can be found in *Teleny*: when Teleny is with the Countess, he manoeuvres her into a position whereby 'having her *a retro*, his whole thoughts were thus concentrated on' Des Grieux; the child conceived during this encounter is, it is suggested, fathered by Des Grieux rather than by the Count or Teleny:

> 'This [child] happened to look neither like the count nor like Teleny.'
> 'Who the deuce did it look like then?'
> 'Like myself.'[73]

While it is unlikely that Pessoa read *Teleny* – when it first appeared there were only two hundred copies in print – he was intimately acquainted with one of the greatest Portuguese novels in the same vein, having accompanied Mário de Sá-Carneiro's *A Confissão de Lúcio* [*Lucio's Confession*] (1913) through its conception and gestation. Although Modernist in style, the atmosphere of *Lúcio* is that of the Decadent aesthetic of the *fin-de-siècle*, and Sá-Carneiro's story bears striking resemblances to *Teleny*, which it would be worth examining in a separate study. To point to a few of these, Lúcio, like Des Grieux, fears descending into madness. Furthermore, Ricardo is possibly an onanistic projection of Lúcio himself. If so, when Ricardo attempts to kill Marta, the event is a murder-suicide. At one point in *Teleny*, the title character says to Des Grieux: 'Who knows – you are, perhaps, my *doppelganger*? Then, woe to one of us! [...] In our country they say that a man must never meet his *alter ego*, it brings misfortune to one or to both'.[74] In its tragic outcome, *Lúcio* enacts the terrible consequences of meeting one's alter ego.

The most significant resemblance between the two novels, in the context of Pessoa's reading of the *Sonnets*, is the possibility that Marta, a spectral female, is merely a vessel for the consummation of the homoerotic relationship between Lúcio and Ricardo.

Mediated by his knowledge of *A Confissão de Lúcio*, perhaps, Pessoa understood that a key component of Shakespeare's *Sonnets* was its use of a woman as an intermediary for male desire. He appropriates the idea for Campos's sonnet – for a sonnet, note, rather than for one of Campos's trademark blank verse poems – dedicated to 'Daisy Mason' (1913). Daisy is asked to inform the speaker's friends, and in particular an anonymous 'pobre rapazito/Que me deu tantas horas tão felizes/[...] a quem eu tanto julguei amar' [poor dear boy/Who gave me so many happy hours/[...] and who I sincerely thought I loved], of his death (*AdC*, p. 58). Her function is to act as a messenger between the two men.

Shakespeare's *Sonnets*, even those in the Fair Youth sequence, often

---

[72] See Katherine Duncan-Jones, 'Introduction', in *Shakespeare's Sonnets* (London: Arden 3rd ed., 1997); Sedgwick, 'Swan in Love: The Example of Shakespeare's Sonnets', in *Between Men: English Literature and Male Homosocial Desire* (New York: Columbia University Press, 1985), pp. 28-48.
[73] *Teleny*, p. 46.
[74] *Ibid.*, p. 91.

tantalisingly avoid ascribing a specific gender to their addressee. Pessoa's description of Antinous's 'bare female male-body' is immediately evocative of the ambiguously gendered Fair Youth, the 'master-mistress' of the speaker's passion. This epithet appears in sonnet 20, the one central to biographical readings of the *Sonnets*, the one Wilde makes so much of in *Mr W. H.*, the one Pessoa annotates, and refers to next to the *Sonnets'* dedication, in his copy of the *Complete Works*. The 'master-mistress' of Shakespeare's *Sonnets* also foreshadows Pessoa's ambiguously gendered terms of endearment for Ophélia Queiroz in his letters to her: 'meu anjinho bébé' [my baby angel], 'Meu Bébé pequenino (e actualmente muito mau)' [my cute little baby (who is currenly very mean)], 'amor pequenininho' [dear little love], 'Meu Ibis chamado Ophelia' [My Ibis called Ophelia], etc.[75] Yvette Centeno posits that such diminutives serve to neutralise Pessoa's love-object:

> Assim Ophélia, aliás logo Ophelinha, reduzida, depressa passa a Bébé (de valor neutro, já não feminino), a Bébézinho (neutro na mesma e ainda mais reduzido), a Bébé-anjinho, em que a des-sexualização mais se afirma, pois os anjos ainda menos que os bébés podem ter sexo...[76]

> [In this way Ophelia, or better little Ophelia, thus reduced, quickly becomes the Baby (of neutral gender, thus no longer female), then little Baby (still neutral and even further reduced), then Baby angel, where the de-sexing is still more evident, for angels and babies have no gender...]

She argues that Pessoa attempts to transform Ophélia into a child, angel or saint, because he could not have a relationship with a woman who did not assume the quality of a dreamscape, a woman who was not dormant and desexed. It could equally be argued, however, that rather than safely neutralising Ophélia's sexuality in his letters to her, what Pessoa in effect does is to transform her into a male beloved. Angels and babies may be perceived to be asexual, as Centeno claims, but in the Portuguese language they both have a masculine gender ('um anjo', 'um bébé').

Significantly, when Campos accuses his fellow heteronym Ricardo Reis of masking, in his poetry, his homosexuality, his case hinges on the masculine ending of a single word in one of Reis's odes, a word ostensibly meant to refer to a female beloved. He argues that the following two lines in Reis's ode 'A flor que és, não a que dás, eu quero' [I want the flower you are, not the one you give], 'é dirigida a um rapaz, pois [...] o pequeno "o" [...] define a coisa' [is addressed to a boy, for [...] the little 'o' [...] settles the matter]:

---

[75] Pessoa, *Cartas de amor a Ophélia Queiroz* [*Love Letters to Ophélia Queiroz*], ed. David Mourão Ferreira (Lisbon: Ática, 1978), pp. 54, 55, 67, 169.
[76] Yvette Centeno, 'Fernando Pessoa: Ophélia-Bébezinho ou o "horror do sexo"' [Baby Ophelia or 'The Horror of Sex'], *Colóquio-Letras* 49 (1979), 11-20, p. 16.

Se te colher avarO
A mão da infausta sphynge[77]

[If you are plucked
By the hand of the unfortunate sphinx]

Campos charges Reis with employing his difficult syntax as a veil of modesty, and argues that the spectral female lovers Reis addresses in his odes are not believable as real women; the same could be said of the famous female spectres in Shakespeare's *Sonnets* and Sá-Carneiro's *A Confissão de Lúcio*.[78]

Beyond appropriating one of the key features of Shakespeare's *Sonnets* for his own homoerotic writings, Pessoa can arguably be shown, by his very choice of subject-matter in 'Antinous', to attempt to provide historical legitimacy for same-sex desire. This was Wilde's intention in writing *The Portrait of Mr. W. H.*, for as Bate argues, he was 'quite aware that his lovely Willie was a *jeu d'esprit*, invented to help make the case for a homoerotic Shakespeare.'[79] Neil McKenna is unequivocal on the point, arguing that Wilde's story was fashioned as 'a manifesto of *paiderastia*, a closely argued dissertation designed to give cultural and historical legitimacy to sex between man and youths'.[80] To this end, *The Portrait of Mr W. H.* emphasises the continuity of homosexual feeling from the past to the present: Wilde makes the link between Willie Hughes and Gaveston in Marlowe's *Edward II*, and associates the homoerotic love depicted in Shakespeare's *Sonnets* with the neoplatonism of Ficino and Michelangelo and the Hellenism of Winckelmann.[81] For the story's protagonists, to study Shakespeare's *Sonnets* is to recognise a personal affinity with the homoerotic passion of Shakespeare and Willie Hughes.

Teleny is also concerned with providing historical legitimacy for same-sex desire. Des Grieux sets out to read all he can find about 'the love of one man for another, that loathsome crime against nature, taught to us not only by the very gods themselves, but by all the greatest men of olden times.' He cites numerous precedents, including the biblical story of David and Jonathan. But the story of Hadrian and Antinous is the supreme example that is evoked throughout the novel. When Des Grieux first falls under Teleny's spell he understands 'the love the mighty monarch felt for his fair Grecian slave, Antinous, who – like unto Christ – died for his master's sake.'[82] Teleny's death, at the end of the novel, re-enacts

---

[77] *Ficções do interlúdio/2-3: Odes de Ricardo Reis* [*Ricardo Reis's Odes*] (Rio de Janeiro: Nova Aguilar, 1976), p. 119.
[78] See Zenith, 'Pessoa's Gay Heteronym?', in *Lusosex*, pp. 35-46.
[79] Bate, *The Genius of Shakespeare*, p. 60.
[80] Neil McKenna, *The Secret Life of Oscar Wilde* (London: Arrow, 2004), p. 145.
[81] On Michelangelo's poems addressed to a man as a precedent see John Kerrigan, 'Between Michelangelo and Petrarch: Shakespeare's Sonnets of Art', in *Surprised by Scenes: Essays in Honour of Professor Yasanuri Takahashi*, ed. Yasanuri Takada (Tokyo: Kenkyusha, 1994), pp. 142-63.
[82] *Teleny*, pp. 34, 17, 4.

this sacrifice, which in light of the earlier allusion to Christ gains added poignancy. The story of Antinous also features prominently in Wilde's poem 'The Sphinx', in which 'The ivory body of that rare young slave with his pomegranate mouth' anticipates Pessoa's description of Antinous's 'lips [...] with opening redness'. Antinous is further evoked in the closing lines of the second part of *The Portrait of Mr. W. H.*:

> [Willie Hughes's] true tomb, as Shakespeare saw, was the poet's verse, his true monument the permanence of the drama. So had it been with others whose beauty had given a new creative impulse to their age. The ivory body of the Bithynian slave rots in the green ooze of the Nile, and on the yellow hills of the Cerameicus is strewn the dust of the young Athenian; but Antinous lives in sculpture, and Charmides in philosophy.[83]

Further to crafting his own poetic version of the story of Antinous, Pessoa overtly cites Shakespeare's homosexuality as a legitimising precedent on at least one occasion. One of the prose pieces he ascribes to Campos is daring enough to argue:

> Shakespeare nos seus Sonetos, apaixonando-se por um mancebo qualquer, foi, como sempre o grande normal que elle era, o representante máximo masculino, o do homem cheio de interesses e attenções para tantas cousas da vida, que não pode gastar tempo na caça ao prazer sexual normal, e porisso o substitue pelo prazer sexual dado pela amizade com outros homens levada ao requinte [...]
> – Essa theoria é phantastica. Com que então, para si, a inversão sexual é de certo modo uma cousa normal?
> = A inversão sexual masculina. (*PC II*, p. 479)

> [Shakespeare in his Sonnets, falling in love with some young urchin, was, like the great natural he always was, the supreme representative of masculinity, of the man full of interests and attentions for so many things in life, who cannot waste time chasing normal sexual pleasure, and therefore substitutes it for the sexual pleasure of the friendship with other men, taken to an exquisite degree [...]
> — That theory is amazing. Do you mean to say that, in your view, sexual inversion is in a sense something natural?
> = Male sexual inversion, yes.]

Pessoa's inverted use of the word 'normal' [natural], in the text above, deconstructs any mask of ideological neutrality. If homosexuality is 'natural', as Campos here implies, then the natural/unnatural binary must be a cultural concept, and an erroneous one at that. Des Grieux comes to the same conclusion

---

[83] Wilde, *Lord Arthur Savile's Crime*, p. 199.

when he realises that he 'had been inculcated with all kinds of wrong ideas, so when I understood what my *natural feelings* for Teleny were I was staggered, horrified.' He reiterates the point that a feeling that is felt to be natural, rather than a conscious choice, cannot be contrary to nature: 'Had I committed a crime against nature when my own nature found peace and happiness thereby? If I was thus, surely it was the fault of my blood, not myself? Who had planted nettles in my garden? Not I.'[84]

Campos's writings subvert the tenuous binaries (sanity/insanity, morality/immorality, normality/abnormality) that led *fin-de-siècle* society to condemn homosexuality as a crime. His poems and *Teleny* alight on the same image for the nature of social morality, that of a suffocating piece of clothing, symbol of oppressive civilisation, around one's neck: Teleny takes off 'his white tie, that stiff and uncomfortable useless appendage invented by fashion only to torture mankind'; Campos, in one of his most homoerotic poems, the ode to the 'grande pederasta' [great pederast] Walt Whitman, pauses momentarily to 'tirar a gravata e desabotoar o colarinho./Não se pode ter muita energia com a civilização à roda do pescoço' [take off my tie and unbutton my collar./One can't be very energetic with civilisation hanging round one's neck].[85]

'Immorality' in Life and in Art

It is significant that Campos's prose piece above should deliberately refer to Shakespeare's sexuality as expressed in the *Sonnets* ('Shakespeare nos seus Sonetos' [Shakespeare in his *Sonnets*]), stopping short of making the leap from literary homoeroticism to real-life homosexuality. Pessoa everywhere makes an acute distinction between the feeling of inversion, which he feels to be natural, and its manifestation in actual behaviour, which he feels is to be condemned. His sharp distinction between 'immorality' in art and in life is of fundamental importance, so it is worth demonstrating by stages.

Pessoa is wilfully paradoxical when he declares, in 'Erostratus', that 'The relations between art and morals are extraordinarily simple, for both the defenders of there being none, and their opponents, are right' (*H*, p. 174). For him, unlike for Wilde, (recall the Preface to *Dorian Gray*) there exists such a thing as immoral art, and it is exemplified by Shakespeare's *Sonnets* and *Venus and Adonis*:

> Of the supreme poets of the world – that is to say, of the supreme artists in the supreme art – there are only two who are to some extent immoral: Shakespeare and Goethe – Shakespeare in the homosexuality of his *sonnets* and the tiresome offshoot of it in *Venus and Adonis*. (yet not in his dramatic works as a whole). (*H*, p. 174)

---

[84] *Teleny*, pp. 33, 86 (my italics).
[85] *Ibid.*, p. 40; 'Saudação a Walt Whitman'. These lines are absent from the poem as it appears in *AdC* (Assírio e Alvim) and Berardinelli's 1990 critical edition, presumably due to doubts whether they belong, but they feature in most early editions of Campos's poetry, such as *Álvaro de Campos: Poesia* [Poetry] (Lisbon: Ática, 1944), p. 9.

The tiresome offshoot of the *Sonnets*' homosexuality is, presumably, the heterosexual 'obscenity' of *Venus and Adonis*. George Brandes, the author of one of the Shakespearean biographies Joyce draws on for Stephen's lecture on Shakespeare, writes that *Venus and Adonis* 'is an entirely erotic poem, and contemporaries aver that it lay on the table of every light woman in London' in Shakespeare's day.[86] Pessoa himself refers to *Venus and Adonis* as 'obscene' in various texts, such as one on the merits and demerits of censorship:

> There are works which are palpably only obscene and not literary at all […] And there are, at the other end, products like *Venus and Adonis*, like so many classical poems and prose-works; the difficulty is greatest when we meet with high works of art which are, not only immoral, but frankly apologetic for some species of immorality.
> It cannot be claimed that the artistic elements involved absolve and extirpate the immorality of the work. (*PETCL*, p. 57)

'Immoral' art is therefore, for Pessoa, that which is either homosexual (as is the case of the *Sonnets*) or obscene (*Venus and Adonis*). It is no coincidence that his own poems 'Antinous' and 'Epithalamium', respectively, are the artistic offshoots of the two different types of artistic 'immorality' he discovers in Shakespeare's poetry. In other words, the 'homosexual' 'Antinous', and the heterosexual but 'obscene' 'Epithalamium', have notable precedents in Pessoa's judgement of the *Sonnets* and *Venus and Adonis* as the same. Suggestive evidence that Pessoa's two poems are a deliberate mirroring of Shakespeare's literary immorality is in his letter of 1915 to the English publisher Frank Palmer, in which he proposes an English-version review modelled on the recently-published *Orpheu*:

> Our review contains certain poems and prose works which are 'objectionable' from a strictly moral standpoint. In the present number the central part of Alvaro de Campos' 'Marine Ode' (Ode Marítima) is in this case.
> The worst which the English number of the review would have is the poem of mine, written in English, called 'Antinous' of which I send you a copy herewith (to avoid lengthy and unsatisfactory explanations). Could a review be sold in England with a poem like this inserted? Fundamentally, it is really not as 'bad' as Shakespeare's sonnets, but no one ever sees things fundamentally. (*Corr I*, p. 190)

Notice how Pessoa here describes 'Antinous' and 'Ode Marítima', arguably his two most homoerotic poems, as immoral: 'bad', but 'not as "bad" as Shakespeare's *Sonnets*'.

Pessoa's pre-emptive defence against the charge of literary immorality, in this letter, by citing Shakespeare's example as a precedent, is reminiscent of Wilde's

---

[86] Brandes, *William Shakespeare*, p. 56.

strategy during his trials, when there was an unrelenting effort to associate him directly with the immoral practices described in his fiction. (The charge of literary immorality was by no means the major evidence against Wilde, but it dod not help his case. Queensberry's Plea of Justification contained the more serious charge that Wilde 'did solicit and incite' a dozen of named individuals and 'boys unknown' to commit 'sodomy and other acts of gross indecency and immorality'. His lawyers had dates, places, and nine different names.) In court, Wilde evoked Shakespeare time and time again as a model for his own homoeroticism; when Carson, the lawyer for the prosecution, read out passages from *The Picture of Dorian Gray* as incriminating evidence of its author's sexuality, asking whether Wilde shared in one of its characters' claims that he 'adored [Dorian] madly', Wilde replied: 'No. The whole idea was borrowed from Shakespeare, I regret to say – yes, from Shakespeare's Sonnets.'

Wilde proceeded in a similar manner in his second trail, when cross-examined by his defence lawyer Gill, in an impassioned speech defending 'The Love that dare not speak its name', the phrase Alfred Douglas had famously coined in his sonnet 'Two Loves' (1892):

Gill: What is the 'Love that dare not speak its name?'
Wilde: 'The Love that dare not speak its name' in this century is such a great affection of an elder for a younger man as there was between David and Jonathan, such as Plato made the very basis of his philosophy, and such as you find in the Sonnets of Michelangelo and Shakespeare.[87]

Even in Shakespeare's day, Richard Barnfield had felt compelled to cite an antecedent for the homoeroticism of his collection *The Affectionate Shepherd* (1594). He had done so by explaining that the poems were 'nothing else but an imitation of Virgil, in the second Eclogue of Alexis', in which a shepherd, Corydon, 'burned with love for his master's favourite,/Handsome Alexis'. [88] Barnfield's disclaimer appeared in *Cynthia* (1595), the only other Renaissance sequence apart from Shakespeare's to include poems directed at a male addressee.[89]

For Pessoa, immorality in art is to be admitted, on the evidence of his poetic appropriations of Shakespeare's example. Not only admitted but positively admired, as the following short, typewritten note about Shakespeare's 'sinful' art, with its gleeful undertone, suggests:

---

[87] *Nineteenth-Century Writings on Homosexuality: A Sourcebook*, ed. Chris White (London: Routledge, 1999) p. 57.)

[88] Cited in Simon Shepherd, 'Shakespeare's Private Drawer: Shakespeare and Homosexuality', in *The Shakespeare Myth*, ed. Graham Holderness (Manchester: Manchester University Press, 1988), p. 97.

[89] Richard Barnfield, *Cynthia, with Certaine Sonnets, and the Legend of Cassandra* (London: Humphrey Lownes, 1595).

Shakespeare and Victor Hugo are the master-sinners. Shakespeare, to speak true, is the worst. He misbehaves himself in the space of a short lyric to a quite French extent.

He is unable to keep still, like a naughty child, which, after all, was what he was among the gods.[90]

Immorality in life, however, is to be condemned, as he clearly states in a recently published text:

A falta de sinceridade do artista de modo algum se deve reflectir na sua vida, que deve obedecer á moral, e ás leis, honesta e burguezamente. Só na literatura é que a immoralidade é permittida, a contradicção sem importancia, e a insinceridade obrigatoria.[91]

[An artist's lack of sincerity should in no way manifest itself in his real life, which should be governed by morality and laws, honestly and pedestrianly. Only in literature is immorality permitted, contradiction of no importance, and insincerity mandatory.]

This is, of course, one more argument for artistic impersonality, a stance which has the advantage of placing an impersonal artist's sexuality, like everything else about his life and behaviour, beyond the realm of critical enquiry.

In one of Pessoa's most anxious attempts to separate his own literary homoeroticism from his real-life sexuality, he admits to the feeling of sexual inversion, but stresses that it does not translate into actual behaviour:

quando digo que sempre gostei de ser amado, e nunca de amar, tenho dicto tudo [...] Agradava-me a passividade. [...] Reconheço sem illusão a natureza do phenomeno. É uma inversão sexual fruste. Pára no espírito. Sempre, porém, nos momentos de meditação sobre mim, me inquietou, não tive nunca a certeza, nem a tenho ainda, de que essa disposição do temperamento não pudesse um dia descer-me ao corpo. Não digo que praticasse então a sexualidade correspondente a esse impulso, mas bastava o desejo para me humilhar. Somos vários d'esta especie pela historia abaixo, pela historia artistica sobretudo. Shakespeare e Rousseau são dos exemplos, ou exemplares, mais illustres. E o meu receio da descida ao corpo d'essa inversão do espírito – radica-m'o a contemplação de como nesses dois desceu – completamente no primeiro, e em pederastia; incertamente no segundo, num vago masochismo.[92]

[when I say I always enjoyed being loved, and never enjoyed loving, I say it

---

[90] *Apreciações Literárias de Fernando Pessoa,* ed. Pauly Ellen Bothe, p. 252. First transcribed and presented in my doctoral thesis *Fernando Pessoa's Shakespeare.*
[91] *Sensacionismo*, p. 286.
[92] Cited in Pizarro, *Entre génio e loucura*, p. 154.

all [...] Passivity pleased me. [...] I recognise the nature of this phenomenon with no illusion. It is a frustrated sexual inversion. It stops in the spirit. However, whenever I reflected upon myself, it bothered me, I was never certain, nor am I certain now, that this disposition of temperament might not one day descend to my body. I don't say I then practised the sexuality corresponding to this impulse, but the desire was enough to humiliate me. We are many of this nature throughout history, especially the history of art. Shakespeare and Rousseau are two of the most famous examples, or exemplars. And my fear of this spiritual inversion descending to my body – the contemplation of how in those two men it did so grounds me – completely, in the case of the first, in pederasty; uncertainly in the case of the second, in a vague masochism.]

Pessoa's words typify the fear of the innate predisposition *fin-de-siècle* sexologists wrote of, some physiological impulse in the brain which might be triggered by external phenomena. Notice how Pessoa does not here imply that he himself is homosexual, like his Shakespeare, but does admit to the feeling of inversion. Kenneth Dover, in *Greek Homosexuality* (1978), posits that there is no sense in the sources available that there was anything wrong for the Greeks in an older man being attracted to a beautiful youth, nothing wrong that is in feeling an explicitly sexual attraction. What was wrong, in the view of Socrates, was the yielding to the feeling.[93] Pessoa appears to subscribe to this notion.

Pessoa's insistence on the difference between 'immorality' in art and in life assumes greater urgency following his encounter with psychoanalysis, which led him to distance himself from his homoerotic writings more forcefully.

Impersonality, Pre-Emptive Strikes, and Decreasing Homoeroticism

A large part of Wilde's defence was based on the argument that literary texts are impersonal rather than a reflection of their authors' personalities. This was true, Wilde argued, even in the case of his seemingly incriminating 'Hyacinth' letter to Alfred Douglas ('Bosie'). When asked whether such sentiments were appropriate, Wilde retorted that the letter was a prose poem, akin to a sonnet of Shakespeare's: 'I think it was a beautiful letter. If you ask me whether it is proper, you might as well ask me whether *King Lear* is proper, or a sonnet of Shakespeare is proper.'[94] He took the precaution of having Pierre Louys prepare a sonnet version of the letter in French, for publication in an Oxford magazine. The result was published in *The Spirit Lamp* (4 March 1883), with an allusion to Wilde's latest play, as: 'Sonnet. A letter written in prose poetry by M. Oscar Wilde to a friend, and translated into rhymed poetry by a poet of no importance.'

As an expression of his feelings for Douglas the letter was lethal, but nobody

---

[93] Kenneth Dover, *Greek Homosexuality* (Cambridge, M.A.: Harvard University Press, 1978).

[94] Cited in Merlin Holland, *Irish Peacock & Scarlet Marquess: The Real Trial of Oscar Wilde* (London/New York: Fourth Estate, 2004), p. 105

had ever been blackmailed over a poem, especially a published poem. As a work of literature, the sentiments in the letter would not, Wilde hoped, be subject to the moral laws that govern everyday life. Following his encounter with Freud's new science, Pessoa would similarly point out, in increasingly anxious letters and critical texts, that Campos and the other heteronyms were completely impersonal; as such, their poetic sentiments were not to be confused with his own, as he assured Gaspar Simões:

> Não há que buscar em quaisquer [dos heterónimos] ideias ou sentimentos meus, pois muitos deles exprimem ideias que não aceito, sentimentos que nunca tive. Há simplesmente que os ler como estão, que é aliás como se deve ler. (*AdC*, p. 131)

> [One must not search for my ideas or feelings in any of the heteronyms, for many of them express ideas I do not hold, emotions I never had. One must merely read them as they stand, which is in any case how one ought always to read.]

It is not incidental that one of Pessoa's most famous explanations of his heteronymic project, the one recalling its generic classification as dramatic poetry and its foundation in his 'madness', hystero-neurasthenia, should appear in his letter of 11 December 1931 about psychoanalysis (*Corr II*, pp. 235-255). Pessoa's insistence on his artistic impersonality was not, of course, merely the result of his encounter with Freudian readings; it is likely that he would have agreed with Carl Jung that Freud's method of interpretation, as Gaspar Simões had begun to employ it, rested upon '"reductive" explanations which unfailingly lead backward and downward, and it has a destructive effect if it is used in an exaggerated and one-sided way.'[95] Furthermore, the facetious tone of Campos's prose piece 'outing' Ricardo Reis, based upon a single letter in one of his odes, suggests that Pessoa is there ironizing the reductive tendency of psychoanalytic criticism.

However, it is significant that the distance Pessoa's Modernist ideal of art as impersonal forges between an author and his poetry should be convenient on a personal level, placing beyond the realm of critical inquiry sentiments that might otherwise be interpreted as real-life beliefs. Maud Ellmann makes a convincing case that impersonality emerged as a doctrine when it did, in part, because it served to 'screen the poet from the prying forms of criticism which accompanied the rise of popular psychology'; if any 'indiscretions crept into their verse they could always disown them as "impersonal"'. She cites Eliot's confession to John Hayward that he had 'personal reasons' for asserting his impersonality, which she takes to mean that 'he was able to confess more freely if he disavowed these confessions as his own.'[96] In the same way, Pessoa is able to express himself more

---

[95] Carl Gustave Jung, *Modern Man in Search of a Soul* (1933), trans. W. S. Dell and Cary F. Baynes (London: Routledge, 2001), p. 49.
[96] Maud Ellmann, *The Poetics of Impersonality: T. S. Eliot and Ezra Pound* (Sussex:

freely by attributing the vast majority of his homoerotic texts, like the majority of his neurotic ones, to the mad engineer. One Campos poem contains the revealing lines: 'Graças a Deus que estou doido!/Isto é uma solução' [Thank goodness I am mad!/That is a solution] (*AdC*, p. 195).

Campos's text on Shakespeare's sexual inversion, as depicted in the *Sonnets*, is doubly impersonal, twice removed from Pessoa 'himself'. First, it is attributed to the fictional Campos, whom Pessoa everywhere describes as an impersonal dramatic character; as such, Campos is permitted certain liberties, which is why he can be less oblique than Pessoa in his defence of António Botto against charges of literary indecency.[97] Second, it is presented as a fictional dialogue, so we cannot even be confident that the nameless narrator of the controversial side of the argument is in fact Campos.

Wilde's plea for the Hyacinth letter's impersonality was not convincing in court. Carson proclaimed in his closing statement that 'a more thinly veiled attempt to cover the real nature of this letter and its history has never been attempted in a court of justice.'[98] At the end of the first trial, the Solicitor-General proclaimed:

> I contend that such a letter found in the possession of a woman from a man would be open to but one interpretation. How much worse is the inference to be drawn when such a letter is written from one man to another. It has been attempted to show that this was a prose poem, a sonnet, a lovely thing which I suppose we are too low to appreciate. Gentlemen, let us thank God, if it is so, that we do not appreciate things of this sort at their proper value, and that is somewhat lower than the beasts.[99]

Douglas himself, after he had turned against Wilde, described it as 'a rotten sodomitically inclined letter written by a diabolical scoundrel to a wretchedly silly youth.'[100] Pessoa's attempts to persuade Gaspar Simões that his work was impersonal also had little effect on the reception of his homoerotic writings. Following the example of Gaspar Simões, who was the first to suggest that Pessoa's 'poesias, por mais "mentirosas" que sejam [...] nunca o são tão completamente que se lhe não possa descobrir o ponto tangente com a experiência real de que partiram' [poems, however insincere they may be [...] are never so insincere that one cannot discover the point that intersects with the real-life experience that generated them], subsequent critics have jumped on the Freudian bandwagon,

---

Harvester Press, 1987), p. 5.

[97] See Castro, 'Oscar Wilde, Fernando Pessoa, and the Art of Lying', *Portuguese Studies* 22, pp. 240-241.

[98] *Irish Peacock & Scarlet Marquess*, p. 262.

[99] Cited in H. Montgomery Hyde, *The Trials of Oscar Wilde* (London: William Hodge, 1949), p. 326.

[100] Cited in Douglas Murray, *Bosie: A Biography of Lord Alfred Douglas* (London: Hodder and Stoughton, 2000), p. 226.

putting Pessoa on the couch and ploughing his poems for their creator's real-life psyche: Blanco's bibliography lists fifty-five different psychoanalytic studies of Pessoa up to 2004. [101] Despite Pessoa's best efforts and deflecting tactics, or perhaps because of them, the critical urge to approach his writings from a psychoanalytical perspective has often proved irresistible.

Pessoa's encounter with psychoanalysis led him to do two further things which are of interest in the context of his reading of Shakespeare's sexuality. First, it prompted him to offer Gaspar Simões a pre-emptive Freudian explanation for 'Antinous' and 'Epithalamium' as artistic sublimations of libido, designed to dissuade the biographer from performing his own:

> Uma explicação. "Antinous" e "Epithalamium" são os únicos poemas (ou, até composições) que eu tenho escrito que são nitidamente o que se pode chamar obscenos. Há em cada um de nós, por pouco que se especialize instintivamente na obscenidade, um certo elemento desta ordem, cuja quantidade, evidentemente, varia de homem para homem. Como esses elementos, por pequeno que seja o grau em que existem, são um certo estorvo para alguns processos mentais superiores, decidi, por duas vezes, eliminá-los pelo processo simples de os exprimir intensamente. [102]

> [An explanation. 'Antinous' and 'Epithalamium' are the only two poems (or, even, compositions) I ever wrote which are clearly what one might call obscene. There exists in each one of us, even in those who do not instinctively specialise in the obscene, a certain element of that nature, whose quantity, of course, will vary from man to man. Since these elements, however weak they may be, are surely a hindrance to some superior mental processes, I decided, on two occasions, to eliminate them via the simple process of expressing them intensely.]

Lucy Newlyn, in *The Anxiety of Reception* (2000), argues that

> anxieties experienced by writers centre as much on the future as on the past – not just because an author's status, authority, and posthumous life are dependent on readers, but because writing exists in dialogue with others whose sympathies it hopes to engage. Readers are as important to writers as their precursors, when it comes to constructing or defending literary identity; and whether they are named, invoked, figured, or idealised, their presence is just as discernible within a given text as are the traces of earlier writings. [103]

Pessoa's aim, in his later dismissive attitude towards both poems, is to convince his readers that, being sublimations of less orthodox inclinations, these

---

[101] Blanco, *Pessoana*, II, p. 78.

[102] Letter to Gaspar Simões, 18 November 1930, in *Corr II*, pp. 219-220.

[103] Lucy Newlyn, 'Preface', in *Reading, Writing, and Romanticism: The Anxiety of Reception* (Oxford: Oxford University Press, 2000), p. vii.

inclinations did not become manifest in any other way. This is consistent with his separation of 'immorality' in life and in art. Sena argues that it is also significant that Pessoa chose to publish the two poems in Portugal, where, being in English, they were likely to attract little public attention, describing them as 'poemas que de facto seria difícil pensar-se que fossem impressos e publicados na Inglaterra, podendo sê-lo em Portugal aonde praticamente ninguém sabia então inglês para avaliar da indecência' [Poems difficult to image could be printed and published in England, although they could be in Portugal, where practically no one spoke English then to evaluate their indecency.] [104] Despite his disclaimer to Gaspar Simões, however, Pessoa was hardly embarrassed by the poems: he kept newspaper cuttings mentioning 'Antinous' from such diverse publications as the *Yorkshire Post* and the *Finance Chronicle*, and even sent copies of *English Poems* to the Advocates' Library in Edinburgh, the University Library in Cambridge and, most ambitiously of all, to the British Museum in London. [105] As we have seen, he also offered the poems to British publishers.

Although Gaspar Simões had accepted Pessoa's explanation of his madness, he was not convinced by his self-explanation as an artist who had, twice, sublimated his repressed desires into poetry. The biographer disregarded Pessoa's explanation for his homoerotic poems in full, writing chapters in *Vida e obra* [*Life and Work*] (1950) with such titles as 'Sexualidade frustrada' [Frustrated Sexuality], 'Aberração e ideal estético' [Aberration and Aesthetic Ideal] and 'Polémica em Sodoma' [Trouble in Sodom]. In the first of these, Gaspar Simões suggests that 'a bela, serena e lacrimosa dor de Adriano perante o cadáver de Antinous [...] funcionará como elemento compensador' [Hadrian's beautiful, peaceful and teary pain before Antinous's dead body [...] functions as a compensation] for Pessoa's repressed homosexuality. [106]

The second effect of Pessoa's encounter with psychoanalysis is that it led him to be less homoerotic in his writings from then on, for it is a salient but unsignalled fact that Campos's poetry becomes less unequivocally 'immoral' from the late 1920s onwards. By 1929, Campos alludes to homosexuality only obliquely, rather than directly as in his early poems, by evoking a seminal work that was much read and discussed in Pessoa's day:

Quero escrever o meu epitáfio: Álvaro de Campos jaz
Aqui, o resto a Antologia grega traz... (*AdC*, p. 389).

[I want to write my epitaph: Álvaro de Campos lies
Here, the rest is in the Greek Anthology...]
'(Escuso de me achar feio, porque os feios também são amados/E às vezes por mulheres!)' [It is useless to consider myself ugly, for the ugly are also loved/And

---

[104] *Poemas ingleses de Fernando Pessoa* [*Fernando Pessoa's English Poems*] (Lisbon: Ática, 1974), pp. 27-28.
[105] See *Fernando Pessoa: Imagens de uma vida*, pp. 90-98.
[106] Gaspar Simões, *Vida e obra*, p. 518.

sometimes even by women!] Campos declares in a poem of 1930 (*AdC*, p. 410). In another of the same year he writes:

> Com que então problema sexual?
> Mas isso depois dos quinze anos é uma indecência.
> Preocupação com o sexo oposto (suponhamos) e a sua psicologia –
> Mas isso é estúpido, filho.
> O sexo oposto existe para ser procurado e não para ser compreendido.
> O problema existe para estar resolvido e não para preocupar.
> Compreender é ser impotente.
> E você devia revelar-se menos. (*AdC*, p. 419)

> [A sexual problem, you say?
> But after fifteen years of age that is indecent.
> A concern with the opposite sex (let us suppose) and its psychology –
> But that is stupid, my boy.
> The opposite sex exists to be yearned for, not understood.
> The problem exists to be resolved, not to create concern.
> To understand is to be impotent.
> And you should reveal yourself less.]

These two poems are more ambiguous than Pessoa's pre-Freudian utterances, for there is at least the possibility, however unconvincing, that their love object be female ('amados/E às vezes por mulheres!'; 'Preocupação com o sexo oposto (suponhamos)'. Pessoa clearly came to feel that he had to exert more caution in the face of Freud's new science, even in the case of his impersonal heteronymic poetry. In another late poem, Campos tellingly pleads for the freedom to exist without being submitted to psychological interpretations:

> A liberdade, sim, a liberdade!
> A verdadeira liberdade!
> [...] Existir sem Freud nem aeroplanos (*PC II*, p. 310).

> [Freedom, yes, freedom!
> True freedom!
> [...] To exist without Freud or aeroplanes.]

Beyond attenuating Campos's poetic expressions of 'perverse' sexuality following his encounter with psychoanalysis, Pessoa offered the following note for the second edition of 'Antinous': 'An early and very imperfect draft of Antinous was published in 1918. The present one is meant to annul and supersede that, from which it is essentially different.'[107] The essential difference is that the second version is less explicit in its homoeroticism.

---

[107] Cited in Zenith, 'Preface', in *Obra Essencial de Fernando Pessoa: Poesia Inglesa*, p. 31.

Sexuality and the Heteronymic Project

As in the case of Shakespeare, Pessoa's sexuality, like his possible 'madness', will remain an open question unless new evidence is unearthed to settle the matter. It is tempting to read Pessoa's marginalia next to the conclusion of one of Hamlet's speeches, the one to Rosencrantz and Guildenstern that begins, 'I have of late – but wherefore I know not – lost all my mirth', as revealing of his lack of interest in sex, for in it the only phrase Pessoa underlined was Hamlet's proclamation: 'man delights not me; no, nor woman neither' (*CW*, p. 955). This could be over-reading, however, for countless readers have been drawn to the same line – Stephen cites it his lecture on Shakespeare – and Hamlet's friends' laughter in response suggests they do not believe him to be immune to the charms of the opposite sex.

The only thing we can know is that Pessoa was able to identify, mentally, with the feelings and themes he discovered in Shakespeare's *Sonnets*, and that he made good artistic use of them in his own homoerotic poetry, particularly that of Campos.

Pessoa's acceptance of homosexuality in art is part of his desire to achieve full self-expression. As Zenith argues in a recent essay on Pessoa and Wilde:

> É natural que Pessoa, desejoso de sentir, experimentar e ser tudo de todas as maneiras possíveis – e isto é verdade mesmo sem Álvaro de Campos, a personificação mais estridente do Sensacionismo que Pessoa reivindicava para toda a família gerada pela sua imaginação – , se quisesse multiplicar também sexualmente.[108]

> [It is only natural that Pessoa, wishing to feel, experience and be everything in every possible way – and this is true even beyond Álvaro de Campos, the most strident personification of the Sensationism Pessoa ascribed to the whole family born of his imagination – wished to multiply himself sexually too.]

The *Orpheu* generation defended the right to explore literary sexuality, like literary madness, in all of its possible manifestations. José de Almada Negreiros begins his poem 'A Cena do Ódio' [The Hatred Scene] (1915) with the words

> Ergo-Me Pederasta apupado d'imbecis,
> divinizo-Me Meretriz, ex-libris do Pecado

> [I raise myself as a Pederast booed by imbeciles
> I make myself a Divine Whore, ex-libris of Sin]

and goes on to proclaim, in the second stanza, the need to 'cantar Sodoma na Voz de Nero!' [sing Sodom in the voice of Nero!] The poem's dedication reads: 'A Álvaro de Campos / a dedicação intensa / de todos os meus avatares' [To Álvaro de

---

[108] Zenith, 'A Importância de não ser Oscar? Pessoa tradutor de Wilde' [The Importance of Not Being Oscar? Pessoa as Wilde's Translator], in *Egoista* [*Egoist*] (2008) 32-36, p. 35.

Campos / The intense dedication / of all my avatars.][109] (The poem was intended for the third issue of *Orpheu*, which never materialized; instead, it was first published in *Contemporânea* in 1923.)

As Cixous defends, 'There have always been those uncertain, poetic persons who have not let themselves be reduced to dummies programmed by pitiless repression of the homosexual element.' She goes on to claim that there can be no invention of the self, in fiction, without a certain bisexuality.[110] There can be no invention of *other* selves without a certain bisexuality, Pessoa might say, in the same way that there can be no invention of other selves without a certain madness, a certain *Bovarysme* (see Chapter 3). In one piece, he says so explicitly, by making the link between sexual inversion and the making of dramatic poetry:

> Na personalidade tudo se liga, se interrelaciona. Não podemos "separar", salvo por um processo analítico conscientemente truncador da realidade, na personalidade de [...] Shakespeare a intuição dramática de, por ex., a inversão sexual. (*PETCL*, p. 113)

> [In a personality everything is connected, related. We cannot 'separate', except via an analytic process that consciously truncates reality, Shakespeare's dramatic intuition from, for example, his sexual inversion.]

This association between dramatic intuition and sexual inversion is misleading, for we have seen that Pessoa deduces Shakespeare's sexuality exclusively from his lyric poetry, the *Sonnets*. Lyric poetry is traditionally perceived to be more personal, confessional, and autobiographical than dramatic poetry, which partly explains (together with a fear of Freud) the contradiction between Pessoa's insistence on the impersonal nature of his own homoerotic writings, and his biographical approach to those of Shakespeare.

'Antinous' is also arguably more 'dramatic' than Shakespeare's *Sonnets* because it is written in the third person, and in English. Robert Bréchon argues that Shakespeare's native language was, for Pessoa, a dramatic mask; if so, writing 'Antinous' in English has the effect of forging a similar dramatic distance between Pessoa and the sentiments described in the poem as that created by Pessoa's attribution of his most homoerotic utterances to the heteronym Campos.[111] The heteronyms are conscious truncations of reality, to echo Pessoa's chosen phrasing, because they are impersonal dramatic others, as Pessoa claims to be true of Shakespeare's characters.

Since Pessoa's readings of Shakespeare's genius, invisibility, madness and

---

[109] Almada Negreiros, 'A Cena do ódio', in *Poemas*, p. 23.

[110] Cixous, 'Sorties', in *Literary Theory: An Anthology*, pp. 351-352.

[111] Robert Bréchon, 'Le masque et l'aveu: l'oeuvre anglaise' [Masks and Confessions: The English Works], *Magazine littéraire* 291 (September 1991); repr. in *L'Innombrable: un tombeau pour Fernando Pessoa* [*The Unnameable: A Tomb for Fernando Pessoa*] (Paris: Christian Bourgois, 2001), pp. 177-185.

sexuality all ultimately draw us to his central approximation between the heteronyms and the Bard's dramatic characters, it is worth exploring in greater depth.

SHAKESPEARE AND THE INVENTION OF THE HETERONYMS

A Little More Than Kin, and Less than Kind: The Kinship Fallacy

Pessoa's readings of Shakespeare, as charted in the previous chapters, establish the Bard as the pervasive underlying presence to his heteronymic project. The analogy this sets up between Pessoa's heteronyms and Shakespeare's characters is seductive, and it was eagerly taken up in Pessoan criticism. Vitorino Nemésio, writing in 1945, describes how Pessoa legitimised his invention of character-authors by comparing them, in all sincerity, to Shakespeare's characters.[1] Jacinto do Prado Coelho, in an article for the *Jornal de Letras* in 1981, argues that Pessoa struggled to discipline and construct himself by placing at the pinnacle of art dramatic poetry, with Shakespeare as its supreme representative.[2] (Prado Coelho claims, quite rightly, that this is an anti-Romantic vision of poetry, but we saw in Chapter 1 that Pessoa's alignment with Romantic readings of Shakespeare was instrumental in its formation.) Alexandrino Severino, in an article of 1990 exploring Shakespeare's presence in Pessoa's work, also focuses on his explanation of the heteronyms as dramatic personalities akin to Shakespeare's characters.[3]

Even independently of Pessoa's view on the matter, Pessoans have approximated the two sets of dramatic characters. João Medina, in 'Hamlet morou defronte da Tabacaria' [Hamlet Lived Facing the Tobacco Shop] (1976), writes that Campos's poem can be thought of as a

> drama estático escrito e sobretudo encarnado por um Hamlet ocultista despejado de todos os seus emblemas e atributos reais, pobre Hamlet lusíada, duplamente desgraçado e desterrado, como português e como discípulo da gnose, escondido numa mansarda a ver as figuras do mundo real que se movem defronte dele, na outra margem ôntica, na Tabacaria.[4]

> [static drama, written and above all embodied by an occultist Hamlet, rid of all his medals and royal attributes, a poor lusiad Hamlet, doubly disgraced and homeless, being Portuguese and a gnostic, hidden in the mansard watching the figures of the real world who move before him, on the other ontic margin, in the Tobacco Shop.]

Notwithstanding the great similarities charted, in the previous chapters, between Pessoa's dramatic art and Shakespeare's artistic genius, it is worth

---

[1] Vitorino Nemésio, 'O sincero fingido', *Diário Popular* (26 December 1945), p. 3.

[2] Jacinto do Prado Coelho, 'Fernando Pessoa ou A estratégia da razão', *Jornal de Letras* (17 March 1981); repr. in *Camões e Pessoa, Poetas da utopia*, pp. 114-118.

[3] Alexandrino E. Severino, 'Fernando Pessoa e William Shakespeare: um estudo comparativo da heteronímia', in *Actas IV*, pp. 13-22.

[4] João Medina, 'Hamlet morou defronte da Tabacaria', *Diário de Notícias* (1 August 1974), p. 7.

pausing to question the validity of the analogy Pessoa himself was the first to propose, especially when it leads to such lyrical flights of fancy. Hamlet and Campos are their creators' most developed dramatic characters, a fact reflected by the emphasis placed on both throughout this book, with interior lives so profound they continue to fascinate. Campos's poetic outlook, for instance in its neurosis, is indebted to Hamlet's (see Chapter 3), and Pessoa responds to Hamlet's most famous soliloquy, 'To be, or not to be', in Campos's poem 'Se te queres matar, porque não te queres matar?' (Chapter 1). To stretch the parallel further, however, is arguably more revealing of our own perceived affinities with either character than of any inherent similarities between the two: most readers uphold Campos as their favourite heteronym, and everyone wants to be a backyard Hamlet. On inspection, there are significant differences between Pessoa's heteronyms and Shakespeare's characters, notwithstanding his continual alignment of the two, the cumulative effect of which is to forge a greater approximation than in reality exists.

Álvaro de Campos is not, as Pessoa claims, a character in a play, precisely because, as he concedes, there is no play. To transpose a physical stage to the purely mental plane of Pessoa's 'drama em gente' [drama in people] is a brilliant imaginative leap, but it breaks down the literalness of the correlation. What distinguishes the heteronyms from Shakespeare's dramatic characters is that they are all writers. Approaching the problem from the opposite angle, if Shakespeare's characters were like Pessoa's heteronyms, they would not feature in plays but author their own bodies of writing. Take Hamlet, for example. We come to an understanding of Hamlet's psychological makeup through his words and actions, or inactions, during the course of the play in which he features. Now imagine that Hamlet, with the psychological characteristics we associate with him because of the play, never in fact appeared in a play. Suppose that, instead, he wrote a book or, better yet, a series of poems and prose fragments with no narrative plot. The supposition is complex, because the only piece of literary writing Hamlet undertakes is his instrumental addition to *The Mousetrap*, but this is precisely the imaginative transposition Pessoa requires us to make if we are to accept his kinship argument wholesale. Alex McNeil, in his essay 'What's in a "Nym?" Pseudonyms, heteronyms and the remarkable case of Fernando Pessoa', is one of few readers to raise the point.

McNeil is not a Pessoa expert. The aim of his essay is to further the Oxfordian cause; its opening sentences read: 'If there's one thing Oxfordians can agree on, it's that Edward de Vere used an alias as a professional writer. His most famous alias, of course, was William Shakespeare.' He even declares, at one point, that 'If Pessoa was aware of the authorship problem, he did not address it', an opinion which even a cursory familiarity with Pessoa's archive would have corrected (see Chapter 2). [5] But McNeil luminously argues that, in order to appreciate the enormous eccentricity of Pessoa's heteronymic project, we must compare him not

---

[5] Alex McNeil, 'What's in a "Nym?" Pseudonyms, heteronyms and the remarkable case of Fernando Pessoa', *Shakespeare Matters* 6 (Winter 2003), 16-20, p. 19.

to the Shakespeare he so admires, but to a hypothetical Shakespeare who, beyond having created the character of Hamlet, spent a lifetime composing a huge body of work under Hamlet's authorship. This is not, of course, what Shakespeare did. It is what anti-Stratfordians like McNeil claim a concealed author did.

Eduardo Lourenço argues that the corollary defining characteristic of the heteronyms is that, further to being poets, they are created by their poems:

> os autores fictícios [não são] *criadores de poemas* [...] os poemas são os *criadores dos autores fictícios*. Na exegese universal de Pessoa os poemas-Caeiro, Reis, Campos são *sombra* de seus fictícios pais quando só o inverso é evidente. Alberto Caeiro, Reis, Campos, mas igualmente Fernando Pessoa 'ele mesmo' são só (e que outra coisa poderiam ser?) *os seus poemas*[6]

> [the fictional authors are not *the creators of poems* [...] the poems are the *creators of the fictional authors*. In Pessoa's universal exegis, the Caeiro-poems, Reis-poems, Campos-poems are *shadows* of their fictional parents, when only the inverse is true. Alberto Caeiro, Reis, Campos, but equally Fernando Pessoa 'himself' are merely (and what more could they be?) *their poems*]

Pessoa has Soares recognise the fact in a memorable passage in *Desassossego*:

> Sou, em grande parte, a mesma prosa que escrevo. Desenrolo-me em períodos e parágrafos, faço-me pontuações, e, na distribuição desencadeada das imagens, visto-me, como as crianças, de rei com papel de jornal, ou no modo como faço ritmo de uma série de palavras, me touco, como os loucos, de flores secas que continuam vivas nos meus sonhos. (*LD*, p. 200)

> [I am, in large measure, the self-same prose I write. I unravel myself in full stops and paragraphs, I turn myself into punctuation and, in chains of images, I dress myself, as children do, like a king in newspaper, or in the way I make rhymes from a series of words, I put on my head, like a madman, dry flowers that go on living in my dreams.]

As Cleonice Berardinelli explains, the heteronyms are texts before they have biographies.[7] The 'personality' Pessoa crafts for each one is retrospective, being projected backwards from the work to the character:

> a *pessoa* de cada criador por ele criado é posterior à criação poética [...] A sua corporificação (se assim posso dizer) se faz nos versos que preexistem a eles como seres com biografia. Esta é feita *a posteriori*[8]

---

[6] Lourenço, *Pessoa revisitado*, p. 29. Original emphasis.
[7] Cleonice Berardinelli, *Fernando Pessoa: Outra vez te revejo... [Once More I See You]* (Rio de Janeiro: Nova Aguilar, 2004), p. 291.
[8] *Ibid.*, p. 264. Original emphasis.

[the *personality* of each creator created by Pessoa comes after poetic creation [...] Their embodiment (so to speak) takes place in the verses which exist before them as beings with biographies. These biographies are crafted *a posteriori*]

Hamlet, in contrast, exists before the play in which he appears, for Shakespeare lifted him from the lost *Ur-Hamlet*. One might retort that Shakespeare's Hamlet, whatever his source, is an individual, independent artistic creation. Even so he exists, conceptually, before his famous opening line, appearing in the list of 'Characters in the Play' before its action begins, and he is on stage for several minutes before he proclaims his first aside. Far from being created by his speeches, Hamlet exists before he utters a word.

Being products of their writings, the heteronyms are characterised by a specific mode of expression as well as by a thematic core and philosophical outlook. Each has an utterly differentiated style. This is true to some extent of Shakespeare's characters, but their speeches vary more in terms of content than technique. There are exceptions, as when Hamlet in his assumed madness turns to the prose more typical of the minor or comic characters in the plays, but as a rule the great speeches of Shakespeare's tragic heroes are presented in iambic pentameter, and in a sophisticated mode of expression. Pessoa writes in one piece that the only thing to approximate a speech of Hamlet's to one of Lear's, Falstaff's, or Lady Macbeth's is 'a subtileza e a complexidade do dizer' [the subtlety and complexity of expression] (*PETCL*, p. 67), but it is precisely the subtlety and complexity of these speeches that makes them immediately recognisable as 'Shakespearean', rather than specific to the character in question.

In everywhere approximating his heteronyms to Shakespeare's characters, Pessoa has blinded many readers to the essential differences between the two. Furthermore, in viewing Shakespeare's art in light of his own, he ingeniously fashions a retrospective projection of affinity, an inversion of the standard direction along which kinship travels.

George Monteiro, in 'Shakespeare, the "Missing All"' (2008), does the same when he argues that Shakespeare's characters should be approached as autonomous poets in the style of Pessoa's heteronyms. Monteiro asserts that 'It is customary to attribute that poetry [Hamlet's speeches] to Shakespeare and not to Hamlet, but our sense of Shakespeare's depersonalization (his disappearing into his characters) is imperfect when we fail to attribute the spoken poetry to those characters that speak it.' His main argument, in this essay, is that Shakespeare's characters should be approached as if they were Pessoan heteronyms:

In the poetry of Alberto Caeiro, for instance, we have poetry presented without dramatic context; it grows out of him and contributes to no play or stage other than that of the life Pessoa has detailed for him. The same thing could be done for Shakespeare's characters: look in the usual dictionaries of quotations (even when such poems are attributed to Shakespeare and not to the characters who speak them, to that extent misleading us, as I see it) and consider them as uncluttered, freestanding poems.[9]

It is debatable whether Caeiro's poetry is indeed presented without dramatic context, for the fictional biography Monteiro refers to arguably provides him with one. And anthologies of the type Monteiro calls for, although rare, do exist: Ted Hughes published in 1971 his *Choice of Shakespeare's Verse*, in which he presents the speeches of Shakespeare's characters outside their immediate dramatic contexts and organised thematically. Hughes's aim, in breaking into 'the sacred precincts of [Shakespeare's] drama' to loot 'portable chunks', is to inaugurate a new way of appreciating Shakespeare, by having us read the speeches of his dramatic characters as if they were lyric poems. Hughes does not, however, argue that the speeches exist, or should exist, independently of dramatic character and context, and his efforts did not lead to a radical reappraisal of the way we approach Shakespeare.[10]

Monteiro's conclusion that Shakespeare's dramatic characters are akin to Pessoa's heteronyms if we approach the former in light of the latter is, by definition, true, and therefore irrefutable. It is legitimised by Pessoa's treatment of Shakespeare, but while it may shed valuable light on Shakespeare's art, it is questionable whether it tells us anything new about Pessoa's. It is, I propose, a 'kinship fallacy', and it was one first perpetrated by Pessoa himself.

Harold Bloom possibly performs a similar inversion to Pessoa's and Monteiro's when he recurrently describes Shakespeare's art, in *Shakespeare: The Invention of the Human*, as being a theatre of the mind. It is not: although Shakespeare's characters have an unprecedented psychological depth, they were all conceived for the theatre, with a physical stage to act upon. It is at least conceivable that Bloom's thinking on Pessoa coloured his turn of phrase when he came to describe Shakespeare's art. The concept of dramatic poetry constituting a 'theatre of the mind' is not, of course, exclusively applicable to Pessoa; the metaphor dates back to Plato and has been employed since, as in Eliot's description of Dante's poetry. But it is not one commonly applied, or commonly viewed as applicable, to Shakespeare.

Retrospective projections of influence are endemic in Shakespeare studies, because Shakespeare anticipates the major concerns of so many later writers and because so many are overwhelmingly influenced by him. Terry Eagleton jocularly declares: 'though conclusive evidence is hard to come by, it is difficult to read Shakespeare without feeling that he was almost certainly familiar with the writings of Hegel, Marx, Nietzsche, Freud, Wittgenstein and Derrida.' [11] The running joke in David Lodge's novel *Small World* (1984) is that a serious-minded scholar is working on a doctoral thesis about Eliot's influence on Shakespeare,

---

[9] Monteiro, 'Shakespeare, the "Missing All"', *Portuguese Studies* 24:2 (2008), p. 49.
[10] Ted Hughes, 'Introduction', in *A Choice of Shakespeare's Verse*, ed. Ted Hughes (1971; London: Faber and Faber, 1991), p. 1.
[11] Terry Eagleton, *William Shakespeare* (Oxford: Oxford University Press, 1986), pp. ix-x.

rather than the other way around.[12]

In short, while the speeches of Shakespeare's dramatic characters can profitably be read as if they were heteronymous poems – Hamlet's soliloquies, which appear at different points in the two Quartos and the Folio versions, seem particularly moveable and detachable – the fact remains that Shakespeare never conceived of them as freestanding poems, that his Hamlets and Lears are not literary writers, much less created by their words, and that they were conceived for the stage rather than for the page. In pointing to these significant departures, McNeil hits upon an important distinction. In his efforts to emphasise the uniqueness of Pessoa's achievement, however, he goes too far in denying precedents.

Modernist Masks: 'Between the true artists of any time there is, I believe, an unconscious community.'[13]

Consciously, in the case of direct influence, or unconsciously, in the case of sharing similar influences, like Wilde's separation of life and art, Pessoa's heteronyms display striking affinities with the other Modernist masks of the period.

Long before the Modernist era, writers and philosophers had experimented with pseudonyms and literary alter-egos – these are widespread in nineteenth-century fiction, and Søren Kierkegaard, in his philosophy questioning the nature of the self, attributes different writings to different putative authors. The idea that there is usually some measure of dramatic distance between authors and their characters is timeless: Leo Spitzer maintains that in the Middle Ages there was already a widely accepted distinction between what he calls the 'poetic I' and the 'empirical I'.[14] Readers of *The Divine Comedy* would have understood that Dante's poetic self was meant to represent the human soul in general, rather than believing that the man himself had journeyed through Hell and Purgatory to Paradise. One of the first modern novels in English, Laurence Sterne's *Tristram Shandy* (1759-1769) makes the dramatic distance between its author and its protagonist obvious.[15] But the Modernists took dramatic masks to another level.

Ezra Pound was one of the first, and one of the most extreme, upholders of the use of *personae*, his word of choice for the concept of poetic masks, and the title of his 1909 collection of poetry. His poems can be highly satirical, downright sarcastic, about their authors, real or imaginary. In *Hugh Selwyn Mauberley* (1920), two alter-egos analyse the first twelve years of the speaker's career and refer to him, in the third person, as a failed poet. One of these poets is 'E.P.', a younger version of Pound; the second is Hugh Mauberley, whose style is more obviously different to that of his author's. This reading is proposed by Hugh

---

[12] David Lodge, *Small World: An Academic Romance* (London: Penguin, 1984).

[13] Eliot, *Selected Prose*, ed. Frank Kermode, p. 68.

[14] Cited in Robert C. Elliot, *The Literary Persona* (Chicago: University of Chicago Press, 1982), p. 5.

[15] Other candidates for the first modern novel include Defoe's *Robinson Crusoe* (1719) and *Moll Flanders* (1722), and Samuel Richardson's *Pamela* (1740).

Kenner in *Ezra Pound* (1951); the chief alternative reading, supported by some of Pound's own remarks about the sequence, as well as textual evidence, would see the first section as 'Mauberley's', and thus employing his voice rather than the poet's. While this reading is persuasive as regards the first section, the voice of the first section of the poem seems to have no consistency with the individual described in the second part.

There is today no book by Pound in Pessoa's library, but he had a copy of the vorticist magazine *Blast* (1915) containing some of Pound's poems, and Pound's name features on a list Pessoa drew up of people he would like to meet.[16] A further point of contact between the two men is Robert Browning, a dramatic poet they both admired: Browning had published his own *Dramatic Personae* in 1855, a collection of dramatic monologues written in different poetic voices. Pessoa transposes to a psychological plane what was, for Browning, primarily an aesthetic concern.[17]

Jung employs the term *personae* to describe, as Helder Macedo explains, 'a forma como o indivíduo se adapta ao mundo ou a maneira que assume para lidar com o mundo [...]. Poderia dizer-se, com um pouco de exagero, que a "persona" é o que na realidade se não é mas que o próprio e os outros acham que se é' [the way an individual adapts to the world around him, or relates to it [...]. One might say, with only a little exaggeration, that a 'persona' is not who we are in in reality, but rather who we, and other people, believe ourselves to be.][18] Macedo applies the term to Pessoa's heteronyms to emphasise their dramatic nature. 'It is probably no mere historical accident', writes the sociologist Robert E. Park, 'that the word person, in its first meaning, is a mask. It is rather a recognition of the fact that everyone is always and everywhere, more or less consciously, playing a rôle. [...] It is in these rôles that we know each other; it is in these rôles that we know ourselves.'[19] Pessoa and his fellow Modernists put at the heart of their poetic visions the belief that one must constantly, like Eliot's Prufrock, prepare a face to meet the faces that you meet.[20]

Eliot's poetry is inherently dramatic, and it is of no small import that he turned his efforts, in later years, to the theatre. 'The Love Song of J. Alfred Prufrock' is a dramatic monologue, 'Portrait of a Lady' a dialogue, and one provisional section-

---

[16] *Escritos autobiográficos, automáticos e de reflexão pessoal*, p. 269.

[17] See Flor, 'Um contexto inglês para Fernando Pessoa' [An English Context for Fernando Pessoa], *Expresso* (12 June 1975). For more on Pessoa's affinities with Pound, see José Palla e Carmo, 'Uma Trindade: Ezra Pound, T. S. Eliot, Fernando Pessoa' [A Trinity], *Colóquio-Letras* 95 (1987), 26-39, and Castro, 'Pound, Ezra', in *Dicionário de Fernando Pessoa*, pp. 677-688.

[18] Helder Macedo, *Nós: Uma leitura de Cesário Verde* [*Us: A Reading of Cesário Verde*] (Lisbon: Editorial Presença, 1999), p. 24. For Jung on 'personae', see *The Archetypes and the Collective Unconscious*, in *Collected Works*, 13 vols. (London: Routledge, 1963), IX, pp. 22-26.

[19] Cited in Robert C. Elliot, *The Literary Persona* (Chicago: University of Chicago Press, 1982), p. 12.

[20] Eliot, 'The Love Song of J. Alfred Prufrock', in *Collected Poems*, p. 14.

heading for *The Waste Land* was 'He do the Police in Different Voices', a phrase taken from Dickens's *Our Mutual Friend* (1864-65), in a scene where the orphan Sloppy entertains his acquaintances with a dramatic reading of the crime news.[21] V. S. Pritchett describes Eliot as 'a company of actors inside one suit'.[22] Maud Ellmann writes that both Eliot and Pound 'spent their careers devising disappearing tricks and new varieties of scriptive self-occultation' [...] 'both efface themselves through masks, personae, and ventriloquy, and the polylogue within their texts impugns the self's domain.'[23] The effect of Eliot's generic bent is, like Pessoa's, to at least distort, and at most make invisible, any authoritative authorial voice. (Recall that Kenner entitled his biography of Eliot *The Invisible Poet*.) Eliot recognised this quality, referring to himself as a 'possum': possums anecdotally play dead, and are thus an appropriate symbol for the giving up of authorial responsibility.[24] There are no books by Eliot in Pessoa's library, and no reference to him has yet been unearthed in his archive, but the two poets insist upon impersonality in their theoretical writings in strikingly similar terms, and strive to achieve it in their poetry with the same urgency.[25]

Yeats is another dramatic poet of Pessoa's generation whose work hinges on the adoption of literary masks. In section II of 'The Tower' (1928), Yeats writes a poetic description of his theory of the mask that is equally applicable to Pessoa's heteronymic mode of creation:

And I myself created Hanrahan
And drove him drunk or sober through the dawn.[26]

As Bernard O'Donoghue first pointed out, Hanrahan can be thought of as a semi-heteronym, for he shares with Yeats major psychological characteristics.[27] A volume of Yeats's early poetry is extant in Pessoa's library, and the latter's archive contains, among numerous references to the Irishman, the draft of a letter to him which Pessoa probably never sent.[28]

---

[21] *The Waste Land: A Facsimile*, pp. 2-18.

[22] Cited in Peter Ackroyd, *T. S. Eliot: A Life* (1984; London: Penguin, 1993), p. 118.

[23] Maud Ellmann, *The Poetics of Impersonality*, pp. ix, 3.

[24] The nickname was Pound's invention, but Eliot appropriated it for *Old Possum's Book of Practical Cats* (1939). His god-daughter relates that he would also sign dedications to her 'O.P' (Documentary on Eliot, BBC 2, 6 June 2009).

[25] For more on Pessoa's affinities with Eliot, see Maria Vitalina Leal de Matos, *Introdução aos estudos literários* [*Introduction to Literary Studies*] (Lisbon: Verbo, 2001), pp. 8-12, and Castro, 'Eliot, T. S.', in *Dicionário de Fernando Pessoa*, pp. 233-234.

[26] Yeats, *Selected Poems*, ed. Timothy Webb (London: Penguin, 1991), p. 131.

[27] Bernard O'Donoghue, 'Fernando Pessoa and W. B. Yeats' (2006), *Portal Pessoa* (www.portalpessoa.net).

[28] For more on Pessoa's affinity with Yeats, see Patrícia Silva McNiell, *The Imperative of Style: A Comparative Study of Fernando Pessoa and W. B. Yeats* (doctoral dissertation, King's College London, 2009), and her articles 'The aesthetic of fragmentation and the use of *personae* in the poetry of Fernando Pessoa and W. B. Yeats', *Portuguese Studies* 19

Joyce's artistic evolution towards the God-like invisibility he considers, like Pessoa, to be the hallmark of literary genius, can be charted chronologically throughout his writings. As Stuart Gilbert asserts, and with Joyce's full authority, his career is a gradual but continual movement away from the constraints of autobiography towards a larger, more impersonal artistic 'freedom'. [29] These reveal a diminishing reliance on autobiographical fact and on the characters Joyce knew, and a movement away from the first-person narration towards a polyphony of competing dramatic voices. In *Ulysses*, we are not provided with a consistent authorial voice in the muddle of competing speakers; by *Finnegans Wake* (1936), the author has refined himself out of his handiwork entirely. Jung was one of many readers full of admiration for Joyce's uncanny ability to impersonally create dramatic others, like Molly Bloom: 'I suppose the devil's grandmother knows so much about the real psychology of a woman. I didn't.'[30]

Joyce's favourite protagonist, Stephen Dedalus, appears in several of Joyce's writings and is, like Bernardo Soares, a limited version of his creator. Joyce attributes several prose pieces and even personal letters to Stephen; one of his earliest stories, 'Eveline', is published under his name, and the famous letter describing Joyce's intention in *Dubliners* ('to betray the soul of that hemiplegia or paralysis which many consider a city') is signed 'S. D.'.[31] Other parallels abound: Soares is a version of his author locked in a specific time and place; Stephen is always a young man, and always in Dublin – as Sydney Bolt puts it, 'Joyce had constructed [in Stephen] a character to dramatize one limited aspect of his personality as a young man.'[32]

Pseudonymous and dramatic masks are also common in Portuguese and Spanish literature of the period. The editors of António Machado's *Poesías* [*Poems*] discovered two apocryphal writers: Juan de Mairena (an embodiment of Machado's philosopher-self) and Abel Martín. [33] Carlos Mesquita created the

(2003), 110-121, and 'Affinity and Influence: The Reception of W. B. Yeats by Fernando Pessoa', *Comparative Critical Studies* 3:3 (2006), 249-267. Earlier studies of the relationship between the two are Ruben García's 'The Unexpected Affinities: W. B. Yeats and Fernando Pessoa', *Journal of the American-Portuguese Society* X:1 (1976), 7-19; Suzette Macedo's 'Mentira, fingimento e máscaras: Alguns comentários sobre Oscar Wilde, W. B. Yeats e Fernando Pessoa' [Lying, Feigning and Masks: Some Notes about Oscar Wilde, W. B. Yeats and Fernando Pessoa], *Colóquio-Letras* 107 (1988), 24-37; and my own 'Yeats, W. B.', in *Dicionário de Fernando Pessoa*, pp. 919-920.

[29] Robert H. Deming, *James Joyce: The Critical Heritage 1928-1941*, 3 vols. (New York: Barnes & Noble), II, p. 538.

[30] *Ibid.*

[31] *Letters of James Joyce*, ed. Stuart Gilbert and Richard Ellmann, 3 vols. (London: Viking, 1957), I, p. 55.

[32] Sydney Bolt, *A Preface to James Joyce* (London: Longman, 1992), p. 91.

[33] See António Apolinário Lourenço, *Identidade e Alteridade em Fernando Pessoa e Antonio Machado* [*Identity and Alterity in Fernando Pessoa and Antonio Machado*] (Braga: Angelus Novus, 1995); António Sáez Delgado, 'Antonio Machado', in *Dicionário de Fernando Pessoa*, p. 424.

imaginary authors Jerónimo Freire and Bartolomeu de Frágoa, Raúl Brandão crafted the literary alter-ego K. Maurício, and *Os Nefelibatas* [*The Dreamers*], by Júlio Brandão, Raúl Brandão and Justino de Montalvão, is attributed to the nonexistent Luís de Borja and R. Maria.[34] Several of Raul Leal's texts display the name Henoch in parentheses; it also features in 'Le Dernier Testament' [The Final Testament] (1918).[35] In the second issue of *Orpheu*, Armando Côrtes-Rodrigues signed pieces as Violante de Cysneiros.[36] As Macedo demonstrates, the speakers in Cesário's poems can be far removed from the authorial self, and his poetic strategy was much admired by Pessoa.[37] Sá-Carneiro, Pessoa's closest friend, explores in his writings the problems of the divided self; his literary fragmentation is more limited than Pessoa's, but it predates the latter's heteronymic explosion of 1914, and it is one Pessoa followed with great interest, as evidenced by their correspondence.

What sets Pessoa's heteronyms apart from the other Modernist masks of the age are the same qualities that set them apart from Shakespeare's characters: the heteronyms are all literary writers who are created by their writings, whereas the masks and speakers of dramatic texts are generally presumed to be speaking, or at most writing a letter. But the influences above provide a sound historical context for Pessoa's development of the heteronyms, which can be viewed as a radical but logical progression of the spirit of the day.

However, Pessoa is not being contrary or obtuse when he recurrently cites Shakespeare, above all other precedents, as the supreme model for the heteronymic project. There are elements of the Bard's dramatic art he is irresistibly drawn to, key characteristics he genuinely admires, and masterfully appropriates, for his own invention of the human.

Dramatic Lights: Theatrical Self-Consciousness

Eliot, in his essay '"Rhetoric" and Poetic Drama' (1919), begins with the commonplace assertion that, in most poetic dramas, the long, moving speeches of the characters are not directed at the audience but to the other characters on stage. In the drama before Shakespeare, and in most drama since, characters speak directly to one another or, in occasional asides and soliloquies, address the audience. But Eliot argues that the most famous speeches in Shakespeare contain a higher rhetorical charge than is called for by the mere exigencies of such communication. Often, what a Shakespearean character is doing is not conveying information, either to the audience or to another character, but rather exhibiting the intensity of his own emotions. Eliot concludes with the insight that 'The really

---

[34] Fernando Guimarães, 'Heteronímia – Poética' [Heteronymity – Poetics], in *Dicionário de Fernando Pessoa*, pp. 327-333.
[35] Fernando Cabral Martins, 'Raul Leal', in *Dicionário de Fernando Pessoa*, pp. 395-397; Mário Cesariny, *O Virgem negra* (Lisbon: Assírio e Alvim, 1989).
[36] Alfredo Margarido, 'Uma Carta quase inédita de Violante de Cysneiros' [An Almost Unpublished Letter by Violante de Cysneiros], *Colóquio-Letras* 117-118 (1990), 117-129.
[37] Macedo, *Nós: uma leitura de Cesário Verde*, pp. 23-25.

fine rhetoric in Shakespeare occurs in situations where a character in the play *sees himself* in a dramatic light.'[38] In a later essay, he cites Othello's final speech as an example of the Shakespearean characters' dramatic self-consciousness:

> What Othello seems to me to be doing in making this speech is *cheering himself up*. He is endeavouring to escape reality, he has ceased to think about Desdemona, and is thinking about himself. [...] Othello succeeds in turning himself into a pathetic figure, by adopting an *aesthetic* rather than a moral attitude, dramatizing himself against his environment. He takes in the spectator, but the human motive is primarily to take himself in.[39]

In other words, Shakespeare's great novelty is that his characters watch themselves think. The soliloquies define *Hamlet*, in particular, and they are at the heart of Bloom's claim that in them Shakespeare invented a new kind of consciousness in Western culture, a meditative, reflective self-consciousness. They display the process of actual thought, as words appear to flow immediately from the inchoate turnings of Hamlet's wavering mind. In *Hamlet*, Greenblatt declares, Shakespeare 'perfected the means to represent inwardness.'[40] Hamlet dominates the play in which he appears, and his is the first great tragedy that is purely interior, purely psychological; for this reason, as Margreta de Grazia argues, *Hamlet* is often hailed as Shakespeare's most modern play.[41] In his 1948 film version of the play, Olivier treats Hamlet's 'To be, or not to be' soliloquy as pure unuttered thought; the ability of film to render Shakespearean soliloquies as internal monologues does much to account for the successful transposition of his plays to the medium.

When Hamlet walks in on Claudius at prayer ('Now might I do it pat, now he is praying') he prevents himself from taking his revenge there and then because of a sudden realisation of its effect:

> And now I'll do it: and so he goes to heaven;
> And so am I reveng'd. That would be scann'd:
> A villain kills my father; and for that
> I, his sole son, do this same villain send
> To heaven. (*CW*, p. 965)

Campos and Soares are also forever pausing to scan their own thought processes. Campos continually qualifies his words, in poetic instances often rendered as dramatic asides. In one poem, he immediately follows a nihilistic

---

[38] Eliot, *Selected Essays*, p. 27.

[39] *Ibid.*, p. 111. It is in this essay that Eliot praises Shakespeare's 'Bovarysme' (see Chapter 3).

[40] Greenblatt, *Will in the World*, p. 299.

[41] Margreta de Grazia, 'Soliloquies and the wages in the age of emergent consciousness', *Textual Practice* 9:1 (1995), 67-92, pp. 80-81.

image – 'Grandes são os desertos e tudo é deserto' [Deserts are vast and everything is desert] – with a deflationary aside on the subjective nature of such sweeping statements: 'Salvo erro, naturalmente' [Unless, of course, I am mistaken] (*AdC*, p. 429). In 'Gostava de gostar de gostar' [I would like to like liking], Pessoa has Campos interrupt a staged dialogue in order to ask for a cigarette, and again to light up:

> Um momento... Dá-me de ali um cigarro,
> Do maço em cima da mesa-de-cabeceira.
> Continua... Dizias
> Que no desenvolvimento da metafísica
> De Kant a Hegel
> Alguma coisa se perdeu.
> Concordo em absoluto.
> Estive realmente a ouvir.
> [...] Obrigado. Deixa-me acender. Continua. Hegel...' (*AdC*, p. 418)

> [One moment... Pass me a cigarette,
> From the pack on the bedside table.
> Go on... You were saying
> That in the evolution of metaphysics
> From Kant to Hegel
> Something was lost.
> I agree entirely.
> I was really listening.
> [...] Thank you. Let me light up. Go on. Hegel...]

Soares is similarly prone to interrupting the free flow of his thoughts to scan his feelings, and to ponder how best to express them. A wonderful example occurs when he alights on an original image for his state of mind: 'hoje, pensando no que tem sido a minha vida, sinto-me qualquer bicho vivo, transportado num cesto de encurvar o braço, entre duas estações suburbanas' [And today, thinking about what my life has been, I feel like some sort of animal that's being carried in a basket under a curved arm between two suburban train stations]. In the very next sentence, he reflects on the image he has just employed, finding it to be defective ('A imagem é estúpida, porém a vida que define é mais estúpida ainda do que ela') [The image is stupid, but the life it defines is even more stupid], before going on to expand the analogy: 'Esses cestos costumam ter duas tampas, como meias ovais, que se levantam um pouco em um ou outro dos extremos curvos se o bicho estrebucha' [These baskets usually have two lids, like half ovals, that lift up at one end or the other should the animal squirm] (*LD*, p. 90).[42]

Some critics of Pessoa, misled by the fact that he should be so little interested in reading or writing plays himself, or perhaps by his description of the

---

[42] Trans. Richard Zenith, in *The Book of Disquiet*, p. 57.

heteronymic project as a theatre of the mind, argue that, unlike Shakespeare, he does not place the heteronyms in dramatic situations. Jacinto do Prado Coelho, in *Unidade e diversidade em Fernando Pessoa* [*Unity and Diversity in Fernando Pessoa*], writes that 'para ser dramático falta a Fernando Pessoa a capacidade de pôr em conflito personagens dinâminas, susceptíveis de alterações profundas sob a acção dos eventos e das outras personagens' [To be dramatic, Pessoa lacks the ability to put dynamic characters in conflict, able to profoundly affect the action of events and other characters]. [43] Sena proposes, in *Da Poesia Portuguesa* [*On Portuguese Poetry*] (1959) that the heteronymic project is essentially non-dramatic. [44] This is highly debatable, for Pessoa's heteronyms interact with each other, and with their author, more theatrically than any other poetic siblings of the Modernist era, save perhaps for the characters in Pirandello's *Six Characters in Search of an Author* (1921), a play which postdates their invention. Furthermore, the heteronyms can be acutely aware of their condition as dramatic fictions, as Eliot suggests is true of Shakespeare's characters.

Campos writes a poem ('Mestre, meu mestre querido') [Master, my dear master] in which he fictionally laments Caeiro's fictional death, and he relates their supposed meeting in 'Notas para a recordação do meu mestre Caeiro' [Notes for the Memory of my Master Caeiro]. [45] The poems Pessoa ascribes to Campos are extremely dramatic, involving staged dialogues; 'Tabacaria' overtly so, with lines that depict Campos's actions, or, rather, his neurasthenic inactions, in the enclosed theatrical space of his room:

> Chego à janela e vejo a rua com uma nitidez absoluta.
> Vejo as lojas, vejo os passeios, vejo os carros que passam,
> [...]
> Semiergo-me enérgico, convencido, humano
> E vou tencionar escrever estes versos em que digo o contrário.
> Acendo um cigarro ao pensar em escrevê-los
> [...]
> Depois deito-me para trás na cadeira
> E continuo fumando.
> [...]
> Visto isto levanto-me da cadeira. Vou à janela.
> [...]
> Como por um instinto divino o Esteves voltou-se e viu-me.
> Acenou-me adeus, gritei-lhe *Adeus ó Esteves!* (*AdC*, pp. 323-6)

> I go over the window and see the street completely clearly.
> I see the shops, the pavements, the passing cars,
> [...]

[43] Prado Coelho, *Diversidade e unidade em Fernando Pessoa*, p. 169.
[44] See Sena, *Da Poesia Portuguesa* [*On Portuguese Poetry*] (Lisbon: Ática, 1959).
[45] Pessoa, *Textos de crítica e de intervenção*, p. 267.

I half rise energetic, convinced, human
And will try to write these verses in which I say the opposite.
I light up a cigarette thinking of writing them
[...]
Then I lean back in my chair
And go on smoking.
[...]
Seeing this I stand up. I go over to the window.
[...]
As if by a divine instinct Esteves turned around and saw me
He waved hello, I shouted 'Hello, Esteves!']

These could be stage directions for an actor.

Soares's book is full of statements hinting at his 'identity' as an actor: 'entro figurante numa tragédia cómica' [I'm an extra in a comic tragedy]; 'Tenho sido actor sempre, e a valer' [I have always been an actor, and for real]; 'Sou uma figura de romance por escrever' [I'm the character in an unwritten novel] (*LD*, pp. 100, 257, 258). In a lengthier passage, he writes:

> Não sei se existo, sinto possível o ser um sonho de outrem, afigura-se-me, quase carnalmente, que poderei ser personagem de uma novela, movendo-me, nas ondas longas de um estilo, na verdade feita de uma grande narrativa. [...] parece que me põem num veículo, como a mercadoria que se envia, e que sigo com um movimento que julgo próprio para onde não quis que fosse senão depois de lá estar.
> Que confusão é tudo! (*LD*, p. 275)

> [I'm not sure I exist, and I wonder if I might be someone else's dream. It also occurs to me, with an almost carnal vividness, that I might be the character of a novel, moving within the reality constructed by a complex narrative, in the long waves of its style. [...] it seems that I've been placed in a vehicle, like freight to be delivered, and that I continue with a movement I imagine is my own towards a destination I don't want until I get there.
> How confusing it all is!][46]

There is much dramatic irony in the way in which Pessoa has Soares continually hint at his dramatic nature, yet fail to ever fully grasp it ('How confusing it all is!'). In other words, it is Pessoa, not Soares, who makes explicit the semi-heteronym's status as a fiction. Part of Soares's tragedy, perhaps, is that he believes himself to be the protagonist of his own story, when in fact he is merely one of several dramatic characters in Pessoa's larger heteronymic play.

Campos, unlike the humourless Soares, is a master of dramatic irony, and thus more acutely aware of his predicament. His self-awareness in this regard is

---

[46] Trans. Richard Zenith, in *The Book of Disquiet*, p. 249.

particularly evident in those poems wherein he examines himself as if from the outside, to the point of addressing himself in the third person. In the poem that begins 'Cruzou por mim, veio ter comigo, numa rua da Baixa' [In a street in downtown Lisbon, a man passed me, came up to me], Campos ends up feeling very sorry for himself:

> Coitado do Álvaro de Campos!
> Tão isolado na vida! Tão deprimido nas sensações!
> Coitado dele, enfiado na poltrona da sua melancolia!
> [...]
> Coitado do Álvaro de Campos, com quem ninguém se importa!
> Coitado dele que tem tanta pena de si mesmo!
> [...]
> Eu é que sei. Coitado dele! (*AdC*, pp. 198-9)

> [Poor Álvaro de Campos!
> So alone in life! So depressed in his sensations!
> [...]
> Poor Álvaro de Campos, whom no one cares about!
> Poor him, who feels so sorry for him self!
> [...]
> I'm the one who knows. Poor him!]

Notice the exquisite self-pity, the 'nobody loves me' feeling. Campos's vision of himself as being slightly ridiculous often borders on the most over-the-top of all dramatic sub-genres, melodrama. By the late poem 'Tabacaria', Campos achieves the difficult feat of making modern life out to be worse than it is, the poem's opening repetition of 'nada [...] nada [...] nada' [nothing] echoing one of the bleakest lines in world literature, Lear's 'Never, never, never, never, never' (*CW*, p. 1018). What prevents this poem from being merely depressing is its speaker's ability to see himself, with self-deprecating flair and dark humour, in a dramatic light.

Transgressing Their Roles: The Heteronyms In and Out of Character

Shakespeare's most memorable characters, adept at seeing themselves in a dramatic light, tend to be irresistibly drawn to play-acting: Iago is not what he is, Rosalind is a boy-actor pretending to be a girl pretending to be a boy pretending to be a girl, Cleopatra plays a part of infinite variety, and Hamlet plays the madman. Richard III begins by declaring that since his physical deformity prevents him from playing the conventional lover, he will play the villain. Richard can, of course, play the lover just as well, as exemplified by his outrageous wooing of Lady Anne over the corpse of her father-in-law, even as she knows that he is responsible for the murder of her husband.

Part of the tragedy of Hamlet is that he does not accept the role he is assigned. His father's ghost orders him to revenge his 'foul and most unnatural murder' (*CW*,

p. 949), in effect casting him in the part of such traditional revengers as the protagonist of Thomas Kyd's *The Spanish Tragedy* (1592). Hamlet appears to accept this fate in his immediate reply:

Haste me to know't, that I with wings as swift
As meditation or the thoughts of love,
May sweep to my revenge. (*CW*, p. 949)

He does not sweep to his revenge, however, but instead, by the end of the scene, admits his unhappiness at what he is cast to perform:

The time is out of joint; O cursed spite,
That ever I was born to set it right! (*CW*, p. 950)

For reasons that continue to generate debate to this day, and which do much to account for the play's enduring appeal, Hamlet is either unable or unwilling to play the typical avenger. Pessoa's heteronyms, too, are prone to acting outside the dramatic roles ascribed to them. Pessoa's propensity to have the heteronyms escape the limitations of their core 'personalities' points to his interest in portraying, like Shakespeare before him, characters who are as imprecise as real people, more complex than comparatively stable Modernist alter-egos like Stephen Dedalus and Mauberley. This is even true of Alberto Caeiro, who on the surface is infinitely less theatrical than the self-conscious Campos.

The first poem in Caeiro's *O Guardador de Rebanhos* [*The Keeper of Sheep*] begins with the striking negation:

Eu nunca guardei rebanhos,
Mas *é como se* os guardasse. (*AC*, p. 21, emphasis added)

[I never kept sheep
But *it's as if* I kept them.]

Its opening stanza contains several corollary similes ('Minha alma é *como* um pastor/[...] eu fico triste *como* um pôr de sol') [My soul *is like* a shepherd/[...] I become as sad *as* a sunset] as developments of the initial one (*AC*, p. 21). Despite the title of the collection, then, Caeiro is no keeper of sheep. As Teresa Cristina Cerdeira argues, the moment a supposed truth is structured from an initial metaphor it loses its validity, 'para navegar no terreno incerto das conjunturas, das possibilidades e não mais das certezas' [to navigate the uncertain terrain of conjectures and possibilities rather than certainties].[47] Once the image of Caeiro as shepherd is established in the reader's mind, however, and in spite of its immediate negation, it is a difficult one to dislodge. A passage from section V

---

[47] Teresa Cristina Cerdeira, *O Avesso do Bordado: ensaios de literatura* [*The Other Side of the Chain: Literary Essays*] (Lisbon: Caminho, 2000), p. 77.

('What the Thunder Said') of Eliot's *The Waste Land* provides a good illustration of why this should be the case:

> Here is no water but only rock
> Rock and no water and the sandy road
> [...]
> If there were only water amongst the rock
> [...]
> If there were water
> [...]
> If there were the sound of water only
> Not the cicada
> And dry grass singing
> But sound of water over a rock
> Where the hermit-thrush sings in the pine trees
> Drip drop drip drop drop drop drop
> But there is no water.[48]

It is impossible to imagine the sound of 'no rain' and 'no water' without first thinking of their opposite; Eliot himself referred to this passage as 'The Rain Song', and its onomatopoeic allusions to rain and water, if only to deny their presence, conversely put them at the forefront of the reader's mind. (A more prosaic example of the effect of poetics of negation is the order: 'Do not think of an elephant.') In the same way, Caeiro's poetics of negation means that our image of him as a shepherd is what endures, notwithstanding our realisation of its metaphorical nature.

In the long poem 'Num meio-dia de fim de primavera' [One noon in late spring], Caeiro describes an imaginary Jesus Christ, as a young boy, coming down to Earth on a ray of sunshine to live peacefully with the poet in his home ('Ele mora comigo na minha casa a meio do outeiro' [He lives with me in my house in the middle of the hill] (*AC*, p. 28). The biography Pessoa sketched for Caeiro states that he lives alone; there is no mention of a Christ-child tenant. Of course, the boy is a metaphor for a number of things, in particular the 'Eterna Criança' [Eternal Child], with his sense of Whitmanesque wonder, that Caeiro strives to be, and this poem is not to be taken as a statement of fact.[49] But the point is that Caeiro is not meant to be thinking in extended metaphors; his poetic vision is supposed to be unique precisely because it derides the usual liberties of poetic license, philosophical systems, and metaphysical or religious symbolism. Such inconsistencies strike an odd note in a collection that otherwise expounds a state of unquestioning

---

[48] *Ibid.*, p. 71.
[49] Maria Irene Ramalho has a wonderful essay about this metaphor: 'O Deus que faltava: the Theory in the Poetry of Alberto Caeiro', in *Fernando Pessoa's Modernity Without Frontiers: Influences, Dialogues and Responses*, ed. Mariana Gray de Castro (Woodbridge: Tamesis, 2013), pp. 23-36.

existence, in tune with the natural world around him, seeing things for what they are without probing any underlying mystical or symbolic content (see, for example, the poem 'Creio no mundo como num malmequer' [I believe in the world as in a daisy] (*AC*, p. 24).

As Cerdeira points out, Caeiro's nakedness is consciously assumed, borne of the effort to deliberately disrobe emotions and rationalisations. As she concludes, 'em Caeiro a inteireza é uma ficção' [In Caeiro, wholeness is a fiction].[50] This applies also to the 'inteireza' of his character's consistency. One poem in Caeiro's *O Guardador de Rebanhos* begins:

As quatro canções que se seguem
Separam-se de tudo o que penso,
Mentem a tudo o que eu sinto,
São o contrário do que eu sou... (*AC*, p. 48)

[The four songs that follow
Are separate from all I think,
Lie about everything I feel,
Are the opposite of what I am ...]

Caeiro concludes the poem by arguing that when one is ill, one is to be forgiven for acting out of character. The explanation is meant as an apology for the uncharacteristic poems that follow, in which he voices wishes contrary to the 'personality' Pessoa creates for him: 'Quem me dera que a minha vida fosse um carro de bois/[...] Eu não tinha que ter esperanças – tinha só que ter rodas...' [I wish my life were an ox-cart/I wouldn't need to have hopes – only wheels]; or 'O luar quando bate na relva/[...] Lembra-me a voz da criada velha/Contando-me contos de fadas' [Moonlight falling on the grass/[...] Reminds me of the old maid's voice/Telling me fairy tales] (*AC*, p. 49, 51). Reis, in a projected preface to Caeiro's poems, also explains the latter's uncharacteristic poems as the product of a bout of illness:

O cérebro do poeta torna-se confuso, a sua filosofia se entaramela, os seus princípios sofrem a derrota que, na indisciplina da alma, representa em espírito o que seja a vitória ignóbil de uma revolução de escravos. O leitor que tenha seguido a curva ascensional de *O Guardador de Rebanhos*, verá, passado esse conjunto de poemas, como a inspiração se deteriora e se confunde. Não se desvia, propriamente: senão que sofre a intrusão de elementos estranhos a ela. (*RR*, p. 139)

[The poet's mind becomes muddled, his philosophy confused, his principles suffer a defeat which, in his undisciplined soul, represent in the spirit the ignoble victory of a slave revolution. The reader who has followed the

---

[50] Cerdeira, *O Avesso do Bordado*, p. 78.

ascending curve of *The Keeper of Sheep* will see how, after that collection of poems, his inspiration deteriorates and becomes muddled. It does not, strictly speaking, deviate: it suffers the intrusion of foreign objects.]

Reis's preface is intended to add to Pessoa's characterisation of Caeiro, and in it he describes his fellow-heteronym as 'quasi ignorante das letras, quasi sem convívio nem cultura' [almost ignorant of literature, almost outside society and culture] (*RR*, p. 46). However, its dedication perversely betrays the fact that Caeiro has literary influences:

Esta obra inteira é dedicada
por desejo do próprio autor [Caeiro]
à memória de
Cesário Verde (*RR*, p. 48)

[This entire work is dedicated
As desired by the author himself
To the memory of
Cesário Verde]

Moreover, Caeiro's poetry displays a clear influence of Walt Whitman and Cesário Verde. Caeiro himself admits his love for Cesário, which has much to do with the latter's insistence on the visual, in one poem: 'Leio até me arderem os olhos/O livro do Cesário Verde' [I read, until my eyes burn/The Book of Cesário Verde] (*AC*, p. 26). In this poem, Caeiro finds a kindred spirit in the poet 'preso em liberdade na cidade' [shackled in freedom in the city] (*AC*, p. 26); he himself, despite his bucolic pose, is erudite: there are even books in Pessoa's library with Caeiro's signature in them, rather than Pessoa's.

In short, Caeiro's poetic vision, as outlined by Pessoa and Reis, is oddly contradicted by both, as well as by his own uncharacteristic, or 'out-of-character', poems. Despite claiming to be anti-philosophical, Caeiro is undeniably a man of letters, and he is interested in metaphysics. Pessoa has Soares point out, in *Desassossego*, that 'quer o saibamos quer não, temos todos uma metafísica' [we all have a metaphysics, whether or not we are aware of it] (*LD*, p. 213); he is wilfully misleading when he has Reis describe Caeiro as 'em filosofia, o que ninguém foi: um objectivista absoluto' [in philosophy, what no one ever was: an absolute objectivist] (*RR*, p. 57).

When Pessoa inserts himself into Soares's story as the latter's fictional literary executor, he declares that he became one of his closest friends ('Fui o único que, de alguma maneira, estive na intimidade dele' [I was the only person who, in some way, knew him intimately]) following their chance encounter (*LD*, p. 41). As Reis falsely claims in the case of Caeiro, Pessoa argues in his preface to *Desassossego* that Soares has no interest in reading; Soares himself makes the same point when he declares: 'Não posso ler, porque a minha crítica hiperacesa não descortina senão defeitos, imperfeições, possibilidades de melhor' [I cannot read, for my hypercritical sensibility only notices flaws, imperfections, things that could be improved] (*LD*, p. 245). But Pessoa's characterisation of Soares as unlettered is completely contradicted in the pages that follow, for in the first half of *Desassossego* alone, Soares makes direct references to Cesário Verde, 'a poesia da Pérsia' [Persian poetry], Shakespeare, António Vieira, a 'dito de Leonardo da Vinci' [saying by Leonardo], his 'leitura dos clássicos' [reading of the classics], Chateaubriand, Lamartine, Horace, Machiavelli, the Romantic poets, Virgil, Amiel, Mallarmé, Verlaine, Carlyle, Rousseau, Haeckel, Kant, Goethe, Socrates, Shelley, Dickens, Plato, Hegel, Verlaine, Pessanha, Chateaubriand, Hugo, Vigny, and Michelet.[51]

Interestingly, when the heteronyms transcend the confines of their given roles, they often enter into those of another heteronym. Soares recognises that one must 'Aumentar a personalidade sem incluir nela nada alheio – nem pedindo aos outros, nem mandando nos outros, mas *sendo* outros quando outros são precisos' [To enlarge one's personality without including anything foreign – neither asking others, nor giving others orders, but *being* others when others are necessary] (*LD*, p. 235; Pessoa's emphasis).

In 'Esta tarde a trovoada caiu' [This afternoon the thunder came], Caeiro expresses a Campos-like desire to feel something that he does not: 'Ah, poder crer em Santa Bárbara!' [Oh, to be able to believe in Santa Barbara!'] (*AC*, p. 28). Following a meditation about what such belief might consist of, he becomes afflicted with the neurasthenic angst associated with Campos and the orthonym (see Chapter 3):

E eu, pensando em tudo isto,
Fiquei outra vez menos feliz...
Fiquei sombrio e adoecido e soturno (*AC*, p. 28)

[And I, thinking about all this
Am once again less happy...
I am sombre and ill and taciturn]

That Pessoa had some difficulty in keeping his heteronyms in check, that is, in character, is reflected by the shifting attributions of his writings, a constant reminder of his presence as the master puppeteer. The orthonymic poem 'Chuva Oblíqua' [Slanting Rain] (1914) is a case in point. In his letter on the genesis of the heteronyms, Pessoa explains it as a landmark poem, signalling his psychological return to 'himself' following his 'inexistence' as Caeiro: 'Foi o regresso de Fernando Pessoa Alberto Caeiro a Fernando Pessoa ele só. Ou melhor, foi a reacção de Fernando Pessoa contra a sua inexistência como Alberto Caeiro' [It was Fernando Pessoa Alberto Caeiro's return to Fernando Pessoa himself. Or rather, it was Fernando Pessoa's reaction against his inexistence as Alberto Caeiro] (*Corr II*,

---

[51] *LD*, pp. 47, 49, 71, 81, 82, 88, 103, 120, 133, 134, 138, 141, 151, 155, 164-165, 173, 177, 202, 222, 224, 229, 243.

p. 343). Readers have followed Pessoa's lead in interpreting the poem in this way: Martinho, for example, argues that in writing it 'Pessoa reagiu de imediato à sua inexistência como Alberto Caeiro, ou seja, [...] interceptou, com sua 'Chuva Oblíqua', a afirmação primária do significante mestre' [Pessoa immediately reacted to his inexistence as Alberto Caeiro, that is, he intercepted, with his 'Slanting Rain', the initial affirmation by the important master].[52] This is testament to Pessoa's myth-making prowess, for upon writing 'Chuva Oblíqua' he initially attributed the poem to Caeiro (with whom it does not sit at all), then to Campos (a slightly better fit), before finally settling on the orthonym.[53]

At one point in *Desassossego*, Pessoa has Soares write:

Criei em mim várias personalidades. Crio personalidades constantemente. Cada sonho é meu imediatamente, logo ao aparecer sonhado, encarnado numa outra pessoa, que passa a sonhá-lo, e eu não.

Para criar, destruí-me; tanto me exteriorizei dentro de mim, que dentro de mim não existo senão exteriormente. Sou a cena nua onde passam vários actores representando várias peças. (*LD*, pp. 283-4)

[I've created various personalities within. I constantly create personalities. Each of my dreams, as soon as I start dreaming it, is immediately incarnated in another person, who is then the one dreaming it, and not I.

To create, I've destroyed myself. I've so externalized myself on the inside that I don't exist there except externally. I'm the naked stage where various actors act out various plays.][54]

These words are extremely problematic if taken to be Soares's rather than Pessoa's. If we ascribe them to Soares, the implication is that he has subpersonalities (sub-heteronyms?) himself. If we ascribe them to Pessoa, the problem disappears, for they square perfectly with his conception of himself as a literary descendent of Shakespeare, adept at impersonally creating dramatic selves, with a tenuous identity of his own; it becomes a further text in which Pessoa theorises on his heteronymic creativity.

Pessoa's indecision over what should belong to Soares's output did much to prevent *Desassossego* from appearing until 1982, almost fifty years after his death. One of his notorious hesitations concerning the book's purview, a wonderful illustration of his heteronymic indecisiveness, is a prose fragment he headed

---

[52] Martinho, *Pessoa e a psicanálise* [*Pessoa and Psychoanalysis*], p. 63; See also Maria José Lencastre, *Fernando Pessoa: uma fotobiografia* [*A Photobiography*] (Lisbon: IN-CM, 1980), p. 8.
[53] In his project for a book called *Antologia do Interseccionismo* [*An Anthology of Interseccionism*], Pessoa's list of poems to be submitted includes 'Poesias de Álvaro de Campos. ('Chuva Oblíqua', – Rei Cheops, etc.)' [Poems by Álvaro de Campos: 'Slanting Rain', King Cheops', etc.)] (*Cartas a Armando Cortes Rodrigues*, p. 30.)
[54] Trans. Richard Zenith, *The Book of Disquiet*, p. 254.

'A[lvaro] de C[ampos] (?) ou L[ivro] do D[esassossego] (ou outra coisa qualquer)' [Álvaro de Campos? Or *Book of Disquiet* (or whatever else)].[55] Campos's output also contains poems of problematic attribution, such as the poem 'Clearly non-Campos!'. The critical edition of Campos's poetry includes a section devoted to those poems its editor considers to be 'Na fronteira Pessoa-Campos' [On the Pessoa-Campos Frontier].[56]

Pessoa is prone to drawing on the same themes, images and conceits across a range of poetic personalities. Campos's motto, 'sentir tudo de todas as maneiras' [to feel everything in every possible way], is the opening line of 'Passagem das Horas', but the phrase also makes its way into the orthonymous poem 'Deixo ao cego e ao surdo' [I leave to the blind and the deaf] cited at the end of Chapter 1. The desire to feel rather than to think also underpins Soares's *Desassossego*, and Soares draws on the phrase on at least one occasion.[57] In the same way, a haunting image in Campos's poetry, featuring in 'Aniversário' [Birthday], 'Tabacaria' and many others, is that of himself as an old rag, a 'trapo'; 'Trapo' is even the title of one of his poems, the one that begins 'O dia deu em chuvoso' [The day became rainy] (*AdC*, p. 431). But the vision of oneself as a useless piece of cloth is not exclusive to Campos, for Soares refers to himself as a 'trapo' on several occasions: 'senti-me de repente um daqueles trapos húmidos de limpar coisas sujas, que se levam para a janela para secar, mas se esquecem, enrodilhados, no parapeito que mancham lentamente' [I suddenly felt like one of those damp rags used for housecleaning that are taken to the window to dry but are forgotten, balled up, on the sill where they slowly leave a stain], he declares at one point, and his single-sentence fragment titled 'Intervalo doloroso' [Dolorous Interval] employs the same image: 'Coisa arrojada a um canto, trapo caído na estradas, meu ser ignóbil ante a vida finge-se' [An object tossed into a corner, a rag that fell onto the road, my contemptible being feigns to the world] (*LD*, pp. 65, 72).[58]

The shifting attributions of Pessoa's heteronymic writings catches him in the act of consciously working out the characters and poetic ranges of his heteronyms. It also points to the heteronyms' lack of a fixed dramatic identity from the start. Their boundaries would remain forever porous. The morphing putative authors of *Desassossego* exemplify their mutable nature, for the book was first ascribed to Vicente Guedes, who later became Bernardo Soares, 'disappearing' himself in the process.

Just as the heteronyms can act out of character, assuming the identities of other

---

[55] Zenith, 'Introdução' [Introduction], in *LD*, p. 14. For more on the changing authorship of *Desassossego*, see pp. 20-23.
[56] *Poemas de Álvaro de Campos* [*Poetry*], ed. Cleonice Berardinelli (Lisbon: IN-CM, 1990), p. 353.
[57] *AdC*, p. 196; *Poesia do eu*, p. 213; *LD*, p. 151: 'Sentir tudo de todas as maneiras; saber pensar com as emoções e sentir com o pensamento; não desejar muito senão com a imaginação' [To feel everything in every possible way; to know how to think with the emotions and feel with thought; to desire little except via the imagination].
[58] Trans. Richard Zenith, in *The Book of Disquiet*, pp. 32, 39.

heteronyms or that of their creator, Pessoa himself impersonates his most self-consciously theatrical heteronym, Campos, in his relationship with Ophélia Queiroz. Tellingly, he also impersonates Shakespeare's most self-conscious dramatic character, Hamlet, in this context, in a perfect illustration of his attraction to Shakespeare's metaphor of the world as a stage, where being and acting are indivisible.

Pessoa, Campos, Hamlet, and the Two Ophelias

Shakespeare's unifying image, throughout his career, is that of man as a player who assumes shifting dramatic roles in 'the great stage of fools' that is the world, as he puts it in *King Lear* (*CW*, p. 1010). Jacques, in *As You Like It*, voices the analogy most famously in his speech about the seven ages of man:

> All the world's a stage,
> And all the men and women merely players;
> They have their exits and their entrances,
> And one man in his time plays many parts. (*CW*, p. 255)

It is likely that the first words Pessoa ever read by Shakespeare were to this effect, for *The Life of King Henry V* was on his high-school curriculum in 1903, when he would have been fourteen or fifteen. The play's opening speech is that of the chorus, who sets the scene for the entry of the actors:

> O! for a Muse of fire, that would ascend
> The brightest heaven of invention;
> A kingdom for a stage, princes to act
> And monarchs to behold the swelling scene.
> Then should the war-like Harry, like himself,
> Assume the part of Mars (*CW*, p. 509)

The chorus goes on to ask the audience to employ its 'imaginary forces' to 'suppose' the stage to be 'The vasty fields of France' and, more significantly, to use their imagination to 'Into a thousand parts divide one man' (*CW*, p. 509). Pessoa's copy of *Henry V* is now in a private collection; a bookseller who once owned it informs me it is profusely annotated in Pessoa's hand.

The image of life as a theatrical spectacle in which men are actors playing a series of parts is not unique to Shakespeare, for it features in classical, Medieval, Renaissance and contemporary sources. Jacques's lines are evocative of an earlier passage in Palingenius's *Zodiacus Vitae*, translated into English in the early 1560s by Barnaby Googe as *The Zodiac of Life*. Googe obligingly offered readers interpretations of the metaphor in his edition, such as the phrase 'The world a stage play' next to the passage below:

> Wherefore if thou dost well discern
> thou shalt behold and see

This mortal life that here you lead
a Pageant for to be.[59]

Pessoa drew a line in the margin next to the following words by Ben Jonson in his copy of Jonson's *Collected Works*, three volumes displaying otherwise few marginal annotations:

> I have considered our whole life is like a Play; wherein every man forgetful of himself, is in travail with expression of another. Nay, we so insist in imitating others, as we cannot (when it is necessary) return to ourselves; like children, that imitate the vices of stammerers so long, till at last they become such; and make the habit to another nature, as it is never forgotten.[60]

Richard Burbage, the tragedian who played many of Shakespeare's protagonists, was described as 'so wholly transforming himself into his part, and putting off himself with his clothes, as he never (not so much as in the tiring-house) assumed himself again until the play was ended.'[61] Pessoa was so good at imitating Campos that he appears to have experienced the same difficulty in returning to himself – whatever 'himself' means in the case of an author who everywhere doubts his own identity, discovering himself to be as invisible a dramatic poet as Shakespeare. Ophélia describes how Pessoa would sometimes impersonate Campos when he went to meet her:

> [Fernando] Dizia-me então: "Hoje não fui eu que vim, foi o meu amigo Álvaro de Campos." [...] Portava-se, nestas alturas, de uma maneira totalmente diferente. Destrambelhado, dizendo coisas sem nexo. Um dia, quando chegou ao pé de mim, disse-me: "Trago uma incumbência, minha Senhora, é a de deitar a fisionomia abjecta desse Fernando Pessoa, de cabeça para baixo, num balde cheio de água.[62]

> [On those occasions he would tell me: 'Today it is not I who came, it is my friend Álvaro de Campos.' [...] He would behave totally differently. Playing the fool, spouting nonsense. Once, he came up to me and said: 'I have a mission, my Lady, to put the abject physiognomy of said Fernando Pessoa, upside down, in a bucket of water.]

---

[59] Palingenius, *The Zodiac of Life*, trans. Googe (1565, book 6, lines 1215-30, *British Library* copy).

[60] Ben Jonson, 'De vitâ humanâ', in *The Works of Ben Jonson*, III, p. 404.

[61] Richard Flecknoe, 'A Short Discourse on the English Stage' (1664), in *Critical Essays of the Seventeenth Century, 1650-1685*, ed. Joel Elias Spingarn (Oxford: Clarendon, 1908), p. 217.

[62] Ophélia Queiroz, *Cartas de amor de Fernando Pessoa* [*Fernando Pessoa's Love Letters*], p. 7.

Pessoa famously impersonated Campos during his single documented meeting with José Régio. Gaspar Simões paradoxically emphasises Pessoa's role-playing when he attempts to describe how ordinary Pessoa was in everyday life: 'Pessoa na intimidade [...] quando não se apresentava a Régio e a mim [...] sob a máscara do "Sr. Álvaro de Campos", era o homem mais urbano e terra-a-terra que imaginar se pode' [In his close relationships, when Pessoa did not introduce himself to me and Régio under the mask of 'Mr Álvaro de Campos', he was the most urbane and down to earth person imaginable].[63] In his 'own' letters to Ophélia, Pessoa also alludes to the continual companionship of Campos in his daily life: 'Tens hoje do teu lado o meu velho amigo Álvaro de Campos, que em geral tem sido contra ti. Alegra-te!' [Today my old friend Álvaro de Campos, who has usually been against you, is on your side. Rejoice!]; 'Como [...] se dá a circunstância de o sr. eng. Álvaro de Campos ter que me acompanhar amanhã durante grande parte do dia, não sei se será possível evitar a presença – aliás agradável – desse senhor' [Seeing as Mr Engineer Álvaro de Campos will have to accompany me for most of the day, I don't know if it will be possible to avoid the company of that gentleman, which is actually agreeable.][64] He has Campos write Ophélia a letter advising her to forget about him (that is, Pessoa): 'aconselho V. Exa. a pegar na imagem mental, que acaso tenha formado do indivíduo cuja citação está estragando este papel razoavelmente branco, e deitar essa imagem mental na pia' [I advise your good self to take the mental image you may have formed of the individual whose citation is ruining this reasonably white paper, and throw it down the sink.][65] In other letters to her, Pessoa refers to himself and to Ophélia às 'Ibis', speaks of a Mr. Crosse, one of his other dramatic masks, and attributes certain sentiments to Campos rather than to himself. In one letter, Pessoa asks, 'Gostas de mim, do Ibis, do Nininho?' [Do you like me, your Ibis, your Nininho?] In another he opens with: 'Não imaginas a graça que te achei hoje á janella da casa de tua irmã! Ainda bem que estavas alegre e que mostraste prazer em me ver (Alvaro de Campos)' [You can't imagine how charming I found you today, at the window of your sister's house! I'm glad you were happy and seemed pleased to see me (Alvaro de Campos)].[66]

Íbis, in particular, could not be a more appropriate name for Pessoa, for the Ibis is associated with Thoth, the Egyptian god of wisdom and magic (Aleister Crowley wrote the *Book of Thoth* in 1940), and he is also the scribe of the gods, one of whose many titles is 'Lord of Divine Words'.

Ophélia relates that, further to masquerading as Campos during their relationship, Pessoa once assumed the part of Hamlet:

Lembro-me que estava em pé, a vestir o casaco, quando ele entrou no meu gabinete. Sentou-se na minha cadeira, pousou o candeeiro que trazia na mão e,

---

[63] Gaspar Simões, *Vida e obra,* p. 392.
[64] *Corr I*, p. 165; *Cartas de amor de Fernando Pessoa*, p. 101.
[65] Letter of 25 September 1929, in *Corr II*, p. 164.
[66] *Cartas de amor*, pp. 83, 100.

virado para mim, começou de repente a declarar-se, como Hamlet se declarou a Ophélia: "Oh, querida Ophélia! Meço mal os meus versos; careço de arte para medir os meus suspiros; mas amo-te em extremo. Oh! Até ao último extremo, acredita!"[67]

[I remember he was standing, putting on his coat, when he came into my office. He sat down in my chair, put down the lamp he carried in his hand and, turning to me, started suddenly to declare his love, like Hamlet did to Ophelia: 'Oh, dearest Ophelia! I do not measure my verses well; I lack the art to restrain my sighs; but I love you extremely. Oh, to the last extreme, believe me!']

Zenith points out that Pessoa borrowed these words directly from Shakespeare's play.[68] The relevant passage appears in a letter from Hamlet to Ophelia, which Polonius intercepts and proceeds to read out to the king and queen:

To the celestial, and my soul's idol, the most beautified Ophelia. –
That's an ill phrase, a vile phrase; 'beautified' is a vile phrase; but you shall hear. Thus:
In her excellent white bosom, these, &c. –
[...]
Doubt thou the stars are fire;
Doubt that the sun doth move;
Doubt truth to be a liar;
But never doubt I love.
O dear Ophelia! I am ill at these numbers: I have not art to reckon my groans;
but that I love thee best, O most best! believe it. Adieu.
Thine evermore, most dear lady, whilst this machine is to him,
HAMLET (*CW*, p. 953)

I posit that it was Pessoa himself who pointed out the parallel between his words and Hamlet's to Ophélia, for this is hardly one of the best-known passages in the play, and it seems unlikely that she should have remembered it verbatim so many years after the event. Furthermore, Pessoa's declaration, as recalled by Ophélia, is not a direct translation of Hamlet's, as is typical of the magpie poet's appropriations: his transformation of Hamlet's bawdy 'groans' into romantic

---

[67] Ophélia Queiroz, 'O Fernando e eu: relato de Ophélia Queiroz, destinatária das Cartas de Fernando Pessoa, Recolhido e estruturado por sua sobrinha-neta Maria da Graça Queiroz' [Fernando and Me: A Portrait by Ophelia Quiroz, the Recipient of Fernando Pessoa's Letters, Collected and Structured by her Great-Niece Maria da Graça Queiroz], in *Cartas de amor de Fernando Pessoa*, pp. 21-22.
[68] See Zenith's editions of *The Selected Prose of Fernando Pessoa*, p. 129, and *Fotobiografias Século XX: Fernando Pessoa* [*Twentieth-Century Photobiographies*] (Lisbon: Círculos de Leitores, 2008), pp. 12, 125.

'suspiros' [sighs] is a particularly deft touch.

The Shakespearean passage Pessoa theatrically makes his own has become more famous, in Shakespearean studies, for Polonius's personal aside than for Hamlet's conventional love poem. After reading the letter's opening sentence ('To the celestial, and my soul's idol, the most beautified Ophelia') Polonius, whose literary pretensions go back to the time when he was considered a good actor 'i'the university', interjects: 'That's an ill phrase, a vile phrase: "beautified" is a vile phrase'. The formatting of Pessoa's copy of the play, rendered above, makes Polonius's brief foray into literary criticism stand out from the surrounding lines, an effect that is lost in most modern editions. In *The Norton Shakespeare*, whose general editor is Stephen Greenblatt, for example, the passage loses the visual impact it has in Pessoa's copy:

> "To the celestial and my soul's idol, the most beautified Ophelia" – that's an ill phrase, a vile phrase, "beautified" is a vile phrase. But you shall hear – "these in her excellent white bosom, these".[69]

We saw in the context of the Shakespearean authorship controversy (Chapter 2) that the first reference to Shakespeare in London's theatre world is an attack in *Greene's Groatsworth of Wit* directed at an 'upstart crow, beautified by our feathers'. Pessoa underlined the word 'beautified' in his copy of *Hamlet*, and translated it, in the margin, as 'embellezado'. There are no other attempted translations on this page of the play. The word 'embellezado' is difficult to decipher with complete confidence, but its final letter appears to be the masculine ending 'o' rather than the expected 'a' (in the line, 'beautified' refers to Ophelia).[70] If so, even as Pessoa appropriates Hamlet's words during his courtship of Ophélia, his mind is partly on the passage as evidence of Shakespeare's biography. This suggests what his impersonation of Campos and Hamlet points to: his theatrical stance towards Ophélia makes his declaration of love somewhat staged, therefore far removed from being a spontaneous, sincere, romantic outburst.

In an intriguing parallel, in *Hamlet* the Player in the *Mousetrap* must necessarily be insincere in order to perform the action demanded of him by the scene he is called on to perform. This is evident from Hamlet's envy at his ability to cry real tears when he is merely acting:

> Is it not monstrous that this player here,
> But in a fiction, in a dream of passion,
> Could force his soul so to his own conceit
> That from her working all his visage wann'd,
> Tears in his eyes, distraction in his aspect,

---

[69] *The Norton Shakespeare: Based on the Oxford Edition*, ed. Walter Cohen, Stephen Greenblatt, Jean Howard, Katherine Eisaman Maus (London/New York: Norton & Company, 2008.), p. 1693.
[70] See *CW*, p. 953.

A broken voice, and his whole function suiting
With forms to his conceit? and all for nothing!
For Hecuba!
What's Hecuba to him or he to Hecuba
That he should weep for her? (*CW*, p. 957)

It is well to remember that the ancient Greek word for actor was 'hypocrite'. This brings us to the age-old connection between dramatic poetry and insincerity, one of crucial importance to our understanding of Pessoa's heteronymic *fingimento* [feigning], which can be freshly reappraised in light of Pessoa's insight into the Bard's enthusiasm for dramatic insincerity.

Dramatic (In)sincerity: Towards an Empsonian Reading of the Heteronyms

The idea that drama is necessarily insincere is an old one: countless writers, from Plato to Bacon to Philip Sidney, all said as much. A contemporary of Shakespeare's condemned Renaissance theatre because of its inherent 'lies':

> In stage plays for a boy to put on the attire, the passions of a woman; for a mean person to take upon him the title of a prince with counterfeit port and train, is by outward signs to show themselves otherwise than they are, and so within the compass of a lie.[71]

The writer of these words denounced the plays of the age because of their inbuilt insincerity, for he felt that lying 'by Aristotle's judgement is naught of itself and to be fled.'[72] Bate argues that Shakespeare, on the contrary, relished dramatic insincerity:

> The genius of *King Lear* is that it was written by a man who was totally unlike his creation. The poetry of a teenager in love is sincere: that is what makes it bad. The key to dramatic art is Insincerity, i.e. that the author should only pretend keenly to feel what he expresses. That way, he can pretend equally keenly to feel the opposite things which he also expresses. He can infect the spectator with the feeling of what it is like to be Goneril as well as that of what it is like to be Lear.[73]

Pessoa would have subscribed wholeheartedly to this appraisal. It is implicit behind his assertion, in 'Essay on Intuition', that 'Falstaff is Shakespeare as truly as Perdita, Iago, Othello, Desdemona are Shakespeare' (*PC II*, p. 194).[74] In a 'Nota esthetica' [Aesthetic Note] , he makes the same point as Bate concerning dramatic

---

[71] Stephen Gosson, *Plays Confuted in Five Actions*, 1582, British Library manuscript sig. E5r.
[72] *Ibid.*
[73] Bate, *The Genius of Shakespeare*, p. 150.
[74] 'Perdita' is here erroneously transcribed as 'Pudita'; see manuscript 14(6)-30.

insincerity, citing his heteronymic poetry and Shakespeare's art as two examples in the method:

> Não é preciso sentir uma cousa fortemente para a dar como fortemente sentida. Basta que a sinta de algum modo e *dê attenção* a como ella se passa. Depois, é uma questão de expressão experimentada fazel-a ter a forma de uma cousa fortemente sentida. Assim a *Ode Triumphal*, e cousas dramaticas./(A arte de Shakespeare é *sã* e *arte* porque mostra esta attenção.[75]

> [It is not necessary to feel something strongly in order to express it as strongly felt. It is enough to feel it in some way, and *pay attention* to how it feels. Then, it is a matter of expression and style to give it the form of something strongly felt. Such is *Triumphal Ode*, and dramatic pieces./(Shakespeare's art is *healthy* and *artistic* because it shows this attention.]

In another piece, he similarly asserts, with Wildean aphoristic flourish:

> Sincerity is the one great artistic crime. Insincerity is the second greatest. The great artist should never have a really fundamental and sincere opinion about life. But that should give him the capacity to feel sincere, nay to be absolutely sincere about anything for a certain length of time – that length of time, say, which is necessary for a poem to be conceived and written.[76]

In other words, as Pessoa would put it most memorably, in the poem 'Autopsicografia' [Autopsychography], the dramatic poet must learn to fake what he truly feels. George Monteiro, Paul Muldoon, and Oscar Pimental have all argued that the central idea of this poem is heavily indebted to Shakespeare's play *As You Like It*, in which the wise fool Touchstone argues that 'the truest poetry is the most feigning'. [77] That these three writers should have reached this conclusion independently shows how powerful the influence is. Pessoa annotated a few sections of *As You Like It* in his copy of the *Complete Works*, although unfortunately not the relevant phrase; he also included the play in some of his plans to translate Shakespeare into Portuguese (see his letter of 1923 to Osório cited in Chapter 1, in *Corr II*, pp. 13-14).

Of course, insincerity is arguably a feature of all art, not just the dramatic: Lionel Trilling expertly surveys its long history in *Sincerity and Authenticity*

---

[75] *Sensacionismo*, p. 414.

[76] *Ibid.*, p. 158.

[77] See Monteiro, 'Shakespeare, the "Missing All", *Portuguese Studies* 24:4 (2008), Paul Muldoon, 'In the Hall of Mirrors: "Autopsychography" by Fernando Pessoa', *New England Review* 23 (Fall 2002), 38-52, p. 42, and Oscar Pimental, 'Experiência em Pessoa' [Experience in Pessoa], in *A Lâmpada e o Passado* [*The Lamp and the Past*] (São Paulo: Conselho Estadual de Cultura, Comissão de Literatura, 1968), pp. 95-98, p. 97.

(1972).[78] Vladimir Nabokov, who was above all a novelist, defined 'the virtues of *all* worthwhile art' as being 'originality, invention, conciseness, harmony, complexity and *splendid insincerity*'. [79] Pessoa, however, having classified Shakespeare's art and his heteronymic project as dramatic poetry (see Chapter 1), speaks almost exclusively of insincerity in this context. As he explains in a letter of 10 August 1925 to Francisco Costa:

> Para mim, pois, a arte é essencialmente dramática, e o maior artista será aquele que, na arte que professa – porque em todas as artes condicionado isto pela "matéria" delas, se podem fazer dramas, isto é, sentir drammaticamente – mais intense – profusa[-] e complexamente viver tudo quanto não é ele, isto é, que mais intensa-, profusa– e complexamente exprimir *tudo quanto em verdade não sente*, ou, em outras palavras, sente apenas para exprimir. (*Corr II*, p. 85)

> [For me, therefore, all art is essentially dramatic, and the greatest artist is he who, in his chosen art – for in every art one can create dramas, that is, feel dramatically – most intensely, profusely and complexly lives everything he is not, that is, most intesely, profusely and complexly expresses *everything he does not truly feel*, or, in other words, feels merely in order to express.]

Little wonder that he should praise Shakespeare, his supreme model of the dramatic poet, for his ability to express insincere feelings through his dramatic characters; in the same letter he writes:

> Não é Shakespeare, talvez, o maior poeta de todos os tempos, pois me não parece possível antepor alguém a Homero; mas é o maior expressor que houve no mundo, o mais insincero de quantos poetas tem havido, sendo por isso mesmo que exprimia com igual relevo todos os modos de ser e de sentir, e com igual alma vivia os diversos tipos psíquicos – verdades gerais *humanas* em cuja expressão se empenhou. (*Corr II*, p. 84)

> [Shakespeare is not, perhaps, the greatest poet who ever was, for I don't believe anyone can surpass Homer; but he is the greatest expressor the world has ever seen, the most insincere of all poets, which is how he expressed with equal depth every shade of being and feeling, and with the same spirit lived the different psychic types – universal *human* truths he endeavoured to express.]

It logically follows that Pessoa should cite Shakespeare's example when attempting to explain his own heteronymic *fingimento*:

[78] Lionel Trilling, *Sincerity and Authenticity: The Charles Eliot Norton Lectures, 1969-1970* (Oxford: Oxford University Press, 1972).
[79] Vladimir Nabokov, *Poems and Problems* (New York: McGraw-Hill, 1970), p. 15 (my italics).

Por qualquer motivo temperamental que me não proponho analisar, nem importa que analise, construí dentro de mim várias personagens distintas entre si e de mim, personagens essas a que atribuí poemas vários que não são como eu, nos meus sentimentos e ideias, os escreveria.

[...] Negar-me o direito de fazer isto seria o mesmo que negar a Shakespeare o direito de dar expressão à alma de Lady Macbeth, com o fundamento de que ele, poeta, nem era mulher, nem, que se saiba, histero-epiléptico, ou de lhe atribuir uma tendência alucinatória e uma ambição que não recua perante o crime. Se assim é das personagens fictícias de um drama, é igualmente lícito das personagens fictícias sem drama, pois que é lícito porque elas são fictícias e não porque estão num drama.

Parece escusado explicar uma coisa de si tão simples e intuitivamente compreensível. Sucede, porém, que a estupidez humana é grande, e a bondade humana não é notável. (*PETCL*, p. 106)

[Owing to some temperemental motive I will not analyse, nor should I analyse, I constructed within me several characters, different from each other and from myself, characters to whom I attributed several poems which are not as I, in my own feelings and thoughts, would write them.

[...] Denying me the right to do this would be like denying Shakespeare the right to express the soul of Lady Macbeth, on the grounds that he, a poet, was neither a woman nor, so far as we know, a hystero-epileptic, or to ascribe him a hallucinatory tendency and an ambition that does not retreat from crime. If this is true of fictional characters in a drama, it is equally true of fictional characters without a drama, for it is permitted because they are fictional, not because they are in a drama.

It seems unnecessary to explain something so simple and intuitively easy to understand. It so happens, however, that human stupidity is great, and human kindness is not notable.]

Pessoa would have agreed with Wilde that 'to censure an artist for a forgery was to confuse an ethical with an aesthetical problem', because 'so-called forgeries were merely the result of an artistic desire for perfect representation [...] an attempt to realise one's own personality on some imaginative place out of the trammelling accidents and limitations of real life.' In point of fact he did agree with Wilde, for he marked these words in his copy of *The Portrait of Mr W. H.*[80] The heteronyms, who provide similar corrective and opposite views to one another, and to Pessoa 'himself', are Pessoa's attempt to realise his personality outside the limitations of real life. In the case of dramatic poetry, synthesis makes little sense. The heteronymic universe is one of coexisting rather than mutually exclusive possibilities, like that of Shakespeare's plays. Does Pessoa contradict himself? Very well, he contradicts himself; to borrow a phrase from Whitman, whose

[80] Wilde, *Lord Arthur Savile's Crime*, p. 153.

influence on him was almost as powerful as Shakespeare's, he contains multitudes. As an enactment of the modern sense of identity, the heteronymic project is the sincerest possible mode of self-expression. As Lourenço argues,

> A genialidade [...] de Pessoa situa-se imediatamente ao nível do 'ontológico' (é ontologia em acto), sendo como é, pura e interminável interrogação sobre o ser múltiplo das 'verdades' ou das 'vivências' em que o pensar nelas as converte.[81]

> [Pessoa's genius lies at the 'ontological' level (it is ontology in action), being the pure and unending questioning about the multiplicity of the self and the 'truths' or 'experiences' that thinking about them transforms them into.]

In a piece attributed to Campos, Pessoa asserts that Shakespeare's performance of the insincerity intrinsic to drama paradoxically makes his art sincere: 'Shakespeare era essencial e estruturalmente factício; e por isso a sua constante insinceridade chega a ser uma constante sinceridade, de onde a sua grandeza' [Shakespeare was fundamentally and structurally insincere; therefore his constant insincerity becomes a constant sincerity, whence his greatness.][82] In a letter of 19 January 1915 to Armando Côrtes-Rodrigues, he applies the same logic to the heteronymic project:

> O que eu chamo literatura insincera não é aquella analoga à do Alberto Caeiro, do Ricardo Reis ou do Álvaro de Campos [...]. Isso é sentido na *pessoa de outro*; é escripto *dramaticamente*, mas é sincero (no meu sentido grave da palavra) como é sincero o que diz o Rei Lear, que não é Shakespeare, mas uma criação dele. (*Corr I*, p. 142)

> [What I call insincere literature is not that analogous to Alberto Caeiro's, Ricardo Reis's or Álvaro de Campos's [...]. That is felt *as another*; it is written *dramatically*, but it is sincere (in my serious meaning of the word), like what King Lear says is sincere, though Lear is not Shakespeare but a creation of his.]

The modern notion of identity, with its intrinsic sense of fragmentation, is captured by Yeats in 'The Second Coming' (1920) 'Things fall apart; the centre cannot hold.'[83] The self in ruins finds its most dramatic representation in Pessoa's explosion into the heteronyms. This crisis of identity, an ongoing ontological meditation on the nature of being or, more usually in the case of Pessoa, non-being, is an omnipresent motif in the poetry attributed to his own name. R. D. Laing describes the 'divided self' as the product of 'a basic ontological insecurity', which, when developed to an extreme, can cause an individual's personality to be

---

[81] Lourenço, *Pessoa revisitado*, p. 23.
[82] *Textos de crítica e de intervenção*, p. 275.
[83] Yeats, 'The Second Coming', in *Selected Poetry*, p. 124.

'profoundly modified even to the point of threatened loss of [...] identity.'[84] The charge of insincerity, inaugurated by Régio's reading of Pessoa, is one often levied against the self-professed faker, but Pessoa everywhere denounces the concept of a fixed, knowable self as a fiction. Lourenço writes: 'A acusação de *artifício* lavrada por José Régio – tanto como por João Gaspar Simões na sua famosa biografia – ficará como uma espada de Dâmocles suspensa sobre a poesia de Pessoa' [José Régio's accusation of *artifice* – like that of João Gaspar Simões in his famous biography – would hang over Pessoa's poetry like the sword of Damocles].[85]

This is not to suggest that the modern scepticism about a fixed or knowable self is a sufficient cause for the creation of the heteronyms – psychological theories of the unconscious mind, including Freud's, explain the former but not the latter. Rather, the heteronyms are perfect embodiments of the divided self, and in this sense a sincere attempt to represent it in art.

Ford Madox Ford, writing in 1930, claimed that 'the novelist must not, by taking sides, exhibit his preferences [...] He has [...] to render and not to tell.'[86] The Modernist practice of showing, rather than telling, like intrusive nineteenth-century writers who comment on their own narratives, is analysed by Wayne C. Booth in *The Rhetoric of Fiction* (1961). In this seminal book, Booth argues that as he writes, an author 'creates not simply an ideal impersonal "man in general" but an implied version of "himself" that is different from the implied authors we meet in other men's works. To some novelists it has seemed, indeed, that they were discovering or creating themselves as they wrote.' He continues,

> Whether we call this implied author an 'official scribe', or adopt the term recently revived by Kathleen Tillotson – the author's 'second self' – it is clear that the picture the reader gets of this presence is one of the author's most important effects. [...] However impersonal he may try to be, his reader will inevitably construct a picture of the official scribe who wrote in this manner.

What better way for the reader to construct a picture of the second selves than to openly describe their physical appearances and give them biographies, as Pessoa does? Booth goes on to argue that 'It is only by distinguishing between the author and his implied image' – something Pessoa makes very easy with the heteronyms, by making his implied authors explicit – 'that we can avoid pointless and unverifiable talk about such qualities as "sincerity" or "seriousness" in the author. [...] A great work establishes the "sincerity" of its implied author, regardless of how grossly the man who created that author may belie in his other

---

[84] R. D. Laing, *The Divided Self; An Existential Study in Sanity and Madness* (Harmondsworth: Penguin, 1959), p. 59.

[85] 'A Fortuna Crítica de Fernando Pessoa' [The Critical Fortune of Fernando Pessoa], in *Fernando, Rei da nossa baviera*, p. 30.

[86] Ford Madox Ford, *The English Novel: From the Earliest Days to the Death of Joseph Conrad* (London: Constable, 1930), pp. 121-122.

forms of conduct the values embodied in his work.'[87]

William Empson, in his groundbreaking *Seven Types of Ambiguity* (1930), effected a transformation in the way that Shakespeare is read. Although Empson does not specifically refer to the problem of artistic sincerity, his argument for the critical acceptance of co-existing, simultaneous, non mutually exclusive interpretations can be profitably applied to our stance towards Pessoa's heteronymic *fingimento*.

Before Empson, Shakespeare scholars and editors had largely pointed to alternative interpretations of words and phrases in his poems, favouring one over the other. Empson warns that the traditional approach to the ambiguity present in Shakespeare's *Sonnets*

> is curious and no doubt wise; it allows a structure of associated meanings to be shown in a note, but not to be admitted [...] So it is assumed, except when a double meaning is very conscious and almost a joke, that Shakespeare can only have meant one thing.

He concludes that 'Very likely the editors do not seriously believe their assumption; indeed I have myself usually said 'either ... or' when meaning 'both ... and'. [88] The effect on the reader, in reading a given annotated passage on Shakespeare, is to hold in his mind the various suggested alternatives simultaneously; if this is the case, Empson argues, then it is likely that Shakespeare also held them, or some of them, as he composed. Empson's revelation is that there is no need to choose between different readings of the lines in Shakespeare's poems, as he demonstrates in his own interpretations of the *Sonnets*.

Stephen Booth, the greatest proponent of Empsonian readings today, states that the notes in his edition of the *Sonnets* are designed to admit that 'everything in a sonnet is there.'[89] These notes run to over four hundred pages, and they admit simultaneous interpretations, teased out in polysemous readings. Booth's aim, like Empson's, is to demonstrate to the reader how Shakespeare's art is a space in which contrary but inseparable reactions are designed to coexist. Keats had already challenged us to approach Shakespeare with uncertainty, rather than with an 'irritable reaching after fact and reason', and developed his theory of 'negative capability' in the context of his thinking on the Bard:

> several things dovetailed in my mind, and at once it struck me, what quality went to form a Man of Achievement especially in Literature and which Shakspeare [sic] possessed so enormously – I mean *Negative Capability*, that is when man is capable of being in uncertainties.[90]

---

[87] Wayne C. Booth, *The Rhetoric of Fiction* (Chicago: University of Chicago Press, 1961), pp. 70-71, 70, 75.

[88] William Empson, *Seven Types of Ambiguity* (1930; London: Random House, 2004), p. 81.

[89] Stephen Booth, 'Preface', in *Shakespeare's Sonnets*, p. xiv.

[90] Keats, letter to Richard Woodhouse, 27 October 1818, in *Letters of John Keats*, I, pp. 386-

The same paradigm shift should be applied to our understanding of Pessoa's project: the heteronyms are both sincere and insincere; sincere expressions of a multiple self, and insincere because they are dramatic poetry.

This inclusive vision can also be applied to the other Modernist masterpieces of the day: *The Waste Land* may be one of the most impersonal poems ever written, but its author later conceded that it contained purely personal sentiments as well: 'Various critics have done me the honour to interpret the poems in terms of criticism of the continental world, have considered it, indeed, as an important bit of social criticism. To me it was only the relief of a personal and wholly insignificant grouse against life; it is just a piece of rhythmical grumbling.'[91] For all his impersonal goals, Eliot had written as early as in 1927 that 'what every poet starts from is his own emotions'.[92] Eight years earlier, describing the proper stance of the critic, he had remarked that 'To understand anything is to understand it from a point of view.'[93]

Pessoa's Shakespeare as a Super-Pessoa

At the beginning of this chapter, I argued that the cumulative effect of Pessoa's constant approximation of his genius to Shakespeare's can lead readers to disregard the essential differences between both sets of dramatic characters. More significantly, I argued that Pessoa fashions a retrospective projection of affinity, contrary to the direction along which influence travels. This is not to deny the fact that Pessoa's heteronymic project, both in its conception and in his subsequent explanations of it, is enormously indebted to his keen insights into his favourite writer's genius. Chief among these are the Shakespearean characters' unprecedented self-consciousness, their awareness of their theatrical natures and consequent tendency to overstep their set roles, and their enactment of the notion of the world as a stage where each man plays many parts. Pessoa's kinship fallacy is an attractive one, and it has been echoed by Monteiro and, possibly, Bloom.

There exists a further fallacy in studies of Pessoa's engagement with Shakespeare: the notion that Pessoa seriously believed he would surpass the Bard's achievement. Three articles all argue that, further to fashioning himself as a 'super-Camões', Pessoa imagined himself to be a 'super-Shakespeare', taking literally his words in one of his essays in *A Águia* [*Eagle*]:

> Paralelamente se conclui o breve aparecimento na nossa terra do tal supra-Camões. Supra-Camões? A frase é humilde e acanhada. A analogia impõe mais: Diga-se 'de um Shakespeare' e dê-se por testemunha o raciocínio, já que não é citável o futuro.[94]

7.
[91] *The Waste Land: A Facsimile*, p. 1.
[92] 'Shakespeare and the Stoicism of Seneca', in *Selected Essays*, p. 117.
[93] 'Imperfect Critics', in *The Sacred Wood* (London: Methuen, 1960), p. 38.
[94] *Textos de crítica e de intervenção*, p. 27.

[In tandem, we conclude that this said supra-Camões will soon appear in our country. Supra-Camões? The phrase is modest and too small. The analogy calls for something greater: let us say 'of a Shakespeare', based on reason, since the future cannot be cited.]

Monteiro writes: 'That Pessoa saw himself as Portugal's Shakespeare, the 'Super-Camões' of the *Quinto Império* [*Fifth Empire*], seems to me beyond questioning.'[95] One of his three section-headings in this article is 'Super Camões? No, Super Shakespeare'.[96] Onésimo de Almeida, in 'Fernando Pessoa and Antero de Quental (with Shakespeare in between)', similarly argues that Pessoa believed he would outclass the Bard's achievement:

> Just as with the *Quinto Império* that the Portuguese would build, by surpassing what the others had done before them in the previous four empires, Pessoa would also be Homer and Shakespeare and Antero – and yes, Camões too. He would then be all of them together, and naturally he would surpass them all.[97]

Rita Patrício, in 'Shakespeare e Pessoa', comes to the same conclusion: 'O que Pessoa anuncia, sob uma máscara camoniana, é um supra-Shakespeare' [What Pessoa announces, under the mask of Camões, is a supra-Shakespeare].[98]

This critical consensus is understandable, for Pessoa's continual approximation of Shakespeare's art to his own has the uncanny effect of making Pessoa sound as if he were the author of *Hamlet*. The heteronyms may not be the straightforward literary descendants of Shakespeare's characters Pessoa says they are, but there is a striking family resemblance.

However, to transpose Pessoa's vision of himself as a 'supra-Camões' to his encounter with Shakespeare is misleading, for Pessoa engages with Camões and Shakespeare in the context of two very different projects. His articles in *A Águia* relate to the ideal that culminated in *Mensagem* [*Message*], that of projecting a mythical past onto the nation's possible future, encapsulated in his vision of the 'Quinto Império'. Camões is clearly the best reference for such a project. He is not an influence, however, in the sphere of Shakespeare's greatest influence on Pessoa, the heteronymic project.

Pessoa uses the two terms 'supra' and 'super' interchangeably: in reference to Camões, he employs 'supra-Camões' in 'A nova poesia portuguesa sociologicamente considerada' [The New Portuguese Poetry Considered Sociologically] and 'Reincidindo' [Restating], 'super-Camões' in 'A nova poesia

---

[95] Monteiro, 'Shakespeare, the "Missing All"', *Portuguese Studies* 24:4 (2008), p. 38.
[96] *Ibid.*, p. 33.
[97] Onésimo T. Almeida, 'Fernando Pessoa and Antero de Quental (with Shakespeare in between)', *Portuguese Studies* 24:4 (2008), pp. 63-64.
[98] Rita Patrício, 'Shakespeare e Pessoa' [Shakespeare and Pessoa], in *Fernando Pessoa: O guardador de papéis*, p. 92.

portuguesa no seu aspecto psicológico' [The Psychological Aspect of the New Portuguese Poetry] and 'Uma réplica ao snr. Dr. Adolfo Coelho' [A Reply to Mr Adolfo Coelho], and refers back to the latter term in a 'Tábua biográfica' [Biographical List] of 1927. [99] In reference to Shakespeare, he implies the appearance of a 'supra-Shakespeare' in the text cited above in *A Águia*. This is echoed by Rita Patrício, while George Monteiro and Onésimo de Almeida speak of Pessoa's intention to be a 'super', rather than a 'supra', Shakespeare. There is a slight, but significant, nuance in meaning between the two prefixes. For Pessoa to imagine himself to be a 'supra-Shakespeare' implies he believed he would be able to transcend the Bard's achievement; for him to imagine himself to be a 'super-Shakespeare' implies his having inherently Shakespearean characteristics, but to a higher degree. Neither is the case.

Pessoa does not fashion himself as a 'supra-Shakespeare' because, unlike in the case of Camões, there is simply no evidence that he believed his own literary achievement would ever match, let alone overshadow, the Bard's. On the contrary, there is evidence that he believed it would not. In the very same year that his articles in *A Águia* appeared, Pessoa writes in a letter to Boavida Portugal:

> erra [...] o professor Adolfo Coelho [...] quando considera *messianismo* a ideia de um super-Camões, isto é, de um poeta máximo, inevitavelmente maior do que aquele poeta verdadeiramente grande, mas longe de ser um Dante ou um Shakespeare. (*Corr. I*, p. 52)

> [Professor Adolfo Coelho is mistaken when he considers *messianistic* the idea of a super-Camões, that is, of an unrivalled poet, who will inevitably be greater than that truly great poet, but far from being a Dante or a Shakespeare.]

In other words, Camões, great poet though he is, will be superseded by a 'supra-Camões': Pessoa himself, as he had posited in *A Águia* and does so here, although not as overtly; however, even the 'poeta máximo' [unrivalled poet] who is to be Pessoa, though inevitably greater than the great Camões, will still not be on a plane with Dante or Shakespeare.

In a letter proposing an English-language review modelled on *Orpheu*, Pessoa informs a prospective publisher that the writings in the Portuguese magazine are good, but not as good as Shakespeare's: 'It is worth learning Portuguese to read [*Orpheu*]. Not that there is any Goethe or Shakespeare in it' (*PIAI*, p. 140). Pessoa's sense of his artistic inferiority, relative to Shakespeare, is echoed in the letter written a month before his death to Tomás Ribeiro Colaço in which he cites his perceived neurosis (see Chapter 3). In it, he also outline plans for the publication

---

[99] *Textos de crítica e de intervenção*, pp. 15-15, 27, 45, 77; *Presença: edição facsimilada compacta* [*Compact Facsimile Edition*], 3 vols., ed. David Mourão-Ferreira (Lisbon: Contexto, 1993) I, p. 250.

of his heteronymous work, and ends by conceding that his art has not reached the dizzying heights of Shakespeare's plays or Milton's poems:

> Reparo agora que estou falando um pouco no estilo de quem vai fornecer *Hamlets* em pílulas ou *Paraísos Perdidos* em comprimidos e não quero que V. vá descobrir até nestas linhas maquinadas de uma carta particular uma daquelas minhas afirmações de valia própria que V. descobriu que eram um dos meus característicos distintivos. Onde diabo foi V. buscar isso? (*Corr II*, p. 355)

> [I now see that I am speaking a bit like one who will dispense *Hamlets* or *Paradises Lost* like pills, and I don't want you to discover in these typewritten lines of a personal letter one of those arrogant affirmations of my own worth that you discovered to be one of my distinctive traits. Where the devil did you get that from?]

When Pessoa turned his hand to crafting Shakespearean sonnets (see Chapter 1), he was proud of his compositions, but he recognised that *35 Sonnets* comprised an instance of purely stylistic imitation of the original. In 'Impermanence', he had declared that 'The sonnet is the type of what our mind can best do', and it was as a derivative exercise that he crafted his sonnets in English (*H*, p. 241). But he came to the deflating conclusion, in 'Erostratus', that

> Shakespeare's phrasing is imitable – it is, indeed, very easy to imitate – but Shakespeare's genius is not. (*H*, p. 193)

Shakespeare's phrasing is only very easy to imitate by one as skilled as Pessoa, but it seems reasonable to assume that the latter, who can rarely be accused of false modesty, here means exactly what he says regarding the untouchable nature of Shakespeare's genius.

Unlike Camões, Shakespeare is an influence towards whom Pessoa displays no discernible anxiety. For Bloom, belatedness is a problem: the precursor has to be confronted aggressively rather than being acknowledged and accepted. This is Pessoa's attitude before Camões, who is not so much as mentioned in *Mensagem*; Pessoa reworks Camões's 'Adamastor' [sea monster] in his 'Mostrengo', and appropriates a line from *Os Lusíadas* for Álvaro de Campos's 'outing' of Ricardo Reis (see Introduction), in both instances making no mention of his source. However, as Bate argues, Bloom's theory of the anxiety of influence omits an alternative stance: 'The hope that one might be a descendant of a great poet may be confidence instead of anxiety.'[100] In this light, Shakespeare is the underlying presence to Pessoa's heteronymic project whom Pessoa openly acknowledges as such; far from inhibiting Pessoa's creativity, he fires it.

---

[100] Bate, *Shakespeare and the English Romantic Imagination* (Oxford: Clarendon Press, 1986), p. 2.

In a wonderful piece titled 'The Defects of Shakespeare', Pessoa pens the following appreciation of Shakespeare's genius:

> This article will probably be considered impertinent. I hope it will. Impertinent people, like children who ask 'why', have at least the advantage of making people think.
>
> Before I found out these faults in Shakespeare, I thought him supreme. After finding these faults, I still think him supreme. I simply think, in addition, that he is not perfect, but that nothing is perfect was absurdly observed by Adam the moment after Eve appeared. I also think, in addition, that Shakespeare is not unsurpassable. Only very young people speak of unsurpassable things. That nothing is 'unsurpassable' was absurdly observed by Eve the moment she saw Adam. But I think he is unsurpassed. I hope this opinion is agreeable to the reader.[101]

Pessoa's notion that his chosen model is, in theory, not unsurpassable, fuels his efforts to out-Shakespeare Shakespeare, with his heteronymic project, in the invention of the human. At the same time, however, his repeated evocation of Shakespeare in the context of the heteronyms contains the implicit recognition that the Bard had reached his intended destination before he arrived there himself.

Beyond not setting himself up as a 'supra-Shakespeare', Pessoa does not conceive of himself as a 'super-Shakespeare' because his readings of Shakespeare tend to be self-referential, even autobiographical, generally discovering in the Bard very Pessoan qualities. It is only following Pessoa's creation of Shakespeare in his own image that he can appropriate him as his chosen model against which to forge, define, and explain the essence of his own genius, the heteronymic project.

Rather than Pessoa entertaining the notion that he was a 'supra' or a 'super' Shakespeare, I venture that Pessoa's kinship fallacy leads him to view Shakespeare, in essentially autobiographical readings grounded in tendentious identifications and self-projections, as, instead, a *super-Pessoa*, a fellow genius and madman who looks much like Pessoa himself. (Interestingly, Monteiro's argument that Shakespeare's characters should be viewed as Pessoan heteronyms, rather than the other way around, seems to support this conclusion rather than the one he arrives at.)

Arthur Quiller-Couch, in his Introduction to the 1921 edition of *The Tempest* that Pessoa owned, writes facetiously in reference to the Shakespearean authorship controversy:

> It has been computed that of the lunatics at present under ward or at large

---

[101] *Apreciações Literárias de Fernando Pessoa*, ed. Pauly Ellen Bothe, p. 239. First transcribed and presented in my doctoral thesis *Fernando Pessoa's Shakespeare*. Bothe suggests 'already' instead of 'absurdly'.

in the British Isles, a good third suffer from religious mania, a fifth from a delusion that they belong to the Royal Family, while another fifth believe [...] that they *are* Shakespeare.[102]

Pessoa drew a line next to these words, but he himself did not suffer from such a delusion. Instead, he was under the illusion that Shakespeare, whose achievement he would never match, had profoundly Pessoan characteristics: that the Bard was a glorified version of himself.

---

[102] *The Tempest* (Cambridge: Cambridge University Press, n.d. [1921]), p. xvii.

Conclusion: An Image of Pessoa's Shakespeare

In his engagement with the Bard's genius, invisibility, madness, and sexuality, the magpie poet appropriates from Shakespeare selectively and tendentiously, and almost exclusively for the heteronymic project. Pessoa's Shakespeare may be a product of Pessoa's absorption of nineteenth-century readings of the Bard, as well as of his Modernist ideal of impersonality, but he is essentially an autobiographical projection. Magpies are one of few species able to recognise their reflection in mirrors, and it is himself he sees when Pessoa gazes at the Bard.[1] Sylvia Plath's daughter Frieda, who keeps a bird sanctuary in Wales, said in an interview that magpies are 'the most intelligent of birds, showing jealousy, mischief and charm.'[2]

Pessoa's Shakespeare takes shape, in Pessoa's appraisals of his genius, as the supreme dramatic poet – dramatic poetry being, not incidentally, the highest form of art – invisible as the God of creation, adept at impersonally creating the different characters he puts on stage. For Pessoa, dramatic poetry is at the pinnacle of the literary genres, a view that explains why, despite his seemingly ambivalent pronouncements about Shakespeare's ability as both poet and dramatist, he places him unequivocally at the centre of his canon. Having created the Bard in his own image, in readings influenced by Romantic character criticism and the Modernist goal of impersonal authorship, Pessoa then upholds him as the supreme model for his own genius, the heteronymic project.

The God-like invisibility nineteenth-century readers ascribed to Shakespeare led to one of the greatest literary conspiracy theories of all time: the Shakespearean authorship controversy, or the debate over whether 'Shakespeare' was in fact a pseudonymous cover for another writer, or group of writers. Although fascinated by the possibility, Pessoa did not seriously entertain the anti-Stratfordian position. Instead, his engagement with the Shakespearean authorship controversy allowed him to probe his trademark concerns, offering him powerful sites of self-reflection in its key sites of contention, such as the disparity between literary genius and a commonplace life. Most significantly, in the context of the authorship controversy Pessoa coined the word 'transpersonalization' to describe an author's ability to step outside himself to create fictional selves, and his most profound engagement with the problem of Shakespeare's supposed invisibility was in the two years immediately leading up to his heteronymic explosion of 1914. The authorship controversy thus provided him with a valuable conceptual space in which to ponder his own brand of invisible authorship.

Pessoa's most original contribution to the Shakespearean authorship controversy is his proposed solution to the problem of Shakespeare's apparent unconcern with the posthumous fate of his genius. In Pessoa's view, Shakespeare's

---

[1] According to a 2008 study at the Goethe University in Frankfurt; the only other species to do so are humans, apes, dolphins and elephants ('Magpie "can recognise reflection"', BBC News website, 19 August 2008: http://news.bbc.co.uk/2/hi/science/nature/7570291.stm).
[2] Cited in Hugo Williams, 'Freelance', *Times Literary Supplement* (22 January 2010), p. 16.

inability to publish was prompted by his touch of 'madness', namely hystero-neurasthenia, the same neurosis he discovered in himself. Pessoa is drawn to Shakespeare's seeming ability to depict, in his dramatic characters, the new mental sciences of the *fin de siècle*, and appropriates the topical thinking on the neuroses for his heteronymic poetry, particularly that of Álvaro de Campos. Furthermore, Pessoa offers the madness he discovers in Shakespeare and himself as the psychological explanation for both men's genius. If, as he believes, genius and madness are inextricably linked, then a touch of hystero-neurasthenia, with an emphasis on the neurasthenic characteristics of the disorder, is the necessary price to pay for their literary greatness, the impersonal creation of dramatic others.

Pessoa's conviction that Shakespeare was homosexual is grounded in nineteenth-century readings of the *Sonnets*, particularly Oscar Wilde's. His approach to the problematic compositions is revealing on a number of scores, and it highlights his penchant for biography and biographical readings, notwithstanding his insistence on impersonality in the case of his own homoerotic writings, for which he appropriates the defining features he discovers in the Bard's. This discrepancy illuminates our understanding of Pessoa's encounter with the most intrusive biographical approach of his day, Freudian psychoanalysis. Following his contact with Freud's new science, in the shape of the inquisitive Gaspar Simões, Pessoa provides competing psychological explanations for his most homoerotic poems, argues for their impersonality with greater urgency, and quietly tones down the poetic 'immorality' of Campos. Furthermore, Pessoa's differing attitude towards Shakespeare's homoerotism and his own reveals his alternative approach to lyric poetry, the *Sonnets*, and dramatic poetry: Shakespeare's plays, and the heteronymic project.

In everywhere approaching Shakespeare's art in light of his own, rather than the other way around, Pessoa falls into what I call a 'kinship fallacy', disregarding the essential differences between the two sets of dramatic characters and fashioning a retrospective projection of affinity contrary to the direction in which influence travels. However, despite the existence of other precedents for the heteronyms in the Modernist masks and dramatic speakers of the period, there are elements of Shakespeare's dramatic art which Pessoa is irresistibly drawn to, and expertly appropriates for his own 'drama in people'. These include the Shakespearean characters' unprecedented self-consciousness, their ability to see themselves in a dramatic light, their tendency to transgress the boundaries of their set roles, and their representation of the insincerity inherent to dramatic poetry.

Pessoa's readings of Shakespeare's genius, invisibility, madness and sexuality are central to our understanding of Pessoa's own work, in particular the invention of the heteronyms. However, although his heteronymic creativity is fired by his engagement with the Bard, he never suggests that he will be able to surpass, with his heteronyms, Shakespeare's achievement in the invention of the human. Far from imagining himself to be a 'supra' or a 'super' Shakespeare, Pessoa is convinced that Shakespeare was a super-Pessoa.

Appendix: Pessoa's Unpublished Texts on Shakespeare Cited in this Book

[76-13, 76-13v]   *Shakespeare*

I propose to investigate, as far as it is possible, what kind of man Shakespeare was. I refer to the author of the works called Shakespeare's.

As there is a 'Shakespeare problem', I shall not use accessory elements except in so far as they bear *exclusively on the *author* of the plays and poems known as Shakespeare's. I shall therefore depend on no biography.

Neither shall I suppose any figure of Shakespeare's to represent, more or less, his creator, or his creator's idea of himself. I shall suppose every Shakespearean figure to be a pure fiction or a *whole.

I shall avoid also 'particular' details, names of places, etc. As no play can be seen to be *altogether* Shakespearean, i.e. in every line, I shall thus limit myself to

(1) the plays as a whole, in their general, typical structures

(2) the 'expression' as a whole, and the unexpressable † not in the things expressed, but in the manner of expressing.

(3) Such details as the only non-*dramatic, personal poems – the *Sonnet* *artist which cannot be taken as symbolic or fictional.

This is therefore a 'detective' criticism.

The Person of Shakespeare
A Study in the Higher Transcendental Detection
A Detective Study

If my study be exact and its conclusions acceptable, I shall have contributed something either to the Shakespeare problem, if there be one, or to the study of Shakespeare, whether there be or not.

In the 1st case I shall be able to put *inquiry on the track of the author of the works. In the first or 2nd, I *shall † reader to have *invented Shakespeare.

[76-14]

Venus and Adonis: 'first heir of my invention.'[1] Is this to be taken as strict truth? Or not? And, if not, can 'invention' have the Latin meaning, 'find'? – 'The first heir of my find?'

What evidence is there of the Shakespearean *touch* before *Venus and Adonis*?

---

[1] Shakespeare, in the dedication of *Venus and Adonis* (1593), describes the work as the 'first heir of my invention.' Anti-Stratfordians of various stripes have claimed from that the phrase somehow signifies that 'Shakespeare' is not the actual name of the author of *Venus and Adonis* but an 'invented' pseudonym. The phrase is also used to try to date Shakespeare's literary activity.

Probably *none*. The Shakespearean *hand* in plays is *later*.[2]

Then, it being natural that the 'first heir' phrase is correct, what age was Shakespeare when *Venus and Adonis* was written?[3]

But what of the 12 plays cited by Meres?[4] Since *Titus* is cited, and this is not Shakespearean, what can be understood?

Shakespeare the actor was certainly an author; probably a fairly competent author on such a level as his. But another 'hand' otherwise 'arranged' his compositions.

'Shakespeare' begins when Watson ceases.[5] – Note.

[76-19]   *The Identity of Shakespeare: A Conspectus of the Problem*

It is one of the strangest logical positions in this unfortunate case that the real or apparent indifference of Shakespeare for his own works – neither publishing them, nor collating them, nor caring what works were published under his name – should be cited as an anti-Stratfordian argument. If this indifference be a fact, it is a fact, and it affects the author, whomsoever he may be. Indeed, it is a stronger argument for the authorship of a man like Shakespeare of Stratford than for any Bacon, Derby, Rutland or de Vere. A spontaneous, precipitate and headlong genius, not trained by position to give himself importance nor educated by learning to give importance to his works, will more readily be careless about those works than the other men who are assumed to have written these works.

The central facts about the Shakespearean works are these: (1) they are composite, in two senses, as being (a) written, in some cases, in what must be considered as collaboration, and in some of these cases, a reasonable approach to the identity of the collaborator can be made, (b) written, in other cases, over original work by another man or men; (2) they are written precipitately and journalistically, in some cases patently for the moment or the urgency thereof; (3) the author cared nothing for collating or printing them, nor for the fact that under his name works not his were foisted on the public.

These facts, which exactly fit the case of (1) an actor-poet, or a poet connected with the theatre, (2) a precipitate and hasty writer, (3) a man of genius who,

---

[2] The first recorded Shakespearean plays are *Richard III* and the three parts of *Henry VI*, written in the early 1590s during a vogue for historical drama.

[3] *Venus and Adonis* was entered into the Stationers' Register on April 18, 1593; Shakespeare would have almost twenty-nine.

[4] Francis Meres (1565-1647) was an English churchman and author. He is especially well known for his *Palladis Tamia, Wits Treasury* (1598), a commonplace book that is important as a source on the Elizabethan poets and more particularly because its list of Shakespeare's plays.

[5] Thomas Watson (1555-1592) was the earliest Elizabethan to make a reputation as a sonneteer. He is mentioned by Meres in company with Shakespeare, Peele and Marlowe among 'the best for tragedie', but no dramatic work of his is extant today.

though conscious of his genius, was at the same conscious of the bad conditions in which he had expressed it, too impatient by nature to revise, too aware of the disparity between his genius and his achievement to care whether the works were published or not, – these facts, I say, are in no sort of congruity with the hypothesis of (a) professed authors, careful of their dignity and of literature, (b) aristocrats, who would not willingly collaborate, nor even easily do so, with common players' poets, (c) learned men, conscious of rules and plans.

[76-20]   *Identity of Shakespeare*

Literature is the art of expressing artificially through words a feeling, or a number of feelings, which have undergone the process, conscious or unconscious, of analysis by thought. Until a feeling has been analysed by thought, and thus reduced to intelligibility to others, it has not reached the literary stage; for that analysis eliminates the element which is purely personal, which is the feeling in itself, and consolidates by intellect the general and transmissible part. This intellectualized feeling is put into words because words are the material of literature. Finally, once put into words, it is so put artificially, such being the condition of all art. The very words art and artifice are related.

The writing of literature involves thus three elements: (1) expression, which is the rendering in as highly intelligent a way as possible of what is felt; (2) verbalizing, which is the careful attention to the material (words) which is used for that expression; (3) construction, which is the disposition of the whole thus produced into as artificially exact a way as possible.

There are, thus, three literary types: (1) the expressionist, (2) the verbal, and (3) the constructive. The constructive type is known as the classical, and the result is logical, frigid and exact. The verbal type tends to the opposite. The expressionist type

The common example of expression is what is called wit. The common example of verbalism is what is called style. The common example of constructiveness is what is called logic.

[76-31]   *Shakespeare-Bacon*

Entre os varios problemas historicos que teem erguido atraz de si uma poeira de interesse, ha trez que, quer em virtude da sua importancia historica, quer por via da sua importancia literaria, teem, mais do que os outros, conseguido apaixonar e prender.

O primeiro – e sem duvida o mais importante, quer porque pertence ao mais importante e intimo de todos os phenomenos sociaes, quer porque seja o de, prisso, interesse mais geral, – é o problema da historicidade da figura de Jesus Christo.

O segundo – de interesse mais limitado, porque corra num campo de erudição fatalmente restricta – é o chamado "problema ou "questão" "de Homero."

O terceiro – de um interesse mais geral, porque os livros que o tratam são mais acessiveis a um largo publico, e por que as obras discutidas são das mais conhecidas em toda a Europa – é o problema da autoria da obra Shakespeareane, ou, pelo menos, parte d'ella.

Tencionamos, n'este opusculo, versar este problema. Como para os que não admittem Shakespeare como autor o candidato mais votado para autor da obra Shakespeareana é Francis Bacon, e como, por certo – pelas razões que no decurso da nossa exposição serão apontadas – este é quem mais argumentos tem em seu favor, o nosso exame da questão recahirá sobre a controversia Shakespeare-Bacon, propriamente dita. Buscaremos expôr qual nos pareça o estado actual d'ella

Como o que especialmente queremos é tornar o problema lúcido para o leitor, não o encararemos chronologicamente, mas seguindo o methodo que mais logicamente concatene os seus elementos componentes. Assim ser-nos-ha possivel dar aos interessados que o ignorem, uma noção concreta e completa de até onde chegou, hoje, o problema Shakespeare-Bacon.

1. Duvidas com respeito a Shakespeare.
2. Argumentos a favôr de Bacon (e Rutland).
3. Contra-argumentação Shakespeareana.
4. □

[Of the several historical problems which have sparked a sprinkling of interest, three, by virtue of their historic, as well as literary, significance, have attracted greater fascination and passion than the rest.

The first – and undoubtedly the most important, because it belongs to the most important and personal of all social phenomena and has, therefore, greater general interest – is the problem of the historical existence of Jesus Christ.

The second – of more limited interest, being in a narrower field of erudition – is the so-called Homer 'problem' or 'question'.

The third – of wider interest, because the books about it are more accessible to a wide readership, and because the works in question are among the best known in Europe – is the problem of the authorship of Shakespeare's works, or, at least, part of them, for those who do not allow that Shakespeare was the their author.

In this booklet I propose to explore the problem, describing what seems to me to be its current state. Since the most popular candidate for the authorship of the Shakespearean works is Francis Bacon, and since he is certainly – for reasons I will give during the exposition – the one with the most arguments in his favour, my examination of the controversy will probe the so-called Shakespeare-Bacon question. I will attempt to describe what seems to me to be its current state.

Since what I most wish is to make the problem intelligible to the reader, I will not approach it chronologically, but rather following the method which links its component parts in the most logical manner. Thus, I will be able to give those who are interested but know nothing about the Shakespeare-Bacon problem a concrete and complete idea of where it is at today.

1. Doubts concerning Shakespeare.
2. Arguments in favour of Bacon (and Rutland).
3. Shakespearean counter-argument.
4. □]

[76-34, 76-34a, 76-34av]   *Bacon a poet?*

We are led, indeed, to the conclusion that Bacon was a poet, and a concealed poet. But we are *not* led to the conclusion that the poet Bacon was 'Shakespeare'.

I am willing to accept *some of the elder poets, – the Peele[6], or Lyly[7] type – as the work of the great philosopher. It would fit in with the unknown activity of Bacon's earlier years. It would fit in with the allusions to Bacon as a poet. It would fit in with the necessary secondariness of Bacon in that capacity.

Bacon's disdain of his poetical labours is comprehensible if they are of the Lily or Peele line. They are then manifestly not of comparison, in referential values, with his philosophical achievement. But the hypothesis is untenable if Bacon's poetry be 'Shakespeare's': The man who was a poet to that height knows to what height he is a poet. Shakespeare is preeminently a *conscious* poet. And he does not despise his work. Whatever his reason might be to hide his authorship, there are none to let the work be published in his lifetime in an imperfect folio, full of errors, containing matter foreign to 'Shakespeare', when the author is in a position of such authority in the state that a simple gesture of his would at once destroy and *prevent the attempt at publication.

[76-57]   *Shakespeare-Bacon*

Henry Green: *Shakespeare and the Emblem Writers*, in *Biblioteca Acadêmica das Sciencias*

• In this work see the numerous, important and unmistakable coincidences between Geoffrey Whitney[8] and Shakespeare.

---

[6] George Peele (c.1558-1656) was a dramatist whose reputation rest upon his treatment of metre, and on his humour. He did much to refine and supple the diction of the drama.
[7] John Lyly (c.1553-1606), alternately rendered as Lilly, Lily or Lylie, was best known for his *The Anatomy of Wit*.
[8] Geoffrey Whitney (c.1548-c.1601) was an English poet who published in 1586 his emblem book *Choice of Emblems*. The work was the first of its kind to give to Englishmen an adequate example of the emblem books from the great continental presses. It was mainly from this book, representing the greater part of emblem literature preceding it, that Shakespeare gained the knowledge of the great foreign emblematists of the sixteenth

- One of the most curious of the coincidences is that between the dedication to *Venus and Adonis* and that to Whitney's book[9] (p. 475)
- p. 221: a *left* arm holding a spear containing 4 wreaths on it. (See, next page, Whitney's lines on the subject). (Do the 4 wreaths, perchance, allude to 4 *plays* then – 1586 – already written?)

[76-58] *Article on Shakespeare in* Encyclopaedia Britannica, *9th ed., vol. 21*

Notes:

All the notes on Shakespeare's knowledge of French and Italian are most interesting.

'Shakespeare derived the story of *Othello* from the untranslated part of this collection' (p. 758) – reference being to *Cynthia's 100 Tales*.[10]

Sonnets published in 1609, though probably begun early. 'Prefixed to Florio's *Second Fruits*, [11] Professor Minto [12] discovered a sonnet so superior and characteristic that he was impressed with the conviction that Shakespeare must have written it. The internal evidence is in favour of this conclusion, Mr Minto's critical analysis and comparison of its thought and diction with Shakespeare's early work tends strongly to support the reality[13] and value of the discovery. In his next work, published 4 years later, Florio claims[14] the sonnet as the work of a friend 'who loved better to be a poet than to be called one' and vindicates it from the indirect attack of a 'hostile critic, H. S., who had also disparaged the work in which it appeared' (p. 756).

century.

[9] Unclear why; Shakespeare's poem is dedicated to Henry Wriothesley, Earl of Southampton, and Whitney's to Robert Dudley, Earl of Leicester.

[10] *Cinthia's Revenge* (1613), an Elizabethan play of problematic attribution, is sometimes cited in the context of the Shakespearean authorship controversy. Alternatively, this could be reference to *Cynthia's Revels*, a play by Ben Jonson performed in 1600 and published in 1601, which Pessoa mentions in manuscript 76A-85 (see below).

[11] John Florio (1553–1625), known in Italian as Giovanni Florio, was a linguist and lexicographer, a royal language tutor at the Court of James I, and a possible friend and influence on Shakespeare. He translated Montaigne into English. *Second Fruits, to be gathered of Twelve Trees, of divers but delightsome Tastes to the Tongues of Italian and English men* (1591) was one of his published manuals including an outline of grammar, a selection of dialogues in parallel columns of Italian and English, and longer extracts from classical Italian writers in prose and verse.

[12] William Minto (1845-1893), Scottish man of letters who published in 1872 his *Manual of English Prose Literature*, and in 1874 *Characteristics of English Poets from Chaucer to Shirley.*

[13] Question mark next to this hesitation; the word appears in the original passage; see following note.

[14] The missing word from the passage Pessoa cites is 'claims'; see the full text of this encyclopaedia entry at <http://www.1902encyclopedia.com/S/SHA/william-shakespeare-31.html>.

Appendix

It is not so much the recurrence of the same images that is to be sought in this comparison, but the analogy of the species of images employed: the recurrence of the same images is but a very minor thing in the Baconian temperament. As Poe, writing in †, noted, the truly great image is *inexhaustible and utterly *rare. This is easily seen in the real impossibility that great dramatists are in of *repeating characters* *themselves. Compare *King *Lear to *Henry V.*

[76-83] *Ben Jonson's Contributions to the Obscurity of the Shakespeare Problem*

De 1576 a 1579 esteve em França.
O caso é que só em 1597 appareceu uma obra[15], fora o pequeno volume dos *Essays*. Até alli que tinha elle feito?

[He was in France between 1576-1579.
The fact of the matter is that only in 1597 did a publication appear, except for the small volume of *Essays*.]

Emerson: *Works* (London: 1883) – vol. 4, p. 420.[16]
Thomas Powell: *Attorney's Academy* (1630)[17]
Mark Twain: Is Shakespeare Dead? (1909)[18]

[15] In 1597, a play co-written with Thomas Nashe entitled *The Isle of Dogs* was suppressed after causing great offence. Arrest warrants for Jonson and Nashe were subsequently issued by Elizabeth's so-called interrogator, Richard Topcliffe. Jonson was jailed in Marshalsea Prison and famously charged with 'Leude and mutynous behavior', while Nashe managed to escape to Great Yarmouth.
[16] The page Pessoa refers to contains Emerson's famous appraisal of Shakespeare, continually cited as an anti-Stratfordian argument: 'As long as the question is of talent and mental power, the world of men has not his equal to show [...] The Egyptian verdict of the Shakespeare Societies comes to mind that he was a jovial actor and manager. I cannot marry this fact to his verse. Other admirable men had led lives in some sort of keeping with their thought; but this man, in wide contrast.' Pessoa misattributes these words to Coleridge in several of his writings on the Shakespearean authorship controversy (see Chapter 2).
[17] Thomas Powell (c.1608-1660), Welsh cleric and writer. In *The Attorney's Academy* he wrote the following poem under a portrait of Bacon, which has been interpreted by Baconians as a reference to his concealed authorship of the Shakespearean canon:
    O, give me leave to pull the curtain bye,
    That clouds thy worth in such obscurity;
    Good Seneca, stay but awhile thy bleeding,
    T'accept what I received at thy reading.
    Here I present it in a solemn strain:
    And thus I pluck the curtain back again.
[18] *Is Shakespeare Dead?* is a short work by the American writer Samuel Clemens, better known as Mark Twain (1835-1910). It explores the Shakespearean authorship controversy bia satire, anecdote, and extensive quotation of contemporary authors on the

Sir Edwin Durning-Lawrence, *Bacon is Shake-Speare* (1910)

[76A-3]   *Shakespeare-Bacon*

Shakespeare's characteristic peculiarities are
(1) His total mental indiscipline
Shakespeare, albeit possessing the qualities which are the very highest mental ones – high synthetic poetic power, absolute intuition of character, complete mastery of expression – is totally incapable of
(1) reigning his subject as a whole,
(2) organizing his plays in a coherent and sequent dramatic form;
(3) containing his tendency to seem in excess of words, into excess of wit and peculiarly of expression, into excess of † and detail.

(2) *His duality of temperament*
Shakespeare is dual in everything
(a) He is in the highest degree † † †
(b) His expression is at the same time in the hightest degree abstract and analytic, and *casual(†) and synthetic.
(c) □

(3) His sexual inversion.

[76A-4]
To what may this mental dispersion be due?
(a) To a constitutional mental disease.
(b) To a state of mind † disease brought about by some † † †.,
(c) To a simultaneous application of the mind to several subjects at the same time.

(a) His one distinctive characteristic is the power to impersonate all kinds of characters; if he has a mental disease, it can thus be but hysteria, for this is the † neurosis, the neurosis that is essentially dramatic and impersonatory.
(b) Only possible if one suffers a lack of † or a † quite complete.

Conclusão: hystero-neurasthenia de Shakespeare.

[Conclusion: Shakespeare's hystero-neurasthenia]

subject; Pessoa owned a copy of the book (see Chapter 2).

Appendix

[76A-26, 76A-26v, 76A-27]   *Shakespeare*

1. The primary argument on which the one-time Shakespeare-Bacon question
– now more fitly to be called the Shakespeare-everyone question – was and is
based is that there is such a disparity between the life and the work of the man
that he can hardly be conceived to be its real author. 'I cannot marry the man to
his verse' was Coleridge's expression of this doubt.[19] It is into the validity of this
argument that I purpose to inquire.

Should it be proved radically invalid; should it further be proved that there is,
on the contrary, a reasonable adjustment between the man and the work that goes
under his name, then only the production of definite and incontrovertible proof
that some other man wrote the works called Shakespeare's can be a relevant
rebuttal. No argument of this sort has yet appeared. We have had, in favour of
divers candidates, fragments of possibilities, nebulae of hypotheses; they prove
nothing as they are, and would tend to prove something only if the primary
argument – the one we are going to consider – were in itself irrefutable. If
Shakespeare were demonstrably not the author of the work called his, then
someone else must have been. Vague approximations and casual hypotheses
would then draw strength for their necessity.

The argument as to the disparity between the man and the work falls under
two heads: (1) the one Coleridge presumably alluded to, that between
Shakespeare's life and character, so far as we know them, and the works under his
name there is no psychological consonance; (2) the one that the works show
several special sorts of learning – classical, legal and others – which Shakespeare
would not have had.

2. The second argument can be at once set aside. It has been all through a forced
argument, based generally on ignorance of Elizabethan literature. It has been
pulverized in abundant detail by the late J. M. Robertson in his Book *The Baconian
Heresy*. Robertson proved (1) that there was no particular learning, classic, legal
or otherwise, in the works, (2) that Elizabethan authors, not particularly learned
themselves, show generally more learning, of all kinds, than Shakespeare of the
Works, (3) that, in particular reference to the legal point, the age was an age of
litigation and interest in litigation and that for that reason legal expressions came
readily to anyone at the time.

But we can go beyond Robertson's confutation[20]. We can set aside the
argument without having read a single Elizabethan book outside the Works, and
even allowing, for argument's sake, the validity of the main points put by the anti-
Stratfordians. This logical content is very evident if we go to it as psychologists.

One thing which patently emerges from the most cursory reading of
Shakespeare is that his mind was an inordinately – we might even say, a morbidly

[19] In fact, it was Emerson's; see Chapter 2.
[20] J. M. Robertson's *The Baconian Heresy: A Confutation* (London: Herbert Jenkins, 1913), a
book in Pessoa's library.

– prehensile and receptive one; he had what Bagehot called, in reference indeed to him, 'an experiencing nature'.[21] Now this highly receptive mind lived, as we certainly know, among scholars, as among men of all types. He could derive from one of his conversations with Ben Jonson as much simulation of learning – in voluntarily intermingled with his rapid inspiration – as could, to a shallow psychologist, give proof of scholarship. He could turn the results of an hour's talk with a lawyer into an exuberance of natural legal expressions that an innocent critic would easily take for a trained lawyer's production. Even for a prehensile mind of no very high quality the simulation of learning, voluntary or involuntary, is extremely easy: a dictionary of quotations is matter enough. I know a man here in Portugal whose knowledge of contemporary French literature is extensive, exact and vivid; so much so that we can hardly imagine that he has the time to read all that. And he does not; he has never read any at all of the books which, with their authors, he so brilliantly and exactly explains and discusses. He simply buys and reads carefully every week the *Nouvelles Littéraires*[22], which is a kind of French *John O'London*.[23] If to this man this is possible, why not to Shakespeare? The argument would have to be reconsidered if real profundity of learning, undoubted profundity of learning, such as we find in Jonson, could be proved of Shakespeare. But that has never been proved; it was on that point that Robertson's rebuttal was definite and complete.

One curious point, raised long ago by Sir George Greenwood, is still left over; it is not a case of learning but of expression. I refer to the ignorance about the habits of birds and some animals which Sir George thought inconceivable in a country-man,[24] linked as it is in Shakespeare with the knowledge of hawking and horsemanship, which, especially the first, are not distinctively yokels' pastimes. It is indeed a curious point but in itself it means nothing. We know nothing about Shakespeare's early life, and the knowledge of hawking may be due to observation of a thing he liked. As to the ignorance of the habits of birds and some animals, the point is irrelevant. Shakespeare, if he was the author of the Works, was not a country yokel in the sense that his life was necessarily bound up with all the things the other yokels were interested in. Apart from this he may not have been interested in birds. Such things happen even in the best regulated countrysides. Not all farmers' sons are interested in farming, as not all bankers' sons in banking. If the ignorance brought against Shakespeare in this respect had been, say, on the simplest things of country life, of the seasons of sowing and reaping for example, then, indeed, the argument might be valid.

---

[21] Walter Bagehot (1826-1877) was a British businessman, essayist and journalist who wrote about literature, government and economics. In *Literary Studies* (1879) he wrote that 'To a great experience one thing is essential – an experiencing nature.'
[22] French literary review 1922-1985.
[23] *John O'London's Weekly* was a weekly literary magazine published by George Newnes of London between 1919 and 1954. At its height it had a circulation of 80,000.
[24] It is unclear whether Pessoa intended to split this word, or if its hyphenation is due to the line length.

Appendix

[76A-46]   *Bacon-Shakespeare*

Durning-Lawrence's Arguments:
Honorificabilitudinitatibus and adjunct crypters.
Signatures of Shakespeare not Shakespeare's.
Ben Jonsons's E. M O[25] and his A[26]
Return from Parnassus[27]
As You Like It
The Tempest
The Stratford Bust
Some sonnets
Hamlet (re Yorick)
Legal phrasing
Ben *Jonson: Discoveries*[28] + † *or *W. S.*[29]
Th. Randolf – reference to Bacon.
George Herbert[30]
Campion
Great Assizes in Parnassus[31]
Shakespeare's correspondence
Ratsei's Ghost[32]
'As the soule of Euphorbus was thought to live in Pythagoras so the sweete wittie soule of Ovid lives in mellifluous and honeytongued Shakespeare, witness his *Venus and Adonis*, his *Lucrece*, his sugared Sonnets among his private friends.'[33]

---

[25] Probably a reference to Ben Jonson's play *Every Man Out of his Humour* (1600).

[26] Probably *The Alchemist* (first performed 1610).

[27] The Parnassus plays are three dramas were produced at St John's College, Cambridge, as part of the college's Christmas entertainments at the latter end of the 16th century. The first play, *The Pilgrimage to Parnassus*, is an allegory about student life; the other two, *The Return from Parnassus* and *The Second Part of the Return from Parnassus*, describe two graduates' unsuccessful attempts to make a living. Authorship of the plays is uncertain, nor is it known if they were all the work of the same man.

[28] *Timber, or Discoveries*, Jonson's commonplace book (1641).

[29] *Poems of Ben Jonson Junior, Composed by W. S. Gent.* (1672).

[30] George Herbert (1593 – 1633) was a Welsh poet, orator and Anglican priest. Throughout his life he wrote religious poems characterized by a precision of language, a metrical versatility, and an ingenious use of imagery or conceits that was favoured by the metaphysical school of poets.

[31] *Great Assizes Holden in Parnassus* (1645), which contains what many claim is a veiled reference to Bacon.

[32] *Ratsei's Ghost or the second part of his mad prankes and Robberies* is an undated pamphlet entered at Stationer's Hall in 1605. In *Bacon is Shakes-peare*, Durning-Lawrence uses one of its allusions as anti-Stratfordian 'evidence.'

[33] An oft-cited contemporary reference to Shakespeare by Meres.

1615 Bacon's name appears as a poet's in Stow's *Annals.*[34]

Mrs. Pott: Bacon's *Promus* – 1883 – 'a monumental work'[35]

[76A-50, 76A-50v]   *Bacon-Shakespeare*

Bacon não é subtil, propriamente: é arguto, □. Profundo, não é. É o que põe o seu escrever, por bello que seja, aquém do de Sir Thomas Browne.[36] É o que lhe tira aquelle tom de poesia que é tão distinctivo do autor da *Religio Medici*.[37] No commum isbellianismo que dê aos dois o commum feerismo de estylo, vê-se que o Chanceller não é senão um exoterico da poesia, que não conheceu, como o medico, aquelles espíritos mais sublimados que cantam, com voz □ demais para humanos ouvidos, do mysterio e da dôr do mundo.

Não sei mesmo de autor que, a ser possivel a hypothese, tanto faria pensar em ser elle o autor da obra shakespeareana como Sir Thomas Browne. A erudição, é certo, era obstaculo fatal; para não tocar na particularidade do jurisconsultismo de phrasear. Mas eu phantasio e faço-me um passatempo deleitoso no mero ponderar do quanto, na essencia reflectiva e □ do magno prosador da Inglaterra, faz pensar no poeta da anterior geração que escreveu o discurso idealisante de Prospero.

O espirito de Bacon é de natureza utilitario e ametaphysico. Analysa muito e medita pouco.

[Bacon is not exactly subtle: he is shrewd, □. He is not profound. Which is what sets his writing, lovely as it is, below Sir Thomas Browne's. It removes the poetic tone so distinctive of the author of *Religio Medici*. In the ordinary Elizabethan

---

[34] John Stow's *Annales, or a Generale Chronicle of England from Brute until the present yeare of Christ 1580* (1580).

[35] After a diligent deciphering of the Elizabethan handwriting in Francis Bacon's *Promus of Formularies and Elegancies*, Constance Mary Fearon Pott (1833-1915) noted that many of the ideas and figures of speech in Bacon's book could also be found in the Shakespearean plays. Pott founded the Francis Bacon Society in 1885 and published her Bacon-cantered theory in 1891. In this, Pott developed the view of W.F.C. Wigston, that Francis Bacon was the founding member of the Rosicrucians, and claimed that they secretly created art, literature and drama, including the entire Shakespeare canon, before adding the symbols of the rose and cross to their work.

[36] Sir Thomas Browne (1605-1682), author of varied works which disclose his wide learning in diverse fields including medicine, religion, science and the esoteric. His writings display a deep curiosity towards the natural world, influenced by the scientific revolution of Bacon.

[37] *Religio Medici* is a book by Browne which sets out his spiritual testament as well as being an early psychological self-portrait. In its day it was a European bestseller, and it brought its author fame and respect throughout the continent.

spirit that gives both the same wonderful style, we can see that the Chancellor is but an esoteric of poetry, that he did not know, like the doctor did, those sublime spirits who sing, with a voice too □ for human ears, about the world's mystery and pain.

I do not know of another author who, if the possibility can be entertained, would be a better candidate for the authorship of Shakespeare's works than Sir Thomas Brown. Certainly, erudition would be a fatal obstacle; not to mention the specific legal phrasing. But I fantasize, and make a delicious passtime in pondering how much, in his reflective and □ essence, the great English prose writer recalls the poet of the previous generation who wrote Prospero's idealising speech.

Bacon's spirit is by nature utilitarian and ametaphysical. He analyses much and meditates little.]

[76A-54]

Remark on p. 136 of Shakespeare's Folio 1623: the different shapes of capitals seem to indicate use of biliteral-† cipher.[38]

Para provar completamente que as obras de "Shakespeare" são realmente de Bacon, não basta se provar pela cifra; resta provar que Bacon não era homem capaz de deshonestamente, e sob cifra, se appropriar de obras alheias... Ahi é que bate o ponto. E a questão não é facil de decidir, em vista do caracter respeitadamente tortuoso de Francis Bacon. – E, sé já assim não é fácil, mais difficil se torna, quando vemos que Bacon se attribui, ou alguém, por cifra, lhe atribui obras de outros poetas dramaticos que poderia, talvez, cada uma d'ellas, ser escripta pelo autor da *Instaurato Magna*[39], mas não *todas* ellas por esse autor.

Ex.[40] the 'Milton's Epitaph on Shakespeare'[41] question: is the epitaph certainly Milton's? Some very *stable metrical □ are very unlike Milton's composition (e.g. line 9).

*Consider 'astonishingness' of *varieties* in *New Atlantis*[42] by Notes to J. M. Robertson's edition of Bacon.[43]

---

[38] Unclear why; the reference is to a page in *Love's Labours Lost*. Bacon's celebrated biliteral cipher, published as an illustrated plate in his *De Augmentis Scientiarum* (*The Advancement of Learning*, 1605), was an arrangement of the letters a and b in five-letter combinations, each representing a letter of the alphabet. Baconians search for this cipher in the Shakespearean works.

[39] Fragmentary and incomplete work by Bacon, the most important part of which is the *Novum Organum* (1620).

[40] Probably short for 'examine', rather than 'excellent' (in Pessoa's marginalia, 'ex' is shorthand for 'excellent' or, more unusually 'example', as in Portuguese.)

[41] 'On Shakespear' [sic] was Milton's first published poem, appearing anonymously in the second Folio of plays by Shakespeare (1632). There it bears the title 'An Epitaph on the admirable Dramaticke Poet, W.SHAKESPEARE', but has no attribution.

[42] In 1623 Bacon expressed his aspirations and ideals in *New Atlantis*, which depicts a utopia called Bensalem.

[43] Bacon's *The Philosophical Works of Francis Bacon* (1905), edited and with an

[In order fully to prove that 'Shakespeare's' works are actually Bacon's, it is not enough to prove a cypher; it must be proved that Bacon was not a an who would, dishonestly, and using a cypher, claim works that were not his... That is the point. And it is difficult to settle that matter, given the respectfully torturous nature of Francis Bacon. And, if it is already difficult, it becomes more difficult still when we discover that Bacon ascribes to himself, or that someone, via a cypher, ascribes to him, the works of other dramatic poets. Perhaps each one of these works might have been written by the author of *Instaurato Magna*, but not *all* of them.]

[76A-75]   *Psychology of the Author of* Shakespeare's *Works*

1. A man with a high intuition of character.

2. A man highly and intimately acquainted with law and legal terminology.

3. A man with an extraordinary imagination, in all directions and to all purposes.

4. A man who commits several errors in geography.

5. A man with an extraordinary fluency, compression and precision of phrase.

6. A man of intense and hardly bridled sensual leanings; extending even to abnormal inclinations.

7. A man of universal curiosity.

8. A man but moderately able to reproduce real cunning, as cunning. (Iago's cunning is not of the subtle kind).

9. A man with intense comprehension of humans and man's character and natures, at least in drama.

10. There is in the drama but little commented and *abstruse reasoning (but many expressions indicating reasoning?); but considerable argument of the legal kind.

11. The abuse of wit and of neat, precise and □ expressions is evident (Cf. Macaulay on Bacon).[44]

12. A man depicting better the clash of sentiment and sentiment than that of intellect and intellect.

13. A man tending in his philosophy to idealism.

14. A man not original in the essential story of his plots.

15. In the plays the alternation of tragic and comic scenes.

16. The symbolic nature of *The Tempest*.

17. □

introduction by Robertson, is in Pessoa's library.
[44] Thomas Babington Macaulay (1800-1859) was a British poet, historian and Whig politician (he was Secretary at War between 1839 and 1841, and Paymaster-General between 1846 and 1848). He wrote extensively as an essayist and reviewer, and on British history. His long essay on Bacon was first published in *The Edinburgh Review* in July 1837.

[76A-85] *Data as to the probable personality of the author of the Shakespearean plays:*

1. In a great number of allusions to him (Quarto), he is referred to by names which involve reference to *a bird* – Sir Oliver Owlets, Sir John Daw, etc. Spenser's Aetion, if to the point, will confirm this, since it mean's 'eaglet'.

2. In a great number of allusions to him (Quarto), he is referred to as being 'a knight'. These allusions include the sonnet in the *Passionate Pilgrim*, written presumably (unless the attribution is wrong)[45] by Shakespeare himself; he there says, of himself, 'A knight loves both'. Cf. Sir Oliver Owlet, Sir John Daw, Puntarvolo ('a vainglorious knight'). In cases where allusion is not distinctly to a knight, it refers still to a person in 'good society', as the Amorphus in *Cynthia's Revels*.[46]

3. In Ben Jonson's inimical allusions to the author of Shakespeare's plays (unless the allusions are wrongly interpreted), the person referred to is always accompanied by a younger friend, as Amorphus by Asotus, Sir John Daw by Sir Amorous La Foole. (This squares with the *Sonnets*).

4. References to Shakespeare are scarce in the literature of the time; but this is chiefly due to the fact that no such notion of the worth of the Shakespearean achievement existed as we might suppose, or would think just. Jonson stood, at that time, in the in which we put Shakespeare to-day.

5. No reference, that we have, separates the poet from the player distinctly. Many do not, indeed, clearly link them, but, such as they are, they allude to Shakespeare as to one about whom no question could exist. They are all above-board.

6. All references to Shakespeare's learning, law-learning and such like are beside the point, and mean nothing. A mind so universally prehensile as Shakespeare's, so able to interpret, to identify itself with anything, and to simulate anything, can simulate all that culture without detection. It will do so naturally. There is no comparison with Burns, who, besides being overrated, was not a peculiarly nimble mind, but a narrow poet.

7. The absolute carelessness of Shakespeare, whoever he was, about his works and their publication, except in a few cases, such as the two poems, means one of the following things, (1) that he did not give his own works that importance which we give them, (2) that he was mentally diseased in some respect of the will and had no artistic scruple, not owing to absence of artistic qualities, but owing to lack of will to put them into action except under a sudden and compelling inspiration, (3) that he simply arranged and altered other men's works and therefore cared little for the fate of the resultant work, which was never wholly his – as the *Sonnets* and the Poems were, (4) that he was away from England, (5) that he had no power to interfere, either through fear or simply through having no power. The last is the last probable hypothesis. – The characters of the published works seems to

---

[45] *The Passionate Pilgrim* is an anthology of twenty poems published in 1599 as the work of William Shakespeare, though his authorship of many of the individual poems in the collection is doubted.

[46] A play by Ben Jonson performed in 1600 and published in 1601.

exclude a careful poet or artist.

8. □

[144D2-16, 144D2-16v, 144D2-17   *Questão Shakespeare-Bacon (Livros)*

[*Shakespeare-Bacon Question: Books*]
B.   *Encyclopaedia Britannica* – artigos [entries on] Shakespeare, Bacon, etc.
     infra. W. H. Smith: *Bacon and Shakespeare: an Enquiry.* London: 1857.
     Delia Bacon: *The Philosophy of the Plays of Shakspeare [sic] Unfolded.* 1857.
     Donnelly: *The Great Cryptogram.* 1888.
     Edwin Reed: *Francis Bacon our Shakespeare.* 1902.
     Pitt-Lewis: *The Shakespeare Story.* 1904.
     Bompas: *The Problem of Shakespeare's Plays.* 1902.
     Sutton: '*The Shakespeare Enigma.* 1903.
A   George G. Greenwood: *The Shakespeare Problem Restated.* 1908 (J Laner
     21/-net)
A   Beeching: *Reply to Greenwood.* 1908.
     Bleibtreu: *Der Wahre Shakespeare.* 1907.
     James Spedding: *The Letters and Life of Bacon.* 7 vols. (1862-74).
     ------------------- : *Evenings with a Reviewer.* 1881.
A   *Philosophical Works of Francis Bacon* – Ellis and Spedding, ed. J. M.
     Robertson. Routledge. 1905.
A   Ben Jonson: *Works*, ed. Gifford and Cunningham. 3 vols., 1903.
A   Oscar Wilde: 'The Portrait of Mr. W. H.' (Tauchnitz).
A   Mark Twain: 'Is Shakespeare dead?' (Tauchnitz).
BAc Sir Edwin-Durning-Lawrence: *Bacon is Shake-spear.*
     Works of Christopher Marlowe, ed. Cunningham.
     Roe: *The Own Story of Francis Bacon.* (American pamphlet)
     John M. Robertson: 'Did Shakespeare write *Titus Andronicus?*'
     Peter Alvor: □
     Dr. Orville Owen: 'Sir Francis Bacon's Cypher Story'. (Gay and Hancock).
     Albert F. Calvert: □
     The Shakespeare Allusion Book – Chatto and Windus – 2 vols., 21/-net.
A   George G. Greenwood: *In re Shakespeare: Beeching v. Greenwood.
     Rejoinder on Behalf of the Defendant* (John Lane, 2/6 net).
     The Collection *The Shakespeare Classics* (sources of Shakespeare's plays),
     Chatto and Windus. 20 vols., 4/-net each.
     The Collection *Shakespeare's England* (Chatto and Windus, various
     prices). Contains some six vols. (including *Allusion Book*).
A.   Mag Thumm – Kintzel: 'Manuscrits de Shakespeare'. *La Revue*, 15 juillet
     1910.
A.   P.-L. Hervier: 'Les Sonnets de Shakespeare.' *La Revue*, 15 julliet 1911.
A.   Cuttings from *Daily Express* (regarding Orville Owen, chiefly). Infra Mrs.
     Pott: *Bacon's Promus.* 1883.

BIBLIOGRAPHY

Primary Sources

Pessoa's Unpublished Texts on Shakespeare
(All at the *Biblioteca Nacional de Portugal*, Lisbon, in Pessoa's archive: BNP/E3.)
76-13, 76-13v
76-14
76-19
76-20
76-31
76-34, 76-34a, 76-34av
76-57
76-58
76-83
76A-3
76A-4
76A-10
76A-26, 76A-26v, 76A-27
76A-46, 76A-46v
76A-50, 76A-50v
76A-54
76A-75 (3 pp.)
76A-85
144D2-16, 144D2-16V, 144D2-17

Books in Pessoa's Library (*Casa Fernando Pessoa*, Lisbon)
A Graduate of Cambridge. [Begley, Walter.] *Is it Shakespeare? The Great Question of Elizabethan Literature Answered in the Light of New Revelations and Important Contemporary Evidence* (London: John Murray, 1903).
Aeschylus. *The Lyrical Dramas of Aeschylus, translated into English Verse by John Stuart Blackie* (London: J. M. Dent and Sons, 1917).
Albino Pacheco. *Degenerescência* (Coimbra: Imprensa da Universidade, 1901).
Anon. [Alfred Egmont Hake and Nicholas Murray Butler]. *Regeneration: A Reply to Max Nordau* (Westminster: Archibald Constable and Co., 1895).
Arnold, Matthew. *Essays in Criticism: Second Series* (London: Macmillan and Co., 1927).
Bacon, Francis. *The Philosophical Works of Francis Bacon*, ed. J. M. Robertson (London: George Routledge and Sons/New York: E. P. Dutton and Co., 1905).
Baudelaire, Charles. *Les Fleurs du Mal* (Paris: Ernest Flammarion, n.d.).
Beeching, H. C. *William Shakespeare: Player, Playmaker, and Poet. A Reply to Mr. George Greenwood, M.P.* (2nd ed., London: Smith, Elder and Co., 1909).
Begley, Walter. *Bacon's Nova Resuscitatio, or the Unveiling of his Concealed Works and Travels*, 3 vols. (London: Gay and Bird, 1905).

Bormann, Edwin. *The Quintessence of the Shakespeare Secret* (London: A. Siegle, 1905).

Carlyle, Thomas. *Sartor Resartus; Heroes; Past and Present* (London: Chapman and Hall, 1903).

Coleridge, Samuel Taylor. *Coleridge's Essays and Lectures on Shakespeare and Some Other Old Poets and Dramatists* (London: I. M. Dent and Sons; New York: E. P. Dutton and Co., n.d. [1907]).

Demblon, Célestin. *Lord Rutland Est Shakespeare: Le Plus Grand des Mistéres Dévoilé Shaxper de Stratford Hors Cause* (Paris: Paul Ferdinand, 1913).

Durning-Lawrence, Edwin. *Bacon is Shakes-Speare* (London: Gay and Hancock, 1910).

Emerson, Ralph Waldo. *Works of Ralph Waldo Emerson: Essays, First and Second Series, Representative Men, Society and Solitude, English Traits, The Conduct of Life, Letters and Social Aims, Poems, Miscellanies Embracing Nature, Addresses, and Lectures* (London: George Routledge and Sons, 1902).

Forrest, H. T. S. *The Five Authors of Shakespeare's Sonnets* (London: Chapman and Dodd, 1923).

Gilfillan, George. 'Shakespeare – A Lecture', in *A Gallery of Literary Portraits* (London: J. M. Dent and Co., n.d. [Introduction dated 1909], pp. 184-215.

Goethe, Johann Wolfgang von. *Werther, Faust, Hermann et Dorothée* (Paris: Ernest Flammrion, n.d. [1832?]).

Greenwood, George. *In Re Shakespeare: Beeching v. Greenwood; A Rejoinder on Behalf of the Defendant* (London/New York: John Lane, 1909).

--- *The Shakespeare Problem Restated* (London: John Lane, 1908).

Harris, David Fraser. *Nerves* (London: Williams and Norgate; New York: Henry Holt and Co., n.d. [1913].

Hirsch, William. *Genius and Degeneration: A Psychological Study* (London: William Heinemann, 1897).

Jonson, Ben. *The Works of Ben Jonson*, 3 vols. (London: Chatto and Windus, 1897-1904).

Lacerda, José de. *Os Neurasthenicos: esboço d'um estudo medico e philosophico* (Lisbon: M. Gomes, 1895).

Lefranc, Abel. *Sous le masque de "William Shakespeare": William Stanley VIᵉ Comte de Derby*, 2 vols. (Paris: Payot and Cie, 1919).

Leland, Charles Godfrey. *Have you a strong will?: or how to develope and strengthen will-power, memory, or any other faculty or attribute of the mind, by the easy process of self-hypnotism* (5th ed., London: William Ryder and Son, 1912).

Lovell, Arthur. *Volo or the Will: What it is; How to Strengthen, and How to Use it* (2nd ed., London: Nichols and Co., 1900).

Lowell, James Russell. 'Shakespeare Once More', in *The English Poets: Lessing, Rousseau: Essays by James Russell Lowell, with "An Apology for a Preface"* (London: The Walter Scott Publishing Co., n.d.), pp. 81-148.

Masefield, John. *William Shakespeare: His Life and Works* (London: Williams and Norgate/New York: Henry Holt, n.d. [1911]).

Mathew, Frank. *An Image of Shakespeare* (London: Jonathan Cape, n.d. [1922]).

Nisbet, J. F. *Marriage and Heredity: A View of Psychological Evolution* (Edinburgh: John Grant, 1908).

--- *The Insanity of Genius and the General Inequality of Human Faculty, Physiologically Considered* (3rd ed., London: Ward and Downey, 1893).

Nobre, António. *Cartas inéditas de Antonio Nobre*, ed. Adolfo Casais Monteiro (Coimbra: Edições Presença, 1934).

Nordau, Max. *Vue du dehors: essai de critique scientifique et philosophique sur quelques auteurs français contemporains*, trans. Auguste Dietrich (Paris: Félix Alcan, 1903).

--- *On art and artists*, trans. W. F. Harvey (London: T. Fisher Unwin, 1907).

--- *Paradoxes psychologiques.* trans Auguste Dietrich (7th ed., Paris: Félix Alcan, 1911).

--- *Paradoxes sociologiques*, trans August Dietrich (5th ed., Paris: Félix Alcan, 1907).

--- *Psycho-physiologie du génie et du talent*, trans Auguste Dietrich (5th ed., Paris: Félix Alcan, 1911).

Pellissier, Georges. *Shakespeare et la supersition shakespearienne* (Paris: Hachette, 1914).

Pessoa, Fernando. *Mensagem* (Lisbon: Parceria António Maria Pereira, 1934).

Rivers, W. C. *Walt Whitman's Anomaly* (London: George Allen and Company, 1913).

Robertson, J. M. *A Short History of Christianity* (London: Watts and Co., 1902).

--- *The Baconian Heresy: A Confutation* (London: Herbert Jenkins, 1913).

--- *The Problem of "Hamlet"* (London: George Allen and Unwin, 1919).

--- *The Genuine in Shakespeare: A Conspectus* (London: George Routledge and Sons, 1930).

--- *The Problem of "Hamlet"* (London: George Allen and Unwin, 1919).

--- *"Hamlet" Once More* (London: Richard Dobden-Sanderson, 1923).

Rosa-Cruz, Frades. *Secret Shakespearean Seals: Revelations of Rosicrucian Arcana: Discoveries in the Shakespeare Plays, Sonnets and Works Printed Circa 1586-1740* (Nottingham: Jenkins, 1916).

Seibel, George. *The Religion of Shakespeare* (London: Watts and Co., 1924).

Shakespeare, William. *The Complete Works of William Shakespeare*, ed. W. J. Craig (Oxford: Clarendon, n.d. [1892]).

--- *The* Tempest (London: Cassell and Co., 1908).

--- *The Tempest: Facsimile of the First Folio of* 1623, ed. Arthur Quiller-Couch and John Dover Wilson (Cambridge: Cambridge University Press, n.d. [1921]).

Shaw, Bernard. *The Doctor's Dilemma; and the Dark Lady of the Sonnets* (Leipzig: Bernhard Tauchnitz, 1914).

Smedley, William. *The Mystery of Francis Bacon* (London: Robert Banks and Son, 1912).

Stoker, Bram. *Dracula* (1897; London: Rider and Co., 1931).

Twain, Mark. *Extract from Captain Stormfield's Visit to Heaven; and Is Shakespeare Dead?* (Leipzig: Bernhard Tauchnitz, n.d. [1909]).

Wilde, Oscar. *Lord Arthur Savile's Crime and Other Prose Pieces* (Leipzig: Bernhard Tauchnitz, 1909).

--- *Le Portrait de Monsieur W. H.* (Paris: Bibliothèque Cosmopolite, 1906).

Woodward, Parker. *The Early Life of Lord Bacon* (London: Gay and Bird, 1902).

Writings by Pessoa and Shakespeare[1]

Pessoa, Fernando. *Alberto Caeiro: Poesia*, ed. Fernando Cabral Martins and Richard Zenith (2001; 2nd ed. Lisbon: Assírio e Alvim, 2004).

--- *Álvaro de Campos: A Passagem das Horas*, ed. Cleonice Berardinelli (Lisbon: IN-CM, 1988).

--- *Álvaro de Campos: Livro de versos*, ed. Teresa Rita Lopes (Lisbon: Estampa, 1993).

--- *Álvaro de Campos: Poesia*, ed. Teresa Rita Lopes (Lisbon: Assírio e Alvim, 2002).

--- *Apreciações Literárias de Fernando Pessoa*, ed. Pauly Ellen Bothe (Lisbon: IN-CM, 2013).

--- *Cadernos I*, ed. Jerónimo Pizarro (Lisbon: IN-CM, 2009).

--- *Cartas a Armando Côrtes-Rodrigues* (Lisbon: Horizonte, 1985).

--- *Cartas de Amor a Ophélia Queiroz*, ed. David Mourão-Ferreira (Lisbon: Ática, 1978).

--- *Cartas entre Fernando Pessoa e os directores da 'Presença'*, ed. Enrico Martines (Lisbon: IN-CM, 1998).

--- *A Centenary Pessoa*, ed. Eugénio Lisboa and L.C. Taylor (Manchester: Carcanet, 1995).

--- *Correspondência inédita*, ed. Manuela Parreira da Silva (Lisbon: Horizonte, 1996).

--- *Correspondência 1905-1922*, ed. Manuela Parreira da Silva (Lisbon: Assírio e Alvim, 1998).

--- *Correspondência 1923-1935*, ed. Manuela Parreira da Silva (Lisbon: Assírio e Alvim, 1999).

--- *Crítica: ensaios, artigos e entrevistas*, ed. Fernando Cabral Martins (Lisbon: Assírio e Alvim, 2000).

--- *Eu sou uma antologia: 136 autores fictícios*, ed. Jerónimo Pizarro e Patricio Ferrari (Lisbon: Tinta da China, 2013).

--- *Escritos autobiográficos, automáticos e de reflexão pessoal*, ed. Richard Zenith (Lisbon: Assírio e Alvim, 2003).

--- *Escritos sobre génio e loucura*, 2 vols., ed. Jerónimo Pizarro (Lisbon: IN-CM, 2006).

--- *Fausto: Tragédia Subjectiva*, ed. Teresa Sobral Cunha (Lisbon: Presença, 1988).

--- *Fernando Pessoa – O Comércio e a publicidade*, ed. António Mega Ferreira (Lisbon: Cinevoz – Lusomedia, 1968).

--- *Fernando Pessoa: 35 Sonnets, Tradução*, ed. and trans. Philadelpho Menezes

---

[1] Excluding the books in Pessoa's library, listed in the previous section.

(São Paulo: Arte Pau-Brasil, 1988).

--- *Fernando Pessoa: Imagens de uma vida*, ed. Manuela Nogueira (Lisbon: Assírio e Alvim, 2005).

--- *Fernando Pessoa: uma fotobiografia*, ed. Maria José Lencastre (Lisbon: IN-CM, 1980).

--- *Ficção e Teatro*, ed. António Quadros (Mem Martins: Europa-América, 1986).

--- *Ficções do interlúdio/2-3: Odes de Ricardo Reis* (Rio de Janeiro: Nova Aguilar, 1976).

--- *Forever Someone Else: Selected Poems*, ed. and trans. Richard Zenith (Lisbon: Assírio e Alvim, 2009).

--- *Fotobiografias Século XX: Fernando Pessoa*, ed. Richard Zenith (Lisbon: Círculos de Leitores, 2008).

--- *Heróstrato e a busca da imortalidade*, ed. Richard Zenith (Lisbon: Assírio e Alvim, 2000).

--- *Livro do Desassossego*, ed. Richard Zenith (3rd ed., Lisbon: Assírio e Alvim, 2001).

--- *O Manuscrito de O Guardador de Rebanhos de Alberto Caeiro: edição facsimilada*, ed. Ivo Castro (Lisbon: Dom Quixote, 1986).

--- *Notas para a recordação do meu Mestre Caeiro*, ed. Teresa Rita Lopes (Lisbon: Estampa, 1997).

--- *Obra Essencial de Fernando Pessoa: Poesia Inglesa*, ed. Richard Zenith, trans. Luísa Freire (Lisbon: Assírio e Alvim, 2007).

--- *Páginas de estética e de teoria literárias*, ed. Georg Rudolf Lind and Jacinto do Prado Coelho (Lisbon: Ática, n.d. [1966]).

--- *Páginas de pensamento político*, 2 vols., ed. António Quadros (Mem Martins: Europa-América, 1986).

--- *Páginas íntimas e de auto-interpretação* ed. Georg Rudolf Lind and Jacinto do Prado Coelho (Lisbon: Ática, n.d.).

--- *Pessoa inédito*, ed. Teresa Rita Lopes (Lisbon: Horizonte, 1993).

--- *Pessoa por conhecer I: Roteiro para uma expedicão*, ed. Teresa Rita Lopes (Lisbon: Estampa, 1990).

--- *Pessoa por conhecer II: Textos para um novo mapa*, ed. Teresa Rita Lopes (Lisbon: Estampa, 1991).

--- *Poemas de Álvaro de Campos*, ed. Cleonice Berardinelli (Lisbon: IN-CM, 1990).

--- *Poemas de Fernando Pessoa 1921-1930*, ed. Ivo Castro (Lisbon: IN-CM, 2001).

--- *Poemas ingleses de Fernando Pessoa* (Lisbon: Ática, 1974).

--- *Poemas ingleses*, ed. João Dionísio (Lisbon: IN-CM, 1997).

--- *Poesia do eu*, ed. Richard Zenith (Lisbon: Assírio e Alvim, 2006).

--- *Ricardo Reis: Prosa*, ed. Manuela Parreira da Silva (Lisbon: Assírio e Alvim, 2003).

--- *Sensacionismo e outros ismos*, ed. Jerónimo Pizarro (Lisbon: IN-CM, 2009).

--- *Textos de crítica e de intervenção* (Lisbon: Ática, 1980).

--- *Textos filosóficos*, ed. António de Pina Coelho, 2 vols. (Lisbon: Ática, 1968).

--- *The Selected Prose of Fernando Pessoa*, ed. and trans. Richard Zenith (New York: Grove Press, 2001).

--- *Ultimatum e páginas de sociologia política*, ed. Joel Serrão (Lisbon: Ática, 1980).
Shakespeare, William. *A Choice of Shakespeare's Verse*, ed. Ted Hughes (1971; London/Boston: Faber and Faber, 1991).
--- *The Enfolded Hamlets: Parallel Texts of <F1> and {Q2} Each With Unique Elements Bracketed*, ed. Bernice W. Kliman (New York: AMS/London: Eurospan, 1996).
--- *Hamlet*, ed. Ann Thompson and Neil Taylor (London: Arden, 3rd ed., 2006).
--- *Hamlet Works* <www.hamletworks.org>
--- *The Norton Shakespeare: Based on the Oxford Edition*, ed. Walter Cohen, Stephen Greenblatt, Jean Howard, Katherine Eisaman Maus (London/New York: Norton and Company, 2008).
--- *Shakespeare's Sonnets*, ed. Stephen Booth (1977; New Haven: Yale University Press, 2000).
--- *Shakespeare's Sonnets*, ed. Katherine Duncan-Jones (London: Arden, 3rd ed., 1997).
--- *Os Sonetos de Shakespeare: versão integral*, ed. and trans. Vasco Graça Moura (Lisbon: Bertrand, 2002).
--- *The Sonnets and a Lover's Complaint*, ed. John Kerrigan (New York: Viking Penguin Inc., 1986).
--- *A Tempestade, seguido de 'O Mar e o espelho' de W. H. Auden*, trans. José Manuel Mendes, Luís Lima Barreto and Luis Miguel Cintra (Lisbon: Cotovia, 2009).

Secondary Sources: Works Cited and Consulted
Ackroyd, Peter. *T. S. Eliot: A Life* (1984; London: Penguin, 1993).
Afonso, Maria João da Rocha. 'As versões portuguesas de *King Lear*', in *Shakespeare*, ed. João Almeida Flor (Lisbon: Fundação Calouste Gulbenkian, 1990), pp. 65-77.
--- 'From Words to Action: Translating Shakespeare for the Portuguese Stage', in *Translating Shakespeare for the Twenty-first Century*, ed. Rui Carvalho Homem and Tom Hoenselaars (Amsterdam/New York: Rodopi, 2004), pp. 162-174.
--- 'Simão de Melo Brandão and the First Portuguese Version of "Othello"', in *European Shakespeares: Translating Shakespeare in the Romantic Age*, ed. Dirk Delabastita and Lieven D'hulst (Amsterdam/Philadelphia: John Benjamins, 1993), pp. 129-146.
Alexander, Catherine M. S. and Stanley Wells (ed.). *Shakespeare and Sexuality* (Cambridge: Cambridge University Press, 2001).
Allan, Mowbray. *T. S. Eliot's Impersonal Theory of Poetry* (Lewisburg: Bucknell University Press, 1974).
Allbright, Daniel. *Personality and Impersonality: Lawrence, Woolf, and Mann* (Chicago/London: The University of Chicago Press, 1978).
Almeida, Onésimo T. 'Fernando Pessoa and Antero de Quental (with Shakespeare in between)', *Portuguese Studies* 24:2 (*The Future of the Arcas*, 2008). 51-68
Anon. 'Lisbon – Teatro Nacional de Sao Carlos', *Planetware*.

<http://www.planetware.com/lisbon/teatro-nacional-de-sao-carlos-p-lisb-tnsc.htm>

Anon. 'Magpie "can recognise reflection"', *BBC News* website (19 August 2008).
<http://news.bbc.co.uk/2/hi/science/nature/7570291.stm>

Anon. 'Shakespeare', *Monthly Review* CV (1824), pp. 398-412.

Anon. (attr. to Wilde et al). *Teleny, or The Reverse of the Medal* (1893; New York: Mondial, 2006).

Appingnanesi, Lisa. *Mad, Bad and Sad: A History of Women and the Mind Doctors from 1800 to the Present* (London: Virago, 2008).

Aristotle. *Poetics* (Cambridge: Cambridge University Press, 1962).

Arnold, Matthew. *Essays in Criticism: Second Series* (London: Macmillan, 1888).

Assis, Joaquim Maria Machado de. *O Alienista e O Espelho* (Rio de Janeiro: Ediouro, 1996).

Athena: edição facsimilada (Lisbon: Contexto, 1994).

Aubrey, John. *Brief Lives Chiefly of Contemporaries set down John Aubrey between the Years 1669 and 1696*, ed. Andrew Clark (Oxford: Clarendon, 1898).

Auerbach, Nina. *Woman and Demon* (Cambridge, M.A.: Harvard University Press, 1982).

Austin, Sarah (ed.). *A Memoir of the Reverend Sydney Smith by his Daughter Lady Holland, with A Selection From His Letters*, 2 vols. (London: Longman, Brown, Green, and Longmans, 1855).

Babcock, Robert Witbeck. *The Genesis of Shakespeare Idolatry 1766-1799: A Study in English Criticism of the Late Eighteenth Century* (New York: Russel and Russel, 1964).

Bacon, Delia. *The Philosophy of the Plays of Shakspere [sic] Unfolded* (London: Groombridge and Sons, 1857).

Baldick, Chris. *The Social Mission of English Criticism 1848-1932* (Oxford: Clarendon, 1983).

Banville, John. 'Emerson, "A Few Inches From Calamity"', *The New York Review of Books* (21 November 2009), pp. 2-4.

Barnfield, Richard. *Cynthia, with Certaine Sonnets, and the Legend of Cassandra* (London: Humphrey Lownes, 1595).

Bate, Jonathan (ed.). *The Romantics on Shakespeare* (London: Penguin, 1992).

Bate, Jonathan. *The Genius of Shakespeare* (London: Macmillan, 1997).

--- *Shakespeare and the English Romantic Imagination* (Oxford: Clarendon, 1986).

--- *Soul of the Age: The Life, Mind and World of William Shakespeare* (London: Penguin, 2008).

Baudelaire, Charles. *Correspondance*, ed. Claude Pichois and Jean Ziegler, 2 vols. (Paris: Gallimard, 1973).

--- *Oeuvres complètes*, ed. Claude Pichois, 2 vols. (Paris: Gallimard, 1975).

Beard, George Miller. *A Practical Treatise on Nervous Exhaustion (Neurasthenia)., Its Symptoms, Nature, Sequences and Treatment* (New York: Wood and Company, 1880).

Benevides, Francisco da Fonseca. *O Real Theatro [sic] de S. Carlos de Lisboa desde a sua fundação em 1793 até à actualidade: estudo historico* (Lisbon: Castro e

Irmão, 1883).

Benjamin, Walter. *Charles Baudelaire: A Lyric Poet in the Era of High Capitalism* (London: Verso Editions, 1983).

Berardinelli, Cleonice. *Fernando Pessoa: Outra vez te revejo...* (Rio de Janeiro: Nova Aguilar, 2004).

Blanco, José. *Pessoana: Bibliografia Passiva, Selectiva e Temática*, 2 vols. (Lisbon: Assírio e Alvim, 2008).

--- 'A Verdade sobre a Mensagem', in *A Arca de Pessoa*, ed. Jerónimo Pizarro and Steffen Dix (Lisbon: Imprensa de Ciências Sociais, 2007), pp. 147-161.

Bloom, Harold. *The Anxiety of Influence: A Theory of Poetry* (New York: Oxford University Press, 1973).

--- *A Map of Misreading* (New York: Oxford University Press, 1975).

--- *The Western Canon: The Books and School of the Ages* (New York: Harcourt Brace, 1994). Bolt, Sydney. *A Preface to James Joyce* (London: Longman, 1992).

Booth, Wayne C. *The Rhetoric of Fiction* (London/Chicago: The University of Chicago Press, 1961).

Borges, Jorge Luis. 'Everything and Nothing', in *Labyrinths: Selected Stories and Other Writings*, trans. James Irby (New York: Penguin, 1964), pp. 242-249.

Bosanquet, *History of Aesthetic* (London: Swan Sonneschein and Co., 1892).

Branco, Camilo Castelo. *Esboço de crítica. Othello, o Mouro de Veneza de William Shakespeare* (*tragédia traduzida para portuguez por D. Luiz de Bragança*). (Porto: Chardron, 1886).

Brandes, George. *William Shakespeare* (London: Kessinger, 1898).

Bray, Alan. *Homosexuality in Renaissance England* (London: Gay Men's Press, 1982).

Bréchon, Robert. 'Le masque et l'aveu: l'oeuvre anglaise', in *L'Innombrable: un tombeau pour Fernando Pessoa* (Paris: Christian Bourgois, 2001), pp. 177-185.

Briggs, Laura. 'The Race of Hysteria: '"Overcivilization" and the "Savage" Woman in Late Nineteenth-Century Obstetrics and Gynecology', *American Quarterly* 52 (2000), pp. 246–73.

Buci-Glucksmann, Christine. 'La place d'Hamlet', in *Tragique de l'ombre: Shakespeare et le maniérisme* (Paris: Galilée, 1990), pp. 147-55.

Bueno, Aurea. 'A verdade sobre a trama heteronímica: o Poeta português Fernando Pessoa não é menos fictício do que o Rei Artur', *Diário de Avisos* (1 November 1984).

Buescu, Helena Carvalhão. *Grande angular: comparatismo e práticas de comparação* (Lisbon: Fundação Calouste Gulbenkian/FCT, 2001).

--- 'Tópicos para o debate', in *Garret às portas do milénio*, ed. Fernando Mão de Ferro (Lisbon: Colibri, 2002), pp. 59-62.

Buxton, John. *Sir Philip Sidney and the English Renaissance* (London: Macmillan, 1987).

Cabral Martins, Fernando (ed.). *Dicionário de Fernando Pessoa e do Modernismo Português* (Lisbon: Caminho, 2008).

--- 'Raul Leal', in *Dicionário de Fernando Pessoa e do Modernismo Português* (Lisbon: Caminho, 2008), pp. 395-397.

Calvert, Albert F. *Bacon and Shakespeare* (New York: Dean and Son, 1902).

Campbell, John. *Shakespeare's Legal Acquirements Considered* (London: John Murray, 1859).

Carlyle, Thomas. *Critical and Miscellaneous Essays*, in *Works*, 18 vols. (London: Chapman and Hall, 1898-1901), XVI.

Carmo, José Palla e. 'Uma Trindade: Ezra Pound, T. S. Eliot, Fernando Pessoa', *Colóquio– Letras* 95 (1987), pp. 26-39.

Carrère, B. *Dégénérescence et dispsomanie d'Edgar Poe* (unpublished doctoral dissertation, Toulouse: University of Toulouse, 1907).

Carter, Alfred Edward. *The Idea of Decadence in French Literature 1830-1900* (Toronto: The University of Toronto Press, 1958).

Castro, Mariana Gray de. 'Fernando Pessoa and the "Shakespeare Problem"', *Journal of Romance Studies* 9:2 (Summer 2009), pp. 11-2.

--- 'Oscar Wilde, Fernando Pessoa, and the Art of Lying', *Portuguese Studies* 22 (September 2006), pp. 219-49.

--- 'Shakespeare, dramaturgo invisível', *Jornal i* (30 December 2009). p. 42.

Centeno, Yvette. 'Fernando Pessoa: Ophélia-Bébezinho ou o "horror do sexo"', *Colóquio-Letras* 49 (1979), pp. 11-20.

Centeno, Yvette K. and Stephen Reckert. *Fernando Pessoa: Tempo, solidão, hermetistmo* (Lisbon: Moraes, 1978).

Cerdeira, Teresa Cristina. *O Avesso do Bordado: ensaios de literatura* (Lisbon: Caminho, 2000).

Cesariny, Mário. *O Virgem negra* (Lisbon: Assírio e Alvim, 1989).

Chancey, George. 'From Sexual Inversion to Homosexuality', *Salmagundi* 58-59 (1982-1983), pp. 114-146.

Cisoux, Hélène. *L'Exil de James Joyce* (Paris: Grasset, 1968).

--- *The Exile of James Joyce*, trans. Sally A. J. Purcell (New York: David Lewis, 1971).

Claretie, Jules. *La vie à Paris: 1881* (Paris: Victor Harvard, 1881).

Clarke, J. Michell. *Hysteria and Neurasthenia: The Practitioner's Handbook* (London: The Bodley Head, 1905).

Cobb, Ivo Geikie. *A Manual of Neurasthenia (Nervous Exhaustion).* (London: Baillière, Tindall and Cox, 1920).

Cochofel, João José. *Grande dicionário de literatura portuguesa e de teoria literária* (Lisbon: Iniciativas Editoriais, 1977).

Coelho, Jacinto do Prado. *Camões e Pessoa, Poetas da utopia* (Lisbon: Europa-América, 1983).

--- *Diversidade e unidade em Fernando Pessoa* (Lisbon: Verbo, 1963).

--- 'Fernando Pessoa ou A estratégia da razão', in *Camões e Pessoa, Poetas da utopia* (Lisbon: Europa-América, 1983), pp. 114-118.

Cohen, Ed. 'Writing Gone Wilde: Homoerotic Desire in the Closet of Representation', *Publications of the Modern Languages Association of America* 102 (1987), pp. 798-823.

Coleridge, Samuel Taylor. *Biographia Literaria or Biographical Sketches of My Literary Life, and Opinions* (Whitefish, Montana: Kessinger, 2005).
--- *Coleridge's Shakespearean Criticism*, ed. Thomas Middleton Raysor (London: Constable and Co., 1930).
--- --- *Collected Letters of Samuel Taylor Coleridge*, ed. Earl Leslie Griggs, 6 vols. (Oxford: Clarendon, 1971).
--- *Marginalia*, in *The Collected Works of Samuel Taylor Coleridge*, ed. Kathleen Coburn (London: Routledge and Kegan Paul,1969-), XII.
Colóquio-Letras 125-126 (June-December 1992).
Coriat, Isador H. *The Hysteria of Lady Macbeth* (New York: Moffat, Yard, 1912).
Corney, Bolton (ed.). *The Sonnets of William Shakespeare* (New York: J. Miller, 1862).
Craig, Maurice. *Nerve Exhaustion* (London: Churchill, 1922).
Crespo, Ángel. 'El paganismo de Fernando Pessoa (Para una interpretación de los heterónimos)', *Hora de Poesia* 4-5 (n.d.), pp. 140-157.
--- *La vida plural de Fernando Pessoa* (Barcelona: Seix Barral, 1988).
Dash, Irene. *Wooing, Wedding and Power: Women in Shakespeare's Plays* (New York: Columbia University Press, 1981).
Dávidházi, Péter. *The Romantic Cult of Shakespeare: Literary Reception in Anthropological Perspective* (London: Macmillan, 1998).
Dellamora, Richard. 'Homosexual Scandal and Compulsory Heterosexuality in the 1890s', in *Masculine Desire: The Sexual Politics of Victorian Aestheticism* (Chapel Hill/London: University of North Carolina Press, 1990), pp. 189-212.
Deming, Robert H. *James Joyce: The Critical Heritage 1928-1941*, 3 vols. (New York: Barnes and Noble).
Desmet, Christy and Robert Sawyer (ed.), *Harold Bloom's Shakespeare* (New York: Palgrave, 2001).
DiGangi, Mario. *The Homoerotics of Early Modern Drama* (Cambridge: Cambridge University Press, 1997).
Dostoevsky, Fydor. *The Brothers Karamazov*, trans. Constance Garnett (New York: Barnes and Noble, 2004).
Dover, Kenneth. *Greek Homosexuality* (Cambridge, M.A.: Harvard University Press, 1978).
Drake, Nathan. *Shakespeare and His Times: Including the biography of the poet, a new chronology of his plays, and a history of the manners, customs, amusements, superstitions, poetry and elegant literature of his age*, 2 vols. (London: Longman, 1817).
Dumesnil, René. *Flaubert et la médecine* (Paris: Societé francaise d'imprimerie et de librairie, 1905).
Dyce, Alexander (ed.). *William Shakespeare: Poems* (London: AMS Press, 1832).
Eagleton, Terry. *William Shakespeare* (Oxford: Oxford University Press, 1986).
Eliot, T. S. *Collected Poems 1909-1962* (London: Faber and Faber, 1963).
--- *The Sacred Wood* (London: Methuen, 1960).
--- *Selected Essays* (New York: Harcourt, Brace and World, 1960).
--- *The Selected Prose of T. S. Eliot*, ed. Frank Kermode (London: Faber and Faber,

1975).

--- *The Waste Land: A Facsimile and Transcripts of the Original Drafts*, ed. Valerie Eliot (London: Faber and Faber, 1971).

--- *To Criticize the Critic* (New York: Farrar, Straus and Giroux, 1965).

Ellenberger, Henri. *The Discovery of the Unconscious* (New York: Basic Books, 1970).

Elliot, Robert C. *The Literary Persona* (Chicago/London: The University of Chicago Press, 1982).

Ellis, Havelock. *Selected Essays*, ed. J. S. Collis (London: Dent, 1943).

--- *Sexual Inversion*, in *Studies in the Psychology of Sex*, 8 vols. (London: Watford, 1897), I.

Ellmann, Maud. *The Poetics of Impersonality: T. S. Eliot and Ezra Pound* (Sussex: Harvester Press, 1987).

Ellmann, Maud (ed.). *Psychoanalytic Literary Criticism* (London/New York: Longman, 1994).

Emerson, Ralph Waldo. *Works*, 12 vols. (London: Routledge, 1883), IV.

Empson, William. *Seven Types of Ambiguity* (London: Random House, 2004).

Estibeira, Maria do Céu Lucas. *A* Marginalia *de Fernando Pessoa* (unpublished doctoral dissertation, University of Lisbon: Faculdade de Letras, 2009).

--- 'Uma perspectiva da *Marginalia* de Fernando Pessoa', *Romântica* 18 (2009), pp. 91-108.

Estorninho, Carlos. 'Shakespeare na Literatura Portuguesa', *Ocidente* LXVII (Lisbon: 1964), pp. 114-125.

Feijó, António M. 'Ricardo Reis, [A flor que és, não a que dás, eu quero]', in *Século de Ouro: Antologia crítica da poesia portuguesa do século XX*, ed. Osvaldo Manuel Silvestre and Pedro Serra (Braga, Coimbra, Lisbon: Angelus Novus and Cotovia, 2002), pp. 467-474.

Ferrari, Patrício. 'A biblioteca de Fernando Pessoa na génese dos heterónimos', in *Fernando Pessoa: O Guardador de Papéis*, ed. Jerónimo Pizarro (Lisbon: Texto Editores, 2009), pp. 155-218

Ferreira, António Mega. *Fazer pela vida. Retrato de Fernando Pessoa, o empreendedor* (Lisbon: Assírio e Alvim, 2005).

Ferreira, Armando Ventura. *Memória dos mitos* (Lisbon: Arcádia, 1971).

--- 'Sequência para Fernando Pessoa', *Contravento: Letras e Artes* 3 (April 1970), pp. 8-13.

Finn, Michael R. *The Body and Literary Form* (Cambridge: Cambridge University Press, 1999).

Flaubert, Gustave. *Correspondence*, 4 vols. (Paris: Gallimard, 1973-1998).

--- *Madame Bovary: moeurs de provence* (Paris: Michel Lévy Frères, 1862).

Flecknoe, Richard. 'A Short Discourse on the English Stage', in *Critical Essays of the Seventeenth Century, 1650-1685*, ed. Joel Elias Spingarn (Oxford: Clarendon, 1908).

Flor, João Almeida. 'Camilo e a Tradução de Shakespeare', in *Actas do XIII Encontro da Associação Portuguesa de Estudos Anglo-Americanos* (Porto, 19-21 de Março de 1992), pp. 179-193.

--- 'Um contexto inglês para Fernando Pessoa', *Expresso* (6 December 1975).

--- 'Fernando Pessoa e a questão shakespeariana', in *Afecto às Letras: Homenagem da literatura portuguesa contemporânea a Jacinto do Prado Coelho* (Lisbon: IN-CM, 1984), pp. 276-.83

--- '*Hamlet* (1887).: Tradução portuguesa de um caso patológico', in *Shakespeare entre nós*, ed. Maria Helena Serôdio, João de Almeida Flor, Alexandra Assis Rosa, Rita Queiroz de Barros and Paulo Eduardo Carvalho (Ribeirão: Edições Húmus, 2009), pp. 184-200.

--- 'Para a imagem de Shakespeare em Garrett', in *Garret às portas do milénio*, ed. Fernando Mão de Ferro (Lisbon: Colibri, 2002), pp. 45-54.

--- 'Shakespeare em Pessoa', in *Shakespeare*, ed. João Almeida Flor (Lisbon: Gulbenkian – Acarte, 1990), pp. 51-63.

--- 'Shakespeare, Rosas e Brazão', in *Miscelânea de estudos dedicados a Fernando de Mello Moser* (Lisbon: Faculdade de Letras, 1985), pp. 233-46.

Ford, Ford Madox. *The English Novel: From the Earliest Days to the Death of Joseph Conrad* (London: Constable, 1930).

Foucault, Michel. *The History of Sexuality: An Introduction*, trans. Robert Hurley (New York: Pantheon, 1978).

Freud, Sigmund. *Collected Papers* (London: Basic Books, 1959).

--- *The Complete Letters of Sigmund Freud to Wilhelm Fliess, 1887-1904*, trans. Jeffrey Moussaieff Masson (Cambridge, M. A.: University of Harvard Press, 1985).

--- *The Standard Edition of the Complete Psychological Works of Sigmund Freud*, 24 vols. (London: Hogarth Press, 1953-1974).

García, Ruben. 'The Unexpected Affinities: W. B. Yeats and Fernando Pessoa', *Journal of the American-Portuguese Society* X:1 (1976), pp. 7-19.

Gaspar Simões, João. *O Mistério da poesia. Ensaios de interpretação da génese poética* (Coimbra: Imprensa da Universidade, 1931).

--- *Novos Temas* (Lisbon: Inquérito, 1938).

--- *Retratos de poetas que conheci: autobiografia* (Lisbon: Brasília Editora, 1974).

--- *Vida e obra de Fernando Pessoa: História de uma geração* (1950; Lisbon: Bertrand, 1981).

Gaultier, Jules de. *Le Bovarysme, la psychologie dans l'oeuvre de Flaubert* (Paris: L. Cerf, 1898).

Gil, José. *Fernando Pessoa ou a metafísica das sensações* (Lisbon: Relógio d'Água, n.d. [1987]).

Glasgow Herald (19 September 1918).

Gollancz, Israel (ed.). *The Shakespeare Classics: Being the Sources and Originals of Shakespeare's Plays* (London: Chatto and Windus, 1907).

Gomes, João Manuel. 'Para acabar de vez com a obscinidade, *Jornal de Letras* (14 June 1988).

Gosling, F. G. *Before Freud: Neurasthenia and the American Medical Community, 1870-1910* (Urbana, Chicago: University of Illinois Press, 1987).

Gosson, Stephen. *Plays confuted in Five Actions*, 1582, British Library manuscript sig. E5r.

Gowda, H. H. Anniah. *Dramatic Poetry from Mediaeval to Modern Times* (Madras, India: The Macmillan Company of India, 1972).

Grazia, Margreta de. 'The Scandal of Shakespeare's Sonnets', *Shakespeare Survey* 14 (1994), pp. 35-50.

Greenblatt, Stephen. *Will in the World: How Shakespeare Became Shakespeare* (London: Random House, 2004).

Greene, Robert [attr.]. *Greene's Groatsworth of Wit* (New York: Barnes and Noble, 1966).

Haller, John S. *American Medicine in Transition 1840-1910* (Chicago: University of Illinois Press, 1981).

Halliwell Phillips, James Orchard. *Outlines of the Life of Shakespeare* (London: Longmans, 1881).

Hammond, Paul. *Figuring Sex Between Men from Shakespeare to Rochester* (Oxford: Oxford University Press, 1997).

--- *Love Between Men in English Literature* (Basingstoke: Macmillan, 1996).

Hardy, Thomas. *Jude the Obscure* (Toronto: Macmillan, 1969).

Harris, Frank. *The Man Shakespeare and his Tragic Life-Story* (New York: M. Kennerly, 1909).

Haventhal Jr, Charles. 'Robert Burton's Anatomy of Melancholy in Early America', *Papers of the Bibliographical Society of America* LXIII (1969), pp. 157-75.

Hazlitt, William. 'On Shakespeare and Milton', in *Lectures on the English Poets* (London: Taylor and Hessey, 1818).

--- *Hazlitt's Essays: A Selection*, ed. Herbert Paul (London: Cassell and Co., 1905).

Heath, Stephen. 'Psychopathia Sexualis: Stevenson's Strange Case, *Critical Quarterly* 28 (1986), pp. 69-79.

Hegel, Georg Wilhelm Friedrich. *Aesthetics: Lectures on Fine Art*, trans. T. M. Knox (Oxford: Clarendon, 1975).

Hermans, Hurb, W. E. Krul and Hans van Maanen. *1894: European Theatre in Turmoil: Meaning and Significance of the Theatre a Hundred Years Ago* (Amsterdam: Rodopi, 1996).

Hilliard, David. 'Unenglish and Unmanly: Anglo-Catholicism and Homosexuality', *Victorian Studies* 25 (1982), pp. 181-210.

Holland, Merlin. *Irish Peacock and Scarlet Marquess: The Real Trial of Oscar Wilde* (London/New York: Fourth Estate, 2004).

Holland, Norman. *Psychoanalysis and Shakespeare* (Michigan: MacGraw-Hill, 1966).

Hugo, Victor. *Cromwell* (Paris: Testard, 1827).

Huysman, Joris-Karl. *Against Nature*, trans. Robert Baldick (London: Penguin, 2003).

Hyde, H. Montgomery. *The Trials of Oscar Wilde* (London: William Hodge, 1949).

Jackson, Heather J. *Romantic Readers: The Evidence of Marginalia* (New Haven/London: Yale University Press, 2005).

Jackson, Kevin David. 'Heteronyms', in *Invisible Forms: A Guide to Literary Curiosities* (London: Picador, 1999), pp. 38-51.

Jakobson, Roman. *Roman Jacobson: Linguística, poética, cinema* (São Paulo:

Editora Perspectiva, 1970).

James, Henry. 'Robert Louis Stevenson', *The Century Magazine* XXXV:4 (April 1888), pp. 869-79.

--- 'The Jolly Corner', *The English Review* (December 1908), pp. 5-35.

--- *Letters of Henry James* (New York: Scribner, 1929).

James, William. *Essays in Psychology* (Cambridge, M.A.: Harvard University Press, 1983).

--- 'The Hidden Self', *Scribner's Magazine* 7 (1890), pp. 361-73.

--- *Psychology: The Briefer Course* (Toronto: General Publishing Company, 2001).

Jameson, Anna. *Characteristics of Women: Moral, Poetical and Historical*, 2 vols. (London: Saunders and Otley, 1832).

Jamieson, Robert. 'Who Wrote Shakespeare?', *Chamber's Edinburgh Journal* (7 August 1852), pp. 14-28.

Jenning, Hubert D. *Os dois exílios. Fernando Pessoa na África do Sul* (Porto: Centro de Estudos Pessoanos, 1984).

Jones, Ernest. *The Life and Times of Sigmund Freud*, 3 vols. (London: Hogarth, 1957).

Jorge, Maria do Céu Saraiva. 'Shakespeare e a literatura oitocentista posterior a Garrett e Herculano', *Palestra* 23 (1965), pp. 56-82.

--- *Shakespeare em Portugal* (unpublished doctoral dissertation, Lisbon: Faculdade de Letras, 1941).

Joyce, James. *Letters of James Joyce*, ed. Stuart Gilbert and Richard Ellmann, 3 vols. (London: Viking, 1957).

--- *Occasional, Critical, and Political Writing*, ed. Kevin Barry (Oxford: Oxford University Press, 2000).

--- *A Portrait of the Artist as a Young Man* (London: Penguin, 2000).

--- *Ulysses* (London: Penguin, 2000).

Jung, Carl Gustav. *The Archetypes and the Collective Unconscious*, in *Collected Works*, 13 vols. (London: Routledge, 1963), IX.

--- *Modern Man in Search of a Soul*, trans. W. S. Dell and Cary F. Baynes (London/New York: Routledge, 2001).

Keats, John. *Letters of John Keats 1814-1821*, ed. H. E. Rollins, 2 vols. (Cambridge, MA: Harvard University Press, 1958).

Kennedy, X. J. and Dana Gioia. *Literature: An Introduction to Fiction, Poetry, and Drama* (New York: HarperCollins, 1995).

Kenner, Hugh. *Ezra Pound* (London: Faber and Faber, 1951).

--- *The Invisible Poet* (London: Methuen and Co. Ltd., 1959).

Kenny, Thomas. *The Life and Genius of Shakespeare* (London: Longmans, 1864).

Kerrigan, John. 'Between Michelangelo and Petrarch: Shakespeare's Sonnets of Art', in *Surprised by Scenes: Essays in Honour of Professor Yasanuri Takahashi*, ed. Yasanuri Takada (Tokyo: Kenkyusha, 1994), pp. 142-63.

Kerrigan, William W. 'The Case for Bardolatry: Harold Bloom Rescues Shakespeare From the Critics', in *Harold Bloom's Shakespeare*, ed. Christy Desmet and Robert Sawyer (New York: Palgrave, 2001), pp. 33-42.

Klobucka, Anna M. and Mark Sabine. *Embodying Pessoa: Corporeality, Gender,*

Sexuality (Toronto/London: University of Toronto Press, 2007).

Knight, G. Wilson. *Myth and Miracle: An Essay on the Mystic Symbolism of Shakespeare* (London: J Burrow and Co., 1929).

Krafft-Ebing, Richard von. *Psychopathia Sexualis*, trans. C. G. Chaddock (Philadelphia/London: F. A. Davis, 1892).

Lacassagne, Zacharie. *La Folie de Maupassant* (unpublished doctoral dissertation, Toulouse: University of Toulouse, 1907).

Laing, R. D. *The Divided Self; An Existential Study in Sanity and Madness* (Harmondsworth: Penguin, 1959).

Larivière, Michel (ed.). *Les amours masculines: Anthologie de l'homosexualité dans la littérature* (Paris: Lieu Commun, 1984).

Lavalée, G. *Essai sur la psychologie morbide de Huysmans* (unpublished doctoral dissertation, Paris: University of Paris, 1917).

Lee, Sidney. *A Life of William Shakespeare* (London: Smith Elder and Co., 1898).

--- 'Shakespeare', in *Dictionary of National Biography* (London: Macmillan, 1897), LI.

--- 'Shakespeare', in *Dictionary of National Biography* (New York: Macmillan, 1897), LI.

Lee, Sidney, Walter Alexander Raleigh and Charles Talbut Onions. *Shakespeare's England: An Account of the Life and Manners of His Age*, 6 vols. (London: Chatto and Windus, 1916).

Lernout, G. Geert and Wim Van Mierlo. *The Reception of James Joyce in Europe*, 2 vols., ed. G. Geert Lernout and Wim Van Mierlo (London: Thoemess Continuum, 2004).

LeWinter, Oswald (ed.). *Shakespeare in Europe* (London: Penguin, 1970).

Lind, Georg Rudolf. *Estudos sobre Fernando Pessoa* (Lisbon: IN-CM, 1981).

Lodge, David. *Small World: An Academic Romance* (London: Penguin, 1984).

Lombroso, Césare. *L'homme de génie* (Paris: Félix Alcan, 1889).

Looney, Thomas J. *"Shakespeare" Identified in Edward de Vere* (New York: Frederick A. Stokes Company, 1920).

Lopes, Maria Teresa Rita. *Fernando Pessoa et le drame symboliste: héritage et création* (Paris: Calouste Gulbenkian, 1977).

Lourenço, António Apolinário. *Identidade e Alteridade em Fernando Pessoa e Antonio Machado* (Braga: Angelus Novus, 1995).

Lourenço, Eduardo. *Fernando, rei da nossa Bavieira* (Lisbon: IN-CM, 1986).

--- *Pessoa revisitado. Leitura estruturante do drama em gente* (Lisbon: Gradiva, 2003).

--- 'Poesia e heteronímia: Resposta (sem metáfora). ao Snr. Prof. Jacinto do Prado Coelho', *Colóquio-Letras* 171 (*Eduardo Lourenço, Uma ideia do mundo*, May-August 2009), pp. 376-387.

Lyn Pykett (ed.). *Reading Fin de Siècle Fictions* (London/New York: Longman, 1996).

Macedo, Helder. *Nós: uma leitura de Cesário Verde* (Lisbon: Presença, 1999).

--- *Do Significado oculto da Menina e Moça* (Lisbon: Moraes Editores, 1977).

--- *Trinta leituras* (Lisbon: Presença, 2007).

Macedo, Suzette. 'Mentira, fingimento e máscaras: Alguns comentários sobre Oscar Wilde, W. B. Yeats e Fernando Pessoa', *Colóquio-Letras* 107 (1988), pp. 24-37.

Madden, J. S. 'Melancholy in Medicine and Literature: Some Historical Considerations', in J. S. Madden, 'Melancholy in Medicine and Literature: Some Historical Considerations', in *British Journal of Medical Psychology*, 72 vols. (London: British Psychological Society (1923-2001), XXXIX (1966), pp. 116-31.

Mahood, Molly M. *Shakespeare's Wordplay* (London: Methuen, 1957).

Maines, Rachel P. *The Technology of Orgasm: Hysteria, the Vibrator, and Women's Sexual Satisfaction* (Baltimore: The Johns Hopkins University Press, 1999).

Manningham, John. *Diary of John Manningham, of the Middle Temple, and of Bradbourne, Kent, Barrister-at-Law, 1602-1603*, ed. John Bruce (London: J. B. Nichols and Sons, 1868).

Marder, Louis. *His Exits and His Entrances: The Story of Shakespeare's Reputation* (Philadelphia/New York: Lippincott, 1963).

Margarido, Alfredo. 'Uma Carta Inédita de Violante de Cysneiros', *Colóquio-Letras* 117-118 (1990), pp. 117-29.

Martinho, José. *Pessoa e a psicanálise* (Coimbra: Almedina, 2001).

Martins, Fernando Cabral (ed.). *Dicionário de Fernando Pessoa e do Modernismo Português* (Lisbon: Caminho, 2008).

Martins, Fernando Cabral. *O Modernismo em Mário de Sá-Carneiro* (Lisbon: Estampa, 1994).

Masson, David 'Shakespeare and Goethe', in *Essays Biographical and Critical, Chiefly on English Poets* (Cambridge: Macmillan, 1856).

Matos, Maria Vitalina Leal de. *Introdução aos estudos literários* (Lisbon: Verbo, 2001).

Maupassant, Guy de. 'Une femme', in *Chroniques*, ed. Hubert Juin, 3 vols. (Paris: Union Générale d'Éditions, 1980), II, pp. 104-113.

McGann, Jerome. *The Romantic Ideology* (Chicago: University of Chicago Press, 1983).

McKenna, Neil. *The Secret Life of Oscar Wilde* (London: Arrow, 2004).

McNeil, Alex. 'What's in a "Nym?" Pseudonyms, heteronyms and the remarkable case of Fernando Pessoa', *Shakespeare Matters* 6 (2003), pp. 16-20.

McNiell, Patrícia Silva. *The Imperative of Style: A Comparative Study of Fernando Pessoa and W. B. Yeats* (unpublished doctoral dissertation, London: King's College London, 2009).

Medeiros, Paulo de. 'Visions of Pessoa', *Cadernos de literatura comparada* (*Poesia e outras artes: do modernismo à contemporaneidade*). 17 (2007), pp. 166-75.

Medina, João. 'Hamlet morou defronte da Tabacaria', *Portugal: Informação* 2:1 (1976), pp. 3-6.

Micale, Mark S. *Approaching Hysteria: Disease and Its Interpretations* (Princeton: Princeton University Press, 1996).

--- 'On the "Disappearance" of Hysteria: A Study in the Clinical Deconstruction of a Diagnosis', *Isis 84* (1993), pp. 496–526.

Micale, Mark S. (ed.). *The Mind of Modernism: Medicine, Psychology, and the Cultural Arts in Europe and America 1880-1940* (Stanford: Stanford University Press, 2004).

Montagu, Elizabeth. *An Essay on the Writings and Genius of Shakespear [sic], Compared with the Greek and French Dramatic Poets. With Some Remarks Upon the Misrepresentations of Mons. de Voltaire* (New York: Augustus M. Kelley Publishers, 1970).

Monteiro, George. *Fernando Pessoa and Anglo-American Literature* (Kentucky: The University Press of Kentucky, 2000).

--- 'Shakespeare, the "Missing All"', *Portuguese Studies* 24:2 (2009). 33-49

Monteiro, George (ed.). *The Man Who Never Was: Essays on Fernando Pessoa* (Rhode Island: Gávea-Brown, 1982).

Monteiro, Maria da Encarnação. *Incidências inglesas na poesia de Fernando Pessoa* (Coimbra: Coimbra Editora, 1956).

Morgan, Maurice. *An Essay on the Dramatic Character of Sir John Falstaff* (London: T. Davies, 1777).

Muldoon, Paul. 'In the Hall of Mirrors: "Autopsychography" by Fernando Pessoa', in *The End of the Poem: Oxford Lectures in Poetry* (London: Faber and Faber, 2009), pp. 222-45.

Muller, Max. *Lectures on the Science of Language* (London: Longmans, 1871).

Munro, John James, Clement Mansfield Ingleby, Lucy Toulmin Smith and Frederick James Furnivall. *The Shakespeare Allusion Book*, 2 vols. (London: Chatto and Windus, 1909).

Murray, Douglas. *Bosie: A Biography of Lord Alfred Douglas* (London: Hodder and Stoughon, 2000).

Nabokov, Vladimir Vladimirovich. *Poems and Problems* (New York: McGraw-Hill, 1970).

Nadeau, Maurice. 'Le cinquantenaire de l'hysterie (1878-1928)', in *Histoire du surréalisme: Documents surréalistes*, ed. Maurice Nadeau (Paris: Seuil, 1948).

Negreiros, José de Almada. *Poemas* (Lisbon: Assíro e Alvim, 2001).

Nelson, James. *Publisher to the Decadents: Leonard Smithers in the Careers of Beardsley, Wilde, Dowson* (Philadelphia: Pennsylvania State University Press, 2000).

Nemésio, Vitorino. 'O Sincero fingido', *Diário Popular* (26 December 1945), pp. 4-7.

Newlyn, Lucy. *Reading, Writing, and Romanticism: The Anxiety of Reception* (Oxford: Oxford University Press, 2000).

Nicholls, Charles. *The Lodger: Shakespeare on Silver Street* (Michegan: Allen Lane, 2007).

Nietzsche, Freidrich Wilhelm. *The Nietzsche Reader*, ed. R. J. Hollingdale (Harmondsworth, Middlesex: Viking, 1981).

Nobre, António. *Poesia Completa* (Lisbon: Dom Quixote, 2000).

Nordau, Max. *Degeneration*, trans. George L. Mosse (New York: Howard Fertig, 1968).

Norton, Rictor. *The Homosexual Literary Tradition: An Interpretation* (New York:

Revisionist Press, 1974).

O'Donoghue, Bernard. 'Fernando Pessoa and W. B. Yeats' (2006). *Portal Pessoa* <www.portalpessoa.net>

Ordóñez, Andrés. *Fernando Pessoa, un místico sin fe* (Madrid: Siglo Veintiuno Editores, 1991).

Orgel, Stephen. *Impersonations: The Performance of Gender in Shakespeare's England* (Cambridge: Cambridge University Press, 1996).

Orwell, George. *The Penguin Essays of George Orwell* (London: Penguin, 1994).

Owen, Orville Ward. *Sir Francis Bacon's Cypher Story*, 5 vols. (New York: Howard Publishing Company, 1895).

Palingenius. *The Zodiac of Life*, trans. Googe, 1565 ed., (London: *British Library* copy).

Partridge, Eric. *Shakespeare's Bawdy: A Literary and Psychological Essay and a Comprehensive Glossary* (London: Routledge and Kegan Paul, 1968).

Patarca-Montero, Roberto. *Concise Encyclopaedia of Chronic Fatigue Syndrome* (London: Routledge, 2000).

Patrício, Rita. *Episódios da teorização estética em Fernando Pessoa* (unpublished doctoral dissertation, University of Minho, July 2008).

'Shakespeare e Pessoa', in *O Guardador de papéis*, ed. Jerónimo Pizarro (Lisbon: Texto Editores, 2009), pp. 83-99.

Pequigney, Joseph. *Such is My Love: A Study of Shakespeare's Sonnets* (Chicago and London: University of Chicago Press, 1985).

Perrone-Moisés, Leyla. *Fernando Pessoa: Aquém do eu, além do outro* (São Paulo: Martins Fontes Editora, 1982).

Pietikainen, Petteri. *Neurosis and Modernity: The Age of Nervousness in Sweden* (Leiden/Boston: Brill, 2007).

Pilling, John. 'Fernando Pessoa (1888-1935)'. *An Introduction to Fifty Modern European Poets* (London/Sidney: Pan Books, 1982), pp. 173-80.

Pimental, Oscar. 'Experiência em Pessoa', in *A Lâmpada e o Passado* (São Paulo: Conselho Estadual de Cultura, Comissão de Literatura, 1968), pp. 95-8.

Pizarro, Jerónimo. 'Antero de Quental, entre contradições e esquecimentos', *Estudos Anterianos* 11-12 (April-October 2003), pp. 57-65.

--- 'Da Histeria à Neurastenia (Quental e Pessoa)', *Conceito* 1 ('Loucura and Desrazão', 2005). 168-178

--- *Fernando Pessoa: entre génio e loucura* (Lisbon: IN-CM, 2007).

--- 'Fernando Pessoa: o génio e a loucura', *Leituras: Revista da Biblioteca Nacional de Lisboa*, 3:14-15 (April 2004-2005), pp. 245-54.

Porter, Roy, and G. E. Berrios, *A History of Clinical Psychiatry: The Origin and History of Psychiatric Disorders* (London: Athlone Press, 1995).

Portugal Futurista, facsimile ed., (Lisbon: Contexto, 1981).

Pound, Ezra. *Selected Poems 1908-1969* (London: Faber and Faber, 1975).

Prawyer, Siegbert Solomon. *A Cultural Citizen of the World: Sigmund Freud's Knowledge and Use of British and American Writings* (London: Legenda, 2009).

Praz, Mario. *The Romantic Agony*, trans. Angus Davidson (New York: Meridian,

1956).

Presença: edição facsimilada compacta, 3 vols., ed. David Mourão-Ferreira (Lisbon: Contexto, 1993).

Prince, Morton. *Psychotherapy and Multiple Personality: Selected Essays*, ed. Nathan G. Hale, Jr. (Cambridge, M.A.: Harvard University Press, 1975).

--- 'Sexual Perversion or Vice? A Pathological and Therapeutic Inquiry', *Journal of Nervous and Mental Disease* (25 April 1898), pp. 237-256.

Queirós, José Maria da Eça de. *A correspondência de Fradique Mendes (memórias e notas).* (Lisbon: Lello and Irmão, 1946).

--- 'Macbeth', *Gazeta de Portugal* (1866).

Quental, Antero de. *Sonetos Completos* (Porto: Anagrama, 1980).

Quinlan, Susan Canty and Fernando Arenas (ed.). *Lusosex: Gender and Sexuality in the Portuguese-Speaking World* (Minneapolis/London: University of Minnesota Press, 2002).

Raine, Craig. 'Whatever Became of Brain Fever?', in *Haydn and the Valve Trumpet* (London: Picador, 2000), pp. 12-21.

Raleigh, Walter. *Shakespeare* (London: Macmillan, 1965).

Rebello, Luiz Francisco. *Dicionário do Teatro Português* (Lisbon: Prelo, 1978).

Richardson, Robert D. *First We Read, Then We Write: Emerson on the Creative Process* (Iowa City: University of Iowa Press, 2009).

-- *William James: In the Maelstrom of American Modernism. A Biography* (Boston/New York: Mariner Books, 2007).

Richardson, William. *A Philosophical Analysis and Illustration of Some of Shakespeare's Remarkable Characters* (Edinburgh: J. Murray/London: W. Creed, 1774).

Ridge, Martin. *Ignatius Donnelly: The Portrait of a Politician* (Chicago/London: University of Chicago Press, 1962).

Rinhaug, Aino. *Perspectives of a Ludicrous Self: A Study of Fernando Pessoa's 'drama em gente'* (Oslo: University of Oslo, 2007).

Rivkin, Julie and Michael Ryan (ed.). *Literary Theory: An Anthology* (London: Blackwell, 2004).

Roditi, Édouard. 'Fernando Pessoa, Outsider Among English Poets', *The Literary Review* 6:3 (Spring 1963). 372-391

Roe, John Elisha. *Sir Francis Bacon's Own Story* (New York: Roycrafters, 1911).

Rosenbaum, Ron. *The Shakespeare Wars: Clashing Scholars, Public Fiascos, Palace Coups* (New York: Random House, 2006).

Rowan, John. *Subpersonalities: The People Inside Us* (London: Routledge, 1990).

Ryan, Judith. *Vanishing Subject: Early Psychology and Literary Modernism* (Chicago: The University of Chicago Press, 1991).

Sá-Caneiro, Mário de. *Cartas a Fernando Pessoa*, 2 vols., ed. Urbano Tavares Rodrigues and Helena Cidade Moura (Lisbon: Ática, 1973).

--- *Céu em fogo. Novelas* (Lisbon: Ática, 1965).

--- *Poemas Completos*, ed. Fernando Cabral Martins (Lisbon: Assírio e Alvim, 2001).

Sacramento, Mário. *Fernando Pessoa: Poeta da hora absurda* (Porto: Inova, 1970).

Santos, Maria Irene Ramalho de Sousa. *Atlantic Poets: Fernando Pessoa's Turn in Anglo-American Modernism* (Hanover/London: University Press of New England, 2003).

--- 'O Deus que faltava: the Theory in the Poetry of Alberto Caeiro', in *Fernando Pessoa's Modernity Without Frontiers: Influences, Dialogues and Responses*, ed. Mariana Gray de Castro (Woodbridge: Boydell and Brewer, 2013).

Santos, Maria de Lourdes Lima dos. *Intelectuais portugueses na primeira metade de Oitocentos* (Lisbon: Presença, 1985).

--- *Por uma sociologia da cultura burguesa em Portugal no século XIX* (Lisbon: Presença, 1983).

Saraiva, Arnaldo. *Fernando Pessoa e o Supra-Camões e outros ensaios pessoanos* (Lisbon: Academia das Ciências de Lisboa, 1987).

--- *Fernando Pessoa, tradutor de poetas* (Porto: Lello Editores, 1996).

Sass, Louis A. *Madness and Modernism: Insanity in the Light of Modern Art, Literature, and Thought* (Cambridge, M.A.: Harvard University Press, 1994).

Schiesari, Juliana. *The Gendering of Melancholia* (Ithaca: Cornell University Press, 1992).

Schlegel, August Wilhelm. *A Course of Lectures on Dramatic Art and Literature*, trans. John Black (London: A. J. W. Morrison, 1846).

Schoenbaum, Samuel. *Shakespeare's Lives* (Oxford: Clarendon/New York: Oxford University Press, 1970).

--- *William Shakespeare: A Compact Documentary Life* (Oxford: Clarendon, 1977).

--- *William Shakespeare – A Study of Facts and Problems*, 2 vols. (Oxford: Clarendon, 1930).

Seabra, José. *Fernando Pessoa ou o poetodrama* (São Paulo: Perspectiva, 1974).

Sedgwick, Eve Kosofsky. *Between Men: English Literature and Male Homosocial Desire* (New York: Columbia University Press, 1993).

--- *Epistemology of the Closet* (California: University of California Press, 1990).

Sena, Jorge de. *Amor e outros verbetes* (Lisbon: Edições 70, 1992).

--- *Estrada Larga* (Porto: Porto Editora, n.d. [1958]).

--- *Fernando Pessoa and Ca. heteronímica (Estudos Coligidos 1940-1978)*, 2 vols. (Lisbon: Edições 70, 1982).

--- 'The Man Who Never Was', in *The Man Who Never Was: Essays on Fernando Pessoa*, ed. George Monteiro (Rhode Island: Gávea-Brown, 1982), pp. 22-39

--- 'Sobre "Benilde ou a Virgem-Mãe" de José Régio', in *Régio, Casais, a "presença" e afins* (Porto: Brasileira Editora, 1977), pp. 104-109.

Serôdio, Maria Helena, João de Almeida Flor, Alexandra Assis Rosa, Rita Queiroz de Barros and Paulo Eduardo Carvalho (ed.). *Shakespeare entre nós* (Ribeirão: Edições Húmus, 2009).

Serrão, Joel. *Fernando Pessoa, cidadão do imaginário* (Lisbon: Horizonte, 1981).

Severino, Alexandrino E. *Fernando Pessoa na África do Sul: a formação inglesa de Fernando Pessoa* (Lisbon: Dom Quixote, 1983).

--- 'Fernando Pessoa e William Shakespeare: Um estudo comparativo de heteronímia', *Actas IV – Secção Brasileira* (São Paulo: Perspectiva, 1990), pp. 13-22.

Bibliography

'Shakespeare Goes to London', in 'Shakespeare', *Encyclopaedia Britannica* (9th ed., n.d.). XXI <http://www.1902encyclopedia.com/S/SHA/william-shakespeare-31.html>

Shapiro, James. *1599: A Year in the Life of William Shakespeare* (London: Faber and Faber, 2005).

Shepherd, David. 'Os 35 Sonnets de Fernando Pessoa vistos por um inglês', *Arquivos* IV:1 (January 1982), pp. 45-84.

Shepherd, Simon. 'Shakespeare's Private Drawer: Shakespeare and Homosexuality', in *The Shakespeare Myth*, ed. Graham Holderness (Manchester: Manchester University Press, 1988), pp. 96-109.

Showalter, Elaine. 'Representing Ophelia: women, madness, and the responsibilities of feminist criticism', in *Shakespeare and the Question of Theory*, ed. Patricia Parker and Geoffrey Hartman (London: Methuen, 1985), pp. 76-92.

Sigel, Lisa. *Governing Pleasures: Pornography and Social Change in England, 1815-1914* (Piscataway: Rutgers University Press, 2002).

Silva, Jorge Bastos da. *Shakespeare no Romantismo Português: Factos, problemas, interpretações* (Porto: Campo de Letras, 2005).

Silverman, Debora Leah. *Art Nouveau in Fin-de Siècle France: Politics, Psychology, and Style* (Los Angeles: University of California Press, 1989).

Smith, Bruce R. *Homosexual Desire in Shakespeare's England: A Cultural Poetics* (Chicago: Chicago University Press, 1991).

Smith, William Henry. *Bacon and Shakespeare: an Inquiry Touching Players, Playhouses, and Play-Writers in the Days of Elizabeth* (London: John Russell Smith, 1857).

Soares, Fernando Luso. *A Novela Policial-Dedutiva em Fernando Pessoa* (Lisbon: Diabril, 1976).

Sobran, Joseph. *Alias Shakespeare: Solving the Greatest Mystery of All Time* (New York: Free/London: Simon and Schuster, 1997).

Spedding, James. *Evenings with a Reviewer: or, A Free and Particular Examination of Mr. Macaulay's article on Lord Bacon, in a Series of Dialogues* (London: Kegan Paul, Trench and Co., 1881).

--- *The Letters and the Life of Francis Bacon, Including all his Occasional Works, Namely Letters Speeches Tracts State Papers Memorials Devices and all Authentic Writings not Already Printed Among his Philosophical Literary or Professional Works*, 7 vols. (London: Longmans, Green, Reader, and Dyer, 1862-74).

Spiller, Michael R. G. *The Development of the Sonnet: An Introduction* (London/New York: Routledge, 1992).

Stead, C.K. *Pound, Yeats, Eliot and the Modernist Movement* (London: Macmillan, 1986).

Stevenson, Robert Louis. *The Strange Case of Dr Jekyll and Mr Hyde*, ed. Jenni Calder (Harmondsworth: Penguin, 1979).

Stoker, Bram. *Dracula: A Tale* (Oxford: Oxford University Press, 1983).

Stoker, Michael. *Fernando Pessoa: De Fictie Vergezelt Mij Als Mijn Schaduw*

(Utrecht: Uitgeverij Ijzer, 2009).

Storrar, P. B. 'Leonard Rayne', in *Better Than They Knew*, ed. R. M. de Villiers (Cape Town: Purnell, 1972), pp. 124-135.

Tabucchi, Antonio. *Un baule pieno di gente: Scritti su Fernando Pessoa* (Milan: Feltrinelli, 1990).

Tamen, Isabel (ed.). *Encontro internacional do centenário de Fernando Pessoa: Um século de Pessoa* (Lisbon: Secretaria de Estado da Cultura, 1990).

Torre, Esteban. 'Fernando Pessoa, poeta metafísico', *Revista de Ocidente* 94 (March 1989), pp. 68-79.

--- *Fernando Pessoa: 35 sonetos ingleses* (Braga: Centro de Estudos Lusíadas, Universidade do Minho, 1988).

Traub, Valerie. *Desire and Anxiety: Circulations of Sexuality in Shakespearean Drama* (London: Routledge, 1992).

Trilling, Lionel. *Sincerity and Authenticity: The Charles Eliot Norton Lectures, 1969-1970* (Oxford: Oxford University Press, 1972).

Verde, Cesário. *Obra Completa*, ed. Joel Serrão (Lisbon: Horizonte, 1988).

Vickers, Brian. 'The Emergence of Character Criticism, 1774-1800', *Shakespeare Studies* XXXIV (1981), pp. 11-21.

Vieira, Yara Frasteschi. 'O discuro erótico nos poemas "Antinous" e "Epithalamium", *Boletim Informativo do C.E.P* dedicated to Pessoa (1985). 67-75

Vieira, Yara Frasteschi and Brian F. Head. '"35 Sonnets": Uma leitura de Shakespeare', U.S.D.P. (1990), pp. 276-81.

Wagner, Richard. *The Art-Work of the Future, and Future Works* (New York: Bison Books, 1993).

Wells, Stanley. *Looking for Sex in Shakespeare* (Cambridge: Cambridge University Press, 2004).

--- *Shakespeare and Co.: Christopher Marlowe, Thomas Dekker, Ben Jonson, Thomas Middleton, John Fletcher and the Other Players in his Story* (London: Penguin, 2006).

White, Chris (ed.). *Nineteenth-Century Writings on Homosexuality: A Sourcebook* (London: Routledge, 1999).

White, Richard Grant. 'The Bacon-Shakespeare Craze', *Atlantic Monthly* (April 1883).

Whitman, Walt. 'What lurks behind Shakespeare's historical plays?' in *November Boughs* (London: Alexander Gardner, 1889), pp. 50-53.

Wilde, Oscar. *The Artist as Critic: Critical Writings of Oscar Wilde*, ed. Richard Ellmann (New York: Random House, 1969).

Williams, Gordon. *A Glossary of Shakespeare's Sexual Language* (London: Athlone Press, 1997).

Williams, Hugo. 'Freelance', *Times Literary Supplement* (22 January 2010). p. 16.

Wimsatt, K. and Monroe C. Beardsley. 'The Intentional Fallacy', in *The Critical Tradition*, ed. David. H. Richter (Boston: Bedford, 1998), pp. 748-756.

Wood, W. Dyson. *Hamlet: A Psychological Point of View* (London: Longmans, Green, Reader, and Dyer, 1870).

Bibliography

Woods, Gregory. *A History of Gay Literature: The Male Tradition* (New Haven/London: Yale University Press, 1998).

Wordsworth, William. *The Poetical Works of William Wordsworth* (London: Edward Moxon, 1849).

Wraight, A. D. *Christopher Marlowe and Edward Alleyn* (Chichester: Adam Hart, 1993).

Wyman, W. H. *Bibliography of the Bacon-Shakespeare Controversy* (Cincinnati: Thomson, 1884).

Yeats, W. B. *Selected Poetry*, ed. Timothy Webb (London: Penguin, 1991).

Yeazell, Ruth Bernard (ed.). *Sex Politics and Science in the Nineteenth Century Novel* (Baltimore: Johns Hopkins University Press, 1986).

Zenith, Richard. 'A Importância de não ser Oscar? Pessoa tradutor de Wilde', *Egoista* (2008). 32-36

--- 'Introductory Note', in *Forever Someone Else: Selected Poems*, ed. and trans. Richard Zenith (Lisbon: Assíro e Alvim, 2009), pp. 13-22.

--- 'Pessoa's Gay Heteronym?' in *Lusosex: Gender and Sexuality in the Portuguese-Speaking World*, ed. Susan Canty Quinlan and Fernando Arenas (Minneapolis: University of Minnesota Press, 2002), pp. 35-46.

--- 'Preface', in *Obra Essencial de Fernando Pessoa: Poesia Inglesa*, ed. Zenith, trans. Luísa Freire (Lisbon: Assírio e Alvim, 2007), pp. 3-15.

--- 'Shakespeare', in *Dicionário de Fernando Pessoa e do Modernismo Português*, ed. Fernando Cabral Martins (Lisbon: Caminho, 2008), pp. 798-800.

Zola, Émile. *The Fortune of the Rougons* (Gloucester: Sutton, 1985).

INDEX

A

Almeida, Onésimo de, 19, 21, 31, 33, 74, 220-21, 248, 254, 262

Assis, Machado de, 33, 121, 249, 254, 262

B

Bacon, Francis, 29, 74-5, 80-85, 88, 91-101, 105-6, 108, 111, 153, 212, 228-9, 230-31, 233-5, 237-40, 242-6, 249, 251, 260-61, 263-5

Barnfield, Richard, 174, 249

Bate, Jonathan, 24, 57, 61-2, 74, 78, 134, 163-4, 170, 212, 222, 249

Beard, George, 116, 126, 249

Begley, Walter, 80, 91-2, 99, 160-61, 167, 243-4

Berardinelli, Cleonice, 128, 172, 187, 206, 246-7, 250

Biographical readings, 153

Blanco, José, 9, 14, 18, 110, 179, 250

Bloom, Harold, 24, 27, 53, 56-7, 61, 189, 193, 195, 219, 222, 250, 252, 256-7

Booth, Stephen, 159, 163, 218, 248

Booth, Wayne C., 217-18, 250

Borges, Jorge Luis, 66, 250

Bothe, Pauly Ellen, 50-51, 54, 112, 133, 175, 223, 246

Bovarysme, 145-6, 183, 195, 254

Bréchon, Robert, 183, 250

Brook, Peter, 61

Browning, Robert, 54, 109, 155, 157, 191

Buci-Glucksmann, Christine, 18, 250

Burbage, Richard, 208

Burton, Robert, 116, 255

C

Camões, Luiz Vaz de, 7-8, 16, 19, 24, 46, 49, 185, 219-22, 251, 262

Carlyle, Thomas, 65, 142-3, 156-7, 161, 204, 243, 251

Casais Monteiro, Adolfo, 14, 69, 245

Castelo Branco, Camilo, 32

Castro, Ivo, 20, 247

Castro, Mariana Gray de, 7, 38, 47, 104, 165, 178, 201, 251, 262

Centeno, Yvette, 169, 251

Cerdeira, Teresa Cristina, 200, 202, 251

Charcot, Jean-Martin, 115, 125, 139, 165

Christ, 64, 104, 105, 170, 201, 230, 238

Ciphers, 82, 100

Coelho, Jacinto do Prado, 10-11, 14, 16, 19, 185, 197, 221, 247-8, 251, 254, 257

Coleridge, Samuel Taylor, 56, 59-62, 84-5, 89-90, 107, 134, 153, 155, 157, 233, 235, 243, 252

Côrtes-Rodrigues, Armando, 42-3, 108, 122-3, 194, 216, 246

Crespo, Angel, 14-15, 252

D

Dante, 46, 49, 53, 157, 189-90, 221

Degeneration, 123-5, 244, 260

Donnelly, Ignatius, 82, 100, 242, 261

E

Eliot, T. S., 23, 40, 63, 126-7, 146, 150, 161-2, 165-6, 177-8, 189-92, 194-95, 197, 201, 214, 219, 248, 251-3, 263-4

Emerson, Ralph Waldo, 23-4, 49, 75, 82-5, 157, 233, 235, 244, 249, 253, 261

Estibeira, Maria do Céu Lucas, 23, 253

Estorninho, Carlos, 18, 31, 32, 253

F

Feijó, António M., 9, 24, 253

Ferrari, Patrício, 13, 23, 161, 246, 253

Index

Index